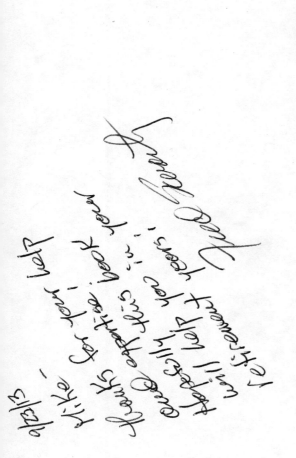

Theft of the American Dream

* * *

*

Understanding the Financial Crisis —
and what you can do to salvage your legacy

J.F. Swartz

iUniverse, Inc.
Bloomington

Theft of the American Dream

Understanding the Financial Crisis —
and what you can do to salvage your legacy

Copyright © 2012 by J. F. Swartz

iUniverse books may be ordered through booksellers or by contacting:

iUniverse
1663 Liberty Drive
Bloomington, IN 47403
www.iuniverse.com
1-800-Authors (1-800-288-4677)

Because of the dynamic nature of the Internet, any web addresses or links contained in this book may have changed since publication and may no longer be valid. The views expressed in this work are solely those of the author and do not necessarily reflect the views of the publisher, and the publisher hereby disclaims any responsibility for them.

Any people depicted in stock imagery provided by Thinkstock are models, and such images are being used for illustrative purposes only.

Certain stock imagery © Thinkstock.

ISBN: 978-1-4759-4911-7 (sc)
ISBN: 978-1-4759-4912-4 (hc)
ISBN: 978-1-4759-4913-1 (e)

Library of Congress Control Number: 2012917386

Printed in the United States of America

iUniverse rev. date: 10/22/2012

To my parents

Jack and Mary

Members of the Greatest Generation, who endured the Great Depression, honorably served the nation during World War II, paid cash for everything, and raised their kids according to those ideals. Thank you.

Contents

Preface

You won't need to be an economics whiz or an investment guru to understand and use the information in this book. But you do need common sense, an open mind, and the ability to abandon the assumption that your savings, retirement plan, or even Social Security will get you through your elder years. Whether you are 25, 50 or 75 years old, you'll need a new way to manage your finances than the one you are accustomed to, and you'll soon understand why you need to begin right now. Your financial future is not guaranteed. 'Theft of the American Dream' will demonstrate how the coming hyper price inflation will overwhelm your old-school plans, making them unworkable. But readers can be assured that financial security can be achieved with individual efforts over and above the services and advice offered by professional advisors. In your hands is a roadmap to do just that.

'Theft of the American Dream' presents a complicated situation in a simplified manner. If some of the information makes your eyes glaze over, don't give it a second thought, because it's the big picture that is all important. This big picture depicts the ongoing insolvency of the United States and the extremely tenuous viability of its currency. These factors will soon render you destitute if you don't properly prepare for the inevitable consequences of financial mismanagement by our leaders.

The Premise

Without question, we are in a much more serious situation than the Great Depression of the 1930's. You'll understand why by the time you finish reading the first part of 'Theft of the American Dream'. You'll have no other choice but to conclude that you have to change the way you think about all things financial, as the un-backed U.S. dollar regime comes to an end. When it happens, guess who will come out on the short end? One way or another, the uninformed and unprepared citizenry will pay; don't even think it would be the politicians, the bankers, or other elites. The game is rigged in their favor, so you need to worry about you, and this book will give you concrete ideas. You'll come to discover that if you follow some of the strategies and moves of the elite, combined with a clear understanding and consequences of past episodes of currency failures, you'll be able to adjust your personal and financial situation accordingly. This will allow you the benefit of surviving the coming financial reckoning.

Please note that 'Theft of the American Dream' will likely offend members of both the Republican and Democratic parties. And no, it was not inspired by the Tea Party or the Occupiers. Unfortunately, President Obama saw things deteriorate badly under his tutelage. He, along with his Democratic majority in Congress for the first couple of years of his presidential term, will take some criticism within these pages. But it's not at all meant to be a political leaning, because prior Republican presidents and Congresses have added to our woes just as handily. Rather, the intended tone is one of a common sense financial bias. This leaning certainly doesn't jibe with the notion that the government and its minions can steer a free market economy, no matter how hard they try to legislate it to their liking. There are always unintended consequences to deal with, and that is a fact that steers seemingly well intentioned legislation off course almost every time. When the Federal Reserve System is added to the mix of central fixers, the results are predictable. The real problem is that the end game of our current money regime is at hand, regardless of the political flavor of the day. The effort here is to give you the truth, tempered by common sense, so that you can survive the coming financial upheaval.

Part one – the situation now

The first step to financial survival is to accurately assess where the U.S. dollar stands in terms of its viability as a world reserve currency and as a medium of exchange for citizens in the U.S. Understanding the problem, placed in our lap by the bankers and politicians, is critical to your defense. This will give you a starting point for survival. *Your future course of personal financial actions depends on an accurate assessment of the viability of your currency.* Unfortunately, that assessment is scary.

Then we'll also take a big picture view of some easy economic lessons. There will be no formulas or heavy theory, just common sense observations based on the overall theme of two very different playbooks for economic growth. By taking a different, yet accurate view of the U.S. financial situation, you'll discover flaws in its playbook that leads to the end of the international use of the U.S. dollar in trade transactions. This fact has a profound consequence for your way of life and standard of living. It is meaningful to each and every individual citizen in the U.S.

We'll then examine how the U.S. Government and the Federal Reserve are in a monetary prison with no way out other than to print money to pay bills. We can't grow out of the problem. Our foreign investors and lenders are running away. The numbers don't work because it is a structural solvency problem for your U.S. government, not simply a temporary cash flow problem. Again, this isn't simply the U.S. government's issue; it directly affects you right now and will even more so in the near future. You'll get the true picture in these pages.

Next, we'll take a common sense look at the *real causes* of our financial crisis that you won't find reported in the mainstream media. The crisis morphed into something much worse than the purported "subprime" loan problem, as originally proposed by various bankers and politicians. This crisis is actually about the jeopardy of having the dollar fail as an effective medium of exchange for both consumers and investors. This is not hype. Houston, we have a problem.

We'll also look at the lunacy of some of the legislation aimed at fixing the economy coming out of Washington DC, and what it really means. It's important to grasp the both futility and unintended consequences of the plans devised by the politicians, so we'll take a closer look at some examples. These moves do not instill confidence for U.S. citizens, job creating business owners, nor for our trading partners.

Next, we'll get to more truths about the so-called recovery of the U.S. economy. There has been no recovery, jobless or otherwise. You'll learn how the politicians and Central Bank deceive people into looking not only at false data, but also at the wrong data. 'Theft of the American Dream' will cut through the smog to show you in pictorial form where our economy really is, and how to make your own assessment of the health or frailty of our country's economic future.

Finally, we'll take a look at what hyperinflation does to an economy and the attending society living through it. We'll examine two examples and delve into what the consequences were for the citizenry. We'll see what everyday people did to survive the onslaught of higher prices and the tragedy for those who did not prepare in advance. In fact, by taking a closer look at the past, you will actually convince yourself to immediately start to act in your own self defense. The measures you'll need to take will be obvious and not that difficult to achieve if you change some of your preconceived notions. You *can* survive what's coming and even negotiate a new personal path to prosperity.

Part two - Personal financial action ideas and concepts

In the second part of the book, you'll get many on-target money concepts to use and how they may be applied by today's regular working or retired citizens, both rich and poor. The idea is to mitigate the impact of the devaluing dollar, outrageous inflation and de facto default of the United States debt which is now in progress.

It is critical to note that both psychological and behavioral changes on your part will most likely be necessary for financial success. *You won't be able to advance your financial situation in a hyperinflationary environment by doing things the same way as you always have.* This is fact, so embrace it for maximum success.

We'll examine investment principles that many people have heard before, but chose to ignore. These principles are used by the elite while the rest of the public remains oblivious to their true value. You will come to understand how the powerful money moves markets, and how to profit from the stealthy tactics of the world's money elite. You'll be able to use this knowledge to seek out investments in tangible assets. You'll discover themes to work with and how to buy right and sell right.

No suggestion about buying tangible assets as an investment class would be complete without a look at the gold and silver market. You'll get some guidelines on buying, holding, and selling gold and silver related assets.

You'll also get pointers on how to search out good stock ideas, the themes to work with, and the right way to time your purchases and subsequent sales. Don't think this is hard. It truly isn't. It just takes a bit of the resource that everyone should have, or can craft for themselves. That resource is time. Spending your time wisely will be critical for your financial survival. You'll also get suggestions on many popular paper assets that are a *must to avoid*.

And of course, there is a chapter on debt. Debt can be a ball and chain to your future plans, or a valuable resource, and we'll examine both sides of the issue.

Part three – your resource guide

Finally, 'Theft of the American Dream' has provided you with a resource guide which will be helpful as a roadmap to your success. This is not something just to browse. This is the gateway to a successful venture into your financial unknowns. The research and screening has been done for you. If you visit even a few of the listed web sites often enough, you'll see what I mean. If you listen to the experts and read their essays, you will be far better off than the masses. These sites cut through all the hype of the politicians on TV, the distractions of the pundits, the barely-scratch-the-surface news broadcasts, and the out and out falsehoods you see in many newspapers and TV news shows. Follow the websites and pros who know the facts. You'll get lists of people who are in the know on any number of financial subjects. They are not Wall Street hype artists or con men, but rather straight shooters of the highest order. Finally, you will get the URL's to plenty of essays and articles on any number of financial subjects. These will round out your understanding of the bind in which we have been placed by the politicians and bankers, and what to do about it.

Footnote

'Theft of the American Dream' is not a book for the college classroom. In an effort to keep readers focused on the big picture I have avoided the use of footnotes, of which there could have been hundreds. References and other citations are found right in the text. The best way to delve into some of the facts and figures presented in 'Theft of the American Dream' is to use the URL's provided in the resource guide. Readers should know that I have assiduously checked my facts using Google search capabilities. If I have made any mistakes, I hereby offer my apologies in advance. Finally, you'll find that some quotes are italicized for emphasis, as the intention is to make a point. We all know that nobody speaks in italics!

JF Swartz

PART I

INTRODUCTION

The seeds of hyperinflation are planted and starting to grow

The moment of truth is coming. That moment will be when the American public catches on to what foreign creditors have already discovered. The devastating effects of the outrageous money creation engineered by the Federal Reserve (the Fed) and overseen by the political elite in Washington DC are headed your way. Central Banks the world over are printing more money than ever before, making the situation even worse. 'Theft of the American Dream' will help you defend yourself against the monetary and fiscal actions by our leaders. These policies have only just begun to erode the purchasing power of your money. But they will suddenly kick in to high gear without warning, potentially rendering you destitute. Even though the timing of explosive consumer price increases is uncertain, the end result is not. That end result is massive inflation, and it is assured. This is not a joke or an exercise simply meant to sell books. This is a crisis of the greatest magnitude, and right now you are in the crosshairs whether you realize it or not.

You are going to have to change your way of life. If you don't do it voluntarily, and in your own way, it will be done for you in a way that could easily devastate your financial well-being, lifestyle, family security, and your retirement. If you have any invested assets or savings, they are in peril right now. You could lose them. Before the purchasing power of your money falls to an unbelievable low, you're going to have to change the way you live, spend, and invest in order to avert personal disaster. You have taken an excellent first step by purchasing 'Theft of the American Dream'. Enlightenment regarding the issues and practical solutions await you.

'Theft of the American Dream' will explain how this time it really *is* different, and what you can do to save yourself and family from total financial destruction. This is not a wild or unfounded scenario. You are about to discover how the idiots in Washington and the thieves on Wall Street have destroyed our way of life, and who gets to clean up the mess. Indeed, the mess can't be cleaned up without massive disruption to our society. You will soon understand how all of the political and financial fixes are just what you *don't want* and certainly *don't need.* You'll also soon be convinced that the purported cause of the problem has not been anywhere near addressed with a permanent solution, and that the risk of a total collapse of your way of life is still very much in play. You simply *must* protect yourself right away. This isn't crazy. The pattern has repeated itself over and over in the history of modern civilization, and it's about to happen again; this time in the United States. You will soon realize that all elements for currency failure are in place for the U.S. dollar. Currency failures wipe out the unsuspecting and unprepared. Don't let this include you.

Chart 1 below will give you some inkling to the premise of a U.S. dollar currency failure. It was produced from data at the St. Louis Federal Reserve website. It shows the growth of the U.S. monetary base from 1918 to 2012. Simply stated, the *monetary base* is the total physical currency (cash) in circulation, together with bank reserves held at the Federal Reserve. It is the base from which the supply of money can be expanded by at least fifteen or more times over through the issuance of new loans by the banking system. *It is the starting point of money creation, not the end result.*

Note that there was a huge expansion of the money supply to pay for World War I and the giant ramp-up in the roaring 1920's - but those inflationary episodes seem insignificant now. Or what about the doubling of the money supply by Herbert Hoover to fight off the Depression before Roosevelt ramped it up even more? It barely shows up in this long term perspective. And you can hardly see the small blip to pay for World War II via government borrowings, as well as for the Great Society expenditures and the Vietnam War in the 1960's. The ramp-up of money creation was on a steady upward trajectory until 1971. Then, the U.S. went off the international gold standard. What do you see after August, 1971? You see a pretty significant increase in the supply of money, causing serious inflation in the 1970's. From the inception of the Federal Reserve System (the Fed) in 1913, until the beginning of the crisis in 2008, the Fed had debased our currency by 96%! But that took 85 years!

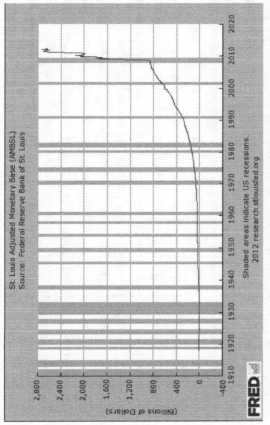

St. Louis Adjusted Monetary Base (AMBSL)
Source: Federal Reserve Bank of St. Louis

Shaded areas indicate US recessions.
2012 research.stlouisfed.org

Chart 1 – Monetary Base (AMBSL):

A 96 percent drop in value (purchasing power) of the U.S. dollar over 85 years is nothing compared to what is happening now. Since the end of 2008, the monetary base has blasted off, literally rising vertically on the chart since we were warned of a "financial crisis" by Treasury Secretary Hank Paulsen in September of 2008. A more than tripling of the monetary base has now occurred in just 4 short years! You don't need an economics degree to see the huge diversion from the inflationary trend of even the past 40 years! *What you see is the germination of hyperinflation!* This is a picture of a dysfunctional and systemically broken banking and financial system.

A quick mathematics note is in order here. Just because the dollar has been devalued by 96% over the past 85 years, don't assume that we only have 4% more to go. Wrong! Using today's value as a starting point, we know that dollar can *easily* lose another 96%, and *it can happen very quickly.* If today's dollar is worth 4 cents in a few more years, think what that will do to your finances! Don't think it will take 85 more years to do so. Just look at Chart 1. The dollar has been devalued by roughly 66% in 4 years from 2008, and this was before *money creation with no fixed end point* was announced by Bernanke in September of 2012. The only distinction to be made is that this debasement has not yet shown up in consumer prices, but it will!

Some financial pundits say that the explosion in the monetary base is not a concern right now, because the money is "sterilized". That means that so far the banks and the Federal Reserve have kept it out of the hands of the public. After all, the way the public can get its hands on the money is through loans. But this view is one of shortsightedness. Remember, these are *excess* reserves over and above those mandated by the Fed and international banking rules established in Basil, Switzerland. Eventually, banks can and will use that money to try to garner much higher return than the measly .25 percent the Federal Reserve now offers them. Once that money leaves the Fed, the race to the currency basement is on. Later, you'll see how the Fed is powerless to stop the money from leaving its hallowed halls, and how the purchasing power of the dollar will be destroyed.

Actually, the situation is much worse than depicted in Chart 1, as you are about to discover. Because our financial system has become a hostage to the out-of-control monetary policies engendered by the Fed and overseen by our elected officials, foreigners have become very nervous and defensive, and will exacerbate our already untenable problem. This assertion may seem like a big jump for neophytes to money matters, but we'll connect the dots for verification as we go forward. Then you'll have a clear picture as to the nature and gravity of the problem.

Ignoring all of the political angles and blather, the fact is that the employment reports and the emphasis on growth of the GDP don't matter very much, compared to the real problem. You'll later discover why this is like giving a person dying of thirst only one drop of water. They are distractions that the politicians and bankers use to keep you in the dark. *The real picture above tells us that our financial system is very broken.* This is a big problem which has everything to do with your future financial security. Don't let the con men in New York and Washington lead you believe otherwise.

How and why could this possibly happen? Simply, since the Great Depression, the Federal Reserve and the U.S. Congress have used the economic playbook of John Maynard Keynes, who espoused a centrally planned way to steer an economy. Now that theory has begun to unravel in ways predicted by another economic theory referred to as the Austrian school. We'll soon explore these theories in simplified terms, and then you'll be able to determine your own course of action to blunt the effects of the coming explosion in prices. But first, let's review some basics about our system of money.

CHAPTER I
HERE COMES THE END GAME

Concern for your financial survival is in play right now

The United States and its citizenry are in a financial crisis. Any news that the purported unemployment rate in the U.S. is dropping, or the Gross Domestic Product (GDP) is supposedly growing doesn't address the real issue. We are not in a run of the mill recession. Our super-leveraged and insolvent monetary system is broken. Politicians point to fudged improvements in the GDP and unemployment rate numbers to convince us that they have everything under control. They tell us they're going to cut government spending. The news media trumpets the lines of the politicians, as you would expect. Unfortunately, if you rely on the mainstream media for your economic news, you are not getting a very clear picture. That's because they focus strictly on a skewed view of the economy and not the financial foundation upon which that economy is built. You are about to get a very different picture of how the money system works and what the moves of the financial and political elite mean to you. First and foremost, citizens need to be concerned about the *foundation* upon which the U.S. economy rests.

Understanding the real issues

Our patchwork financial system has been rigged together with manipulation of asset prices, money printing, currency swaps, interest rate swaps, smoked and mirrored accounting tricks, and side bets; all overseen by the Federal Reserve. The objective of 'Theft of the American Dream' is to explain what is really happening so you'll understand what you'll need to do. Our money is devaluing before our very eyes, regardless of what you hear from Washington and Wall Street. This means your dollar buys less and less. And the trend is about to accelerate in a major way because of outrageous money creation. So far, none of the fixes have worked. But they have had numerous negative effects; and your personal money decisions will need to focus on that fact.

The U.S. dollar has been the world's reserve currency since the end of World War II. This means that international trade transactions amongst all industrialized countries have up until now required the use of U.S.

dollars for settlement payments. The dollar earned that privilege because at the time the agreement was reached at Bretton Woods, New Hampshire in 1944, the U.S. had not only the biggest stash of gold to back its currency for this purpose, but it also had the world's strongest economy. But things have changed quite a bit over the years. Countries world-wide have begun to lose confidence in the stability of the dollar's value because we are producing far too many of them to pay for an unearned standard of living and unfunded government promises.

It's not obvious to most people, but our U.S. dollar is unofficially *and rapidly losing its favored world reserve currency status. This is a very big deal.* The confidence of U.S. citizens and foreign countries alike has kept it in its reserve status since the end of World War II. But it's different now. It was forecasted in conversations and planning at the 2009 World Economic Forum in Davos, Switzerland. Vladimir Putin of Russia carried the torch for a new reserve currency system, with his proposed implementation plan to start as soon as possible. Putin knows the U.S. has a systemic problem, and that therefore systemic change must occur. But readers should know that Putin was simply a messenger. Consider that the International Monetary Fund (IMF), most Oil Producing and Exporting Countries (OPEC), the United Nations (UN), and the outgoing President of the World Bank have also called for the decoupling of world-wide trade transactions with U.S. dollars. It's not been reported nearly as widely in the U.S. press as it has outside of the U.S., but trade settlement transactions in other than the dollar have become commonplace the world over, and the trend accelerated as we entered 2012. How great is a reserve currency that other major economies of the world don't want to use? Not too great, unfortunately. Time is not on the side of the U.S. dollar. The unfortunate translation is that time is not on your side either. It's a train wreck in slow motion 3D HD video.

The U.S., the European Union, and the United Kingdom (UK) have big economic problems caused by too much debt, and soon their currencies will be relegated to the second tier. You can't keep pumping blood into a massively hemorrhaging patient forever. At some point a gaping hole has to be repaired or death will occur. As referenced above, Putin was vocal on the dangers of a U.S. debt dominated economic model, and offered a new plan, involving the currencies of Russia, China, Germany, and Saudi Arabia. What do you notice about this? These are countries which have vast resources, either in the productivity of their people and manufacturing facilities, national savings, or their natural resources. They also have low sovereign debt levels. Will a new reserve currency actually be implemented? Who knows, but it doesn't really matter. Any sovereign trading partners can accept payment by any means they desire. They don't need any stamp of approval to dump the U.S. dollar. What does matter though is that the United States has lost its grip on the strength of its world economic leadership. Leadership is not about military might anymore; it's about economic might, as China has proven.

The core of the problem

The very basis of our economy and its underlying financial system is the U.S. dollar. The dollar has gradually evolved away from the gold and silver content it had upon the nation's founding into the fiat currency we have today. *Fiat money* can simply be defined as money that is dictated by government fiat, decree, or order as that instrument which is to be accepted for all public and private transactions. It is backed by nothing, other than the good faith of a government to make good on its redeemable nature. Under the Constitution, money was to be based on a specific measurement of gold or silver, or even notes that could be exchanged for same. But now the problem is this: what would our dollars be redeemed for now? The answer is - nothing! The days of getting gold or silver in exchange for your paper money are gone.

Since there is no longer anything of actual value, or standard, backing the currency, it can be produced at will on the whim of the Central Bank, with the usual nod by the politicians. How do they do it?

At the root of the fiat scam is *fractional reserve banking*. Very simply, this allows banks, including our Federal Reserve, to maintain on hand only a tiny fraction (or as little as 6%) of the deposits customers have made. By law, banks can loan out money in amounts far in excess of their actual custodial customer deposits. If you were to deposit $1000 into a new bank account, the bank can loan out $940 of that money. The recipient of the loan then deposits the $940 into his bank account (even if it's the same bank that made the original loan), and then at least 94% of *that* money can be loaned out. And the process goes on and on. At the height of the high times pre-2008, some banks held as little as 3 cents for every dollar they created and lent out for customer loans. What is worse, the 3 cents the banks did have was of questionable value, consisting of toxic financial investments and side bets. The word toxic has become a popular description for bank assets that are worth far less than they originally were, or what is shown on the books. Further, the Federal Reserve Bank works the same way!

In fact, many of the side bets are done via the use of structured investment vehicles (SIV's). These are entities created on paper that allow banks and other institutions to make side bets that don't show up on the books! They are referred to as *off balance sheet*. The problem is that there are contingent liabilities associated with the SIV's. That means that if they lose the bet, the bank that created the SIV has to cough up the money that *will* show on the books in the form of dramatically less reserves on hand! Most of the biggest banks in the U.S. and around the world operate in this fashion. Not only that, it is likely that the Fed runs more than one set of books as well, given that $16 trillion of loan activity (on a $2.8 trillion balance sheet!) was discovered as part of the Dodd-Frank financial reform bill enacted in 2010. For readers who aren't accountants, a balance sheet keeps track of assets and liabilities, and is supposed to count everything such that both sides of the tally *balance*. A bank can't possibly have a $2.8 trillion balance sheet after having doled out $16 trillion in swaps or loans. This is an outrage! The Fed is far less than transparent and not telling Americans the extent to which it is creating new money! The bankers and politicians would lose their job if they were to tell the truth, but here it is: our financial system *is built upon a Ponzi scheme of the highest order!*

But that's not all. The Federal Reserve has become the lender of last resort to the world. That means it gets to create money to its heart's content, while citizens can only sit by and pay for the exercise in the form of higher prices. Because the U.S. dollar has been the world's reserve currency, up to this point there has been plenty of demand for dollars. But that is changing, and this fact is ominous for consumers in the U.S.

What the heck is a dollar, anyway? Let's investigate. Looking on the top of a dollar bill, there's a big fat clue: "Federal Reserve Note". *That dollar is actually a loan from the Federal Reserve.* The notes are signed by both the Treasurer of the United States and the Secretary of the Treasury. Does the U.S. government owe money to the Federal Reserve Bank? The answer is yes. And how can we expect that an IOU is legal tender, for all debts, private and public, as the bills state? The answer is that the U.S. government mandates it! However, *it depends on the confidence of the public to make the system of trading IOU's actually work.* Even though our government mandates that the dollars we spend be *accepted* as payment for a debt, goods, or services, it does not preclude citizens from using alternative methods of payment for tender and acceptance. If you offer a dollar, the recipient *must* accept it. If you offer a different form of payment, it may or may not be accepted at the discretion of the recipient. And, in terms of international acceptance, *confidence is absolutely the critical factor.*

You undoubtedly agree that a dollar just won't buy what it used to, whether your time frame is 4 or 40 years. All you have to do is go to the grocery store or gas station. Prices have become so high because of the excess volume of dollars that have consistently been cranked out by the Fed over the years. And as you have seen in the introduction, that money creation has gone into hyper-drive. The super-fudged Consumer Price Index (CPI) numbers show depreciation in the value of the dollar of over 96% since 1913, but that's before the upcoming explosion in consumer prices! Even the Federal Reserve's own numbers admit to 2500% inflation since it started its game in 1913. The politicians are overseeing the bankers depreciate the value of your money into nothing! And now it's set up for a disappearing act!

Inflation is not a pretty concept. It is the worst kind of tax a citizen of any country can endure. But in the history of civilization, the record is clear. Literally, every currency that was ever issued by a country that was not backed by something real (referred to as commodity money) has been inflated away into worthlessness, only to have the issuing government either fail, or start over again with a new monetary system. We'll look at examples later. Indeed, in the history of the United States, this re-start has occurred more than once. And it's the regular people, not the elite, who are devastated when it occurs.

What is inflation?

The relative supply of anything determines its value. The more you have availability of an item, the less each of those items are worth. Money works the same way. So believe with certainty that an expanded supply of money will ultimately result in higher prices for the tangible goods that we want to buy. That's because the more of it there is, the less value each unit of it has. This isn't theory, this is fact. In plain terms, that spells inflation. *It is a fact that inflation is a monetary phenomenon that causes rising product prices. Increasing the amount of available money is the cause, and rising consumer prices are the result of excess money creation.* Conversely, deflation has to do with a shrinking supply of the money stock. Money supply can shrink by debt default or by contraction by the Central Bank. Sometimes this contraction can even manifest itself in lower prices due to less availability of money to spend, causing less demand.

The United States continues to undergo the greatest money expansion in world history. This will ultimately lead to extreme price increases. The end result is already assured, as in – a done deal. If there is any positive aspect to our pending disaster, it's that it takes time for the new money to work into the system. Right now we are in the gestation period, which can work to our benefit if we are willing to properly prepare.

In an inflationary environment, sellers of products and services have to make up the deficiency in value in the form of a higher price charged to the buyer, because the currency appears to be worth less to the seller! The price of OPEC oil is a prime example of price inflation caused *in part by currency inflation*. Of course, supply and demand factors also account for price movements.

Having stated the above, please realize that you could have rising prices without monetary inflation, just as you could have falling prices without a decrease in the money stock. But *you can't have monetary inflation without eventually having tangible asset prices escalate*; and this fact is what the bankers and most politicians don't want you to know. In fact, they use any number of strategies and ploys to keep you in the dark.

We've heard a lot of deflationary fears in our economy since 2008, but those fears are unfounded. Ben Bernanke, the Fed Chairman, wants to have a 2% inflation target. But he deceitfully uses the term "inflation" when targeting prices, when in fact the U.S. monetary base has increased more than 300% since the crisis unfolded, as we know. A lot of pundits say now that inflation is not a problem because some prices are dropping. But if money is hoarded and not put into circulation, like what the banks and many corporations did for the first few years into the crisis, of course it could have the effect of seeing some prices drop. Or, if the big money holders have decided to invest their funds elsewhere around the globe, that doesn't mean the increased stock of money will affect U.S. consumer prices right away. But this is strictly a temporary phenomenon.

Inflation – the chosen path to default on government promises

We have come to the point of reckoning that puts our smiling bankers, politicians and bureaucrats in Washington DC in a box, with no good chance for escape. The bottom line is that they can't pay for the promises they have made over the years. This means that the United States only has four basic choices to get back on permanent, prosperous path, and none of the choices are good. Any one of them will cost the citizenry its lifestyle, while the powers in Washington, DC get to pick the poison of their preference.

The *four choices* are: 1) Grow our way out of the problem with a miraculous new industrial revolution in conjunction with a massive amount of new tax revenue; 2) Enact massive cuts in government spending, including reneging on Social Security and Medicare; 3) Declare that the U.S. would immediately default on its debts in the form of Treasury issues, then start fresh with no debt; or 4) Simply print up more money to cover promises and other expenses.

Politicians and bankers would have you believe that our economy can grow out of our debt problem. This is guaranteed not to happen under current regulatory and tax law regime, as the numbers just don't work. The industrial base and technology necessary to make that happen don't exist in the U.S. anymore. The regulatory environment and wage structure is simply not competitive with the higher growth areas of the world, witnessed by the outsourcing of tens of thousands of factories and tens of millions of jobs. Of course the United States is a world leader in innovation and technology. And of course the U.S. has been through tough times before. But government expenses on everything from defense to entitlements have overwhelmed our ability to pay for our current and future commitments. So let's briefly examine the three remaining choices to see how we can deal with the promises we've already made.

It is patently obvious that the massive cuts in government spending needed for the survival of our financial structure will never happen. This path to survival is untenable, as the consequences of the public reaction would be revolutionary. The politicians would never do it. Promises like Social Security and Medicare would need to be reneged upon. We know that President Obama had a commission look into the matter of debt and finances of the U.S., but he totally ignored their findings in proposing his 2012 budget. And yes, we know the Republicans, the Tea Party, and even some Democrats have gotten on the bandwagon to cut spending. But nothing they'll be willing and able to do will help alleviate the very real, pending debt explosion and resulting stealth default. The needed immediate and massive spending cuts can't be made for political and societal reasons. And dumping some of those expenses on the states wouldn't help the middle class, since they'd be paying that tab as well. So massive cost cutting just won't work. It would certainly even cause massive civil unrest, as in Greece or the "Arab Spring" countries.

This leaves only two methods to deal with our debts and future promises. It's just the timing and methodology that are in play. Defaulting on the U.S. national debt is a given, period. How could that be? It has to be because the debt spiral is unsustainable. Debt default is not at all unusual. In fact, a default in one fashion or another has been involved with each and every fiat currency regime in the history of the world. The U.S. dollar regime will end the same way, and it's already started. The method the U.S. has chosen is a *process*, not an event.

Of course, the quickest method of dealing with oursized obligations would be an honest, straight up default as the one which occurred in 2001 in Argentina, with the U.S. thumbing its nose at creditors worldwide and reneging on Social Security and Medicare promises. The money is just not there. There is no Social Security "lockbox". With this type of default, the U.S. could announce to the world that we would only pay, say $.25, $.05 or even $.00 per dollar of debt (or whatever the number may be). This method would create instant chaos, a huge loss in the buying power of the dollar, and the loss of a civil society. This happened in Argentina in 2001 when it decided to de-peg its peso from a 1 to 1 ratio with the U.S. dollar. An immediate devaluation would have immediate adverse effects. A U.S. dollar centered economy and financial system would cease to exist in its current form. A new system would have to be built. It would not be the way to go if you were a politician or a banker.

That leaves us with the last choice for dealing with our debts and future promises. The government can make the debt less and less burdensome by creating more and more new money, as was done in Weimar Germany in after World War I. The old debt is inflated away in favor of newer, debased debt at your expense! In other words, *new money is created to pay off old debts!* Citizens pay for this old debt by way of higher prices which reflect the loss in value of the paper money. The value of the stuff you want to buy isn't really isn't worth more; your money is worth less! It's like legalized theft to which the public doesn't object, to the delight of the bankers and many politicians! These folks thrive on the *spread* between the old, higher borrowed value and the newer, lesser repaid value!

So this is the chosen path to debt management and prosperity in the United States: pay the debt back and keep promises with dollars that are less valuable than those that were borrowed or promised in the first place. This isn't a radical statement, as this is precisely what is happening. Our foreign creditors have taken notice and have become reluctant to fund more loans to us. This means that we now must resort to both overt and covert quantitative easing (QE) instead. This QE money creation, aka federalized counterfeiting, has a guaranteed result. As the world repudiates the dollar, U.S. citizens will pay dearly in the form of unexpectedly explosive increases in prices on most goods they need.

A currency war arises

Unfortunately, it is much worse than just profligate U.S. money printing. The world money stock has grown huge, as the top twenty economies in the world (the G-20) set on a coordinated course of "stimulus" in addition to defending their own brand of fiat with the printing presses. And there are many foreign banks and sovereign countries which need to be bailed out so the presses have to keep cranking out the fiat paper.

The currency war is now front and center. A lower currency value has the effect of making domestic products cheaper in overseas markets, fostering higher exports. In the fall of 2010, President Obama announced to the world that we plan to double our exports within 5 years! Does this mean that we'll double our manufacturing capacity to dig out of the recession? No, it means that the plan is to devalue the dollar to make this goal a reality! A lower dollar value makes U.S. manufactured goods cheaper overseas. What do you think is the reaction of other industrialized nations to this policy? They print up money too to defend their own currency, keeping it at their desired value against the dollar, so that *their* exports keep pace. No fewer than 23 industrialized countries have fought back at the U.S. by printing more money of their own. This is profound! Not everyone can increase their exports! Not everyone can keep printing currency without vast worldwide ramifications. But everyone can indeed devalue their currency at the same time! So the world is now stuffed with lesser-value cash than ever before that can be deployed anywhere in the world with a few clicks of a computer mouse.

History has repeatedly shown that the financial prosperity of any country is directly tied to the viability, strength, and acceptability of its money. But when the currency becomes debased, the confidence in the financial system erodes, and economic prosperity disappears at the citizen's expense in the form of inflation. We also know that those who first control this newly created money benefit the most because they can spend it before prices rise. In fact, they can even hoard the newly created money hoping for lower prices in their targeted purchases. This way they can do even that much better when they ultimately decide to release it for purchasing assets on the cheap. Unfortunately, those at the end of the food chain for dollars take it on the chin when prices have already risen due to the huge wave of new money hitting the marketplace. These are typically middle class citizens, and they are the ones who pay the ultimate price in the form of vanishing purchasing power as the realization of the scam surfaces and the confidence in their money is lost. The problem accelerates as citizens try to spend their money more quickly to avoid certain price increases in the near future.

Fiat money value measurements are flawed

Some financial pundits, most Central Bankers, and even the politicians rely on the *Dollar Index* as a measure of relative value against other currencies. But readers should understand that examination and dependence on the Dollar Index as a true measure of comparative value against other currencies is yet another diversion of the truth by the financial elite. The index is comprised of six currencies: the Swedish Krona, the British Pound, the Swiss Franc, the Canadian Dollar, the Euro, and the Japanese Yen. So what do all of these have in common? They are all creating new money like crazy, that's what. This has the effect of making the U.S. Dollar look more stable than it actually is. But the critical point is not just about the Fed's profligate debasement of our currency. The real point to be made is that virtually all industrialized nations, including the Swiss, the last bastion of Western financial stability, are inflating their currencies. In fact, an examination of the money supply of the central banks of 8 of the largest economies in the world shows a *tripling* of the balance sheets (3 times more money). That is correct. The money supply in these eight economies went from about $5 trillion total to over $15 trillion from 2008 to 2011. The biggest jump was in the fall of 2008 at the onset of the crisis. And these figures don't even reflect the $1 Trillion Euro injection of new money into the European Banking system at the start of 2012. Nor does it consider the many other major economies doing the same thing. There is no evidence of a shortage of printer's ink, so don't be deceived by the stability of the Dollar Index.

But you may ask, what does this really mean? It means that we have many multiples of fiat units worldwide than we had just a few years ago. Has the volume of commodities, food, and the building block materials for manufactured goods increased by the same many multiples? No; not at all. But the fact is that the world *has recently added hundreds of percent more money that will ultimately chase roughly the same amount of goods.* That spells super inflation in prices for the things we want to buy!

Has the population increased? Of course, putting even more demand on those goods, particularly for necessities such as food and fuel. This added demand will also act as a great force for higher prices. We have entered a vortex of hyperinflation. It's like a perfect storm. And the real problem for U.S. citizens is that the U.S. government is stuck with the need to continue to print more money! The larger point is that you should simply *disregard the Dollar Index as a value determinant of the purchasing power of your dollars.*

So, how do you compare the value of the dollar against other paper money? Where is the basis of value? How do you know what the dollar is really worth, and what it will buy? *The price of gold is the index of truth.* Gold has served as real money for thousands of years. It has always functioned as and has been considered to be money until 40 years ago! Over the long run, gold has always maintained its purchasing power, no matter what the brand of fiat currency. That's the very reason that gold has risen relentlessly against every brand of modern currency, although not necessarily in equal percentages. The printers keep printing, but the gold miners have no chance at all to keep up! It's no contest, as gold production only adds about 1.5 percent per year to the overall supply of the precious metal.

But gold isn't the only determinant of real value. To consumers, practically any tangible asset is what they will soon use as a dollar value determinant. That's because there will be tremendous increase in the prices of all tangible assets as the problem accelerates when newly created money chases tangible assets the world over.

The financial elite and the hoarding of the "power money"

It is well recognized by any honest observer that too much debt and easy credit at all levels led to financial excesses, political promises, creative new betting vehicles, and extreme speculation that need to be somehow dealt with now. Vast new money stocks had to be created. This newly created electronic money doesn't just chase the markets. No, this money *controls* the markets, at least in the shorter term price movements. And much of the trading is done by computers which are programmed with heavy doses of math and technical analysis that try to anticipate supply and demand price points to their maximum advantage. Computers are now able to move the markets in ways that have no basis in consideration of supply or demand of the subject assets.

That fresh new money which is hoarded by governments, equity funds, pension funds, hedge funds, large corporations and other institutions is what can be considered to be the *power money*. It can move worldwide in an instant, affecting any market it touches. And when the U.S. Fed Funds rate (for bank borrowing) is set between 0 and .25 (1/4) percent for a period of years, we see a phenomenon called the *dollar carry trade*. This is simply the borrowing of dollars by large financial institutions at virtually no interest cost, and hoarding or investing those dollars elsewhere for a higher return than the cost to carry the loan. Much of these borrowed dollars have to be sold to convert to another currency of choice before landing in their intended resting place, putting more downward pressure on the value of the dollar. And as long as the interest rate on the loan is low and the dollar value is muted, the game continues.

Why would the financial elite hoard the new money? The idea is to temporarily keep it out of circulation so that it doesn't chase the targeted assets they want to buy, driving the price higher. In a tough economy with escalating prices for many consumer goods, the investment money of the little guy becomes scarcer. This means that many investment sectors will actually drop, even though doing so in an inflationary environment. By waiting to spend their stash, the power money can pick up their targets more cheaply. But once they spend the money, subsequent users of those funds will experience higher prices due to excess supply of the fiat paper that just came into circulation.

Meanwhile, the ordinary U.S. citizen can't get the normal access to credit that he has come to expect, putting a severe damper on the economy at home. Rightly or wrongly, that citizen has come to learn how to consume from the equity in his or her home, but now the well is dry. The *people money* has dried up, while the amount of power money has grown exponentially bigger, ready for deployment.

Foundation now built for hyperinflation of consumer prices

There is a distinction between inflation and hyperinflation. Sure, money printing will eventually and most definitely have a huge impact on consumer prices, regardless of the blather to the contrary from Federal Reserve Chairman Ben Bernanke and his 2% target. But price *hyperinflation* is a different animal. It can be both anticipated and guaranteed at a certain point, caused first and foremost by the lack of confidence in the value of the purchasing power of the brand of money being spent. Once user confidence is gone, money will be quickly unloaded for tangible goods. The faster this money turns over and over, the higher prices get. Hyperinflation is about the *demand to unload an unwanted currency* more than it is a demand for tangible assets, and there is a definite psychological factor involved.

The demand for tangible assets by the world's financial elite has commenced. Tangible asset prices will rise accordingly, depending on how much money chases the various asset classes. Typically an asset class coveted by the financial elite is commodities, the *building block assets.* These are the assets that are needed to produce consumer and industrial products, such as iron ore, crude oil, timber, copper, silver, cotton, and the list goes on and on. The demand on the raw materials causes the cost of the end products to be higher. Otherwise, the producer would have to shutter the business or product line due to the lack of a profit margin.

What will you do when prices rise relentlessly on the items you want to buy? You'll stock up on staples that you can find at a good price, just like everyone else, depleting the shelves in the stores. You'll not keep as much money in the bank, favoring its use to buy necessary items, albeit at higher prices. As the prices get even higher, you'll spend even more on stockpiles, reducing your cash that much more. Think of it as a game of *hot potato with cash!* That's what the power money does, and you'll do the same. As mentioned, this hyperinflationary scenario has happened twice before in American history, and it's going to happen again. It simply cannot and will not be avoided. Too much money outstanding chasing a relatively stable base of products guarantees it.

The bottom line

Do you really believe that money printing aka quantitative easing (QE) will get the U.S. back on its monetary feet? Do you think that inflation is not a problem, and that deflation is something you should be worried about? Unfortunately, the propaganda about the monetary policy moves coming out of Washington DC is a total lie! The consequences will be dire, regardless of what you hear from the Treasury Secretary, or the Chairman of the Fed and their band of thieves. Not only will you discover proof positive in these pages, but you'll also find out that their supposed concern for the well-being of the taxpayers is total baloney. That's right: all of the untested moves and adventures into unchartered financial waters will directly and negatively affect you! Fed Chairman Ben Bernanke claims to be an expert on the Great Depression and its solutions. You will soon learn how laughable this notion is in light of the facts surrounding our

Theft of the American Dream

current situation. Our financial crisis could lead directly to the destruction of your standard of living, and your way of life.

But if we are supposedly on the road to recovery, why posit that the financial system is set to fail? Because not only is the *cause* of the crisis still with us, it has also gotten markedly worse since it first became apparent in 2008! Using freshly printed paper money to cover over the symptoms (i.e. the losses) of the real problem just won't cut it as we fast approach a disintegration of the function of the U.S. dollar. A currency crisis of confidence is now upon us, and it will cause very dramatic consequences.

We are in a crisis of a lifetime. Is it worse than the Great Depression? Yes, most assuredly. *You will experience what the end game of an un-backed currency regime feels like!* What we had in the fall of 2008 after the demise of investment bank Lehman Brothers was the first sign of a broken financial system. This was not a sign of a run of the mill recession. Consequently, the bankers and politicians were scared into outlandish fiscal and monetary moves, unlike this country has ever seen. They now claim we are on the road to recovery. They're talking about the economy, and lying about it too, as you will discover. 'Theft of the American Dream' actually refers to the destruction of financial underpinnings of the United States, which will come directly out of your pocket. The end result will *not* look like it did coming out of the 1930's. This is the feared *crack up boom*, the phenomenon dubbed by the Austrian economic theory, and you are in the eye of the storm. Now it's time for a simplified explanation of this theory. Just know that the end result will render the U.S. fiat dollar worthless and will usher the U.S. into a second tier economy. But as in any crisis, there is opportunity. Let's build a base of knowledge before getting into personal survival techniques and suggestions.

* 18 *

CHAPTER 2
JOHN MAYNARD KEYNES
VS. THE AUSTRIANS

Who knows how to create real wealth?

In this chapter we'll examine two economic schools of thought regarding fiat currency and debt created money. In a capitalist system, wealth creation is the key to government tax revenues and further productivity and product innovations across a wide spectrum of goods and services for the consuming public. This is the starting point of your financial edification. You won't need any economics background for this chapter, just common sense.

The school of economic thought used by the U.S. government and the Fed was envisioned by John Maynard Keynes, referred to as Keynesianism. The other school to which we'll refer is simply called the Austrian school, as the academics who originally espoused it in the 1800's were from Austria. Keynesianism uses "central planning" to manage an economy, while the Austrian school emphasizes free market directives controlled by consumers.

A lot has changed in the past 100 years or so under our Federal Reserve System, but unfortunately those changes would not include the cessation of the scheming by the bankers and politicians. The United States government has tried to use the Federal Reserve System to steer the economy since the depths of the Great Depression. However, the lack of fiscal discipline and the reliance on easily created money has distorted our capitalist free market and its underlying financial system. This fact will dramatically affect all things financial and economic, including your little piece of the pie. The beginning of the end actually happened on August 15, 1971 at the time of Richard Nixon's denouncement of the international gold standard. Prior to that, any country that wanted to convert its dollars into gold from the U.S. Treasury could do so upon demand. This option has long since disappeared. We are currently experiencing the only time in history that every country in the world is run on a totally un-backed fiat currency regime. This fact sets up a simple question and discussion for this chapter.

That question is: *Can an effectively and efficiently regulated free market make its own financial determinations, or should the government elite and central bankers make those decisions for it?* The answer to this question is critical. The politicians (with the exception of a very few) and bankers have been fighting to keep their Keynesian ideas going all along the way, even when it is showing major stress fractures at its foundation. Now that foundation has become irreparably damaged. It cannot be fixed unless we are willing to start over. If we don't, it will destroy the American dream and our way of life. If we do, the shorter term pain will be horrendous, but the longer term gain will be the continuation of our freedom for our children and grandchildren. The choice is ours, but we'll definitely suffer tremendously either way. The piper demands payment in one fashion or another.

Savings versus debt: freedom versus bondage

Based on the thinking of the Austrian school, one should consider two important points. First, *savings and wealth creation is critical for long term survival of our capitalist way of life* and the enjoyment of an advanced standard of living. Second, *spiraling debt accumulation is death to the need and desire for freedom*, as it becomes more and more burdensome until it ultimately crushes the debtor. Debt accumulation is the opposite of savings and wealth creation. Even though the use of government or personal debt can seem like an easy fix to a problem in the short term, it cannot possibly lead to permanent prosperity, unless its use is stopped and reversed by paying that debt off. Debt can be a wonderful tool if it comes with a plan for repayment and the accumulation of wealth in the process. But absent that plan, it becomes a noose.

Savings and wealth accumulation means freedom of choice in how that wealth is to be utilized, which in turn is crucial to long term political freedom. Savings is freedom, just as debt is oppression. Savings allow us to make choices, while debt necessarily makes choices for us. Having money in the bank gives us tremendous flexibility in the analysis and selection of our purchase and investment options, both personally and governmentally.

True savings and wealth cannot be printed into existence. It must be created through value production of a viable business, and subsequent acceptance of that value by the consumer. It must be earned and saved. The most important thing to realize is that the investment of our prior savings for the production of further capital formation and savings is the way to national wealth, prosperity, and the continuation of our freedom.

The Austrians demonstrate that it is critical to allow the natural level of economic activity control itself. It espoused *capital formation* (savings) as the key to long term economic security, growth and prosperity. This means that a depression should be allowed to seek its natural end, including business and bank failures. But why should we have cycles of boom and bust in the first place? The Austrians are able to demonstrate that there was nothing in the capitalist market system that could explain away the boom and bust cycles of the economy *other than* debt expansion and contraction. Absent unabated debt creation and government intervention policies, the economy would self-correct as it went along, on more of a steady upward glide path than the rollercoaster ride caused by fiat debt expansion and contraction. Monetary inflation makes the depression necessary.

While the Austrians can explain how to avoid the real damage of debt expansion boom and bust cycles while still achieving prosperity, the Keynesians simply tell the government and bankers how to remedy their own mistakes, primarily through money creation, hiding the truth for political expedience. This is the key distinction. Not only do Keynesians like new debt, they need the new debt to perpetuate their theory. The Austrians would rather save and reinvest into productive enterprise, creating a base for capital formation and further wealth accumulation. *Very simply, Keynesians need debt for growth while Austrians eschew it.*

Capitalism can work wonders if left to its own devices. It doesn't need help, or safety nets. All it needs is to be left to the markets of consumers to make the fateful decisions. This does not mean there should be no rules. Regulations are certainly necessary, but only if their impact is fully researched and understood prior to implementation. With effective regulation, success is still there for the taking, as is failure. Both individual entrepreneurs and big business are on trial daily and the rewards can be handsome, just as the punishment can be brutal. But in the end, a free market capitalist system ensures that the consumer is satisfied, the economy gets stronger, government is paid for, and the standard of living is enhanced for all. And the success or failure of any capitalist society rests in the discerning minds and choices of the citizen consumers.

Take cover!

After the Great War (now referred to as World War I) the U.S. entered into a severe depression by 1920. The Fed was still pretty new, and it basically did nothing, after having doubled the money supply to fund the War. The depression ended very quickly, with virtually no interference from government or the Fed. In fact, the government reduced expenses as a policy response! But then the party really started as the Fed ramped up the money supply again during the Roaring 20's. When the inevitable correction came, the U.S. Central Bankers were blamed for aggravating this Great Depression by holding money out of the commercial banking system. And the politicians didn't help matters either. Their regulations and fiscal actions under the Coolidge, Hoover, and Roosevelt administrations caused the boom, and then helped to prolong the bust. It was all guesswork, and many ad hoc programs just didn't work. By 1936, both the bankers and the politicians needed a playbook, so to speak. Enter John Maynard Keynes.

John Maynard Keynes became very popular in the U.S. after the publication of his book 'The General Theory of Employment, Interest, and Money' in 1936. The Great Depression was in progress, and the politicians and bankers of the day obviously didn't want it to happen again in the future. After all, the sales pitch to the American public in 1913 in favor of the Federal Reserve System in the first place was to provide for an elastic supply of money, thus managing through potential future panics. The proponents had to get a handle on how the government, in conjunction with the Federal Reserve, could make things better in the event of another actual or threatened depression or panic scenario, and the promise was to keep prices stable and to have full employment. So, Keynes became a rock star when the bankers and politicians thought he had all the right answers.

Keynes gave the bankers and politicians cover for what they wanted to do: attempt to manipulate the economy through fiscal and monetary policy. In this context, *monetary policy* can simply be defined as controlling interest rate movements, the supply of money, and the member bank reserve requirement levels, so that the Central Bank could try to achieve the desired economic result in the U.S. economy. These moves have effects on business growth, employment, and as a result, on consumers.

Additionally, *fiscal policy* can be defined as those actions by the government affecting economic conditions, such as more borrowing, more spending, and additional taxation or other regulatory action affecting money and its use. So the bankers and politicians had finally found cover with Keynesianism, since now they had an academic assert that they could increase the stock of money with impunity in an effort to effectively steer the economy. The bankers and politicians were thrilled at this development, as it seemed to have all the answers. All the government had to do, with the help of the Fed, was to attempt to guide the economy down the narrow road between the boom and the bust using money creation and interest rate manipulation as highlighters on the roadmap.

So Keynesianism became all the rage after 1936 as the stodgy Austrians faded to the background. But they were never successfully refuted. Indeed, they seem to be coming to full vindication in the current worldwide financial crisis. But the politicians and bankers still hold tightly to the Keynesian solutions and ways. Unfortunately, the Keynesian solutions of the 1930's do not, nor will they ever effectively address the problems we face today. The situation today is so very different than the 1930's, and much more pervasive. The bailout nation will get sicker until it dies. The Austrians show how this comes about, which is what hyperinflation is all about in the context of a fiat currency expansion in its latter stages. Now the price must be paid, even though the politicians and bankers don't acknowledge that fact to the American public.

Unfortunately, John Maynard Keynes is the still the guru to whom the politicians and bankers look for guidance on how to run an economy. The Fed employs hundreds of Keynesian economists, but none in the Austrian discipline. Fed Chairman Ben Bernanke had become the head cheerleader prior to the onset of the crisis. Indeed, for decades it has been assumed that all would be well if the ideas of Keynes were followed in a financial crisis, but Professor Bernanke now oversees the end of the fiat regime with quite inventive fixes that Keynes would never have conceived nor imagined. Forget the fact that there weren't supposed to be any more panics after the establishment of the Federal Reserve System. No, now they would be called depressions, and after the Great Depression, they were then called recessions, as it sounded better. But no matter what they are called, they are all due to the misallocation and unbridled expansion of the money supply in defiance of natural consumer market forces. The elasticity of the currency that the bankers so desperately wanted never actually retracts. It just keeps building and building. This is inflation, and it most definitely has an end game, a very bad one. We know that this bad ending has happened to 100 percent of all fiat currencies in world history. The record is perfect.

Inflation and enforcement of the fiat

Of inflation of the currency, Keynes, in his 1920 book 'The Economic Consequences of the Peace' wrote:

"Lenin is said to have declared that the best way to destroy the Capitalist system was to debauch the currency...Lenin was certainly right...There is no subtler, no surer means of overturning the existing basis of society than to debauch the currency. The process engages all the hidden forces of economic law on the side of destruction, and does it in a manner which not one man in a million can diagnose."

Take heed from the gentleman who wrote the bible of the bankers and to this day serves as their guiding light! Even now we teach Keynesianism in our college classrooms to the exclusion of the Austrian theory under the presumed assumption that if the government likes it, it must be right!

Inflation is the most insidious of all taxes, and it is monitored and guarded by the Internal Revenue Service. Without the IRS, the fiat currency game would be over, as the citizens would find their own medium of exchange. The mediums of choice for many a society for thousands of years have been gold or silver. It should interest the reader that even the doctor of fiat currency demonstrated how tax regulation is a critical element in the inflationary robbery of the people. In his 1920 book referenced above, Keynes states:

"Should government refrain from regulation the worthlessness of the money becomes apparent and the fraud can no longer be concealed."

Here Keynes was referring to the absolute necessity of having a function of enforcement of the fiat, which is done in the U.S. with tax collection under the aegis of the Internal Revenue Service. It is the policeman that directs public compliance with the fiat currency mandate. Can we really consider Keynesian economics to be a valid form of economic theory for the benefit of regular citizens? It has been totally discredited with our current crisis, given that every trick (and then some) in the Keynes playbook has been tried without successful results for a true and lasting economic recovery. We have however, succeeded in a vast expansion of the monetary base and a record amount of U.S. government debt. Has Ben

Bernanke run out of tools in his black bag? If so, what economic theory is the right one, and can its efficacy be demonstrated?

Fatal flaws

What are the basic subjects that any capitalist economic theory must address? It must address *employment, money, and interest*. The Austrians could easily and effectively offer correct answers to the problems posed by the Keynesians and their attending perverse monetary logic. Let's dig into this question with a bit of common sense.

Over 75 years after the discovery of the cover of Keynesianism, we have found that the Keynes solutions to normal business contractions had fatal flaws. It has become plainly obvious that the economy cannot be centrally managed without long term ramifications. Firstly, the theory was developed when there was a U.S. and international gold standard, which no longer exists. There are no longer controls on money creation. The gold standard served its purpose until the 1960's. Secondly, it only viewed the prescribed solutions over too short a timeframe, given that it short-circuited the normal capitalistic treatment of interest rates and the supply of money, critical to savings and wealth building. In other words, it was a feel good solution for the economic issues of the day, and it assumed that it could always do more in the future, no matter what. But make no mistake here. Even though Keynes acknowledged inflation in his solutions, he found it easy to blame consumers for inflation by saying they were spending too much, causing escalating prices. This is only partially true. Consumer demand can increase prices simply due to a demand/supply imbalance, but that is not inflation, as most people have been led to believe. Finally, the extreme level of leverage at financial institutions and the attending creative new instruments for betting and risk off-loading along with synthetic ways to keep interest rates low could never have been conceived by Keynes. Computers have seen to the wizardry in a new and scary way.

Regardless of modern financial engineering, we find the real flaw, and a critical admission by Keynes in the preface to the German edition of his 'General Theory' book of 1936 in which he unequivocally states:

"Nevertheless the theory of output as a whole, which is what the following book provides, is much more easily adapted to the conditions of a totalitarian state, than is the theory of production and distribution of a given output produced under conditions of free competition and a large measure of laissez-faire."

Does it get any clearer than this? Do we have to go any further with the point that trying to boost production by increasing the stock of money and fiddling with interest rates does not work for the benefit of a capitalist system, but is better suited to totalitarianism? It is really sad that sneaky bankers have pulled the wool over the eyes of the American public with the help of unwitting politicians. Let's now take a cursory look at some Austrian school proponents, and what they believed.

Ludwig von Mises (1881-1973)

The Austrian school of economics was well known in the 1930's, but pushed aside. It had originally been developed by Carl Menger (1840-1921). By the 1930's a famed proponent of the theories espoused by Menger was Ludwig von Mises. He was one of the very few economists during the boom of the 1920's who correctly predicted the Great Depression. He also predicted that Roosevelt's New Deal would actually prolong the Depression, which was only much later proven correct. And he even anticipated the severe conditions we suffer today as evidence of the feared and final *crack-up boom*. We will soon confirm that the U.S. will suffer this ultimate disaster as the moment of truth comes into view.

Von Mises believed that there were two very basic tenets to a sound monetary policy. The first was that *actual wealth had to be produced, not borrowed*. That seems pretty reasonable. The second was that the *savings from the produced wealth had to be directed to the production of goods that the consuming public desired the most*. This would produce a profit, generating that much more additional wealth. But he cautioned that the production had to match the actual desires of the consumer. If this were not the case, distortions would occur and some businesses would fail. However, the profit and consumption cycle could repeat itself through the generations if it were left to its own ability to adjust itself. The cycle would go on and on. This is a pretty simple explanation for a theory that took a lifetime to develop, but the outline of the economic progression is: innovative ideas, the assumption of risk, production, then profit (and subsequent tax revenue to the government), then more innovative production, then more profit. And it was all controlled by the choices of consumer. If there would be no demand, there would be no profit, so the necessary failure of that product or service *had* to occur.

The "crack-up boom" was the phrase that Ludwig von Mises used to describe a currency collapse. It may be best to understand how this crack-up boom is defined on the Mises.org website. It can be found on the website in chapter 8 in the Introduction to Austrian Economics:

"The decision not to halt the credit expansion eventually must lead to what Mises has called the "crack-up boom", *characterized by a general flight into real values and the collapse of the monetary system.* In the later stages of the expansion the additions to the money supply must be increasingly accelerated as market participants have come to expect ever increasing prices. At some point, the system of monetary exchange must break down. Consequently, *to continue the easy-money policy in order to avoid the otherwise inevitable depression must bring about an even harsher fate: the collapse of the monetary system and the market economy,* with its great advantages of specialization and division of labor."

If you want to read it from the famous Von Mises himself, these scary words appear in his book 'Human Action' (1949):

"There is no means of avoiding the final collapse of a boom expansion brought about by credit expansion. The alternative is only whether the crisis should come sooner as the result of voluntary abandonment of further credit expansion, or later as a final and total catastrophe of the currency system involved."

It seems pretty clear that the path chosen by the Washington politicians and money mavens is that of desperation and further expansion of the money supply, as demonstrated by all the new spending, borrowing, QE, twisting, guarantees, bailouts, and zero interest rates. This does not bode well for U.S. citizens who use the money as it is inflated into oblivion!

More Austrian School proponents

The study of the origin of wealth is basic to the Austrian school of economics. It was actually Friederich A. Hayak (1899-1992) who spread the Austrian word with even newer and enhanced theories in the 1930's, in both the U.S. and Britain. He had been a protégé of von Mises in Vienna, attending the famed *'Privatseminar'* along with several eminent economists of the day. In the early 1930's both Hayak and Keynes debated their theories in the 'Economic Journal'. Even though Hayak was well prepared to refute the fallacies and holes in the Keynes theories, directly confronting Keynes in a public forum was not his cup of tea. Keynes was a charmer with plenty of rhetorical skill, and this left the Austrian Hayak very overmatched.

But nonetheless Hayak was later awarded the 1974 Nobel Memorial Prize in Economic Science. What was the reason for the Prize? Hayak was recognized for demonstrating how the various machinations of interest rate movements enacted by central banks gives the boom and bust cycle its life, and that these cycles are not caused by a free market. This says it all, don't you think? He was also able to demonstrate how *ultra-low interest rates set by the whim of central banks actually destroys capital*, exactly the opposite of what is desirable. Does this sound familiar, with the Fed guaranteeing its zero interest rate policy (ZIRP) for at least 6 years? Ask savers how their capital is being destroyed. Ask consumers how inflation destroys their capital. Austrians show how the free market should set the rates for money which would reflect its value in the marketplace.

Another economist in a long line of Austrians was Murray N. Rothbard (1926-1995) who succeeded Ludwig Von Mises and Frederic Hayak as the torch-bearer. In his 1969 essay 'Economic Depressions: Their Cause and Cure', he details the basics of an Austrian approach. He writes of good entrepreneurial forecasting, or an effective assessment of risk which leads to better profits, stating:

"The market economy, then, is a profit and loss economy, in which the acumen and ability of business entrepreneurs is gauged by the profits and losses they reap. The market economy, moreover, contains a built in mechanism, a kind of natural selection that ensures the survival and flourishing of the superior forecaster and the weeding out of the inferior ones. For, the more profits reaped by the better forecasters, the greater become their business responsibilities, and the more they will have available to invest in the productive system. On the other hand, a few years of making losses will drive the poorer forecasters and entrepreneurs out of business altogether..."

Successful risk takers represent the very basis of capital formation. This is the critical wealth creation in the form of the survival of the fittest in the business world, and is critical to a free and successful capitalist society.

There have been scant few members of Congress who are even aware of Austrian economics. But one, former Representative Ron Paul of Texas, has been quite vocal on the subject and accuses the Federal Reserve System as having caused most of today's problems.   He states:

"At least 90% of the cause for the financial crisis can be laid at the doorstep of the Federal Reserve.   It is the manipulation of credit, the money supply, and interest rates that caused the various bubbles to form.   Congress added fuel to the fire by various programs and institutions like the Community Reinvestment Act, Fannie Mae and Freddie Mac, FDIC (Federal Deposit Insurance Corporation), and HUD (Housing and Urban Development) mandates, which were all backed up by aggressive court rulings."

Mr. Paul also reminds us of that which has been the mantra of the Rothschild's (the dominant family of European banking) for over 250 years, saying:

"...understand that political power is controlled by those who control the money supply. Liberals and conservatives, Republicans and Democrats, came to believe, as they were taught in our universities that deficits don't matter and that Federal Reserve accommodation by monetizing debt is legitimate and never harmful.   Inflating the money supply and purposely devaluing the dollar is always painful and dangerous."

It is unfortunate that Mr. Paul never got serious consideration in Washington, nor in the media.   And when 2012 Republican Presidential candidate Rick Perry likened the money printing of the Fed's Ben Bernanke as almost "treasonous" he got excoriated by the political pundits and the mainstream press. But if viewed from an Austrian School perspective, one could argue the point!

So can we say that the both the politicians and the bankers want to inflate the currency for their own benefit? Yes.   Of course, it is possible that the guilty parties may not have known the damage they would cause in their quest for power and largess.   Remember, even Keynes acknowledged and agreed that the best way to destroy a capitalist system is to debauch the currency.

The origins of wealth

Now we know: *business* is the source of all genuine wealth and the true engine for savings in a capitalist society, not the government.   The entrepreneurial business owner is the guy who creates the wealth in this country, and the world. That's just how it works. It's about good businessmen creating good values in products and services for people so they are compelled to consume. Nobody has forced the consumers to buy that product or service. Think about this, as it's really a critically important point. The source of wealth is the creation of products or services that the consumer *wants to buy.* Those products can't be poorly made, or dysfunctional for the advertised use, and plus they have to be affordable. The products and services must satisfy the needs of the buyers in more than one way. Products have to be able to improve the life of the consumer, all at a cost that is thought to be worth it to the buyer, right? And the only way a product can be brought to the market is if an entrepreneur can make a profit on it. If a guy starts a company and can't make money on his idea, how long will he stay in business? The answer is obvious.

Clearly, it is the entrepreneur's job to make sure he/she can make a profit on a product or service that he brings to market for consumers. If the guy can't make a profit by risking the time and money, why bother? Common sense dictates that a profit motive has to be part of the formula to even bother to assume the risks to bring a product or service to market.

Too many talk show pundits and newspaper op-ed pieces rail on the businessman and how greedy and out of touch he is to the needs of the regular people. Agreed, there are certainly a lot of them who won't give back to the community and the less fortunate. And there is undoubtedly way too much greed in business, no question about it. Further, too many CEO's have gotten compensation growth that has far exceeded the growth in his workforce or profits to the company. How can outrageous compensation packages be justified at the expense of the workers or consumers? Greed puts some entrepreneurs in their own self-centered world, ignoring their neighbors, employees, and environment. This is morally wrong. But this doesn't mean that capitalism doesn't work for the betterment of society, because clearly, it does. *Business is the one and only source of wealth, and by extension, the one basic source of tax revenue.* This is a conceptual crux of the Austrian argument. The mindset of a good, ethical and caring entrepreneurial businessman is the guy we need to understand, because he is the engine of the economy and the source of economic salvation, no matter what.

Innovation and risk assumption = wealth creation and increased living standards

Why was it that the middle class in the 1950's and 1960's meant that dad had a decent job that paid enough for mom to stay home with the kids? Because they could afford to do it! Half a century later, it requires that both spouses enter the workforce to support that same household. And now we find that many of the two worker families still have trouble keeping up. What happened? Our standard of living has been given a major haircut through long term inflationary forces, while wages have definitely not kept up.

Why is it that Japanese products of the 50's in America were thought to be cheap (lower quality), and were avoided? Because they *were* lower quality, but not low priced enough for widespread acceptance! So what has changed so much that the American consumer now demands, for instance, more Japanese or even Korean cars instead of the Big 3 U.S. automaker products? Because they perceive that the value is better, so much so that they feel compelled to buy. The point is that the success or failure of the product is directly related to the potential consumer acceptance of that product. It is a fact that about 70% of the American economy is directly related to consumption by individual citizens. That's right; the spending of regular people on everyday needs and wants comprises about 70% of the GDP (Gross Domestic Product, the measure of total annual money spent in the economy) of the United States. When the consumers speak, the economy listens.

Please realize that *the consumer market is always there for innovation in any for-profit enterprise, and the public has proven that it is willing to pay for this innovation. This is particularly so when the innovation improves the standard of living, or gives the consumer a feeling that he received added value. The sale of this added value is the very source of wealth.* The huge success of the Apple I-Phone in the middle of the crisis is a perfect example. An entrepreneur will always step in to fill any void in the desires of the consumer; and he is willing to risk his capital to try to get a superior return. Remember, the entrepreneur is also a consumer and citizen, so there is a lot of common ground on which he can look to fulfill your needs and wants at a competitive price, while still being able to realize a profit. Conversely, consumers see innovation as an improvement to their living standard. This innovation leads to added value for the consumer. Everybody is happy.

What many of the detractors of businesspeople, including many politicians, fail to take into account is what it really means to be an entrepreneur. *It's about risk.* That's right, the risk. Businesspeople need to mitigate their risk in every way they can, but the bottom line is that they must put their own money (borrowed or otherwise) at risk to bring a product or service to the marketplace that someone actually wants to buy; and at a price that allows that risk-taker to get a return in both his time and money. Trying to carry the product for as much expense as it takes, and for as much time as it takes is a huge risk. Remember, the entrepreneur can't control either the time or the success variable with absolute certainty. Add to that the fact that the only certainty in the sale of a product at any level of profit is ultimately up to the consumer himself. After all, if you don't like the product, or if you don't want to buy because you think it costs too much or is too cheaply made, you the consumer, decide the success or failure of that product, not the entrepreneurial businessman!! That's his risk.

Profit motive is just as important as business failure

There is a very basic reason for a profit motive in a capitalist society; to pay for the risk assumed by somebody else. Risk is critical to progress, as with no risk the status quo would rule. There would be no innovation absent a profit motive. With no risk and subsequent profit motive, there is no progress, and no increased standard of living. That's just the way it is. This fact has been demonstrated time and time again in the history of the world. This is why socialist or communist, or any other sort of collectivist system is always doomed to failure. The weight of the lack of reward for risk taking is tantamount to encouraging the status quo, eliminating savings incentives, spreading any gains to the masses, and eventually relegating any economic progress to the trash bin. Without economic vitality, no society can survive. Pick any failed country in the history of the world, and you'll find that absent real national wealth it did not and could not survive.

Suppose the businessman has spent his money on an idea and for whatever reason, he can't make it. The sales just are not there. He can't recoup his real expenses, to say nothing of the time he has spent in vain. Maybe he could try to make up the lost money some other way, with some other product. But he cannot ever make up his lost time. He risked a part of his life on earth to bring a failed product to the market. That was his risk. But that is his way. He is willing to assume that risk in order to try to realize a profit. This time the risk didn't pan out. Now he must decide whether or not to stop doing business or otherwise give up on the product, both of which have caused a loss of money, and more importantly, the loss of time. The public has spoken: his product is not wanted. He made a bad bet, for whatever reasons.

Now, true capitalism demands that something be done. And that something cannot be in the form of help from the government. This is so because the government's only source of help would come from money taken from others in the form of taxes, or borrowing from one to give to another. Neither of these choices do anything to promote wealth creation; in fact, they do just the opposite. So the failure of a business which made a bad decision must occur. A new idea must come with new innovations, and the risk process must repeat itself. This process guarantees that either there will eventually be profits, or otherwise the inevitable losses will come. End of story. Capitalism has spoken.

The notion of bailouts is really foreign to the entrepreneurial business owner. It seems to the entrepreneur that government involvement leads to mediocrity and the status-quo; just the opposite of a highly profitable enterprise. Think about it. Bailouts only serve to reward substandard business practices, and reward greed, allowing them to perpetuate themselves. Further, it creates a moral hazard to the taxpayer, because the people running our large institutions take risks that they may otherwise not have taken because they know their mistake will be fixed by the government! So, it becomes clear that bailouts subvert capitalism. Not only that, innovation takes a back seat. Innovation leads to added value to the consumer, for which they will most definitely pay. A system dependent on bailouts or special concessions (like zero interest rates) is no longer capitalism, it is something else. Privatizing profits, but socializing losses is just plain stupid. It's like trying to direct the evolution of a species: it just doesn't work!

Without serious change to the failing business operation and plan, or simply poor judgment, nowhere will any bailout work for the production of wealth. What we have had with today's financial mess are numerous massive bailouts using borrowed money; and they have been done without the necessary structural and systemic changes necessary to make them work. And simply changing the figurehead at the top isn't enough. Translation: All we have done is to borrow money to perpetuate the same flawed operations which will likely result in more losses into the future.

Looking at the bigger picture, a bailout actually misallocates money to the less efficient operation and keeps that same capital away from another potentially much more efficient entrepreneur. It prevents a new guy with a better idea from coming in to fill the void with better plans, better technology; his own money (as opposed to public money), more productivity, and ultimately a better product at a lower price. Bailouts perpetuate a losing proposition instead of favoring innovation. They subvert progress, and usually happen for political expediency, not for good economic sense.

The media and the politicians tell us that bailouts have to happen because the entity getting help has lost so much money, they are *too big to fail*; and it would be for the good of the people and the economy to give the cash injection to the ailing patient, right? Well, not exactly. The mantra of too big to fail is just a politician's way of looking to buy votes and keep the power of the status quo. Most of the businesses that are too big to fail are actually *too big to save!* You see, the lost money is actually still out there as payment for the various parts of the goods or services rendered. Money had successfully entered the pockets of other entrepreneurs on the other side of the transactions. You know, that would be the guys who received the money from the guy who lost it. Very simple; the money changed possession. No, it didn't get burned up in the fireplace! Oh yes, it is definitely still out there. One man's loss is another man's gain. So doesn't it irritate you that, as a country, we now decide to make the American citizens pay for putting money into the pocket of both sides of the profit and loss equation? This is absolutely nuts! And it sure isn't capitalism.

The labor force and consumers: a price to pay

Let's not forget about the risk incurred by the labor force. The entrepreneur must hire employees, and this cost has to be baked in to the formula for profits. This is part of the risk borne by the business owner. But the risk actually comes back to the workers, the employees, as well. They are also subject to the laws of supply and demand. Artificially mandated wages and benefits have to be competitive, or the long term sales prospects for the products the laborers make will not be good. If the cost of labor is too high so that the product in question has to be priced higher than its competitors, sales will suffer, as will the production line; consequently, there will be less demand for those workers. They will have to accept lower wages and benefits, or be laid off for some period of time. This isn't due to the malevolence of the owner; it's just that their services are worth less to the business owner who has a product he can't sell for profit. Why would he make more of the same? He can't and won't, so the labor is not needed.

A perfect example of this high price of labor and its consequences is the Detroit automakers prior to the government bailout and/or bankruptcy. The wage scale on top of the legacy costs (retiree benefits) of the union had simply priced itself out of work compared to its foreign competitors, even when those competitors make their cars right here in the U.S. But the market is able to correct itself, in that the union employment statistics would go up if their wages and benefits came down. This isn't a political statement; it's just how the free market is supposed to work, and does work. If the union workers demand more benefits for medical or retirement, who will pay? The consumer must ultimately pay in the form of a higher price for the product! The business owner must look at the numbers at every turn, and make judgments on profitability. This always directly affects price to the end user, which always effects consumer demand in some way. This isn't a failure of capitalism; it is how it works successfully.

Also to be factored into the cost and profit formula is compliance with government regulations, including taxes. The job of the entrepreneur is to find the most efficient and cost effective ways to pay all the expenses of doing business and bringing wanted products to the marketplace at an affordable price. Remember, *affordability and desirability is decided by the consumer*, not the producer! Citizens have to realize that if they want the government to look after the environment with additional regulation, or if they want the government to bring in more revenues from profitable businesses in the form of higher taxes, or they want to somehow change the compensation of the risk takers, they are the ones who will somehow pay that tab. This payment could come in the form of higher prices, or even in the form of the removal of a marginally profitable product or service from the market, with an adverse effect on employees. The entrepreneur has no guarantees, so she will do what she can to mitigate her losses. But if losses do occur, she will have adjust or move on to plan B. Risk takers are not in business to continue to subsidize time and money on unprofitable products or services.

Is your Government a profit center?

Can the government go out and create wealth? Does the government have to take any financial risk in anything it does? Not really, as it spends money sent in by the taxpayer, and if it screws up or otherwise needs more money it can raise taxes or borrow what it needs from the Federal Reserve. Remember, the government is only a two trick pony. It gets money from the printing press (via debt and the Fed), or from taxes; it doesn't go out and earn it like citizens do. That's it, just two possible sources of cash. Remember, *wealth creation is the basis of a successful economy*, and it's instructive to see where our government fits into the picture.

No matter what a government agency calls itself, no matter which House of Congress, no matter if it is state, county, or local government, these folks are in the practice of spending your money, not making you money. These entities are supposed to be there for the common good, and should never decide to get into attempts at profit-making. Fine, use our tax money to distribute to the best causes, but don't try to compete with the risk takers. As a group, politicians and government bureaucrats have *never* proven the ability to be better managers than are found in the for-profit world. They have a long track record of mediocrity, and that's being kind.

Politicians and bureaucrats don't have the mindset for creating wealth. If they did, they'd be in the private sector. If they really had the mindset and aptitude to make big money, they'd make a heck of a lot more money by running a successful business or being a money mover on Wall Street than they would as a politician. So why do we look to them for economic guidance? This is a prescription for disaster! The big problem is not the failure of the free enterprise system; rather it's the failure of the interventionist policies that the no-clue politicians and empowered agency bureaucrats create! These people just don't have the mindset of businesspeople, and they prove it with each new move they make or law they pass in the form of unintended consequences or lack of budgetary control.

The bottom line is that governments at all levels in the United States get their funds from the for-profit world, as it should be. They are not in the risk for the opportunity of profits business. Entrepreneurial businesspeople drive the profits that will ultimately be taxed for providing revenues to the government. The higher the profits, the higher the tax paid to the government. We desperately need growth in tax revenues, and the way to get it is to foster higher growth in for-profit enterprises through value creation for consumers in the form of technological advances. Government income should not grow to the level of government expenses by borrowing the difference, which is the way it's been for years. Sure, it works for today, or this month, or this year. But it won't work long term, and that's easy to prove! In fact, in terms of the experience of your representative form of government here in the U.S., it is being proven right now! So we can be assured that the government will never be in the business of creating true wealth. Encourage and foster through good and effective policy, maybe; but not created with higher tax rates or the printing press.

Here's an example. At the Capitol building, a new visitor's center was recently completed. A few years back, our friendly Congressional leaders decided they needed this center to better control, screen, and educate the public as they visited the Capitol. This seemed like a good idea. The cost estimate at the beginning of construction was $71 million. When the project was completed, the report card came in. The project took three years longer than it was supposed to and came in over budget. How much over budget? Well, the total cost was $661 million, bringing it in at over 800% over budget! What do you think of this management of the project right under the noses of Congress? It was pretty pathetic, right? So how would you guess Mr. Obama's stimulus plan to improve the country's infrastructure and boost employment fared? You probably know the answer, but if not you'll soon find out! The word boondoggle comes to mind.

Wealth creation of non-profit organizations, the service sector, and the consumer

Do non-profit organizations create wealth or provide tax revenues to the government? No. But that doesn't mean that a non-profit organization can't make profits. In fact, the most successful NPO's are self-sustaining, having revenues and positive cash flow. The U.S. tax code may refer to them as 501-C(3) organizations, but they are simply a device to get common good types of projects and initiatives to people, places, and things that are in the interest of society to help. For the most part, these organizations are funded from private donations, other non-profit money, from their own for-profit projects, and from government money. In some cases, they actually do create enough value in a way that will actually make them profitable, but generally they are at least partially funded by the government or other non-profit entities like foundations. The question is what is their *original source* of the donations? From the for-profit business world, that's where. Whether the donations come from a church, an individual, a foundation or otherwise, the original source of the donation is a business.

Does the service sector of the economy create wealth? We must give credit where credit is due. To the extent that a service is rendered to satisfy part of the process to bring a wanted value to the consumer market, that service would help to create wealth. OK, so maybe many service businesses simply trade dollars for another service, or cash. How about the guys going to the golf course for 18 holes? Money is exchanged, but there is nothing to show for it, except for some lost balls and a few broken tees. To the owner of the course, he has to pay himself and his groundskeepers so the golfers will keep coming to his course. But where is the wealth creation? He may not have created wealth directly, but he may well have saved some of his revenues after paying his expenses. Savings is wealth, to be used another day, and it can certainly be achieved through the sale of a service. But on the consumer side, that service is *consumed and gone forever*. There is no lasting benefit to the consumer for a service that he/she has bought. It is a fleeting, feel good or even necessary expense, but it can't be used by the consumer to create more savings or wealth.

Of course employees of all types, as consumers, can create wealth for themselves by saving, not borrowing. Consumers create their own wealth by earning more than they spend. Once the money is saved, that particular individual is free to determine what he or she wants to do with that saved wealth. *Savings is freedom of choice. Debt is not.* Savings is critical to a successful capitalist society, no matter at what level it occurs. All of the saved money originates from a successful for-profit business no matter how you slice or dice it.

Review of Austrian solutions

Very simply, the *only* origin of wealth is running a profitable business, in any and all forms. Please remember that local, state, and Federal governments in the United States get their funds from the for-profit world, as it should be. They are not in the risk and reward business. Entrepreneurial businesspeople drive the profits that will ultimately be taxed for providing revenues to the government. The higher the profits, the higher the tax paid to the government. If we need a growth in tax revenues, and the way to get it is to foster higher growth through value creation for consumers and technological advances by business and entrepreneurs. Government income should not grow to the level of government expenses by borrowing the shortfall, particularly when it knows it cannot repay the money!

Stop the presses! The Austrian theory would propose that the government stop inflating immediately. The government must not prop up, bail out, offer backstops, or offer loans to failing businesses, as all this does is allow the disease to grow. The government should not interfere in the control of wages and/or prices, as all this does is distort the feedback in terms of product sales, an acute and effective mechanism joining consumers and the business owner. Nor should the government try to stimulate consumer spending via low interest rates and tax rebates, or spend additional monies on its own growth, as all this does is to add more debt to unproductive segments of the free market. And certainly, the government should not try to inflate itself out of the depression/recession, as this just adds to the imbalances.

To the extent that the government ignores these basic Austrian tenets, the painful adjustments that will eventually come will be that much worse and capital formation will continue to decline. The less policy actions are enacted by the government, the faster the eventual recovery that leads to more wealth building. Laissez-faire with fair and effective regulation is the best policy for capitalism. Only the entrepreneurs can build the necessary wealth building capacity for long term growth and stability, not the government.

You can now see that the notion of capital formation is all important, because without it we must relegate ourselves to borrowing for the basics. This is true of our own individual financial situations as it is the U.S., state, and local governments. Why not create more wealth from money that has already been earned and saved, instead of paying interest to a third party? *The debate lies in the difference between capital formation and debt creation.* Which is desirable in the long run? You know the answer, but how the heck can we get there from here? We must go through the withdrawal symptoms.

Just remember, *REAL WEALTH CANNOT BE PRINTED.* Wealth must first be earned, and then saved for further investment. There is no other way. Yes, money can be borrowed to pay for current expenses, or for investment purposes, but ultimately it has to be paid back. It is fundamental that the rules of economics apply to both citizens and the Federal government in much the same way.

Finally, remember that you are the government and the government is you. It is a reflection of what you have built over time, and its bad habits and actions will come back to haunt you. The reckoning day of the crack up boom is fast approaching, while the financial oligarch's ply their craft at the expense of the American people, under the watch of many economically dim witted politicians. Now let's take a look behind the curtains for better understanding of the truth and the fallacies behind the machinations engendered by the bankers and politicians.

CHAPTER 3
THE MOMENT OF TRUTH

Political and financial leadership is not evident

The Federal Reserve may be complicit in the financial difficulties of the United States, but its enabler is Congress. If Congress has to borrow money to keep its promises to the American people, the money has to come from somewhere. If there are not enough lenders, the Fed has to step in. Consider this quote:

"The fact that we are here today to debate raising America's debt limit is a sign of leadership failure. It is a sign that the U.S. Government can't pay its own bills. It is a sign that we now depend on ongoing financial assistance from foreign countries to finance our Government's reckless fiscal policies."

The premise seems pretty straightforward, as we suffer leadership crises regularly on display any time the two political parties in Congress clash over money, spending, and the national budget. Do you think this instills confidence throughout the world that the dollar will remain of value in the face of outlandish money creation to cover the U.S. deficit spending? Will foreigners continue to foot the bill for us? The answer is *no*, to which the facts in this chapter will attest. Readers need a source for the above quote. If you said March 16, 2006 on the floor of the U.S. Senate, you would be correct. The speaker was none other than the self-incriminating Barack Obama.

Mr. Obama then went on to define more truths about the consequences of continuous debt accumulation:

"And the cost of our debt is one of the fastest growing expenses in the Federal budget. *This rising debt is a hidden domestic enemy*, robbing our cities and States of critical investments in infrastructure like bridges, ports, and levees; robbing our families and our children of critical investments in education and health care reform; robbing our seniors of the retirement and health security they have counted on".

Mr. Obama spoke the truth in 2006, and the robberies to which he referred are ongoing and accelerating! The national debt for the entire history of our country up to the time of Mr. Obama's Senate speech was about $8 trillion. By the summer of 2012, it had doubled to $16 trillion.

If there were ever a time for the truth in Washington DC, it was during the great "debt ceiling" debate of the summer of 2011. It was bad enough that the debt ceiling was raised just enough to get past the 2012 elections, but the biggest problem with the temporary solution was that it didn't attack the real issue, and that is the insolvency of the United States. Sure, Congress supposedly cut about $2.5 trillion of spending for the next 10 years. Now we are supposed to be happy that the additional debt accumulation for those 10 years would only be an estimated $7.5 trillion instead of an additional $10 trillion. Even with the cuts, the debt will continue to grow. And did the politicians account for interest rates escalating to pre-crisis levels? Of course not! When rates rise to normal, historical levels again, the added interest cost alone on a national debt of $16 trillion would overwhelm the proposed savings by double or more! Did Congress assume that the economy would grow at a slower pace than it did pre-crisis, in the face of the largest tax increase in U.S. history slated to begin in 2013? Of course not! It assumed a growth rate to match the high-end experience of the 1990's, which then would clearly make interest rates rise dramatically! But that was before thousands and thousands of manufacturing facilities were transplanted to China starting in 2000, and before the U.S. had literally the highest corporate tax rate in the world! Then, did Congress account for the $75 trillion in promises made for "entitlement programs" such as Social Security? Of course not! Money will still have to be created out of thin air in the form of new debt for those costs. The debate was much ado about nothing! The proposed cuts, if they are actually made, would be a drop in the bucket and *would do absolutely nothing to resolve our national insolvency.*

The truth of the matter is that *the faster we default on the debt we cannot pay, the faster the road to recovery.* A dramatic and instant adjustment of writing off some or all of the public debt in the U.S. would cause an instant depression. But it would clear the decks for vibrant wealth accumulation and growth in a new economy with a much more solid fundamental structure; and no debt! This strategy would eventually be a good thing for the citizenry after the initial economic shock cleared. But it would be death to the banks and the holders of U.S. debt. And the poor politicians would likely be tossed out of their cushy and high-privileged jobs by the electorate.

The United States will default on its debt, and in fact *we are defaulting on our debt right now*. This stealth type of default is euphemistically called *Quantitative Easing* (QE). It used to be called "monetizing the debt". Bernanke's "Operation Twist" is simply a variation on the same theme. Next it will be called "GDP targeting" or some other stupid moniker to disguise the truth. No matter what, it is simply printing money to keep our promises. This is inflation at its finest! The more the country inflates, the less that debt is worth, and the less it costs the country to repay. The only problem with the plan is that it actually hides the most insidious effect, and that is that the U.S. citizen pays a heavy toll in the form of higher consumer prices. The delayed effect of the price increases makes it hard for most people to connect the dots back to money printing. But the ploy is really marvelously simple, and the people have to be distracted not to understand. This is the very reason that the politicians and bankers try to obfuscate the truth. They really don't want you to get it, and have become masters at defining the debate away from the real issues.

This time it really is different!

Ben Bernanke spoke the truth in his January 13, 2009 speech at the London School of Economics, stating:

"...fiscal actions are unlikely to promote a lasting recovery unless they are accompanied by strong measures to further stabilize and strengthen the financial system. *History demonstrates conclusively that a modern economy cannot grow if its financial system is not operating properly*."

These words seem to indicate that the U.S. needs to reduce debt, engender strong fiscal responsibility, and maintain balanced budgets. Further, Bernanke admitted that a solid financial system is critical to a healthy economy. But what would those strong measures to further strengthen the system look like to Mr. Bernanke?

"...more capital injections and guarantees may become necessary to ensure stability and the normalization of credit markets."

He suggests more borrowing to solve the excess debt problem? Print more "guaranteed" wallpaper money to hide the cracks in the system?

That's right; more donuts will be served at the fat farm! How is the patient to lose weight? To Mr. Bernanke's credit, he did cite three ways to remove troubled assets from the banking system, none of which were enacted, as we'll discover later.

The fact of the matter is that our politicians and Central Bank are trying to drive the economy by looking out the rear view mirror. This means that Bernanke and his crew are trying the tired old solutions that the bureaucrats and historians have told generations of Americans will work. It is so obvious that not only are their prescriptions not healing the patient they're actually making the problems much worse, as demonstrated by Austrian economic theory. This crisis is so large and so different, that the solutions espoused by John Maynard Keynes and followed by our government and its money masters have gotten overwhelmed, and the end of the U.S. dollar hegemony is at hand.

Even Bernanke had a light bulb turn on during the conclusion of a speech on October 4, 2010 at an annual meeting of the Rhode Island Public Expenditure Council in Providence, when he stated:

"In the past few years, the recession and the financial crisis, along with policy actions taken to buffer their effects, have eroded our fiscal situation."

He admitted that the stimulus spending with borrowed money has put us deeper into the hole. Keep in mind this statement was *after* the Fed had spent about $1.5 trillion of fresh new money buying up garbage loans that had crippled some financial institutions. Later, he went on to announce yet another $900 billion QE program for U.S. bond buying, which pundits called QE2. Why would the Fed have to buy U.S. Treasuries with fresh new money? What happened to the free market? Nothing happened. *The problem is that there are not enough buyers!*

Buyers strike in focus

The fact of the matter is that the U.S. has need for not only new debt issuance, but it also needs to roll over that debt which is maturing. Traditional buyers of that kind of volume simply don't exist. Part of the reason is that the vast quantity of money needed (over $4 trillion in 2012 alone) isn't available for investment at all time low rates. But more importantly, *the foreign sources of loans to the U.S. are disappearing due to their loss of confidence in the stability of the U.S. financial structure and the future value and viability of the dollar.* In the same speech noted above, Ben Bernanke put the situation this way:

"Almost by definition, unsustainable trajectories of deficits and debts will never actually transpire, because creditors would never be willing to lend to a country in which the fiscal debt relative to the national income is rising without limit."

Mr. Bernanke clearly states the reason for the buyer's strike against U.S. Treasury issues, and this fact is going to cost us our standard of living. How is that? By the end of 2011, the numbers had come in: the Fed had to buy fully 61% of the new U.S. Treasury debt for the year! To say that this is a disaster in the making would be quite an understatement. The money to buy the bonds associated with this debt came from thin air! Then, Mr. Bernanke went on to say:

"What we do know, however, is that the threat to our economy is real and growing, which should be sufficient reason for fiscal policymakers to put a plan in place for bringing deficits down to sustainable levels…"

Mr. Bernanke clearly puts the onus on the politicians to bring down expenses. Unfortunately, the leadership vacuum in Washington DC precludes this from happening. The main concern appears to be to get a solution that lasts through the next election cycle.

Have our biggest customers for the purchase of U.S. government securities actually begun to exit the U.S. Treasury market on a wholesale basis? Possibly, but most do not announce their intentions and the reported levels of their investments in U.S. debt issues are not necessarily accurate. Yes, some of our traditional big buyers have stopped buying or even started to sell off bits of their portfolios. *And many of the largest customers are now accumulating the T-bills instead of the T-bonds. This is yet another early warning of trouble.* That's because the T-bills are a cash equivalent with a short maturity (like 30, 60, or 90 days), with very little room for principal erosion if rates rise or the dollar devalues. This "power money" can be deployed immediately, anywhere in the world. And the holders wouldn't lose much in interest payments, since rates are so low anyway. It is simply a parking place for funds meant for another purpose. But when the T-bills mature, the Fed has to come up with the money to pay off the debt, and the source of that money could likely be the printing press if new investment money doesn't appear.

In contrast to a T-bill, a T-bond is a much longer duration instrument with plenty of potential for principal loss. It is an investment that many buyers have begun to boycott. Why do you think Bernanke's new strategy after the two rounds of QE was called "operation twist"? His twist idea was simple. He could sell the Fed's portfolio of short term T-bills to the traditional buyers of the T-Bonds, and use the proceeds to buy the longer dated bonds to keep the demand up and rates down! This was yet another temporary game to squeeze the life out of any market generated interest rates escalations. But it's like trying to keep a beach ball underwater at the same time it is being inflated even more. You'd bet on the ball coming to the surface every time, just as you'd bet on interest rates rising eventually, destroying the principal value of the bonds.

The fact is that any country that counts on borrowed money for survival is beholden to those doing the lending. In recent years, our traditional sources of loans have come from China, Japan, Great Britain, and the oil (OPEC) countries. We were perceived as a good risk because of our reserve currency status and our vibrant consumer economy, and they had plenty of U.S. dollars to invest. Our fiscal policies have been a question for years, but now they are out of control, giving more than a pause to our traditional creditors. So where do we now stand with these sources of money?

China can you spare a dime?

Most economic policies in today's industrialized countries are not very well thought out, since most of these countries are run by bureaucrats who really don't understand what they need to understand; either that or they simply can't change the system. And their advisors who do understand most likely don't want to make any waves for fear of losing access and power.

One exception could be that of *China*, which had earned wealth for itself through its own innovation, the stealing of U.S. technology, super low wages, lower costs and a better business plan. And yes, their labor cost is virtually nothing compared to our union pay scales and fringe benefits. But we must now confront reality in this global economy. This is our competition, and the unions, business owners, and government need to adapt to that. Many businesses in China are state owned, but still, as a country and as an economy the United States has to deal with this. The fact is that the Chinese have now become the world's financial powerhouse. Their country balance sheet proves it. They are supposedly biggest holder of U.S. debt, as they have invested just some of their savings by loaning money to the United States.

Many financial pundits and even some of the Chinese finance ministers would have you believe that the Chinese have no choice but to buy and hold U.S. bonds. But they most certainly do have a choice, and that is to search for effective alternatives to the investment of their national savings. Meanwhile, they are parking their spare cash in T-bills, as explained above. They have moved in this direction after repeatedly warning the U.S. that its monetary policies are not in China's best interest. Of course they aren't! Why would the Chinese or any other creditor want their investment inflated away?

This leads us to look at what the Chinese have started to do as the U.S. has ramped up the printing presses. No publicly announced guarantees to placate China have been forthcoming from the Obama administration, shaking the confidence of the Chinese even more. But old-time currency traders have a time tested axiom: Plan your move opposite to what the official line from the government is. Rather, try to ascertain what they're actually doing. The Chinese indicate that they have no choice but to continue to buy U.S. bonds, but they then go world-wide to spend their excess U.S. dollars on natural resources. Did they borrow the money for their acquisitions? No, they already had it saved in large part in U.S. bonds, and are reinvesting both at home and abroad.

In fact, the Chinese have made deals for purchasing vast quantities of commodities for use far into the future, all over the world. From all over Africa, to Russia, to Brazil and Canada, the Chinese are locking in their supply chain for the long run. They've even bought up huge tracts of U.S. farmland. And they are entering into agreements to pay for most of these investments by unloading their excess U.S. dollars. This is *not good* for U.S. consumers, because as there become less demands on the dollar, it will depreciate, creating more potential for hyper-inflationary forces.

And, why wouldn't China lock in those industrial supply chains now? Weren't industrial commodity prices quite low when the Chinese started to buy? Yes! Not only that, we the U.S. consumers have paid for this supply chain for the Chinese, by our deficit spending as consumers and as a nation. That's why the trade deficit does matter. All it does is redistribute our wealth to other nations in exchange for things like flat screen televisions. And these other nations can use that newfound wealth to create more wealth. Meanwhile, what we do in the U.S. is to use debt to create more debt. This is very clear to the Chinese and they show it by diversifying away from the dollar.

Read what the President of Brazil, Luiz Inacio Lula da Silva had to say in front of a Chinese trade delegation in Beijing on May 19, 2009 when discussing a proposed Joint Action Plan between the two countries:

"It is absurd if two important trading nations such as ours continue to carry our commerce in the currency of a third nation."

So what did China and Brazil do about it? They dumped the dollar as the settlement currency. This is not doom and gloom Chicken Little scare, as it has already happened! China has now replaced the U.S. as Brazil's largest trading partner. Neither of them needs the dollar as a settlement currency anymore! This is disastrous for the dollar, and for the United States. By the way, Brazil is one of the top five economies in the world.

Another clue to the death of the dollar is that China starred to circulate Yuan denominated bonds when the U.S. ramped up its money presses. But why would China issue bonds when they have so much national savings? To establish a market, that's why. As these bonds get more widely accepted, they become direct competition to U.S. Treasuries. In other words, demand for U.S. Bonds will drop, and acceptance of the Yuan as a viable alternative currency will increase.

Additionally, the Washington Post had a blockbuster news article on December 27, 2011. The lead read:

"Japan and China will promote direct trading of the Yen and Yuan without using dollars and will encourage the development of a market for companies involved in the exchanges..."

Readers should note that China is Japan's largest trading partner, not the U.S. Again, this means is that the dollar will no longer be used to pay for the trade deals on either side. This is yet another nail in the coffin, if you will.

Not only that, while Americans were celebrating Independence Day on July 4, 2012, China and Australia announced that they would now bypass the dollar as their settlement currency. Under the new agreement, the currencies of the two countries will be mutually convertible, which holds vast negative consequences for the U.S. dollar. We may soon have to celebrate July 4th as Dependence Day!

By 2011 China, for the first time since the turn of the century when it was still a bit player in international finance and with just a small portfolio of sovereign funds, finally had shown a net reduction in U.S. bond holdings. In a ChinaDaily.com article dated March 3, 2012 we got more confirmation of genuine concern out of our biggest customer. The article states:

"China has many reasons to reduce its exposure to the U.S. dollar, such as low yields and the monetary easing measures adopted by the U.S. government, which could lead to inflation that could erode the value of those holdings', said Wei Liang, a researcher with the China Institute of Contemporary International Relations. The increasing volume of outbound investment may also have directly affected the amount of money invested in U.S. debt, Wei said."

Simply stated, the Chinese are increasingly investing their savings elsewhere!

A final note on China and its investments: it only divulges what it has done after the fact. Readers should note that it has doubled its gold reserves from 2009 to 2010, and continued to buy gold by the boatload through 2011 and 2012. Shipments from Hong Kong to mainland China had exploded skyward. Additionally, they have ensured that all gold produced in China stays in China, and China is the world's largest gold producer. Does this tell you anything? They have also announced that no silver mined in China will leave China.

Financing from Japan?

Well then, how about Japan; can we count on that country to pick up the financing slack for our deficit spending? The Japanese also have tremendous amounts of their country savings invested in our bonds, in fact, more than any country for years until China came of age. But their economy is in bad shape too, dropping fully 15% in the first quarter of 2009, even before their disastrous earthquake. You can be assured that due to the huge tsunami and nuclear disaster in Japan, there is no way that they're in any financial position to buy more U.S. bonds *unless* they printed up yen to swap for dollars from the Fed in a back door collusion!

The G-20's nations met on how Japan was going to handle its tsunami reconstruction. They agreed on a global QE program to sop up the bonds the Japanese government and insurance companies had to sell. Just look at the tracking charts. Japanese ownership of U.S. bonds fell dramatically after the disaster. Readers should not confuse this with their new deal with the Chinese mentioned just above. That deal is for trade transactions, not investment of savings dollars. And it gets even worse. As part of the announcement of local currency trade with China, the Japanese also cut similar deals with India, Indonesia, the Philippines, and South Korea. Uh, this is *not* dollar positive, folks.

Financing from Great Britain?

Third in line for the traditional big owner of U.S. debt is Great Britain. Its economy is in shambles, and the pound sterling is at great risk. A quick look at the price chart of the pound looked like a fishing line into a pond as the crisis unfolded. The Brits can use the Bank of England much as we use the Fed, since they don't use the Euro currency. If they need more money they can just print it up like we do in the U.S.! We can be assured that at least some of the freshly printed money by the British will be used to buy U.S. bonds at the same time they have massive deficits of their own to deal with. But they have no savings to buy anything.

Can we keep borrowing the OPEC money?

Fourth in line for traditionally big purchasers of U.S. debt is OPEC, the oil producing cartel of exporting countries. They became extremely frustrated at the precipitous drop in oil prices in 2009, putting a severe negative impact on their budgets. Surpluses to buy bonds are not to be found; plus the fact that they are furious at the financial engineering that went into the dramatic drop in oil prices. No, the oil states won't be adding to their portfolio of long term U.S. bonds, either. They may park some cash into T-bills, but that would be for convenience.

Actually, it gets worse. The Gulf Co-operative Council, located in Saudi Arabia, has made efforts for an evolution into a Central Bank for the Saudi's, Kuwait, Qatar, and Bahrain, with a common asset backed currency for its members. Even though the Group has publicly stated that they would peg the value of the new currency to the dollar, it will still put a damper the demand for dollars. Forget the talk of the peg to the U.S. dollar, as pegs can and do change with the whims of the politicians. Again, this is very bad news for the petro-dollar, pointing to further deterioration of value. It appears that after 60 years or so, many nations in the Middle East are getting tired of being under the economic thumb of the United States, and they are getting tired of having their oil paid for in devaluing dollars.

Finally, the reserve currency of the world has been the dollar, and its biggest use has been to pay for oil in every corner of the globe. These countries can see how debased the dollar has become. What would you do if someone printed up money to buy a resource that you had? The simple answer is to raise the price, or ask for a different form of payment! President Obama should not need a special commission to study higher oil prices. All he has to do is to look at his own printing presses for part of the answer. So now the big oil producing countries have entered into agreements to trade that oil in other currencies as well. There will be much less demand from that quarter, and this fact *will have a profound negative impact on you.*

Temporary relief from European Union capital flight

By mid 2012, the economic and financial situation in Europe had become dire. Depositors began to pull their money out of the banks in many European countries as bailout packages for Greece, Spain, and Italy got bogged down due to widespread political pressures from the better economies in the Union. Bank depositors feared for the viability of their Euro currency as the interest rates went into negative territory. This meant that they actually had to pay some banks to hold their money. So when the Germans and Swiss enacted negative interest rates, money flowed into a perceived bastion of safety, the U.S. Treasury 10 year bond. This presented Bernanke and his crew a bit of a reprieve, as the ten year yields dropped dramatically due to a new and unexpected source of funding. These folks absolutely rushed to loan the U.S. their hard earned savings at a sickly interest rate of less than 1.5% for 10 years. For those who might wonder, this is what a bubble looks like. The final stages are manifested by having the dumb money jumping in without regard to risk after a 32 year bull market! This is a classic sell signal. When the big money decides to sell Treasuries, the end of the dollar regime will be at hand, and hyperinflation will begin. When could that happen, and how low can rates go in the interim here in the U.S.? The movement of the money holds the answer. When the demand abates, a rout in bonds could ensue as interest rates rise.

U.S. bond dealers choking on inventory

The U.S. uses 20 bonds dealers to buy its unsubscribed new debt. Unfortunately, by 2012 these banks became so loaded with inventory that they began to curtail their loans to traditional commercial customers. This meant that rates on commercial loans either escalated or at best stayed the same as the rates on U.S. government issues dropped. This is not a normal phenomenon, and it does nothing to help businesses with necessary expansion or development funding. The result is lagging growth in the economy. Government demand for money is displacing demand from the wealth creators and taxpayers. This is exactly the opposite of the prescription needed. The Fed and the U.S. government are in a box from which the only escape is depression and destruction of the middle class via currency debasement.

Can retail investors pick up any of the slack in the future?

Maybe, albeit temporarily. U.S. investors have shown no burning desire to do so, particularly since the higher guarantee limits are became effective at the FDIC insured banks and as well as with previously uninsured money market funds. Unfortunately, those added guarantees are slated to vanish by the end of 2012. However, historically the biggest traditional U.S. based sources of funds to buy government bonds have been banks, pension plans, insurance companies, mutual funds, money market funds, and households. What every one of these have in common, is that since 1995 they have *all shown a steady decline* in investing in U.S. government bonds as a percentage of the total debt outstanding. This means that their buying has not kept up with the growth of the debt load! They are buying, but not enough.

The proof is in the actions of the Federal Reserve

Nobody in Washington will admit to a buyers strike on U.S. Treasury bonds. They point to surveys on how much value Japan, China, and Great Britain and others have in our debt instruments. But these surveys are not precise. They are estimates. The fact of the matter is that there would be no need for the Fed to buy up the excess supply of bonds if the demand was sufficient. But it's not. That's why the Fed has to do programs like quantitative easing and operation twist. Somebody has to loan money to our government, so the Fed must step in with fresh new money. Not actually having the money to do such heavy buying, they have to use newly created funds via the printing press. Here's a picture of the activity since the crisis started:

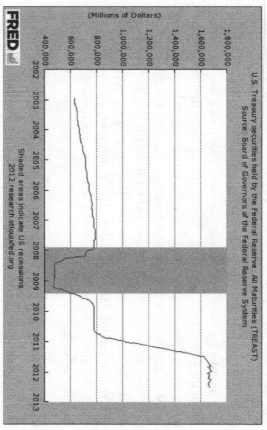

U.S. Treasury securities held by the Federal Reserve, All Maturities (TREAST)
Source: Board of Governors of the Federal Reserve System

(Millions of Dollars)

Shaded areas indicate US recessions
2012 research.stlouisfed.org

Chart 2 – US Treasuries held by the Fed (TREAST):

As readers can see, from the bottom of the recession in 2009, the Fed added fully $1.2 trillion to its portfolio of Treasury issues. These are bonds that no-one else would buy! Note the dip in the portfolio starting about 2008. What is that? That was the Fed *selling top quality U.S. securities to pay for toxic assets which it bought up from selected financial institutions.* Never before in the history of the Fed has this been necessary. And readers should also note that the chart above only shows part of the Fed's portfolio. What aren't shown on this chart are the approximate $1.2 trillion of toxic waste on its books as of 2012, as well as the other unknown trillions that are *off balance sheet.* This is why you can tell your neighbors that our financial system is partially backed by worthless, non-performing IOU's! By the way, the Fed is leveraged at over 30:1, meaning it has actual cash backing of about 3% of its obligations. Does this give you confidence in its viability and by extension, the viability of your dollars?

The cover story falls apart

When the Fed started on its second round of Quantitative Easing, it did not tell people that the government didn't have enough suckers to buy its debt. But it did come up with 2 headline purposes of the QE2; more jobs and lower interest rates. Do these reasons pass the smell test? Not to a knowledgeable observer. Let's look at the jobs goal first. If the Fed buys government debt, no matter who it buys from, how can Bernanke assert that this will create jobs? Is it because the seller of the bonds now has money to spend? Hey, if the seller of the bonds wanted to create jobs, he could obviously sell his bonds to *anyone* to raise the cash to do so. He wouldn't need the Fed. Remember, these are U.S. government bonds we are discussing, not some debt from Myanmar.

The fact is that bond dealers are the ones who have the biggest stash of the bonds in question. There are twenty primary bond dealers for U.S. debt, and fully 12 of them are foreign banks. If fact, they are the ones that have the obligation to find the buyers so that the Treasury auctions go smoothly and are fully subscribed. If they can't find enough buyers, then they have to step in to fill the void, and as mentioned, they are up to their necks in inventory. So the bond dealers would be the first place the Fed would go to buy back those long term bonds. And what do the bond dealers, or anyone else for that matter, do with the cash proceeds? It would be very likely to reinvest those dollars into selected stocks or commodities. The money would go to where the return is higher than the rate of inflation, naturally. OK, that's fine. Let the bond dealers pump up the certain stock issues or commodity markets. If the stock market goes up and a business owner or entrepreneur somewhere feels the wealth effect, will this make him hire new people? You tell me! The argument seems tenuous at best, as it *consumer demand* or technological advances that creates the need to hire, not higher stock and commodity prices.

If a sharp investor uses the sale of bond proceeds to buy commodities for instance, he will likely see those prices rise due to the excessive money being poured into a relatively fixed market, whether it is soybeans or copper, or whatever. Will the rising value of his commodity portfolio cause him to create jobs? That's a big fat no. The point here is that Bernanke has *no control* over where the money goes after he spews it to the seller of the bonds. So how can he tell us it will encourage job growth? The connection is shaky for sure, as there is no solid economic proof that the new money will go to the folks who would add to the employment rolls. It is far more likely that it will go to more speculation in some market somewhere around the world. One thing we do know for certain. Foreign banks have received newly printed money for selling their bonds back to the Fed at all time high prices! They will not be sitting on the depreciating dollars; they will put them to use, and that's the truth about quantitative easing!

What about the second goal of using the QE to keep interest rates down? Again, all the reader needs is the ability to think and use some common sense to discover the answer. We already know that the principal value of bonds is at 30+ year highs, making the yields pretty darn low. Bond principal value moves inversely to the direction of interest rates. The fact is that the notion that the Fed would be creating electronic money to buy bonds is a *major* sign that the top of that market is in. Remember, bond buyers are extremely sensitive to the ravages of inflation. So if Professor Ben wants to buy a portfolio of bonds at all time high prices with fresh new money, what would a smart bondholder do? He would sell bonds for sale due to monetary inflation, that the Fed can't keep up with the offers to sell? The principal value drops due to lack of demand, and yields rise. And again, the Fed is stuck overpaying for the bonds. This is not theory, but fact.

Indeed, after Bernanke announced the QE2 initiative, his targeted 10 year bonds began to drop in value. The translation is that more sellers appeared than buyers! With days of his announcement, yields *rose* over ½ percent. Gee, it appears that the plan didn't instantly work as he thought! Both objectives of the plan were doomed to failure in the long term. Only when the European banking system began to implode did the new rush into the perceived safety of U.S. Treasuries bring rates back down, with the likely assist of interest rate swaps. Without getting into the intricacies of interest rate swaps, just know that these instruments put an *artificial, theoretical, or synthetic demand* on the targeted bond issues.

The biggest truth arising from our financial system crisis is that, due to our extreme experimentation with fiscal and monetary policies, many potential buyers have been scared off and will not likely return. Why won't they come back? Simply, they have lost confidence in the ability or desire of our leaders to make prudent moves with our financial system and our economy. This problem has been building for 40 years, and can't be fixed without systemic disruption and the wipe-out of the American middle class via hyperinflation.

The fallacy of the "exit strategy"

In an attempt to comfort the American public that there would not be a forthcoming inflation problem due to the profligate money creation, Bernanke granted an interview to the popular '60 Minutes' TV program on December 5, 2010. It was telling that he had to go on the program to sell his ideas to the American public in the first place. Actually, this was his second visit to the program. During the interview *Bernanke insisted that the U.S. was not printing currency to buy U.S. debt.* However, this argument is as shallow as they come, as it simply rests on semantics. True, the bonds are not paid for with green currency, but rather an electronic credit to the seller's account. Could the seller then go to the bank to get his green cash? Of course! But that wouldn't even be necessary, just as it's not necessary for you to pay cash for all of your household bills. Just use checks or electronic withdrawals, and it accomplishes the same thing, right? It would be no different for the seller of the bonds.

Additionally Bernanke guaranteed that he had just the solution to keep inflation out of the equation. After all, that is the basic argument of the critics, asserting that more money in circulation will certainly promote serious inflationary pressures. Here we go again. How do you tame the price inflation caused by excess money printing? There are actually 2 choices: *raise interest rates* substantially as Paul Volcker did in the late 1970's, or *take the newly created money back into the Fed.* If rates are raised, this encourages people and businesses to spend less and invest and save more. Hoarded money has a tendency to put a damper on purchases, and consequently prices. The second way to contain inflation is to take the money back into the Fed. How is that done? Sell the Fed's agency bonds, T- bonds, and toxic assets it had previously bought, back into the marketplace. Aha! Let's look at the result or prospects of enacting either choice.

Professor Bernanke can't possibly raise rates without dealing a death blow to the staggering U.S. economy by placing an added burden on homeowners and anyone else needing or using credit, without raising the government borrowing cost and exacerbating the deficit even more, and without raising rates is to contain, just as in Japan since 1990! The Professor should take a remedial course on the Japanese financial situation.

Even Alan Greenspan, in a 'Meet the Press' interview in the fall of 2010, agreed that the 10 year yield had to stay under 4% otherwise the economy would be in more serious trouble than it already is. Do you wonder why the Fed *had to* enact Operation Twist in September, 2011? It's an idea not used since 1961 to take the proceeds from the sale of short term T- bills to buy mountains of 7-10 year bonds at all time high prices. This is yet another clue that the system is very broken!

And how do astute, big money investors react to interest rates that are lower than the admitted and acknowledged inflation? They either switch to a different currency or rush out to re-invest their money elsewhere due to the assured loss of purchasing power by staying the course. Either way, there is less demand to hold the dollars, making it worth that much less.

Well then, how about the *second option* for containing inflation? That would be that the Fed could sell some of its toxic toxic assets and Treasuries back to investors and banks, which dumped them with the Fed in the first place at record high prices! This would result in less money floating around in the economy. Remember, a big portion of this "stuff" on the Fed balance sheet is the same stuff for which it paid 100 cents on the dollar! So what is it worth? This is a good question: what is a bad bet worth? What is a loan worth on which no payment is being made? No, you don't need a math or econ degree to know the answer! If a debtor can't pay the interest, how is he going to repay the principal? He can't, and most certainly won't! The point is that the Fed has the toxic waste because no-one else wanted it at *any* price!

Do you really think the banks will use their excess reserves amounting to well north of a trillion dollars to buy back the trash they have already unloaded at 100 cents on the dollar? There is no way. They may buy up smaller failing banks with the help of FDIC loss sharing, or they may go into the markets to speculate. Heck, they may even make more business loans to qualified borrowers, but they won't be buying Fed assets. And even if the Fed decided to sell its best assets in the form of Treasuries, it would still have to use the money to buy up new U.S. debt that foreign investors won't buy. So it is quite clear that eventually extreme leverage on the excess money shown in Chart 1 will hit the streets of America by some means.

The conclusion is quite simple: *there is no viable exit strategy to pull the extreme money creation back out of the U.S. economy.* The Fed is cornered, all due to failed policies of the past coming home to bite, and bite hard they will. The bottom line is that price inflation will soar due to the monetary inflation that is already in play, and it is a world-wide phenomenon.

Chapter 4
What They Don't Want You To Know

The truth about the origins of our financial crisis

In 2008, what started out being called the subprime crisis morphed into a recession, and then into a financial crisis. And then with deteriorating business conditions all around the country, it was still referred to as a recession and nothing worse. Forget about the fact that it took financial authorities almost a year to acknowledge that all was not coming up roses for the U.S. economy. After the so called recession was supposedly over, we heard that the jobless recovery was an expected turn of events. This is ridiculous.

The politicians and financial authorities want you to believe that the United States economy is *strong*, and that you should have confidence that our leaders can and will fix whatever the economic problems are. By the time you finish reading 'Theft of the American Dream', you will know better. The more the politicians and bankers fiddle with fixes on issues they don't understand, the worse the big picture scenario gets for our financial system, regardless of the short term feel good solutions enacted to date. *A representative government by definition can't fix a free market economy*, although it sure can mess it up and keep it from its own natural devices for some little while. But it cannot put off the final reckoning of policies which have gone awry and continue to compound upon themselves because of constant Rube Goldberg repair efforts.

Now we'll examine several points of interest that are *serious contributing factors to the weakness and mal-structure of the U.S. financial system, and that in reality led us to the most severe financial crisis in the history of the U.S.* Our economy is suffering because our financial system is broken. Remember, it's about the concern and viability of our financial system, upon which the consumer economy is built. It is the resulting ramifications of the big picture issues which will soon demonstrate their ability to crush you financially. Knowing the truth will lead you to a better financial defense. The public usually doesn't get the whole truth and nothing but the truth, but here is.

The truth about over the counter derivatives

The great financial crisis is not simply about loan packages in U.S. housing market mortgage debt having gone bad; it is much deeper than that. The layers of side bets (more benignly called derivatives by the bankers) on these mortgage backed securities are hard to fathom, and clearly contributed heavily to the depth of the problem in causing the credit markets to lock up and usher in the demise of many financial institutions. But what happened to all the bailout money and financial help from the Federal Reserve? Simply stated, it was used to pay off side bets and to boost reserves, not loan to citizens for normal transactions!

A derivative contract gets its value, or loss, from some external contingency. The derivative contract itself has no value until that underlying event comes to be. These contracts have traditionally been traded on an over the counter (OTC) basis because they are private party transactions. There has never been an exchange or central clearinghouse to make them marketable. Not only that, the side bet can be made by someone who has little or no control over the underlying event that is the subject of the bet.

As an example, let's say that you'd like to bet that your next door neighbor's (#1) house will burn down, and you (#2) want to make some money if it does. Say one of your other neighbors (#3) on the street thinks you are crazy, and says he'll pay both you and #1 if #1's house actually does burn. But before he does so, you're both going to have to pay him an up-front insurance premium before he takes on the risk. Fine, you say, and the deal is struck. You cough up the up-front premium in cash, amounting to a small percentage of the total you hope to eventually collect. Now neighbor #3 is on the hook if house occupied by #1 burns to the ground, and you (#2) get paid big if it does, even though the house isn't even yours. So we have 2 people involved in a bet that are not even party to the event in question. Number three is happy because he just pocketed your up-front payment to him, and he likely won't pay off anyway if the house burns because he has already palmed off the risk to someone else, just to hedge his bet. Meanwhile, #1 thinks he has insurance coverage in the event of a catastrophe. And you, now thinking that maybe you were wrong and the house will never burn down, found some other sucker to pay you to take your side of the deal. It is messy for sure, but all very legal. By the way, there is a minor detail with all this betting, and that is that very little if any *collateral* has been put up to back the loser's obligation.

Now apply this game to the international market for money, debt payments, and interest rates, and you've got the picture. This is how the banks and Wall Street firms make hundreds of billions of premium dollars on hundreds of trillions of side bets. They make bets to garner the up-front money, and the only fool getting burned is the one stuck with the obligation when the triggering event occurs. This is how companies like AIG lose big money; taking the wrong side of the bets. If they bet poorly enough, they go under (think Lehman Bros.). And if they were a giant financial firm, repercussions of a default by one player reverberates throughout the world, making that firm too big to fail in the eyes of our central bankers and political leaders. But don't think insurance companies are the only dupes in the game. Many states, counties, cities, investment companies, pension funds, hedge funds, corporations, sovereign wealth funds, and numerous other types of entities convinced of the easy money games are now on the hook for hundreds of trillions in potential losses. There literally isn't enough collateral or money in the world to cover them.

Both the creation of more layers of bets, as well as the financial crisis, is ongoing. The Washington DC crowd has done nothing to target the real problem, but they'd like you to believe all will be well with some money printing and tweaking of regulations. Unfortunately, they can't fix those private derivative contracts which have already been put into place; they can only affect those which would be coming on stream at some point in the future by setting up standards and a clearinghouse for price and terms transparency. Further damage to the financial system is assured, regardless of new legislation.

What is far worse than the credit default swap market (side bets on defaults by creditors) is the interest rate swap market, which has yet to explode. By 2010, the credit default derivatives market was only about 6.6% of the total (about $40 trillion), while interest rate contracts comprised a huge 84.4% (about $500 trillion) of all derivatives. Interest rate swaps are side bets on the direction of interest rate movements. In fact, these swaps can be and indeed are used to help to keep rates low, because they have the effect of creating artificial demand that really isn't there. It's like synthetic demand, if you will. JP Morgan Chase Bank, the bank of the U.S. government, is the biggest bank in this game, and it had to fess up to what it claimed was a hedge on a $2 billion loss in May, 2012. But we also have to give credit to Morgan Stanley, which added fully $8 trillion of interest rate swaps to help professor Bernanke with his operation twist idea to drive rates even lower in the fall of 2011. After that, Moody's rating service gave them a 2 notch downgrade, requiring them to put up more collateral in the event of a mishap.

If interest rates have literally been dropping in the U.S. for over 30 years, there is only one long term direction they can now go, and that is *up*. The interest rates across the board are stretched to the downside so much that when the system gives, rates will rocket higher, finally forcing financial firms and the entire U.S. economy into the deepest pit of insolvency. It is a guaranteed event. Only the timing is in question.

For context on how pervasive the derivatives market really is, just know that it dwarfs the total amount of financial instruments in all markets around the world combined. Let's do some simple math. All stock markets world-wide added up to a value of about $36 trillion by the end of 2011. This was after the big rally coming off of the lows of 2009. But the world-wide bond market is a lot bigger, totaling roughly $72 trillion. So what are the total values of side bets? The number is estimated to be well north of $1 quadrillion (a thousand trillion, or a million billion if you prefer!). Granted this is the notional value (face value) and would include both sides of the bets. Most of these derivatives are created on Wall Street, and have to be settled in U.S. dollars. Where will those dollars come from? Guess! Remember, bets on the direction of interest rates dominate this pending disaster, and make the credit default swap problem that began with the onset of the subprime mortgage market problem look like a non-issue. This market has had no regulation since its inception in the 1990's, and it is hugely profitable for the winners, estimated to be in the neighborhood of $35 billion per year alone in up-front premiums for the fat cats on Wall Street.

When the yields for 10 year bonds head north, watch out! That will be the siren signaling the end of our financial regime set up in 1913, and totally bastardized since 1971. The 10 year Treasury bond is that benchmark which is used for many interest rate setting purposes. This experience will be orders of magnitude worse than the first round of the crisis from 2007-11. The Fed is desperate to keep rates low, as the entire house of cards depends on it. Below, check out this interest rate chart going back to 1981. What you are looking at is another picture of a broken financial system along with its attending capital destruction. The lower rates go, the more capital is subsequently destroyed. If you can borrow

U.S. fiat money for practically nothing, then how valuable is it? Think about that!

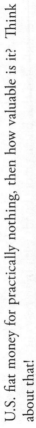
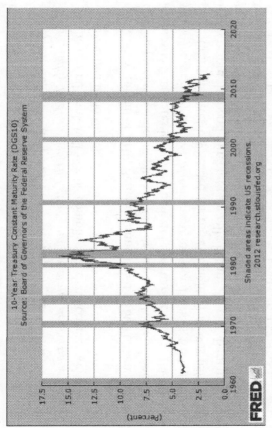

Chart 3 - Ten year Treasury rate (DGS10):

But on the flip side of the problem, as rates increase, the U.S. budget (and other deficit countries) gets strained even more because it has to pay higher interest on its debt and has nothing to show for it other than a bigger deficit! Even Alan Greenspan weighed in on the problem, when in a March 27th, 2010 Bloomberg interview, he stated:

"But if the 10-year note and say the 30-year bond yields begin to move up, in other words, the 10 year note begins to move aggressively above 4%, it's a signal that we are in difficulty. There is basically this huge overhang of Federal debt, never seen before. It's going to have a marked impact eventually, unless it is contained, on long term rates. That will make a housing recovery very difficult to implement and dampen capital investment as well."

Mr. Greenspan was eloquent and guarded in this remark. He was merely referring to the cost to the U.S. government to cover the interest payments. The fact is that it was a major understatement, in that the financial world as we know it will disintegrate due to derivative exposure if the 10 year rates get above 4%. How can the Fed possibly try to keep this key rate down? Print more money and keep buying those T-bonds!

On the same date as the quote above, Dallas Fed head honcho Richard Fisher indicated that buying more bonds with fresh new currency would not be an option, stating;

> *"Monetizing the debt via Fed purchases of government bonds, inevitably leads to hyperinflation and economic destruction, and the central bank will not be complicit in that action if we were pressured to do so."*

Well, by the fall of 2010, Bernanke announced a $600 billion program to print money in order to put artificial demand on 10 year bonds, in an attempt to keep rates low. And how did the market react? The 10 year yields *immediately headed higher*, meaning bond prices were dropping dramatically as investors headed for the exit sign! This was telling, but it was before the bond purchases actually began. In fact, Bernanke used more like $900 billion to create demand on the T-bonds, and indeed, the rates stayed relatively low on a historic basis. But when the program ended, then what? More of the same, but in hidden fashion, straining the bond market beyond any semblance of free market values with the use of interest rate swaps.

This strain on the low yielding bonds will not and cannot continue without massive infusions of money that has to come from somewhere. If you were a big time investment guru or in charge of China's bond buying, would you buy U.S. bonds at all time low interest rates, meaning all time high prices? There is no way! So, what has to happen is to create artificial demand, either with over the counter (OTC) derivatives, or money printing. Either method will definitely spell the end of the fiat U.S. dollar. It's guaranteed. And if we let the market deal with it by not having the government or the Fed intervene in one fashion or another, rates will rise dramatically, putting an arrow in the heart of the U.S. economy and its citizens. This is also guaranteed. *We are in big trouble here, with no way out!* It's called being painted into a corner in cartoon land. But they don't want you to know this.

What sounds like a legitimate market, albeit highly leveraged and risky, can also be used for nefarious purposes. Without getting into detail here, let's pose a scenario which likely happens with regularity. Suppose a hedge fund is highly leveraged with loans. Let's say that the lender bets against the hedge fund's ability to easily pay back those loans on demand as the deal may require. Then let's say, as a lender who has bet against his customer's ability to pay back the loans, forces the payback of the loan within the terms of the agreement.   The lender could make life very difficult for the borrower, all the while making money on the side bet against him!   The truth is that over the counter derivatives endanger our financial system and is simply a game for big money and suckers.   These instruments do nothing to move the U.S. economy along in a free market direction.   In fact, they aid in doing just the opposite.

The truth about our private central bank

The Federal Reserve System is a self-regulating, for-profit enterprise and is privately owned by the big for-profit banks, most of which have foreign stockholders.   Granted, the operational and political structure of the Fed makes it practically a government entity, but that's just as bad.   Since the Fed is owned by private banks, the relationship is a bit too cozy and unseemly for anyone who digs beneath the surface.   The Fed exists to help the banks and to assist the government in stealing your purchasing power to subsidize its own spendthrift existence, period.   It has nothing to do with servicing the American taxpayer.   All the outrageous experiments by Bernanke and his ilk purported to help move the economy in the right direction have literally done nothing to encourage stable prices or help foster more employment for the benefit of the American public.   All that you see (contrary to what you hear) is every attempt to keep the shaky U.S. financial structure intact.   But the public heard the cry of too big to fail and were scared into absorbing the continuing losses.

The too big to fail financial firms are the ones that had to undergo the stress tests to ensure their viability.   These are the ones that got first dibs on the Troubled Asset Relief Program (TARP) money, the $700 billion bailout cooked up in 3 handwritten pages by then Secretary of the Treasury Hank Paulsen.   We'll delve into that scam shortly.   The bankers who instigated the outrageous leverage that led to the credit crisis are the ones who control the money policies and the purported solutions of recharging themselves with more fiat money, with your approval!   And the Fed is supposed to regulate them!   The fox is to guard the henhouse?   What is worse, they then asked citizens to bail them out with borrowed money at an interest cost; which needs to be paid back by taxpayers to …them!   This is crazy.   No wonder they want the American public to be happy but oblivious.   They line their pockets with money that they have loaned to us!   It would be bad enough if it came out of national savings.   But it doesn't.   It has to be borrowed, and the interest cost is mounting to unmanageable levels.

Do you know what the interest payment was on the 2011 $1.2 trillion (that's $1.2 million-million by the way) budget shortfall? That would be roughly $32 billion ($32,000 million) just in interest payments each and every year for as long as it takes to pay that money back. And that is just for the deficit for 2011! But how much is the interest payment on the total national debt of $15 trillion by the end of 2011? At the current ultra-low rates, it comes to only a measly $300 billion or so, *every year*! Remember, the budget deficit for all of 2008, which was the largest in U.S. history up to that time, was only about $450 billion. So can't we make a case that, from 2009 and beyond, a huge chunk of the budget deficit was basically paid to the debt holders (the Fed, foreigners, bond dealers, and to a lesser extent U.S. citizen' portfolios) in the form of interest? Absolutely! Stated another way, *we are borrowing the money to pay the interest!* Do you borrow the money to make your mortgage payment? How long will that strategy last?

The Federal Reserve System was unconstitutionally established to control the issuance of our money. And it gets paid annual interest for every dollar that exists. The Federal Reserve funds the Federal deficit if there are no other saps to buy up the government's IOU's. Who do you think gets to collect the interest on those T-Bonds they own by exchanging them for paper fiat dollars? Yes, it's the Fed. Admittedly, the Fed gives an annual refund of left over money back to the Treasury Department to keep the politicians quiet, but this is a pittance compared to what it takes in. After all, the Fed has bills too! Unfortunately, our foreign creditors don't give refunds!

So what is a dollar anyway? The simplest definition is found in Webster's dictionary. It indicates that it is "the monetary unit of the U.S., equal to 100 cents." Boy, that' helpful! Ok, how about a second definition … "a piece of money worth one dollar". Well, that clarifies it, doesn't it? It seems that Americans are entitled to know and understand exactly what the value of a dollar really is. After all, it is specified in the Constitution that it needs to be based on a gold or silver standard of weight and measure. And surely it was immediately after the ratification of the Constitution of the United States, in conjunction with the Coinage Act of 1792, which has never been repealed. But let's get back to the Fed.

Actually, the very words "Federal Reserve System" seem pretty misleading at best. After all, the Federal Reserve System has nothing to do with ownership by our Federal Government. OK, it is beholden to the politicians, but it is fighting desperately to maintain its independence (read power and influence).

And the word "Reserve" is a bit misleading, in that there are *no reserves* in the traditional sense of having the gold or silver to cover all the debt (money). The Fed had traditionally kept U.S. government securities as the vast majority of what it could call reserves. And now, a large proportion of the reserves that are there are subprime, non-performing loans bought by the Fed from – well, that's a secret. It is kept secret so that seller of toxic waste looks better financially to its stockholders and the American public. Remember, it's about confidence. The Fed had run so low on its reserves of T-bonds that it had to print more money to keep buying new bond issuances. After all, it needs to have money to cover what President Obama described as *"trillion dollar deficits for years to come"*. The bottom line is that *our financial system is now partially backed by assets of extremely questionable quality and value.*

And then the last word, "System", is also misleading, in that it really isn't like a traditional system at all, but rather run almost entirely by the New York Fed, along with its Federal Open Market Committee (FOMC). The word system is supposed to instill confidence that the U.S. is protected by some big, all-encompassing entity. But it's not like you can go ask Ben Bernanke for a car loan; well at least not yet. So why worry, right? After all, it says right on the dollar that "this note is legal tender for all debts, public and private".

There was one courageous Congressman who wanted to audit the Federal Reserve for the first time in its existence. That was Ron Paul of Texas, with HR 1207. By 2010, he had gotten over 300 co-sponsors for the bill, and it initially looked like it would fly through Congress. But alas, by the time Barney Frank of the House and Chris Dodd of the Senate got done with it, it was a shadow of its former self, and basically a non-starter. Dr. Paul indicated that the biggest objectors, including Ben Bernanke, to his bill trumpet that Congressional oversight over the Fed would be government interference in the free market. But his retort is easy, and Congressman Paul sounded like an Austrian economist, stating;

"This argument shows a misunderstanding of what a free market really is. Fundamentally, you cannot defend the Federal Reserve and the free market at the same time. *The Fed negates the very foundation of a free market by artificially manipulating the price and supply of money–the lifeblood of the economy.* In a free market, interest rates, like the price of any other consumer good, are decentralized and set by the market. The only legitimate, Constitutional role of government in monetary policy is to protect the integrity of the monetary unit and defend against counterfeiters."

For a clear understanding of the issues regarding the Federal Reserve, one could read Ron Paul's book 'End the Fed'. Ron Paul proposed going back to a sound money policy. But the American public seems oblivious and apathetic, unable to get its arms around the nature of the problem and its consequences. Hopefully, 'Theft of the American Dream' will help you in that regard.

The truth about fiat money

Fiat money is the problem, not the solution. We've already touched on this subject, but we should explore a few more points that are not well understood by the populace. Fiat money is based on a promise, but it is not a medium of exchange with intrinsic value in and of itself. Fiat money is mandated by decree of the government, thus the term *fiat*. The declaration mandates that this or that piece of paper is to be used to settle transactions. So there is a big difference between a *medium of exchange* such as gold and silver as mandated under the U.S. Constitution, as opposed to *legal tender* which is recognized as our mode of settlement; modern fiat currency.

Ever since the U.S. Constitution was enacted, big money bankers have tried to encourage, cajole, or even force (with success) our government to borrow money at interest. Even though there is no specific provision in the Constitution for this type of borrowing by government, it has been found necessary to do so because of the high cost of territory expansion, financing our wars, to help the less fortunate both at home and abroad, to cover the unfunded liabilities (promises) made by our government to any number of causes (like Medicare or Social Security), to bail out failed big money interests, and to fund what we now call pork barrel projects. But by now we are choking on the debt of ill-advised spending for the last 100 years or so, and have to keep the patient alive with the untested strategies of the bankers and politicians.

In the past, any citizen could take paper money to the bank and expect to get paid some weight of gold or silver. Gold and silver were Constitutional money. But that ended in 1933, immediately upon the inauguration of Franklin Delano Roosevelt (FDR). So now we use fiat money, and that is the crux of the problem. It's easy to create when there is no intrinsic value or commodity reserve behind it to keep it under control. In today's crisis, the proposed solution and fix applied to every financial problem is more borrowed fiat money. More guarantees, more bailouts, and more stimuli will not make the problem go away, it only makes the situation that much more dangerous. It has simply prolonged the agony until the day of reckoning, which is now upon us. So we now have the biggest bubble in the history of civilization, that of the government money boom, making our money worth much, much less than it used to be worth.

Consider a well circulated 1963 Franklin half dollar. This coin was widely circulated in the 1950's and 1960's. Clearly, when it was issued and put into circulation, it was worth fifty cents. The coin was struck in 90% silver, consisting of about .36 of an ounce of the shiny white metal. In 1963, silver was pegged at a value of $1.28 per ounce. So that fifty cent piece had about 46 cents worth of silver in it. At a price of about $36 per ounce of silver, that makes this coin worth over $13.00 in today's market. Please realize that this does not refer to any "rarity" or collectible numismatic value, but rather only the silver metal from which it was struck. It now has substantially more value than the fifty cents face value. Using the $36 dollar per ounce of silver for calculations, this comes in at roughly 2600% inflation in about 45 years! Would you go out and spend this fifty cent piece today? No way! You'd rather spend the debased, close to worthless paper money, wouldn't you?

China experimented with fiat paper money around 800 AD with no success long before it caught on in the West. But a more modern concept of paper money can be traced back to the goldsmith days in Medieval Europe. Goldsmiths were known for the store of gold they held for themselves, as well as for others. They had to be trusted, since most people had no other alternatives for the storage of their wealth. People not wanting to carry around or store their hoard of gold and silver to make purchases would deposit them with a local goldsmith, acting somewhat like a bank. The goldsmith would issue a receipt for the person's deposit, redeemable on demand. And depending on the reputation and reliability of the goldsmith, the depositor found that he could simply use his deposit slip (currency) to pay for needed goods and services. That way he wouldn't have the problem of going to get his gold or silver to buy something. Just pay for it with a piece of paper, backed by his stash of gold and/or silver, redeemable at the goldsmith shop by the holder on demand.

Well, the goldsmiths weren't stupid, or necessarily ethical. They found that since people would infrequently come in to get their gold, they could easily put out more paper receipts into circulation than the bullion they had backing them up. Who would know, particularly when the backing was that goldsmith's own holdings of the precious metals? This issuance of excess gold receipts was done in the form of loans. With this system, they could control the amount of currency in circulation. Then, by reducing the currency in circulation (requiring repayment by the debtor), it became easy to force borrowers into insolvency, and the goldsmith could foreclose on the debtor's property used as loan collateral. The system worked in cycles to perfection, impoverishing debtors and enriching the goldsmith. One of the most noted and successful goldsmith of his time was Amshall Bauer (later changed to Rothschild) and the grandfather of Nathan (owner of the Bank of England in the early 1800's when it went on the gold standard), and the patriarch of the Rothschild dynasty. This dynasty has controlled gold, money and banking throughout Europe for centuries.

You can call it a war on terror, or earmarks, or entitlements, or homeland security, or tax rebates, or unfunded mandates, or corporate bailouts, or any other designation. The fact is that if the United States spends money that it doesn't have, that creates a deficit, which creates a loan, which creates inflation and interest. Hey Federal Reserve, just print up some more money, and we'll give you a fiat IOU! But in fact, the Fed and commercial banks don't even need to bother with printing the money on paper anymore. All they have to do is issue computer entries. Nonetheless, this *is* inflation. But it gets worse.

At the onset of the crisis, there was a problem with uninsured bank deposits over $100,000 per depositor, whether perceived or real. No problem, the government decided to insure them to a higher level. Was there an issue with a money market fund going under the $1 share price? No problem, as the bureaucrats just guaranteed the value of all money market funds. Is the FDIC running out of money with which to insure bank deposits? No problem, just print up more. Is the Pension Benefit Guarantee Corporation going broke, unable to guarantee the billions of pension benefits for existing and future retirees? Check, start the presses. Are the banks failing? Give them more fiat money! Or what of the auto companies, are they going bankrupt? That's an easy one; just take them over with government money, and receive stock ownership and control. You know, buddy up with the unions and bring on the prosperity. But that's not all we can fix with computer entries or printed fiat money.

Can we force interest rates to the basement? That's easy; buy the Treasury bonds in the open market, creating demand, lowering rates. How you ask? Just buy more ink and keep the printing press going full tilt! Do we want to prevent foreclosures in the housing market? How about trying to renegotiate those loan terms and conditions for the homeowner? But if the bank has to lower the interest rate, won't that make them even less solvent than they already are? No problem, give them the difference from the government checkbook. Do we want to remove the toxic assets from the banks with money from investors? Simple, just guarantee them against loss with fiat money funding. And how do we fix the slowing economy? We can fix that with borrowed stimulus spending, right? If that doesn't work we can just give it a shot of QE! Are the taxpayers hurting and need a shot of fiat adrenaline? Just give them a dose of tax rebates from the Treasury confidence coffers.

Folks, this is a fiat currency bubble in the making, and it can only end badly, just as every other currency bubble in history has. We'll look at examples a bit later. You don't think it can happen here? You'll bet your financial life on it if you're in doubt. The U.S. debt situation is much worse than those! In fact, it is the most outsized national debt in the history of the world. The myth that it can't happen in America is being exposed. In fact, the problem is here now! All of the symptoms above point to a currency failure. But it gets worse!

You were previously told that Social Security was fixed until at least 2029, when the money coming in was going to be less than the money going out, right? But the financial crisis has caused so much unemployment, that *Social Security for the first time paid out more than it received in 2010, and that trend continued in 2011.* But it is actually worse than that, as there is no set-aside lockbox for the money put in from withholding taxes over the years. The fact is that these entitlements are pay as you go by the U.S. government, as the trust fund has long been plundered of its money for running the annual government expenses. The only thing left in the Trust Fund to pay for these programs is a big fat U.S. government IOU. The money has long been spent, replaced only with a promise to pay. Fiat money will have to be used to make good on these obligations to the tune of tens of trillions of dollars! So how high is your confidence level on how much your savings dollars will buy going forward in time?

There is a great book called 'Days of Destiny', published in 2001 by Pulitzer Prize winner James McPherson and Alan Brinkley. It picks out dates in American history which have come to prove to be turning points in any number of subjects, even though many of these dates and their significance were of no particular note at the time. For instance, there was October 19, 1781, which is actually pretty obvious; this was the date that the Continental Army defeated the British in the battle of Yorktown, leading to the States in America to forming themselves into a Republic. The most recent date reviewed in the book was June 14, 1973. This was the date that molecular biologists had announced to the world how the study of DNA could be accomplished in a functional way and be used to transform the study of the human body.

What was curious was that the authors skipped over Sunday, August 15, 1971. This was the day that Richard Nixon "closed the gold window" to the international community of trading partners. You see, prior to this date, ever since the Bretton Woods accord in 1944, the world had used the U.S. dollar as the reserve currency. This meant that trade settlements, and other contractual obligations would use the dollar as a means for settlement the world over. This made the dollar the king of currencies, and it would be accepted worldwide. Why would this be? It was due to the fact that by 1944, the United States had, by an overwhelming margin, the highest amount of gold reserves on the planet. It was also due to the fact that the economic engine of the United States was unmatched anywhere in the world. So we as a nation made the dollar as good as gold. Any country that wanted to redeem its dollars in gold was accommodated by the U.S. Treasury, all at a price of about $35 per ounce of the shiny metal.

After World War II, the U.S. economy stalled for a while once all the defense spending ceased. Some consider this stall out as actually the last gasp of the Great Depression; albeit temporarily interrupted by the great deficit spending and stimulation of manufacturing base for defense for the War. At any rate, the United States turned this tremendous manufacturing capacity to the needs at home, now being stoked by returning soldiers in their need to get on with their lives. So from the late 40's into the 50's and beyond, life in America was good. There was a lot of growth, consumer prosperity, and low inflation.

But the 1960's changed things. The Vietnam War was very expensive, as was the "Great Society" and "War on Poverty" policies of Lyndon Johnson. Deficit spending coming out of Washington DC started to be noticed by the international community, as the U.S. had to inflate its money supply to fund those deficits. They saw the monetary inflation taking hold as politics trumping sound economics. Fearing that the dollar would be worth less than they had come to expect, they began to request gold in exchange for their dollars, as assured by the Bretton Woods agreement.

By 1971, the paper for gold redemptions had gotten out of hand, and the U.S. gold reserves were dropping in a frightful manner. The stash of 20,000 tons of gold in 1960 had shrunk to only about 9,000 tons at the time of Nixon's decision. So Nixon led the U.S. in a default on the Bretton Woods agreement, and would now permanently deny the international community the right to redeem dollars for gold. That right has never returned. Even though Nixon acknowledged the monetary inflation, he instituted wage and price controls anyway, blaming the problem on OPEC. Then, with the controls in place, Nixon stated "We are all Keynesians now", referring to the J.M. Keynes theories of how a government could manipulate money supply and monetary policy to keep the economy going. *The reader needs to realize that since 1971, the entire world has transacted business with fiat currencies! This has never happened before in world history, and it has everything to do with our crisis.*

To say that this repudiation of the gold standard was a bad idea would be a gross understatement. Once the wage and prices controls were lifted, inflation roared. Gerald Ford tried to put a lid on the rising prices with his WIN (Whip Inflation Now) buttons in soliciting the help of all citizens, but the response from that quarter was extremely tepid. But we have to credit Mr. Ford. On October 8, 1974, he gave a speech to a joint session of Congress and elucidated numerous ideas and actions to curb inflation. It is instructive to quote a couple of important and salient points, both of which pertain more today than ever. First, Ford stated:

"Winning our fight against inflation and waste involves total mobilization of America's greatest resources–the brains, the skills, and the willpower of the American people."

The point is that the American people have to care enough and understand our situation well enough to demand, and get, the right action out of not only Congress but also themselves. Today's problems are so much worse than in the 1970's, yet only a small segment of the population gets it.

In closing, Ford went on to say:

"...I say to you with all sincerity that our inflation, our public enemy number one, will, unless whipped, destroy our country, our homes,

our liberties, our property, and finally our national pride, as surely as any well-armed wartime enemy."

This statement is as powerful and truthful as it gets. But that was about 40 years ago. Just know that currency destruction ramps up, taking time to lay the groundwork. But once it starts, it continues until the devastation is complete. This inevitable demise is quickly approaching for the U.S. dollar.

With the gold standard abandoned, the issuance of new of fiat money became the policy of choice, as the politicians and bankers could now enjoy the fruits of their labor. The more money that was printed, the more bankers could lend on their low reserve requirements, and the more politicians could spend in their home states to buy more votes for the next election cycle. The detachment of gold as a valuing device was the key to the off switch of the printing press.

Gold and silver soared in price in the late 1970's, and interest rates went to the ozone layer when Paul Volcker used a high interest rate policy to tame the inflation. And tame inflation he did. Savers were rewarded with super high rates on CD's, while the principal value on Government bonds got crushed. That's right; people who had loaned money in good faith to the U.S. government during the inflationary times would see their principal severely eroded. Those who waited until the bonds matured to cash out found their purchasing power severely impaired, worth far less than they had loaned. The dollar just wouldn't buy as much as it had previously.

As Ronald Reagan came into office with his supply side economics ideas, taxes were cut with the passage of TEFRA in 1981, but the Congress didn't have the political will to rein in spending. The $50 billion dollar annual budget deficit that ensued was the outrage of the day. By 2009, the Federal budget deficit had ballooned to $1.4 trillion, or $1400 billion, if you prefer. That translates into an explosion in the growth of the budget deficit of 2800%, all paid for with fiat money.

Fiat money cannot survive. It *never* has in any country at any time in history and it never will. Once the confidence in the money scam is broken, it can't be repaired or replaced without the major surgery of severe currency devaluation and a return to some sort of standard for backing. *This* is what the bankers and politicians fear the most. This would render them helpless. This would take their profligate greed away. This would remove the curtain behind which the Wizard of Oz shows his frailty and lack of magical powers. It is the most serious game in the history of our nation, and it is happening right now, on our watch. But the money elite prefer that you not know the desperation and consequences of the struggle to keep the entrenched system alive.

The truth about the international nature of money movement

This is a very critical element of both the current condition and future demise of the U.S. fiat money financial structure. Money isn't contained by borders. There are no immigration controls on it. Fences and security guards can't hold it hostage. Computers see to that. Governments have tried to contain it at times, but that has always led to disastrous consequences for its national economy. If you ever hear that Congress is considering the undertaking of currency controls, enactment would spell doom for the U.S. economy and your cost of living. Very simply, this would likely restrict dollars from moving out of the country. But it would not restrict them from moving into U.S. based assets, forcing prices much higher.

Throughout world history, wherever there has been trade, there has been a requirement to move money; and until August 15, 1971, that could have involved the movement of physical gold and silver. Sure, paper chits and IOU's were used for convenience, but precious metals were always behind those chits should some country want their payment in a tangible asset instead of a paper promise.

It is too simplistic to think that trade transactions alone create international money flows. That is a factor, but more important to our discussion is that *money tends to flow to where wealth is being created, and away from areas that present obstacles to that creation of wealth*. Money will flow to the currency or country that appears to present better value to the investor. If the currency is undervalued, money will come into that currency. If it is overvalued, money will leave for greener (no pun intended) pastures. The relative value of one currency versus another is all important. What a government does to affect its currency value relative to others is also all important. *When debtor nations engage in competitive devaluations of their currencies to generate more exports, it is suicidal to true wealth creation and the subsequent growth of tax revenue*. Government policy has everything to do with currency value, money flow, and wealth creation in that it can make it easier, harder, or virtually impossible to achieve the sought after wealth. And of course the value of a currency has everything to do with a successful investment. If any given investment is rising when measured in all currencies, this is a huge sign that it is a genuine bull market, and it should seriously be considered for all portfolios.

It is a definite problem though when there are politicians passing laws while having no concept of the international consequences. They look at a specific problem in their domain, and try to solve it with new legislation. This is often a recipe for disaster; and will very rarely work as they hope and perceive. It will always have consequences that were not intended or imagined. This is because they truly don't understand the movements of money, the flow of capital that is washing around the world looking for opportunity. It is both financial acumen and human psychology that is the key to the money movements. You can call it greed for the next big thing, or fear of control and regulation; but the big money will flow to the area best suited for profit. In physics, you have likely heard the axiom that for every action there is an equal and opposite reaction. Well guess what? In money matters, it's the same theory!

Generally, a bull market in any investment or asset price develops in stages. The very big, very connected, and very smart money gets in first. These are the people or organizations to first act on recognized value, and they invest accordingly. They are the ones who have control. Then the traditional institutional money, like insurance companies or investment banks enters the picture. They see an uptrend in progress. They establish their position, many times with other people's money and some of their own, and ride the trend until the public catches on. The third stage comes when the public gets involved. The big money gauges the interest of the public, and many times whips up the enthusiasm of the retail investor. Heck, you may even be shocked to learn that the pros would lie and manipulate the market to keep the mirage of super profits going, so the fools feel good about getting in at the top (think U.S. Treasuries)!

The power money then sells its position to the last man standing who doesn't do any homework. Now, to whom does the retail investor sell when he's lucky enough to realize a profit? That would be the last fish in line before that particular market tanks. This same scenario happens over and over and over again. The retail investor is the last to catch on to the game. But *this is what bubbles are all about; the timing of the movement of money based on the regression of the knowledge held in that particular market.* The pros get to sell to the dummies who don't understand what they're doing! Alas, they believe what they're told! And then the fish sell to other fish until the pond is depleted of dumb money, while the power money has long fled the scene to other investments ripe for profit in anywhere else in the world. For our purposes, the idea is to get in while the dummies are still sleeping. Then you can *sell* when you hear the idea to *buy* at a cocktail party! Just remember that the smart money doesn't flaunt their targeted investments until they are all in. It is then that the public hype starts.

Money movement is not just an international phenomenon, as it happens similarly in the domestic economy. You can see it in your own town. Look at real estate. Why do the homes in some neighborhoods sell quickly, while others with similar features sit on the market for an inordinate amount of time? How did the real estate bubble happen? How did the bubble pop? Or look at the retail stores at the mall, or those that surround that same mall. Why do some go out of business, while others expand? Or go to the grocery store. Why are some of the items depleted, while other shelves are full? All of these questions can be answered in the same way; it's about money movement, or lack thereof. Of course there are always external factors that encourage people and businesses to spend or invest their money in the way they have chosen. It's not done without thought and purpose. Whether the reason for the purchase of one house in favor of another due to better schools; or one grocery item rather than another due to a sale, *the external factors are the key to understanding where the money is going.*

This same theory can be applied to the investment markets. Whether it be stocks, bonds, mutual funds, Exchange Traded Funds (ETF's), Real Estate Investment Trusts (REIT's), utilities, gold, oil, international investments, or anything else, money moves the markets one way or another. The more the money flows, the more prices will move, both up and down. For every move in any market, there are reasons for that movement. Why is the price of one company's stock rising, while a competitor's is falling? Many various factors force the money to move, which could be due to a better opportunity, or even in reaction to a negative happenstance.

So why wouldn't the huge flow of international money act any differently? It doesn't! Whether it is due to tax codes, Congressional legislation, agency rules and guidelines (like those established by Security and Exchange Commission or the Commodity Futures Trading Commission, or even the Environmental Protection Agency for instance), Supreme or Appellate Court decisions, or Central Bank policies regarding money printing or interest rates, both the domestic and international capital flows will certainly react dynamically. This is particularly true when bureaucrats have been empowered to make the rules without having the requisite knowledge to truly understand the consequences of their actions. This will prove out once again with the Dodd-Frank Wall Street Reform and Consumer Protection Act signed into law on July 21, 2010. Unfortunately, the law grants any number of government minions the power to make new rules that suit their views of how the investment world should be or act.

Sovereign debt issuance and payments also depend on international money movement. Sovereign debt is that which is owed by governments. Who holds that debt and who is at risk is the question. Thus far, the solutions to the financial crisis that started in the U.S. as a subprime mortgage problem are about saving the banks, both foreign and domestic, and not the respective economies. But debt too is a subset of the money movement in this discussion. It is critical to note that what happens in foreign countries has ramifications at home. Excessive debt with the need to finance and refinance without the requisite collateral is a contagion, and the U.S. will ultimately prove it is not immune from the problem.

The current crisis could be compared to the 1931 experience with a European bank going down and dragging other banks and countries down with it. This time will be no different, other than the size of the disaster. That's right; the problem in Europe will not be contained. So far, it has spread from Greece, to Ireland, Spain, Portugal, France and Italy. Great Britain and the United States are next. Readers should know that when debt starts to go bad, and more debt money is needed to fill the void, the intelligent money recedes from the risk. Debt money gets harder to find, and the solution for the fiat currency regimes is to print money to fill the void. The European Central Bank has been running its press too. This will have dire consequences for the debtor nations, as you will see. Just watch the news and see the riots over government belt tightening in Greece. No country can escape from debt mismanagement, and the U.S. will prove to be the poster child for these lessons.

Let's follow an example of bad fiscal management and the resulting consequences of the reduction in the flow of money from overseas. When U.S. banks have to foreclose on a home due to a debtor default, it has the effect of depressing real estate prices. When foreclosed properties are put up for sale, prices drop in the immediate area. Because home equity drops for the survivors, they spend less. Businesses and consumers alike then pay less in taxes. Government gets less money coming in, creating all sorts of problems, particularly if it continues to spend more than it takes in. If it does continue to spend, this creates more interest cost than it can afford.

If it raises taxes to try to create more income, consumers spend even less as businesses have to raise prices to cover the added cost of the new tax. If government cuts expenses, there are real human costs and suffering. There isn't as much money flowing as there was previously.

It's a cycle that is not easily broken, and is extremely destructive. If real estate prices have no impetus to rise, the malaise will continue for years. Given the oversupply of homes, both held by the banks, held by people just waiting to sell, and the changing demographics of the baby boomers needing to downsize, in the U.S. this situation is not an easy fix. This is a generational problem, and the easy foreign money applied to the housing market is now history. It's a totally different game now that the housing bubble has popped. The psychology of the homeowner has been radically altered. The lack of equity of the homeowner restricts his spending. The foreign money that supported the bubble through the use of CDO's (packages of loans) has moved elsewhere. These facts will negatively affect real estate in the United States for years to come.

The point of this section is to set up for later consideration some of the moves both Congress and the Fed have enacted as *reasons* for international money to flow in a manner that it has. Not only is it likely that you don't even know what the big money is doing; you also likely don't know what the true consequences of this money movement are. The fixes enacted have and will continue to have disastrous consequences for citizens and the United States government due to the reaction of powerful money interests of both the domestic and the international community. They'll now act very defensively in terms of what they will do with their money. This defensive posture has dire consequences that the bankers don't want you to know, and that most politicians don't even understand.

The take-away from this section is simple. *Everything that the politicians and bankers do to affect any aspect of monetary or fiscal policy in the United States has international ramifications.* We do not live in a vacuum in the U.S. We are simply a part of the whole. If we take large actions, we'll see large reactions. Currently, Congress and the Fed are taking the largest, boldest, and most untested actions in the history of the world. This is no joke. The retail investor must expect large reactions, understand their meaning, and then act accordingly.

The truth about the education of the U.S. populace

The politicians and the bankers don't want you to know what you don't know. The American public has a major educational deficiency. This could be interpreted as primarily as apathy, narcissism, or even a misplaced sense of privilege. One might blame the problem on our educational system. Whatever it is, the bottom line is that our schools don't really teach what is necessary for people to help themselves or their beloved country to survive in a manner consistent with the dreams and ideals of the Founding Fathers. There is no indoctrination in any visible form. This doesn't mean brainwashing; it refers to a way of thinking about the responsibilities as a citizen of the U.S.; an attitude of patriotism combined with a desire to be educated, and informed enough to participate and provide input. We must educate our future leaders now, and the understanding of our money system is at the very foundation of true leadership!

Why can't we take a second look at what we are teaching our kids from the earliest of ages? Why can't education be seconded at home? It may seem corny but we should engender a love of country, Constitutional ideals, sound monetary ways, and fiscal responsibility. Throw in a constant dose of regular discussion and enlightenment of the issues of the day, and of how the political system is supposed to work verses how it actually works, and someday things may change. But that someday will be too late. People have become too complacent, or just downright lazy. Narcissism has become the American way, and it has contributed to the mess we're in. Attitudes can and do change, usually under extreme circumstances. Effective education would help in the quest for the needed attitude adjustments. The problem is that time is not our friend, making easy solutions impossible, and financial hardship guaranteed.

Maybe what looks like apathy by citizens is just that, because they think the politicians will take care of us. Or it could be likely that the populace just doesn't believe that their vote or say so means anything. This will certainly be true until the crisis really hits home with force. That's when the social unrest will become extreme. This could be when a grass roots effort for real change will occur.

Mr. Obama ran on his first Presidential campaign on change that we can believe in, but unfortunately his team of advisors was comprised of many of the same tired politicos and policy wonks who have become embedded in the Washington culture all along. Worse, the financial policies of Obama perpetuate the status quo, and have indeed exacerbated the problems. This is not the change that is needed. This is not a partisan Democrat or Republican leaning, but rather a patriotic leaning, where now there is very little. What is being done for the good of the country? The words we hear on the news sound so very good and encouraging, but the political actions don't match. The only solutions one hears these days are the marvels of more regulation, more government meddling, and more deficits, all funded with fiat money.

Most of the politicians are just as undereducated on the financial issues of critical importance as the general population. This is because they always have the need for votes in the back of their minds. And the need is always there for the power and prestige. This is not a prescription for national success. Rather, it is a roadmap to the destruction of our standard of living, our economic security, and our freedoms as prescribed in the Bill of Rights. Severe degradation of our society is at the end of this road, but the public seems oblivious that we are traveling this very road right now with the toll booth in sight.

Your government is desperately afraid of having the public know how the financial system works for fear of it coming unraveled, leading to the demise of their entrenched power in the Legislative and Executive branches of government, along with their partner in the theft, the Federal Reserve. The dumber the public the better, in order that they can continue with control of the powers and largesse they bestow upon themselves.

The powers that be want you to think that our monetary system is so complicated that there is no way you can understand it. Of course it's complicated, but the basics certainly aren't. You can't spend more than you've produced and saved. If you think you can, you are simply wrong. We know you can't borrow forever, particularly when the lenders have vanished. The laws of sound economics do not change depending on whom or what is applying them to a given situation. A principle is a principle. A law is a law. But that's even not the major point.

We now have in Washington DC a major political system that has entrenched itself. Why is it that most of the incumbents get re-elected? Do you think gerrymandering has anything to do with it? You know, that's redesigning and redrawing the Congressional district boundaries so that the majority of voters for the incumbents are certain to fall within that particular district! Have you taken a peek at the look of these Congressional districts? Do so, and you might be surprised. If it doesn't make you laugh it will make you cry. These are not designed to represent the mass of the people, but rather they are designed to include or exclude those citizens who are thought to vote in predictable ways, either for or against a particular party. But that is only part of the problem.

Think about this for a moment. Using approximate numbers, the estimated 2008 population of the United States was 304 million people.

Of those, we had a total of 169 million registered voters, but this likely includes some who were illegal, or even dead. They also count those in our protected territories such as Puerto Rico, Guam, and Samoa. So, about 56% of the population was able to vote. Of that 56%, about 54% of these folks were registered as Democrats, while 46% were Republican, Independent, or other. In the 2008 elections, about 62% of the registered voters turned out to vote, and of course, the Democrats took control of the country with wins in both houses of Congress and the Presidency. So what is the point? *The point is that only roughly 19% of the U.S. population was able to effect complete control of all 304 million people.* Basically, this comprised just 62% (turnout) of the 56% (registered) of the 54% of the winning party (Democrats). So you don't think every vote counts? Forget about the politics of the parties, as this statistic is a travesty no matter how you slice it. Do you think the populace has allowed our system of government to become dysfunctional with this type of statistic?

Polls taken after the budget deadlock in the summer of 2011 indicated that the public approval rating of Congress is actually lower than George W's was at its nadir; that is, about 10%. And fully 90%+ of the populace was against the TARP banking and financial rescue package, yet the politicians passed the monster anyway. Had they bought into their own line that the system was about to implode? Or were they merely trying to maintain the status quo for their own benefit? Do you think that there is only one course of action that could have been taken? Were they telling us there was no other way? If we have a major problem that Congress, the President, and the financial leaders think can be fixed in a jiffy with a wink here and a nod there, why didn't they fix it prior to it becoming critical? They didn't see it coming you say? Well then how do they know enough to enact the perfect fix? They don't! Doesn't this indicate a major disconnect to you? The root cause is a lack of relevant education by both an entrenched political system of self-satisfaction first and foremost, combined with a system of bribes (aka campaign contributions) from special interest groups. Add to the mix a compliant and/or apathetic citizenry, many of whom are not educated enough on critical issues to make good choices at the polls, and you have the perfect financial storm in your face.

Readers should understand how cheaply politicians can be bought by the money and influence of special interests and lobbyists. Actually, this is nothing new. Indeed, a foreigner actually participated, guided, bribed, and wrote the language used to demonetize silver in 1873, in effect stealing half the wealth of a vast number of U.S. citizens. That was a glaring example. And another was the expertise of Paul Warburg in the critical language that brought the Federal Reserve into existence. A modern day example is the Affordable Care Act health care bill, the flagship legislation of the Obama administration. Do you know that much of the language was written by the health care industry, along with the pharmaceutical company lobbyists and various other special interests? Do you think any members of Congress stayed up late at night to craft a 2700 page bill in their spare time? Of course they didn't. The special interests helped because they wanted to ensure that they were taken care of. Do you want proof? Check out the stock price charts of the health care companies leading up to the vote and after the final passage! Case closed!

Add to the mix the ingrained power structure of the Congress and its cozy relationship with the lobbyists on K Street, and we end up with a big mess. No wonder Congress has super low approval ratings. No wonder they don't care about what the public wants. It has become irrelevant to them! They can do whatever works best for them to stay in office, while the public suffers. But what then is the root cause? Simply, the accountability must come back to the electorate, the people. We've allowed it to happen through our own ignorance and lack of concern, for whatever the reasons. From the derivatives, spawned by fiat money cranked out by a private central bank, to the dysfunctional Congress, over the years, *U.S. citizens have allowed the crisis to unfold by their lack of education, attention and concern.*

What did Thomas Jefferson say about the necessity of education?

"Educate and inform the whole mass of the people…They are the only sure reliance for the preservation of our liberty."

Our way of life is at stake and we should heed Jefferson's words! Remember, the more we count on government to fix our problems for us, the more is paid in lost liberties afforded us under the Bill of Rights. A quick perusal of the Constitution is quite enlightening on how far we have strayed, and how this has affected our individual rights! You may want to check it out, along with the Federalist Papers. It will either make you sober or drive you to drink!

There was an article published in May of 2009 by a Russian columnist in Pravda, the state run newspaper, which makes our situation here in the U.S. very clear for the world to see. The problem is that the American people don't really understand the longer term consequences of what is truly happening. But others who observe these things from afar certainly do, particularly those who have already been through it.

In the first sentence of his essay, author Stanislav Mishin states:

"...the American descent into Marxism is happening with breathtaking speed, against the backdrop of a passive, hapless sheeple..."

Ouch! The author referred to a cross between sheep and people! He says that the first reason is that the people have been:

"...dumbed down through a politicized and substandard educational system..."

This is hard to argue. He goes on to say how many have had their faith in God destroyed, contributing to the problem. Further, he notes that the country seems to be controlled by a cabal of financial oligarchs who are taking the powers and duties out of the hands of Congress. After the author's short review of some of the ridiculous initiatives Congress considered for the financial control of various corporations, he goes on to review the fact that Prime Minister Putin, at the G-20 meeting in April:

"...warned Obama and U.K.'s Blair not to follow the path to Marxism, since it only leads to disaster."

The Russians certainly ought to know about the failings of Marxism! In closing, the author proclaims a painful statement and warning to all Americans who have donned rose colored glasses:

"The proud American will go down into his slavery without a fight, beating his chest and proclaiming to the world, how free he really is. The world will only snicker."

Conclusion

We've just examined five facets of our financial system that have led us to a crisis situation. But what are the American people told were the causes of our subprime debacle and subsequent recession? Let's take a look at the cited causes of the crisis from a layman's viewpoint, not hampered by political considerations or Beltway spin! With this knowledge, we can then understand the folly of the efforts to fix the glaring symptoms of our systemic illness.

CHAPTER 5

THE BUILDING BLOCKS TO CRISIS

Let's pick on easy targets for the blame

In this chapter we'll take a look at the issues most touted by the politicians and the media as causing the financial crisis that surfaced in 2008. We've already examined the result of our crisis, and that is money printing to cover our debts. But getting to that point didn't just happen; just as it cannot now be stopped without a financial system implosion. Getting to the point of printing money to pay bills took years of work by the bankers and politicians, and getting out of it will require even harder work, with very poor choices from which to choose.

The facts surrounding the financial crisis give us plenty of things to think about. It was kicked off by the seemingly benign problem loans in the subprime category. Subprime loans refer to those transactions that were made to people who were less than stellar credit risks, buying homes that they really couldn't afford, accompanied by low payments due to abnormally low interest rates. Many of these loans became to be known as NINJA loans, based on borrowers with no income, no job, and no assets. These loans became the patsy in the eyes of the politicians and bankers. But this is only a starting point for discussion. Let's look at the situation.

A guy wants to buy a house for the family. He goes to the bank for the loan and gets it. But the bank doesn't want to tie up its capital on a lousy 5% mortgage, so it offloads the loan to investors. But the bank needs help in selling the mortgage. Here come the Wall Street investment bankers. They have investors all over the world with mega-bucks, much of it borrowed. So those investors need assurances that those home loans will actually be paid back. Enter the rating agencies, Standard and Poor's, Moody's and Fitch. With a high rating from supposedly the best rating agencies in the world, who's going to worry?

So the loans are packaged up by the investment banks according to their credit-worthiness. But certainly not all of these millions of loans could possibly be rated AAA, right? Of course not! So enter the credit default swaps. This sounds complex, but just think of it as an insurance policy that would pay the investor if the loans went bad. It's a derivative contract; it pays if something occurs that isn't supposed to.

One of the biggest participants of the credit default swap insurance policies was AIG. The insurance company was on the hook because it was insuring the lousy mortgage with its own AAA rating. But with the insurance in place, this homeowner's loan now looks to the investor like it is gold plated, and he'll get his money back eventually. Little does the investor or the insurance company realize that these AAA rated securities are fraught with risk because the family was in a home they couldn't afford that they paid too much for in the first place, which only looked affordable because of low teaser front end interest rates. This off-loading of questionable loans became so profitable for banks that they then decided that no down payment loans could also be workable. They were going to sell the loan anyway, so what did they care? Finally, they were running out of fish, so next they invented "low doc" mortgages. These low documentation loans didn't even require income verification, just the word of the guy buying the house. Now we've gotten the picture, and can play the blame game.

A cursory examination of the building blocks to crisis below will give us a clearer picture of our travels on the road to perdition. Please note that there are plenty of fingers that need to be pointed, some rightfully so, while others are a smokescreen, as you will discover. Unfortunately, even the legitimate contributing factors are simply peripheral to the basic causes of our financial implosion that is now in progress. Let's look at the scapegoats, both legitimate and otherwise.

Failure of the Capitalist Free Market Processes

Here is a good quote, uttered by President George W. Bush in a CNN interview:

"I've abandoned free market principles in order to save the free market system."

This may be the stupidest, most ridiculous, and laughable statement ever made by any leader of the capitalist free world.

A failure of the free market system had nothing to do with the financial crisis. It is actually the very opposite. Because of all the meddling by the government instituting stupid fiscal policies, like trillion dollar stimulus plans funded by borrowed money, or tax rebates sent to the taxpayers after having been borrowed, and with all the ill-conceived practices of monetary engineering by the Federal Reserve and the always backward looking regulation coming out of Congress, this reason hardly deserves page space but it needs to be addressed because of the frequency of its use.

This is basic: *true free markets are self-correcting!* The more interference from allowing natural market forces to take their course, the more distortion builds. This *does not* mean there shouldn't be rules and regulations. But too many senseless ones cause problems. The distortion arises because the free market has a tendency to avoid onerous rules to find an easier, but legal, way to profit. It has to do with legal innovation where none was previously necessary before political meddling occurred. That distortion ultimately has to be corrected in one fashion or another. There is no endorsement of either fraud or greed here. It is simply elucidating the stupidity of Congress in thinking they can regulate something which they really know nothing about, and the unintended consequences that the regulated fix then causes. This goes for the Federal Reserve as well, proven by the fact that its hundred years of experimentation is showing major stress fractures!

It is the intervention into the free market that causes misallocation of funding and investment. The culprit is pointing its finger away from itself, which is normally happens in Washington DC. You see, the actual damage to the economy is not necessarily the bust phase, but rather an artificially induced boom which is not sustainable. It sucks away capital which could have been used to create more income and wealth in a more profitable enterprise.

As Thomas Woods, the author of 'Meltdown' eloquently describes it:

"The problem is that in the wake of Fed-induced misallocations of resources we wind up with structural imbalances, a mismatch between the capital structure and consumer demand. The recession is the period in which the economy repairs this mismatch by re-allocating resources into lines of production that actually correspond to consumer demand. The modern preoccupation with levels of spending instead of patterns of spending obscures the most important aspect of the question."

Here's a perfect example. After the dot.com bubble burst in 2000, Alan Greenspan and his merry pranksters at the Fed wanted nothing hinting of a recession. So they repeatedly cut interest rates. By the end of 2001, the rate had been cut 11 times, and ultimately ended up at 1 percent by 2004. Easy money was all the rage. Now where was the bubble to go?

Into housing! We had the only recession in history where housing starts didn't decline. The boom was on. Buyers were encouraged to buy houses and flip them for a profit. Builders could borrow on the cheap and get in on the fun. That was exactly what happened and it worked; until it didn't. Bust again, only this time much worse than it had to be due to the mal-investment in the housing stock.

The newest crisis is on and it's unprecedented in scale. What is the remedy? Mr. Bernanke came to the rescue with lower rates yet again, this time to 0% on the Fed funds rate, an all-time low, for what is promised to be at least 6 years. Please note that Japan has tried this for years, and it never worked. Japan has been in an economic slump for over 20 years running, with debts of 200% of GDP and growing after numerous failed tries at stimulus. The free market doesn't cause slumps, but fiddling with the free market does!

President Obama, on the eve of his attendance at the G-20 summit in April of 2009, spouted the rhetoric that Washington Keynesians and bureaucrats just love to hear:

"I'm a market oriented guy, but not when I'm faced with the prospect of a global meltdown."

Here we go again. Let's just incite the masses, ignore history, and go with the flow of more government intrusion into the free markets. After all, the politicians wouldn't want to be blamed for any pain to their constituents!

Ronald Reagan had it right when he said that government was not the solution, but rather the problem. The problem with government policy is that it consistently fails to anticipate the unintended consequences of its actions, and then enters into some self-preserving state of denial when things go wrong. Have you noticed that it's never the fault of the politicians or the bankers? No, it's always somebody or something else.

Wall Street Greed

Who could argue with this one as a contributor to our crisis? To the outrageous greed, we can add malfeasance at best, and as the facts have become obvious, fraud at its worst. The big problem is that the instruments used to generate profits for the fat cats on Wall Street are very complex. Even many of the investment bankers didn't understand the future impact of their decisions, being blinded by the opportunity for the big fees and oversized compensation incentives. As it turned out, the five biggest stand-alone Wall Street investment banks needed financial help in order to survive. Lehman Brothers didn't get it and they are gone.

The culture of greed was primarily fed by the prospect of huge profits from legalized (or should we say non-regulated) gambling. Instead of the old-time model of making deals with regular business customers with a regular amount of security behind the loans and with loss reserves at the ready for possible mistakes, the process was subverted. Just gamble and make side bets, and try to hedge those bets so someone else would pay off if something went wrong. The culture changed, as did the risks involved, and credit default swaps and interest rate swaps made the whole scam fun and profitable.

Sure, the derivative swap deals bought and sold by the Wall Street biggies were complicated. But that didn't stop them from churning those products to their maximum compensation advantages. The guys on Wall Street made billions of dollars in compensation. The attraction of this kind of money made a lot of them not really care what they were selling, nor how it was done. Just give them the product, because they had an unending stream of new suckers on the line from all over the globe! So, as it is in many a sales organization, the compensation design drives the sales, regardless of the product.

There were 5 major stand-alone investment bank players in the swaps game on Wall Street: Goldman Sachs, Lehman Brothers, Bear Stearns, Merrill Lynch, and Morgan Stanley. None of them exist today as stand-alone investment bank entities. Bear Stearns was digested by JP Morgan with the help of billions of dollars of your money. Bear was forced into liquidation as other investment firms ganged up against its losing positions. It did not help their case that they were the only major investment firm that refused to help with the Long Term Capital Management (LTCM) bailout in 1998. The refusal to cooperate ate at the craw of Hank Paulsen, Treasury Secretary under George W. Bush. Paulsen had been CEO of Goldman Sachs when LTCM went down, and he helped with the bailout on behalf of Goldman Sachs in conjunction with Merrill Lynch, Morgan Stanley, and Lehman brothers. Bear Sterns didn't participate, so Paulsen was now able to extract his pound of flesh. Plus, JP Morgan could now take care of the outrageous and outsized naked silver short position that helped keep precious metals prices low. That position was taken over from Bear Sterns. It worked for a couple of years, but when silver took off to the upside, JP Morgan took it on the chin, booking huge losses when they had to buy back the silver at much higher prices. Getting out whole was impossible.

Lehman Brothers was allowed to fail, which the Treasury and Hank Paulsen later realized was a mistake. Of course Lehman got what the free market capitalist system requires, and it appears to have set the credit crisis in motion. Then, Bank of America had to buy Merrill Lynch to save it, after having itself been given a large cash transfusion with your TARP funds. Goldman Sachs and Morgan Stanley had to re-cast themselves as regular banks so they could tap into both the government largess and support from the Federal Reserve. Finally, Morgan Stanley worked out a deal with Smith Barney to mitigate its losses and bring in more retail investors.

The point is that now the Wall Street investment banking crowd has gotten absorbed by other entities, most of which could not make it on their own with the possible exception of Goldman Sachs. After all, Goldman Sachs is the ultimate insider in world-wide finance and has an inside track around Washington DC.

But the consolidations and bailouts haven't stopped the flow of bonuses as the banks rushed to pay back TARP money so they could write more derivative contracts, manipulate markets and continue the search for more suckers. Does Congress really believe that they can regulate them into order? These companies are in the money business. They know how the game is played; indeed, they invented the game, and continue with new adaptations on a regular basis as the rules change. Regulations are to be damned; the money kings are always a step ahead. There is absolutely no way that the "wizards" in Congress such as Barney Frank and Chris Dodd, or even good intentioned people like Ron Paul, could possibly keep up.

But it gets worse. With a high water mark of about 8 thousand hedge funds cluttering the investment scene and with leverage from the investment banks and other big creditors of upwards of 50 times actual equity, things really got distorted. This leverage means that the hedge funds brought only 2% of investor money to the deal, with the rest being borrowed. Hedge funds are for the super-rich and were very lightly regulated. And the hedge fund managers share in the profits of their funds to the tune of 20% or more. So it is their job to speculate and lock in a profit when it is there. The investment bankers aided and abetted the scheming by providing the huge loans for the super leverage of the hedge funds, but ended up cutting them loose and calling in the loans when things hit the wall in the fall of 2008. This was in the same time period that the stock market did the nose dive. With no loan money available, and a call-in of loan balances by the investment bankers, the hedge funds had to liquidate in a major way, and the American public saw themselves getting a 40 to 50 percent haircut on their investment portfolios. The market crash didn't just happen. It was "managed", as was the price of oil both on the way up to $147 per barrel, and all the way down to $30 during that timeframe. Greed by the money elite was a big factor.

Readers should not confuse this financial engineering as a form of capitalism. No, this was more like a form of legalized fraud prompted by extreme greed, by knowing the rules and working around them. Like the hot potato game, don't get stuck with the hot potato, just pass it on quickly. Or maybe musical chairs would be a better analogy. Just don't get stuck standing and holding the bag, as many foreign investors and AIG did. Greed has been displayed in its ugliest form before the crisis, during the dark days, and still is now.

Lack of regulations

Do you think that $5.2 billion would buy a lot of influence in Washington DC? According to Harvey Rosenfeld, the President of the Consumer Education Foundation, for 10 years from 1999 to 2009, the financial sector in the U.S. gave $1.738 billion in campaign contributions to Congress. In addition to that, these same folks gave $3.441 billion to almost 3000 Washington lobbyists. The goal was to curry favors from Congress for deregulation, and it worked. Now the taxpayers have to clean up the mess. Let's not be naïve here. One of the biggest causes of the greatest financial mess since the Great Depression was the buying of influence in Washington DC.

As a consequence, the regulatory environment was lacking. In 1999, Congress repealed the *Glass-Steagall Act* with the enactment of the Financial Services Modernization Act. It was followed by the Commodity Futures Modernization Act in 2000 which had passed by huge margins in both the House and Senate, and actually deregulated over-the-counter derivatives. This was a big deal, and effectively allowed the power money to operate unchecked. The demise of Enron was the first sign of trouble caused by this deregulation, followed by the implosion of Bear Sterns and Lehman Brothers. Then AIG, Citigroup, Bank of America, Fannie Mae, and Freddie Mac went onto life support before having to be bailed out as a result of the legalized form of gambling, along with Federal Reserve support of financial institutions around the world.

The Glass-Steagall law was enacted during the Great Depression to keep banks out of the investment and insurance business, and conversely, to keep insurance and investment firms out of the banking business. It was a slap in the face of JP Morgan at the time, as its insiders ran the Federal Reserve then. It seemed like a pretty good idea to the politicians, and it worked to control the shenanigans, conflicts of interest, and out-and-our fraud. For the most part it worked for years.

Granted, some laws were enacted along the way since the 1930's which eroded the effectiveness of Glass-Steagall. One was a 1970 law which excluded publically traded companies from membership in the New York Stock Exchange. Membership would guarantee an entity a seat on the exchange, as opposed to simply having the privilege of having its stock traded there. So when the private, member investment banks were allowed to go public while still retaining their seats on the exchange, they had a huge source of funding for selling their own stock to investors. Goldman Sachs was the last of such investment banks to go public in 1999. This allowed them to raise tremendous amounts of new capital which they could use for any number of new investment scams, or schemes.

The repeal of Glass-Steagall allowed financial firms like Citigroup to emerge; a new animal was born and there were really no laws on the books that could adequately deal with what transpired. This was certainly to be expected. Amazingly, between 1980 and 2005, there were about 11,500 mergers and acquisitions amongst financial firms. This had the effect of creating mega money firms with the extreme concentration of investment capital to go along with it. A few of these firms got so huge they were deemed by our esteemed Paulsen/Geithner Treasury Department and Bernanke Federal Reserve as too big to fail. The failure was that of your government allowing them to get that big, with no controls, in the first place! And you thought the politicians could regulate the money elite?

Now the investment banks could turn their risky loans into investment products, which had been precluded when Glass-Steagall was still in effect. They invented things like packages of loans called CDO's (collateralized debt obligations) to be backed by CDS's (credit default swaps). And away they went. It was great. More and more big-time investors, including Sovereign Wealth Funds joined the party as investors. Sovereign Wealth Funds are investment monies owned by foreign governments. Heck, as mentioned earlier, both the firms and the investors didn't even know their own risks, but the party and the profits were just too fun to resist. So once the gig was up, do you wonder why foreigners became more than a bit perturbed? They were duped in a major way by slick operators on Wall Street because the regulations were not adequate to match the financial engineering activity.

And don't forget that one of those slick operators was the CEO of Goldman Sachs, one of the major players in the game. In fact, it was Goldman Sachs that bet against its own mortgage backed securities offered for sale to its customers, knowing full well that they would drop in value, securing big profits for the firm. They even purposely put a package together that was virtually guaranteed to fail, then sold it as good stuff, while at the same time betting on its demise. And who was the CEO overseeing these moves? Oh, a guy named Hank Paulsen. You know, that was the guy who became Treasury Secretary, and made sure that his buddies at Goldman got $10 billion of your money out of the TARP funds. Is this sort of like the fox watching the chicken coop? Only in America, land of opportunity! We won't forget that Goldman subsequently paid back the TARP money, but it sure didn't have to pay back that $19 billion it squeezed out of AIG. That's right, about $7 billion was extracted from AIG before it went down, then at least $12 billion more out of the government money which you provided to buy almost 80% of AIG. Amazingly, this $19 billion was paid to Goldman Sachs at 100% on the dollar of what was owed. When was the last time you heard of a bankrupt firm fully making good on its obligations to just one of its many creditors while the others got stiffed? Like, never?

Even during 2010, fully three years after Bear Sterns went down, and when regulation of over the counter derivatives and clearinghouse methods were being seriously espoused by the Treasury Secretary Geithner, what did he suggest? Regulations looking forward! Readers must realize that a forward looking plan would totally ignore the problems, lack of transparency, and valuation methods of the $1.2 quadrillion of face value derivatives already on the books worldwide. So our fearless leaders never saw the crisis coming and had no clue as to how to effectively deal with the crisis. But then they claimed to devise just the plan for going forward?

It is doubtful that any new rules, regulations or strategies that the government and the Federal Reserve would ever come up with would be free market. They've implemented fully 25 programs since the onset of the crisis, and there is no proof yet that anything has worked. How will we know if something worked? Don't worry, the politicians and bureaucrats will tell us!

Leverage

Our crisis is all about leverage, which is just a fancy word to denote borrowed money with not much collateral to back it up. Commercial banks, investment banks, insurance companies, and the hedge fund crowd thought they had this one mastered, but it's actually a reason for the billions of dollars in losses. The idea is to use a small amount of investor money as collateral for an ever expanding amount of loans, to try to make even more money. Let's say your hedge fund has 40-1 leverage. Basically that means that you have made investments that are 40 times greater than the money you actually have. It also means that if your investments go down a measly 2.5%, you are out of money. Pay back the loans and you end up with nothing. But the idea is to make money, right? Yep, and that would be big money. If things go the right way and you get a 10% return on the overall investment, after you pay back the money you have borrowed, you have actually made a 400% return on the money that you really did have in the first place. That's leverage!

Leveraged investing is a great game unless it doesn't work. In the above example of 40 to 1 leverage, if your stocks go down say, like 40% as they did in 2008, you've lost a lot of borrowed money, to the tune of 14 times the amount of money that you started with. Somebody has to cough up the cash on that loss. Should it be the U.S. taxpayer who has to pay off a bad bet by the greedy Wall Street crowd? Well, apparently your government decided that firms like Goldman Sachs and AIG represented a systemic risk and therefore had to be bailed out with your money. Remember too, that the losses we are talking about reside as profits in somebody else's pocket!! Thanks to you, many of the bets have been paid off! But the super-leveraged derivative side betting continues in a big way.

Tainted Ratings Agencies

Let's make this really simple here. There are 3 ratings agencies that provide the vast majority of quality ratings for any number of investment products. They include Standard & Poors (S&P), Moody's, and Fitch. The purpose of these firms is to look at the financial statements and other information of the companies or investment products in question, and then assign a rating, so investors have some clue as to its credit-worthiness. For instance, a bond with an AAA rating is as solid as you can get, supposedly. Then the ratings go down the scale to AA, then A, then BBB, etc. By the time you get to D, you need to think default.

How does a company go about getting a rating? Why, by paying a fee to the rating agency, of course. This in and of itself, in good times, is subject to the questions of propriety, right? Obviously, one has to wonder how objective an agency can be with a customer who brings it billions of dollars in fees to rate their various products. Would you expect the rating agency to shoot itself in the revenue foot? No! Are these firms regulated as to an effective review process? Of course not!

Throw into the mix the lack of understanding of the product being rated, and one really begins to wonder. But if the holder of a credit default swap such as AIG, which has an AAA rating, is as good as gold, wouldn't their contract to make good on a default of a package of mortgage loans be also as good as gold? Well, the ratings agencies thought so, but they have been found to be wrong to the tune of $180 billion (AIG bailout) of taxpayer money. To say that the ratings system abetted our financial crisis is accurate.

Tainted Regulators

This chapter wouldn't be complete without mentioning the folks in Congress and other Washington bureaucrats who had the oversight responsibility. Let's start with Barney Frank, Chairman of the House Finance Committee from 2004-2010, and Christopher Dodd, Chairman of the Senate Banking Committee when the crisis hit. No one should have a big problem with politicians being slow on the uptake regarding the financial crisis. After all, they are human. But when the uptake is in the form of huge campaign contributions from those they are supposed to be watching, things get a bit unseemly. These men pounded the table in the late 1990's that there was no problem at Freddie Mac and Fannie Mae, and no further regulatory action was necessary. What is worse, Frank contended for years that any possible financial problems by Freddie and Fannie would pose no risk at all to taxpayers. Well, he was slightly off, as we had an initial commitment of $200 billion to cover losses, which has now become an *unlimited* commitment according to Secretary Geithner at Christmastime, 2009, when no-one was watching or listening. The cesspool of bad loans will never see the light of day now that they've got the government to hide the truth from the taxpayers. And what about the mortgage loan with super favorable terms reportedly received by Dodd from Countrywide (the failed feeder sub-prime mortgage broker to Fannie and Freddie), that most other citizens wouldn't get? Would that shade his regulatory opinions?

Reportedly about $ 1.5 trillion ($1500 billion) was unaccounted for somewhere within the HUD bureaucracy prior to the crisis! This money is not in losses in the traditional sense of the word; rather it is unaccounted for and it was funneled through HUD offices during the Papa Bush and Clinton years. Read that as misappropriated, aka gone! At best we could call Congressional overseers naïve and ineffective, at worst, bought and paid for. How can that kind of money come up missing without anyone having a clue as to its whereabouts? Where were the regulators?

What did the Securities and Exchange Commission (SEC) do to stem the tide of outrageous leverage used by Wall Street investment houses? It let *them* decide how much money to put aside for loss reserves! This was not a good idea. To see an agency of the government have a budget increase of 200% over the first decade of the twenty first century and not get anything to show for it seems pretty typical for our government. It was subsequently discovered that thousands of pages detailing the results of many of their investigations went through the paper shredders. This leads to suspicion by taxpayers, if not disgust. Who the heck knows what these folks are actually doing with all that money? Coddling friends? Looking the other way if the facts aren't to their liking?

And let's not forget to throw in the blind eyes of SEC Chairman Chris Cox. Maybe he thought he was going to get some lucrative job on Wall Street after his stint at the SEC ended. For what reason would he have gotten rid of the uptick rule related to short selling stocks, which allowed them to cascade faster than they normally would in the fall of 2008?

Short selling is selling stocks that you have borrowed. What the uptick rule does is to allow shorting only when the last price traded in a stock was up over the previous trade in that stock. The uptick would not keep stocks from dropping. That's not the point. The point is that with no uptick rule, stocks went down like avalanches, building more pressure the lower they went. Sharks piled on more selling as prices dropped, instead of having to wait until the price rises. This made many additional billions for the big money interests who can make stocks plunge with computer algorithms.

And why didn't Cox do anything about the outrageous amount of naked short selling, which is selling borrowed stock, but not actually borrowing that stock in order to sell it? You know, pretend you have it, and then sell it as a book entry without having to produce any documentation? To naked short sell is to sell something you don't have, nor having the ability or desire to borrow. This is blatantly illegal, and easy to prove. Even Cox admitted in 2006 that there were a lot of holes in the regulations, but he chose to do nothing. By 2008, the shorting got so bad that Cox banned short selling of 799 financial institutions, effectively choosing to enforce the law for these select companies.   What about the other thousands of companies?

Here's just one example, that of IBM.   In 2009, IBM had a total authorized issuance of 1.3 billion shares.   So why, when we count up the shares in 2009 owned by large block traders, such as banks, insurance companies, and mutual funds, do we come up with 1.6 billion shares outstanding?   Naked short sales account for the 300 million share discrepancy.   These were non-existent shares that had been sold into the market place by unscrupulous banks, traders or hedge funds, aided and abetted by their brokers or investment bankers, and of course, the SEC. Do you think selling 300 million shares would make the price go down? Of course! But this is just one high profile example.   There are hundreds more. The SEC chose to do nothing.

Did you ever hear of Bernie Madoff?   He was the guy who made-off with reportedly $60 billion or more of investor's money, all while being watched and examined by the SEC. It makes you wonder if the examiner who looked at the Madoff activities eight times was a bit nearsighted because of the fact that he was married to Bernie Madoff's niece.   What does this say about the regulators?   Congress wants more regulations, but the regulators don't enforce the laws already on the books! It seems they choose to prosecute the small guys, while leaving the big guys alone.

Now we come to Cox's successor, appointed by Mr. Obama. Mary Schapiro is an interesting study. Here is a woman who left the Financial Industry Regulatory Authority during a period of flagrant violation of trading regulations by big firms.   This was after having been in charge of the Commodity Futures Trading Commission (CFTC) under President Clinton.   This is the same Commission that wouldn't regulate the gross manipulation of metals futures undertaken for years on a daily basis by JP Morgan and about 6 other big financial firms.   These guys are the brokers and agents of the U.S. Government via the Exchange Stabilization Fund (ESF).   The ESF is a Treasury Department operation charged with "stabilizing" (aka manipulation) markets where they see fit, so apparently it gets a pass.

Community Reinvestment Act (1977)

Now let's point another finger. The Community Reinvestment Act (CRA) is a law that was touted by some pundits as being an enabler of the housing meltdown. And it was. This was the law that bankers had to deal with to get more mortgage money out to the lower income segment of society. The politicians decided that everyone who wanted to experience the American dream of home ownership should be able to do so, regardless of economic realities. Typically these loans went to the working class neighborhoods that were under a state of slow decay, which had previously been red-lined (avoided) by the banks. In order for everyone to achieve the American dream of owning a home, Congress decided to mandate that banks make this type of home loan to certain lower income customers and in areas that previously they would not touch. Even though this sounded admirable, the results were predictable.

Banks were not thrilled about making such loans at first. Along with the CRA beginning during the Carter administration, many community groups were also government funded to make certain that the banks did their civic duty. Groups such as ACORN (Association of Community Organizations for Reform Now, President Obama's former legal client) sprouted up. Banks were routinely hassled by such groups anytime they wanted to change business direction, or otherwise grow their branch count. Many banks would buy off the community groups with funding, which further strengthened these organizations. By 1994, a new law was passed to make it easier for banks to merge and acquire other banks, which was a clarion call for the community groups. Their watchdog activities went into overdrive, as did bank loans to the depressed neighborhoods.

The banks just didn't start to make loans to the lower income neighborhoods out of goodwill. Under President Clinton, many government agencies issued nasty ultimatums to lenders to relax loan standards for low income individuals. In fact, on April 15, 1994 the Federal Register shows an entry for the 'Policy Statement on Discrimination in Lending' published by the Clinton Interagency Task Force on Fair Lending. This directive was signed by the Housing and Urban Development (HUD) Secretary Henry Cisneros, the Attorney General Janet Reno, and even Fed Chairman Alan Greenspan. The directive stated:

"Applying different lending standards to applicants who are members of a protected class is permissible."

Even though this initiative was based on a Boston Fed study concluding that racial discrimination was the culprit, red-lining by the banks and mortgage companies was now green-lined, so the chase for subprime loans was on! Our leaders signed an initiative to promote more subprime loans!

Then, HUD pushed both Fannie Mae and Freddie Mac to buy the resulting subprime mortgages so that lenders would have more capital for additional subprime loans. What was the end result? Unfortunately, now that we citizens own Freddie and Fannie, we've had to make good on $177 billion worth of guarantees on defaulted loans as of the end of 2011, and the damage is growing each and every calendar quarter. This is a prime example of an unintended consequence.

In 1995, the Clinton administration began to put more pressure on banks to make more of the loans, asserting that if a buyer would go through a credit counseling program, this would suffice as a satisfactory underwriting tool to determine mortgage loan worthiness. Forget about income verification and credit history, there was now a new paradigm! By the time credit default swaps were invented, these types of loans could be off-loaded to foreign investors under the guise of an AAA label. So that segment of the loan market took off, particularly when the Greenspan Fed dropped rates in the early 2000's. It worked great – until it didn't! By 2003, the poster child for shaky loans was Countrywide, the largest lender in the nation, with fully $600 billion of subprime loans made. By the time the credit crisis was in full bloom, Countrywide was insolvent, and was merged into another problem child, the Bank of America, now partly owned by the American taxpayer.

Even though the politicians would like you to believe that the CRA, along with its subsequent tweaking, was not really a problem, the facts are that the housing bubble hid the effects of the law until the market blew up. And the fuse was the extremely poor repayment performance of the subprime loans.

Moral hazard engendered by Greenspan

You probably haven't seen much of this excuse for the crisis in the newspapers or on TV news, but the financial pundits see it like this: After the dot. com bubble burst, Fed Chairman Alan Greenspan made it an unofficial policy for financial firms that the Federal Reserve could step in if private firms made bad investments (bets) and needed help.

So it was obvious to Wall Street that they would be able to take more risk, and keep the hefty profits that risk generated, but would be saved by the Fed if things went bad. This is the very definition of moral hazard, and it came to pass with the nationalization of some of the country's largest banks. Even the Financial Times newspaper pointed this out in 2000 citing "*a destructive tendency toward excessively risky investment supported by hopes that the Fed will help if things go bad.*" Keep in mind that this was during the same timeframe that Greenspan repeatedly pounded the table against regulation of the OTC derivatives market. Has the halo come off the sainted and revered Mr. Greenspan? But we can't just blame Mr. Greenspan for the guaranteed backstops. The good Professor Ben Bernanke has taken the effort to an entirely new level with his currency swap lines, bailing our banks all over the world.

China's Monetary Policies

The biggest laugh of all was when Hank Paulsen accused China of instigating our financial problems with its ill-advised savings policies along with its control of its currency. At the time, the Chinese had invested upwards of $800 billion into our Treasury bonds, stoking the credit crisis, when they should have been spending that money on American goods and services, per Paulsen. He also accused them of artificially keeping their currency low compared to the U.S. dollar. How dare they do that? This smokescreen is the most ridiculous thing coming out of Washington in quite some time. Talk about pointing fingers! Did the Chinese authorize the U.S. to go into debt? Who would Paulsen expect to buy the massive volumes of the bonds? Would that be the U.S. public? Doubtful, since they were encouraged to go out and spend their stimulus checks at the mall instead of saving them!

Paulsen preferred that the Chinese spend more money on American goods, and that by manipulating their currency, they were hurting the trade prospects of other countries, particularly the U.S. The only manipulation (if that's what you want to call it) the Chinese did was to print money to keep the Yuan level with the Dollar Index. In other words, as we printed money so did the Chinese in defense of their own currency, so their exports would flow without a hitch. It worked to perfection as U.S. consumers loaded up on Chinese goods.

Later, Tim Geithner accused them of manipulating the currency as one of his first acts as Treasury Secretary. This wasn't too bright on his part, and that's being kind to the man. Aside from the fact that the Chinese know darned well that for years the U.S. tried to keep the Dollar Index within a well-defined channel by manipulating the gold prices (remember the Clinton strong dollar policy?), our leaders have also made it very clear that the dollar will fall dramatically with the profligate printing of currency coming out of Washington DC. A falling dollar makes our exports cheaper, and our imports (read Chinese products) more expensive. Then, poor Tim had the unfortunate experience of being ridiculed to his face by Chinese college students when he was trying to explain how safe the U.S. dollar was for Chinese investment!

The point is that China has a tremendous balance of trade surplus, especially from the U.S., and it has to invest those dollars somewhere. Do we twist the arms of the American consumers to buy Chinese goods with money from their home equity lines of credit? What are the Chinese supposed to buy with those billions of dollars they get from us? It's not like we have that many factories left in this country for stuff they might want. Many of our factories have packed up and left for friendlier wage, tax and regulatory environs, such as…China.

If that were not enough, President Clinton gave China *most favored nation* trade status once it became a member of the World Trade Organization (WTO). So what is China supposed to do with its dollars? This is a *critical* question, and has everything to do with the reserve status of the U.S. dollar. Up until 2010, China had lent a big portion of its savings back to the U.S. by purchasing Treasury notes and bonds. Yes, they have loaned it back to the U.S. to fund our continued deficit spending! This temporarily had the effect of avoiding the quantitative easing measures instituted by Mr. Bernanke at the Fed. Antagonizing the Chinese by trying to cajole them into more spending and borrowing like we do in the U.S. has gotten us nowhere. Expecting the Chinese to fall into the U.S. line is lunacy.

It's clear that Chinese fiscal and monetary policies are working for them. Our fiscal and monetary policies are not working for us. We have only ourselves (i.e. our politicians and bankers) to blame, not the Chinese. Readers should not think that this is a defense of the Chinese brand of the state capitalist system. But we must deal with reality. The point is that just because we have a bad habit of spending borrowed money on stupid stuff, doesn't mean that other countries should be expected to do the same. The Pied Piper theory doesn't work. Once again, the bureaucrats point the finger away from the real source of the problem.

Conclusion

Now we've looked at the most often cited blend of causes of the great financial debacle. The U.S. got its first hint of trouble with the demise of Bear Sterns back in the spring of 2007, but trouble became front and center with the failure of Lehman Brothers in the summer of 2008. Anyone who has been following the crisis is led to believe that things can be fixed with the wisdom and guidance of the Washington DC crowd. If you are included among the believers, you are betting your lifestyle and retirement plans on it. Let's check into why this is true by examining the facts and figures on the TARP bailout and the economic stimulus planning. These two ideas were the first and best attempts the politicians offered to turn things around for the U.S. economy, so a review of the facts ought to lead us to some solid conclusions as to their efficacy.

Chapter 6
Cover It Up With A Tarp

Smoke and mirrors behind the curtain of your banking system

Now we'll look at the maneuvers that the bankers and politicians enacted starting at the time that the fragility of the financial system became public, the fall of 2008. We know that the bankers, financial elite and even politicians, were telling us it was the end of times and the financial system was about to crash and burn. If we didn't act right now, and in a big way, the financial system would be doomed. *This was true at the time, and still is very true.* But did we get saved, or enslaved? How did your Congress and the banking elite actually try to fix our economic ills? You will soon find out. This knowledge is all important to your defensive financial plans for the future. If the 2008 episode wasn't well known, the Great Debt Debate in the summer of 2011 brought it out in bold headlines: the U.S. Congress is dysfunctional. Let's see what happened and what it really means to you.

Sometimes realism sounds like pessimism. The proposed Troubled Asset Relief Program (TARP) solution and its subsequent implementation gives us a good look at not only the folly of Congressional economic fixes, but also the process resulting in mega largess for the beneficiaries. The beneficiaries were not, nor ever were intended to be the American people. Rather, the bankers and politicians were looking to save themselves. It is true that the American middle class could be wiped out in a currency and systemic bank failure. But TARP was actually an attempt to save the banks and our monetary regime, not you. Unfortunately, the fact is that nothing has been fixed!! Not only is the banking system irreversibly broken, but so is its biggest customer, the U.S. government. This is not a good combination for you, your family, and your finances!

The opening salvo

On Thursday evening September 18th 2008, Ben Bernanke and Hank Paulsen made an unusual visit to Capitol Hill to brief Congressional leaders on their vision of the scope of the financial problem we (they) were facing. The picture on the front page of the Washington Post the next morning said it all. Nancy Pelosi looked like a deer in headlights. She had clearly bought in to Paulsen's scare tactics. And Chris Dodd said on a 'Good Morning America' segment the next morning that the leaders were told *"that we're literally maybe days away from a complete meltdown of our financial system."*

It's interesting that our politicians decided to call the bill for bailing out the banking industry TARP - as in cover-up. The Troubled Asset Relief Program was the first in what has proven to be a series of disastrous fiscal and monetary measures instituted by Congress, the Treasury Department, and the Federal Reserve to supposedly fix our troubled economy. Don't you use a tarp to cover over things that need protection? Why does a free market banking system need such cover? Can't they fend for themselves, or otherwise fail and go bankrupt, just as a capitalist system would have it? Why do "we the people" have to pay for their lack of acumen in their own business?

The sales pitch was that TARP was supposed to buy up all the bad debt held in the banking balance sheets, so they could free up capital to loan more money to the already over-leveraged American public and financial businesses. If banks had to maintain those bad assets on their balance sheets, the losses involved would occupy the availability of money they could lend, due to reserve requirements. There would be no money to lend! So why not use government money, borrowed from the Fed, to buy up those toxic assets and that would be the perfect solution, right? Yes, kill two birds with one stone. Eliminate the bad assets by having the government pay the banks cash for them, automatically increasing cash and reserves by virtue of the fact that no more bad loans would be on the balance sheets; plus the banks would then have some of the sale proceeds to loan out yet again! Wasn't that a great idea? Good old American ingenuity comes through again.

How were the taxpayers to get repaid for the loan? Oh ye of little faith; when the toxic assets increased in price to full value again they could then be sold back to the banks, or even to worldwide investors, and everybody would be whole again. Lets' continue our short trip down memory lane to see how TARP came to be, exactly what it's done to solve the real crisis, and what that means to you.

When the Senate Banking Committee held its hearing on September 23, 2008, it was moderated by Senator Christopher Dodd. The purpose of the hearing was to gather enough information to determine whether or not to bail out the banking industry with a massive bill. This 5 hour hearing featured testimony by both Fed Chairman Ben Bernanke and

Secretary of the Treasury Hank Paulsen. Frankly, some of the assertions and admissions by these two men were astonishing, so some comment is instructive here. Then we'll look at what actually happened after the bill was passed, so get ready for some fun and games, Washington DC style.

The setup

Let's pick on Mr. Bernanke first. Keep in mind this is the man who, not 3 months earlier, called the credit crisis only a $100,000 billion problem. He just knew at the time that the subprime problem would be contained, and it wouldn't affect the rest of the economy. Mr. Bernanke also assured us that the recession would end in the early part of 2009; before he changed his mind to say that we would then recover by late 2009. He thought a zero interest rate policy (ZIRP) on Fed Funds would be just the solution! Only in January 2012 he admitted that the rate would have to stay in the basement for 3 more years, because the so-called recovery wasn't happening. It was pretty obvious that if he did have a clue as to the depth of the crisis, it wasn't politically acceptable for him to give any hints.

One shocking takeaway from Bernanke's testimony was that he suggested that hold-to-maturity value (the original 100%) of the toxic assets be paid to the banks. Pay a dollar for something that is worth 30 cents at best? This seemed crazy, but it's exactly what he ended up doing! This choker would have us assume that all of the bad loan portfolios would be paid back in full in order for the American people to come out of the deal whole. Well, if they were in a huge loss position at the time, what would lead Mr. Bernanke to think that by some miracle the toxic assets would become current and appreciate to 100% of true value at the bitter end? That would just never happen. But Bernanke assured us that "...this is a pre-condition for a good, healthy recovery of our economy."

For now, let's assume that this is true that the loans would be made good to the penny. Bernanke offered absolutely no theory, evidence, hints, or past history as to why this would be the case. He couldn't. He went on to say that: *"The situation we have now is unique and new."*

This seemed true enough, since the OTC derivatives market in CDO's and CDS's is fairly new and had never imploded before; so Bernanke thought that this time it really was different! It is well known that Bernanke is a student of the Great Depression of the 30's, but if the current problem is that unique, what made him think his plan would work? We can only assume that as leader of the financial system, he had to *appear* as though he knew exactly what to do.

Actually it was Hank Paulsen who carried the burden of the sales pitch for much of the hearing. Yes, this would be the same Hank Paulsen who was CEO of Goldman Sachs during the time that the Credit Default Swaps came into being, and he made Goldman Sachs a big participant in the game. Make no mistake about it, Paulsen knew all about the risks inherent in CDS's. He and his firm profited handsomely when the times were good, and when the derivatives could be sold world-wide to naïve investors with more dollars than sense. Then he bugged out to become Treasury Secretary under George W. Bush. Of course, Paulsen was an old time Washington DC player, having gotten his first job out of Harvard Business School working for none other than John Erlichman. Naturally, some readers may not know or remember the name Erlichman. John Erlichman was in charge of the "plumbers" in the Nixon White House, who did the dirty tricks for Nixon against any number of political adversaries. Paulsen was at ground zero then. But once the walls came down around Nixon, and Haldeman and Erlichman had to resign as part of the big Watergate cover-up, Paulsen headed for Chicago to get his start in the investment business with Goldman Sachs in 1973.

Mr. Paulsen began his testimony on that September 23, 2008 by telling us how appalled he had become at the apparent lack of regulation pertaining to Credit Default Swaps which he had discovered when he became Treasury Secretary. Right away, one became skeptical. Here's a man who presided over hundreds of billions of CDS business, and he did not know what the regulations were, or were not? To prove the point, he said: "The regulatory system was built for a different structure".

Paulsen went on to say that the taxpayers were already on the hook for the problem anyway, so Congress should just go ahead and give him what he was requesting, and that he would handle everything with the utmost care. He claimed that the buy-back program (of the toxic assets) would be a voluntary program, and that only those institutions that felt it was worthwhile would do it. Gee, it seems that those that wanted to voluntarily dump the bad loans would not have to be asked twice, especially if they were to receive full value for defaulting loan portfolios! But the Senators were still concerned that there was a problem with bailing out private banking companies, particularly those who had made a practice of doling out loan money to less than credit-worthy borrowers, then dumping some of those lousy loans on unsuspecting investors, including other countries around the world. But Mr. Paulsen reassured the Senators, saying: "This is not about the companies it's about the American people." Well, that sounded good. The only problem was that it later became clear that this was patently false!

Democratic Senator Chuck Shumer of New York was a vocal advocate of doing the TARP in tranches, or baby steps. That would give money to the Treasury a little at a time, and Congress could evaluate as it went along, and make changes or cut off the supply of funding if necessary. But Paulsen would hear none of it. He wanted them to promise all the money now, asserting that we: "…need market confidence and need the tools to work with."

There's that word "confidence" again, the ever critical and crucial ingredient to the U.S. and worldwide Ponzi money scheme. He expressed concern that it would be a "grave mistake" not receive the whole wad all at one time.

Then Republican Chuck Hagel of Nevada stepped up to the plate. He asked Paulsen about his vision as to how the oversight of the taxpayer money would be handled. Seven hundred billion dollars was multiple orders of magnitude more money than Congress had used to bailout out or spend on anything, ever. Here's where Paulsen lied with the straightest of faces. Paulsen assured the panel that he needed and wanted oversight. He wanted to operate the bailout with great transparency, which would be broad based, with some parts being more narrowly focused. Paulsen then said: "If it works like it should, it's not an expenditure it's an investment."

However, he then went on to say that there would be no profit sharing once everything was resolved. This is very curious. One must wonder how many investments he sold at Goldman Sachs on which the customer did not expect a profit on such a speculation. However, it was apparently OK for the American public to simply hope to get their money back with interest.

Paulsen seemed genuinely concerned that the banks could not be allowed to fail because of the lack of regulatory structure. At least, that's what he claimed. He did not address the fact that regardless of regulation, the risk takers at the banks expected to get bailed out because of precedents set by Alan Greenspan when he ruled the Fed. But the fact is that both he and Bernanke knew the risks involved either with or without a bailout. But as to the proposal on the table, Paulsen said: "I have not said that the taxpayer is not at risk."

If the truth were known, Paulsen didn't want to see banks fail due to the certainty of the ramifications to the U.S. financial system and its concomitant economy, which neither he nor Bernanke would detail. That outcome could be, and very probably will be, the complete *do-over of our monetary system regardless of TARP*. But any conjecture on the future machinations and attempted fixes by the bankers and politicians at this point would be fruitless.

A big warning signal

It was not disclosed to the public, but on September 15th, 2008, starting at about 11AM and just a week prior to the big rush for TARP money, fully $550 billion was withdrawn from U.S. money market funds within two hours. A run on the system had started, but the hole was quickly and quietly closed by the Treasury for fear of the loss of public confidence. It got Paulsen's attention in a hurry, and the Treasury then pumped $105 billion back into the system. *This* was what led to the guarantee of up to $250,000 per account in money market funds, announced by Paulsen in a press release on September 19th. These facts were supported by Congressman Paul Kanjorski (D-Pa), Chairman of the House Capital Markets Subcommittee. This event happened concurrent with the oldest money market fund in the country, the $63 billion Reserve Primary Fund, "breaking the buck" due to exposure of Lehman Brothers bonds in its fund. The phrase "break the buck" refers to the fact that each share of the fund, which normally would always be worth a dollar, was now valued at less than a dollar! This was a wake-up call for the investment community, and somebody got very nervous to the tune of $550 billion! Somebody lost confidence.

In Paulsen's press release announcing the guarantee of money market assets, which had previously never been guaranteed, he told the American public that the illiquid mortgage assets in the banks were choking off the credit flow, which could have significant ill-effects to the U.S. financial system. But he never mentioned the run that had happened a few days prior. He went on to say:

"The Federal Government must implement a program to remove these illiquid assets that are weighing down our financial institutions and threatening our economy."

So he had effectively set the bait, telling the American public that the toxic assets had to be removed from the banking system. The switch would come after the bill passed.

The plan, the plan

The Congressional leaders then decided to wait for Paulsen to draft a plan for Congress to consider. Dodd explained:

"We have got to deal with the foreclosure issue. You have got to stop that hemorrhaging. If you don't, the problem doesn't go away. Ben Bernanke has said it over and over again. Hank Paulsen recognizes it. This problem began with bad lending practices. Those are his words, not mine, and so this plan must address that, or I'll be back here in front of a bank of microphones at some point explaining the next failure."

So, seemingly everyone was on the same page. But, then things got strange. Years elapsed after TARP passed, proving that the foreclosure issue was still very alive and very well. Many banks were by then up to their eyeballs in repossessed homes, and millions of homes were part of the "shadow inventory" in the banking system. So what went wrong with the bailout?

Paulsen's proposal consisted of a 3 page, $700 billion plan that would exempt him personally for any and all wrong-doing or second-guessing as to what he did with the money. Well, that one did not fly, so the House drafted its own version of the $700 billion plan. When the public got wind of it, according to Congressman Ron Paul, a Rasmussen poll found that only 7% of the public supported it. It was voted down in the House; and the U.S. financial system was still standing. So the Senate took charge, added some pork-barrel spending directed to the right Senators and the measure got enough votes to get it passed. It should be noted here that they still gave Paulsen free reign, as the bill contained a huge "get out of jail free" card stating:

"Decisions by the Secretary pursuant to the authority of this Act are non-reviewable and committed to agency discretion, and may not be reviewed by any court of law or any administrative agency."

Then, on September 24th, 2008, Ben Bernanke testified before the Joint Economic Committee, chaired by Chuck Schumer of New York. This was an interesting event also, and gives us a clue as to the twisted thinking of the good professor Bernanke. Representative Kevin Brady of Texas suggested to Bernanke that he should let the free market be free and then it would correct itself. But Bernanke took the approach that the country needed the help of the Fed and Treasury to discover what the sale price of those illiquid assets should be, so that private enterprise could come in and help the government get them off the books of the banks.

Of course, Representative Ron Paul of Texas lost it! He said that the illiquid assets were illiquid because they weren't worth anything; a hard statement to refute. So Bernanke finally had to agree that government price fixing would be counterproductive and that a good price discovery process had to somehow be found. Paul went on to assert that the Fed wasn't smart enough to fix prices of the assets in question, and that the free market should be able to do it with great efficiency. Gee, that sounds so... logical. So we have a great idea that the Fed Chairman didn't think of; just let the buyers and sellers decide the prices they'd settle for in buying and selling the toxic assets!

Readers should understand that the Treasury and the Fed were then and still are scared to death of a good price discovery of bank assets, as it would reveal systemic insolvency. That is correct; established prices will reveal the fact that many, many more big banks are insolvent than admitted by the powers in Washington, which would lead to total chaos both on Main Street and on Wall Street. Readers should remember the fact that no cleanup of the financial structures of the U.S. can occur without massive dislocation and disintegration of the whole system. The money mavens can't possibly cover all the current and potential future loan and derivative losses and systemic insolvency, but they're giving it a go!

Finally, Bernanke said that he did not expect the $700 billion dollar TARP injection of taxpayer money to be inflationary. How could this NOT be inflationary? Well, just don't let banks loan out the money, that's how. But we weren't supposed to know that.

Ultimately, under the threat of Martial Law whispered behind closed doors, the House finally passed the TARP legislation on the second go-around, but with a caveat innocently planted during debate. The final bill only gave the Treasury one half at a time, and the second half was to come after seeing how the first half was working. By that time, Mr. Obama would be in office and the second $350 billion became his baby. The country was now to be saved! This begs the question why subsequently Obama kept pinning the whole TARP plan on Bush, when he was the one who got to decide on the disposition of the second half of the money, including the auto and insurance company buyouts!

So now it looked as though the Treasury would get the money it needed to buy all those toxic assets so as to get the banks in good financial shape to lend again. But what happened? The first half of TARP was gone, but no toxic assets were bought by the Treasury! Instead, Paulsen decided to simply make what he characterized as "investments" in 9 big banks. He simply gave them money in exchange for newly issued preferred stock! It was now party time for the recipients of the windfall! But it was worse than that.

The recipient banks could now use some of that money to act as predators to buy up weaker and smaller banks at pennies on the dollar, and they would be rewarded for doing so. How so? They'd buy the good assets of the failed banks under an FDIC guarantee, and let the FDIC make up the losses on the balance of the bad assets, that's how. Good deal, right? So the toxic assets from little banks went into the FDIC cesspool, and the good stuff went to the already dead big banks with TARP cash. But didn't both Paulsen and Bernanke tell us that the toxic assets had to be removed from the banks for the economy to recover? And where was the vast majority of the toxicity? The big banks with TARP money! So what else could help to get dead big banks with TARP money to buy good assets from bad little banks? Tax benefits!

The Treasury Department runs the Internal Revenue Service. It enforces the tax laws; it is not supposed to make tax laws. But it did so anyway by giving the big banks with the new found money a new goodie. On September 30, 2008, the Treasury repealed a 22 year old law which denied acquiring companies the ability to write off the losses of the companies they had bought out. Section 382 of the Internal Revenue Code had been enacted by Congress in 1986 to eliminate fat tax write-offs in the process of buying another company with losses on the books. But Paulsen decided to allow the write-offs anyway in the case of a bank buying another failing bank. This would be a major windfall, and an incentive to get big banks to buy smaller ones. This was done *prior* to TARP being passed, and immediately after Paulsen was pleading for the money to buy toxic assets so the banks could start loaning money again. No wonder Paulsen wanted that "get out of jail free" card! He was effectively working a con on Congress and the American people!

The switch

Let's get back to basics. A bank has assets, its loans to customers. And it also has liabilities, such as its deposits and stock outstanding in the hands of the stockholders. The stock outstanding is a *liability* because it represents a pledge against its assets. The stockholders own the loans, both good and bad. So when the TARP plan calls for buying up toxic assets from the banks, it refers to purchasing those bad loans and non performing CDO's from the banks, so the bank doesn't have the problem anymore. It would then have more cash to loan out; and no more non-performing loans on the books, right? Good. We've seen the bait; now it's on to Paulsen's switch.

The Senate had already passed the TARP legislation, and then it was sent back to the House for another try. The House has a procedure to clarify any nebulous provisions of a bill being discussed. If, during the debate, an issue or question comes up as to the meaning of a passage within the legislation, the clarification of that passage during debate goes into the record as the way the passage of the bill is to be interpreted. The TARP legislation generally allowed for the Treasury to purchase only distressed assets, but it also referred to "any other financial instrument", leading the Congress to assume that this could have referred to any number of over-the-counter derivatives like interest rate swaps or credit default swaps.

Representative Jim Moran of Virginia asked about buying up troubled the assets, and if the purchase of stock was to be considered as an allowable way to get cash into the banks. The issue was not clear in the language of the bill since it referred to "assets". The intrepid Barney Frank sprang into action and stated:

"I can affirm that…It is not simply buying up the assets, it is to buy equity, and to buy equity in a way that the Federal Government will be able to benefit if there is an appreciation."

So the deed was done; the Act would allow for the Treasury to buy both assets *and* liabilities of the banks. This begs the question of why the bill was not then sent back to the Senate for clarification, debate, and another vote, but such are the marvels of our system. The switch became law, and Barney came through for the benefit of his campaign contributors once again.

What happened to the first tranche of the TARP money? Nine large banks got the first $125 billion immediately. Ninety five billion dollars of this money went to primary U.S. bond dealers. That would be brokers who raise money for the government. The totals are ugly: Citigroup, JP Morgan, and Bank of America each got $25 billion, and Goldman Sachs and Morgan Stanley each got $10 billion. Let's see, Morgan Stanley could now pay out its bonuses totaling almost $10.7 billion for 2008! Forget about the company losses, the employees need spending money, and it came in the form of the TARP bailout!

According to an analysis in the Washington Post, fully 52% of the first $125 billion of TARP money paid out to the 9 pet banks would go to pay three years-worth of dividends to the stockholders. Now that sounds like a good deal for taxpayers, doesn't it? But let's be fair to Mr. Paulsen. At least he got preferred shares from the banks that would yield a 5% dividend to the taxpayer. But that's as good as it gets. Paulsen got no voting rights associated with these shares, no seat on the Board for a taxpayer representative, and no warrants for upside potential as Barney had promised. And let's not forget about the fact that, during the same timeframe, Warren Buffet cut a deal with Goldman Sachs for preferred shares yielding 10%. So why couldn't Paulsen get his buddies at Goldman to give the taxpayers the same kind of deal? Do you think the government is ever capable of providing the taxpayer with any sort of a good deal? Why do we continue to look to our economically under-educated politicians for help? Investment bankers do what they do, but why do the citizens have to clean up the mess?

Let's do a quick review of how the 5 big Wall Street investment banks performed from 2004 to 2008. The market value of the stock of these 5 institutions dropped $83 billion during this timeframe. This was not good, leading the man on the street investor to believe that these companies just didn't do too well. But wait, the total compensation to employees of these firms was fully *$239 billion* during this same timeframe! The TARP legislation allowed the CEO's to rob the piggy bank and screw the shareholders!

The joke's on us!

"The facts have changed." This was Paulsen's explanation of his diversion of the first half of the TARP funding for an entirely *different* purpose than what was discussed in his press release and his testimony in the House and Senate hearings to consider the TARP legislation. Have you ever known the facts to change? Facts are, well, reality. Now, maybe someone's knowledge of the facts changes, or maybe circumstances change giving added significance to our knowledge of the facts, but the facts don't change. So when Paulsen told the American people over and over again that the facts changed, either he was lying, or he just didn't know what he was talking about in the first place. How is your confidence level?

What is curious is that Paulsen appeared, albeit slowly and dishonestly, to have taken the lead from the Bank of England. Perhaps it was his intent all along; perhaps not. At any rate, the Bank of England (British central bank) had already decided not to buy up the toxic assets from its member banks. Instead, it would inject the cash in exchange for an equity stake. But it would also require recipient banks to lend that money to its customers. OK, a model around which to fashion the use of the TRAP money, with exceptions of course. And that *major* exception was to ignore the needs of American citizens and business owners looking for loan money, in favor of parties, bonuses, dividends, and bank consolidation. No TARP money was ever loaned out. No toxic assets were ever purchased. The Fed took care of some of that with fresh new money, plus it had to unload a huge chunk of its top quality Treasury Bonds to make it happen as we've already seen.

Elizabeth Warren, a Harvard Law School professor, was head of the TARP oversight committee that called for a revamping of TARP on February 5, 2009. It took her over 3 months to delve into the inner workings of the program, and she accused the Treasury (Paulsen) of misleading the public. That is shocking! We're not talking about the bait and switch just described. Now we're talking about the overpayment for the preferred shares that the Treasury arranged to purchase. Paulsen assured overseers that he would drive a tough bargain and get a fair price for the shares with plenty of transparency. In a Senate Banking Committee hearing, Warren stated: *"Treasury simply did not do what it said it was doing."* She further stated that the bailout was: *"...an opaque process at best,"* and that Paulsen: "...was not entirely candid."

Warren discovered that the Treasury paid $254 billion for bank stocks worth $176 billion in value, a shortfall of $78 billion, representing pure profit to the banks. We are not referring to the 9 pets, but rather 319 other banks, 230 of which subsequently ran out of money again. This is not to say that all these banks are U.S. banks. We weren't allowed to know. Witness the Bloomberg and Fox News Freedom of Information Act requests for information regarding the disposition of the TARP money (who got what), which got stonewalled for some while by both the Treasury and the Fed.

One of the best jokes on the public was the fact that this TRAP plan had to be passed right away. No delay, no politics, it had to be done immediately. Congress swallowed the line, and acted in undue haste to pass the most reviled financial measure under the U.S. fiat money regime.

But then, after Paulsen spent the first half of the money, he said that it could take *years* to see if it worked or not. Great, we needed it right now, or there might be Martial Law, blood in the streets, a depression. But we won't know for years if it worked or not. This sounds so…uneducated. It seems that it would have been in the better interest of the American people to take a little time and craft a tighter piece of legislation? But no, Huckster Hank had made the sale to the gullible U.S. Congress!

Turbo Tax Tim takes command

Tim Geithner, the new Treasury Secretary under President Obama, and a Robert Rubin (former Treasury Secretary under Bill Clinton and CEO of Goldman Sachs) protégé, announced the development of the second half of the TARP program on February 10, 2009, and assured the public that it would be much different under his watch, but was either unwilling or unable to provide too many details at that point in time.

As background, Geithner was employed by Kissinger & Associates from 1985 to 1988. As readers may recall, Henry Kissinger was the Secretary of State under Richard Nixon. Geithner worked his way up to the top post at the New York Fed in 2003, after having done stints with the Council on Foreign Relations as a Senior Fellow in the Economics Department, and a consultancy with the International Monetary Fund (IMF), where he made income which he failed to report on his tax return. He intimated that confusion about the tax preparation software Turbo Tax was the problem.

As President of the New York Federal Reserve, Geithner implemented the economic and monetary policy for the United States government through his control of the Federal Open Market Committee (FOMC), and in fact had control over the entire Federal Reserve System. So here is a critical point: for several years, Geithner was uniquely qualified as head of the New York Fed to see and prevent what was to eventually become the worst economic crisis in the history of the United States. So how did he do regulating the banks? Where was his warning? Where was his leadership and guidance?

Here's a quote from the New York Fed's website:

"…the New York Fed implements monetary policy, supervises, and regulates financial institutions and helps maintain the nation's payment systems."

One must realize that the New York Fed is the *lead* bank of the 12 Fed branches scattered throughout the country. It has oversight over the entire system, and implements the operations of the Federal Open Market Committee (FOMC), which does the actual market intervention work to implement its monetary policy.

One more quote from the website is instructive, and telling:

"One of the reasons for the establishment of the Federal Reserve System was to *forestall a repeat of the liquidity crises and financial panics* that occurred sporadically in the United States before 1913....The objective of their activities is *to ensure the financial strength and stability of the nation's banking system.* The New York Fed conducts on-site and off-site examinations of member depository institutions..."

Was someone sleeping at the controls? The Fed has publicly admitted that it failed in its one task of forestalling a liquidity crisis. Forestall means to prevent by doing something ahead of time, according to Webster's dictionary. Ok, they get an "F" for forestalling. What about those supposed bank examinations? What happened to the caretaker when the outrageous amounts of derivatives were being touted as a legitimate way to make obscene profits at the big banks, instead of the tried and true method of making good loans?

Shouldn't we, the public, be outraged that the man at the helm of the New York Fed was simply not doing his job, putting our entire financial system at risk? What happened? He got kicked into the Secretary of the Treasury position for his vast experience. Geithner has proven over and over again to be inept at best, but then we looked to him to administer stress tests on the 19 biggest banks in the country after they had been spoon fed the TARP money? Wasn't Turbo Tax Tim supposed to be doing this anyway years ago, to forestall a problem? Well, that was then.

Now it was time to have Geithner bring his expertise to the U.S. Treasury Department. He had been charged with a couple of initial priorities. He needed to make sure that the banks were solid in order to keep public confidence up, and he also had to devise a way to get the toxic assets out of the banks without the use of TARP money. The first objective could be handled with adroit use of smoke and mirrors, and also by deflecting the real issue over to the supposedly recovering U.S. economy; but the second was much more difficult, reality being what it is.

The TARP funding was about gone, having been spent on everything from banks to insurance and car company bailouts, and Congress had no more appetite for giving more money to the banks after having reviewed the public opinion polls. What was a Treasury Secretary to do? How about an exercise in attempting to restore the confidence of the public in their banking and money system? The first and most very basic question that should be asked in a free market economy is: why is all of the maneuvering necessary in the first place? After all, haven't the regulators been on the job for years and years? They have, but then again they haven't.

The tests were passed with gimmickry

The stress tests of the big banks after the TARP handouts were a farce. They were meant to do one thing and one thing only, and that is to con the American people into believing that the banks were solvent. The theory is that this would keep up the confidence of the public, so that they would continue to go to the malls to spend their paper money, boosting the economy.

The highly touted and successful stress tests were done on the 19 biggest banks in the U.S. after they received their TARP money. Do you have renewed confidence in the knowledge that they all passed with flying colors? Granted, a few of the biggies had to raise a measly $75 billion or so. But that was relatively easy.

What has happened to the crisis and the toxicity once we were told all was well? It lives and has gotten larger. The big banks are not simply suffering from a liquidity crisis (temporary cash flow issues) as we have been led to believe. The fact is that they are insolvent (read bankrupt), and nothing has been done to change this fact. Don't be fooled by the fact that banks are holding record reserves at the Federal Reserve, as we know from the monetary base shown earlier in Chart 1. Their stock values have weakened dramatically. The excess reserves picture is demonstrating how weak our financial system really is. This proves how distressed bank portfolios really are. But that's Ok, because Professor Bernanke can print money to infinity, as he assured us in September, 2012. Unfortunately, this is a picture of a dysfunctional banking system and it proves the point of extreme stress cracks!

The toxic assets are still on the balance sheet at the banks because the regulators are allowing the banks to value these assets in full. How can portfolios of non-performing loans, with payments not being made, be worth the same as they were to start with when hopes were high and payments were current? They are not, and indeed can never be, as the ability to pay is gone and will not return. The stress tests were never meant to do anything other than to appease the naïve American public into believing that all is well again with our flawed and bankrupt banking system.

The confidence game with the stress tests took two steps to pull the wool over the eyes of the American public. Step one was to make a big deal that the banks were now in good shape once they passed the test. When you were in school, did you ever hear of the teacher changing the questions *during the test?* That's what the money mavens did! The banks complained that the benchmarks were too onerous, so those benchmarks were changed while they were being given the stress test. Indeed, the numbers were run assuming a high of 8.5 percent unemployment, and the fact that the recession would be over by the end of 2009. Both of these assumptions were subsequently disproven.

Also, the stress test did not take in to account those losses that the banks were certain to incur after 2010. The Alt-A and Option Arm home loan resets were to peak in 2011, and more than 20 million home mortgages nationwide were "upside down" by then. Not only that, there are a slew of commercial mortgages set for rollover before 2014 which were glossed over. A large percentage of these are also underwater. So the regulators looked, but not very deeply! It's like taking a close up photo. Things look much different if the photo is taken from 1 foot away versus 20 feet away. But that was the only way to make the dire situation inside the banks look normal!

Step two of the con entailed a couple of accounting sleights of hand. The FASB people (U.S. Financial Accounting Standards Board) were under pressure to eliminate the *mark to market rule* concerning the bad bank assets, and they finally caved in. Prior to the change, banks had to write down the bad loans to their true market value, requiring more reserves to be put up. That made sense. But now the banks would be allowed to value the lousy performing loan assets at whatever level they wanted. This method is called *mark to model, thus allowing banks to value the toxic assets at 100% or more of the original value!* It is actually a mark to fantasy! But it gets worse. Many banks which had previously and appropriately taken losses on marked down assets were now allowed to mark them back up! What does that mean? It means that the banks (like Citigroup, for instance) could now show a *profit* on a non-performing loan, and that is exactly what they did!

The above paragraph discusses loan values that were owed to the bank. What about the loans that the bank itself owed and had to pay back? Here's where part B of the accounting gimmickry comes into play. Banks in financial trouble have obligations too. The market decides what those obligations are worth, given the individual bank's ability to pay. So if the liquidity and solvency of any given bank comes into question and the free market discounts the value of those obligations due to shaky probabilities of getting repaid, then the bank that owes the money to someone else gets to show a *profit* on the amount of the loan obligation that the market has discounted because the bank is in trouble! In common terms, *they get to show a profit because they have an impaired ability to pay back an obligation. So if they don't have to pay what they owe, it's a profit!* Both Morgan Stanley and Bank of America made a big deal over their illusionary $1 billion profits in the second quarter of 2010 using this accounting gimmick! Does this give you a great deal of confidence in our money system?

Lo and behold, due to accounting scams, the banks were profitable again; they were able to spin their stock prices higher with TARP money (we'll get into the mechanics of how it was done later in the book when we talk about the stock market), and now the banks could sell more stock to the public because they could demonstrate profit making ability! Done, and done. Now they could give back the TARP money so that they wouldn't be under the watchful eye of the Fed and Treasury. Done; now, let's give ourselves a new round of bonuses! Done! Isn't banking fun again, now that the crisis is over?

But actually, it's not over. Over 140 banks had failed in 2009, with even more than that going down in 2010, and more in 2011, albeit fewer than the prior two years. After all, the FDIC couldn't close too many more banks, as they were out of money to pay their guarantees. But what did *all* of the failed banks have in common? They all had stated assets well in excess of true value, most to the tune of 40% or more. And, of course, the FDIC has taken into its custody many toxic assets from these banks. We know they can't sit on them like a bank can and pretend how valuable they are, so what do they do? They'll auction them off later, and the fun will start anew. This is when we see the rats scatter once again, as the true prices of the toxic assets will be discovered. Many banks will then be forced into reality; more losses will follow necessitating the use of more reserves. That could result in less loan money going to the public sector.

By 2012, more testing had to be done. After all, banks had been able to borrow as much money as they needed for virtually nothing which helped them build their stash of cash. This was when a big deal was made of the fact that 15 out of the 19 biggest banks passed the test. The other 4, including the government owned Ally Bank had to raise more money somehow. Readers should note that Ally Bank was the former GMAC financing arm of GM, which became a commercial bank when the government took over GM. It's too bad the bank continued to make sub-prime car loans to prop up GM's car sales. Three years after the government takeover, it still didn't have the necessary cash to cover its potential liabilities!

The test included a higher threshold for a lousy economy to see if the banks could handle the pressure, and Mr. Geithner and the Fed Professor told the world how wonderful things were in the U.S. banking system. But wait! Did they do a test for a rising interest rate environment? We know the answer, and it is *no*. Higher interest rates would implode the system due to the extreme exposure to interest rate swaps (OTC derivatives), as we already know. So let's just test for what we know will pass! Done, and done!

Plan B for toxic asset disposal

Regardless of value, the toxic assets remained nestled in the bank file cabinets. What could a Treasury Secretary do about that? After many months of uncertainty, Treasury Secretary Geithner finally announced the Public-Private Investment Program (PPIP) which was basically plan B to get the toxic assets off the books of the banks. At long last, we finally got *the* plan that the U.S. economy was waiting for, since the TARP was never used as Hank Paulsen assured us it would. The new idea was to designate up to $1 trillion in private investment funds in order to buy up toxic assets at prices that were to be determined by the market. Unfortunately, this plan was dead on arrival, even though the government was to guarantee fully 93% of the private investment in the asset purchases. Actually, the taxpayers are very lucky the plan didn't fly.

We have to wonder *why* it was dead on arrival. If the banks could unload their bad assets, and the investors were to receive a virtual non-recourse guarantee that the government would cover losses, why it didn't work? Again, *the banks didn't want to sell the bad assets, because they didn't want real price discovery.* This would have let the American public see that they were actually insolvent, after having to write off tremendous losses when the sale transaction actually took place. Pull the curtain back to expose the Wizard? Never! Don't ever show those losses, or they'd be out of business without any way to raise the additional reserves needed! End of that story.

The reason given by the financial powers that the PPIP never gained traction was that banks were able to go to the marketplace and sell more stock to get the money they needed. That means they diluted the shares already owned by investors, rendering them with less of an ownership cut of the banks in question. How could the banks ever hope to raise more money this way? They passed the stress test, and forced their stock prices higher, so new investors thought all was now OK. But what do you think the banks did with the TARP money? They were able to invest it in anything they wanted, and did so without the knowledge of the public through the use of "dark pools". Now they could put in bids on their own stock, forcing the prices higher in preparation for sales of new issues to the public. It's called "pump and dump" in the business.

Damned lies

"If you tell a lie big enough and keep repeating it, people will eventually come to believe it. The lie can be maintained only for such time as the State can shield the people from the political, economic, and/or military consequences of the lie."

This is a Joseph Goebbels quote, who was the infamous Hitler henchman in charge of propaganda during the Third Reich era. It must actually work, since Hitler got away with quite a bit without any trouble from the German citizens. And it has worked quite well in the U.S., at least for the last 40 years.

The Fed refused to divulge the details on loans and security under 11 of its inventive programs which have never been tried in its history. Three years later they did provide some detail, after major cajoling by Congress and the passage of the Dodd-Frank legislation. The programs totaled over $16 trillion in loans! And where did the end result of the money movement ever appear on the balance sheet? It didn't. Congressman Ron Paul proposed to audit the Fed, having a huge majority in the House as co-sponsors of his legislation. But the bill got merged and ended up with no teeth at all. He wanted to know who got the money with all the various Fed programs, and what the security is behind the solid U.S. fiat dollar.

Alas, our financial system is now partially backed on subprime debt, or worse, credit default swaps and CDO's gone bad. Will it be possible to get the complete truth out of our central bank? No. If the American public learned the truth, the confidence game would be over. It was Henry Ford who said:

"It is well that the people of the nation do not understand our banking and monetary system, for if they did, I believe there would be a revolution before tomorrow morning."

The Financial Reform that really wasn't

Almost 2 years elapsed since "the end of the world as we knew it" would be addressed in the form of a financial reform bill coming out of Congress. The 2700 page monster was called the Restoring American Financial Stability Act of 2010, commonly referred to as Dodd-Frank. Of course, we had to have the stimulus package first; and for sure the Health Care Reform bill, along with the Cap and Trade initiative which flew through the House before getting stalled in the Senate. OK, now let's get on to fixing the problems that resulted in the huge and landmark financial crisis. A quick look how each of the causation factors was addressed in the Dodd-Frank legislation is instructive.

The new legislation required derivatives to be traded in exchanges and clearing houses; gives powers to the bureaucrats to shutter failing financial firms; allows the bureaucrats to make the rules as they go along without Congressional approval; and creates a consumer protection infrastructure. It is certain to generate plenty of unintended consequences. Many of the details and fiddle fixes will likely take years to perfect to the liking of the bureaucrats charged with such initiatives. Suffice it to say, the legislation will be like going to the doctor and having him treat your symptoms, instead of the actual malady causing those symptoms. It won't really do anything other than disguise the true problem. And by the time the lobbyists finish, it will likely be a shell of its former self.

In a July, 2010 article, Ezra Klein of the Washington Post put it very succinctly when he stated of the financial reform:

"…think of the difference between public health and medicine: the bill is medicine-it's primarily about helping the doctors who figure out when you're sick and how to make you better. It doesn't dramatically change the conditions that made you sick in the first place. *Many of the weaknesses and imbalances that led to the crisis escaped this regulatory response.*"

Isn't that the way Washington usually works? What this reform means to you is the all-important point. Let's move on to demonstrate the glaring flaws of the legislation, given what the politicians and bankers really don't want you to know.

The first element that had the appearance of efficacy was the "Volcker Rule". This was an initiative suggested by former Fed Chair Paul Volcker that somewhat mimicked the Glass-Stegall Act in that it would not allow banks to speculate for their own account with many risky investments and side bets. As we know, many investment banks had outrageously successful profits from their proprietary trading (prop desks) departments, and used these profits to help stabilize their balance sheets that became decimated as the crisis hit in 2008. Fortunately, the trading by the prop desks that could have led to taxpayer loss guarantees would now supposedly be banned.

In fact, the prop desk speculations seemed to disappear so quickly after the passage of the law, and before the Volcker Rule was to take effect fully 2 years later, that one has to be curious. Did the banks take their business elsewhere, or find other ways to disguise the activity off balance sheet? Maybe, but only time will tell. An April 9, 2012 article by Bloomberg regarding the trading activities of JP Morgan's London office states:

"While the firm describes the unit's main task as hedging risks and investing excess cash, four hedge fund managers and dealers say the trades are big enough to move indexes and resemble proprietary bets..."

It would appear from reading this article that the side bets and price management efforts were simply moved to a different location where the rules were more benign. In fact, a month later, it was revealed that JP Morgan suffered a huge loss on one of their "hedge" investments (hedging was allowed under Dodd-Frank), which brought CEO Jamie Dimon under the microscope. He called it a hedge, but the purpose of a hedge is to offset the potential loss on another bet. If your hedge goes down, the other bet should go up. Oops, maybe it wasn't a hedge after all!

At any rate, the politicians haggled over the terms of the Volcker Rule so much that to get it passed, they had to make exceptions. And the exceptions were exceptional! Banks could still invest in hedge funds, private equity funds, along with U.S. Treasuries, Freddie Mac and Fannie Mae bonds, and municipal bonds. This is a loophole so big that the Volcker rule is too weak and almost worthless according to reform advocates. What do the politicians think hedge funds and private equity funds do?

They speculate and make side bets with borrowed money! But this was just a sideshow compared to the main flaws in the Dodd-Frank bill. Here are some of the apparent and glaring flaws:

Problem number one: Just because new side bets will now be out of the closet and more transparent with pricing mechanisms and a clearinghouse, that doesn't mean that the $ 1.2 Quadrillion in derivatives on the books already will disappear, come into the clearinghouse, or somehow be retroactively fixed so they won't blow up. Many simply can't be regulated and won't go away, as they do not conform to the new guidelines; and existing contracts cannot be changed. Get ready for the meltdown in the $400+ trillion market in interest rate swaps when the bankers lose control and the world-wide free markets in government bonds exert their forces on interest rates. It will dwarf the problem caused by the meltdown in credit default swaps in 2008. When this happens, as it most likely will, it will be the end of your fiat U.S. dollar regime. Then it will likely result in what happened to the Continental dollar in the Revolutionary War or in the Southern States toward the end of the Civil War with the disintegration of the Grayback. Vast new sums of money will have to be created, and U.S. citizens will run from the prospect of getting paid in dollars, just as foreigners are now doing.

Problem number two: Fiat money is still alive, and still not well. Have you heard any discussion of the stoppage of the printing press? Have you heard any discussion of backing our currency with gold and/or silver as the constitution demands? Maybe you heard it out of Ron Paul along the Republican Presidential primary campaign trail, but the media and Washington DC types treated him like a red-haired stepchild. Paul's message was both ignored and ridiculed as impossible. Have you actually seen real spending being slashed to the bone in Washington? It won't happen. The power elite in DC will have nothing of this discussion or implementation until the end game actually forces them to do so. Consider symptoms of the end game as the repudiation of the U.S. dollar all over the world, having those dollars come back into the U.S., resulting in the repudiation and destruction of debt (the banker's worst nightmare) and hyperinflation (the consumer's worst nightmare) at home at the same time. The stage is perfectly set for these events to unfold.

Problem number three: The Federal Reserve System remains intact, with not even a hint of reform in the Dodd-Frank bill. Not only that, the bill adds to its responsibilities in more ways than ever. We know the Fed is the tender of the fiat currency, the regulator of the banking system, and the organization that had blinders on all the way through the crisis. It is the organization that has been doing financial experiments faster than a mad scientist in his basement lab. To say that the many moves have been trial and error would be spot on. The very source and facilitator of the problem gets a free pass, and indeed does so with more power than ever before. In fact, it even gets to further coddle several "too big to fail" banks. This means that no matter how poorly those banks are managed or how much money they lose by ill-fated scheming, they will never be forced into bankruptcy. They will get fully bailed out with…your money. They will get even too bigger to fail. This is a moral hazard at its finest.

Problem number four: The international movement of electronic money is alive and well. Not that it should be regulated or cut off in any way: it shouldn't! If controls were placed on the movement of money out of the U.S., the end would be nigh. But either way, because we are barely hanging on with our reserve currency status, the international nature of money movement guarantees that we U.S. citizens will eventually be financially doomed when the dollars have nowhere else to go internationally except back to the U.S. Sure, those dollars can be spent in Africa to bid up natural resources for instance, but wherever they are dumped will cause a price spike in the related tangible assets, resulting in a spike in prices at home. By 2011, this was quite evident.

Problem number five: The Dodd-Frank bill contains, and will prove to add, far more consumer protections. Even though this may sound good, it is a disaster from the standpoint that the populace may well think that they are being protected. This is a problem. The best protection is self-education, and subsequently acting accordingly. If we as citizens once again expect the bureaucrats to watch out for us, then we will most certainly get what we deserve. The intended and unintended consequences of any such new rules and regulations devised by uneducated bureaucrats would likely be worse than no regulation at all. Let the consumer/investor beware!

Problem number six: Many banks will get much bigger! Whether it was intended or not, the Dodd-Frank legislation puts tremendous pressure on the small banks. They are having a much tougher time remaining competitive due to the additional costs of complying with the new regulations. Not only does the Fed's low interest rate policy put pressure on their margins, but the new mandate to keep a certain percentage of loans on their books instead of selling them adds to that pressure. Additionally, the capital requirements have become stricter. So what is a small bank to do? Look for a bigger white knight and sell out while there is still some value remaining in the company? And, this is exactly what is happening, as small bank mergers and acquisitions soared by 2012. Why should consumers care? Because the competition will be more concentrated, and the bank offerings to the public will become that much less competitive!

Problem number seven: This is probably the worst of outrages; the Dodd-Frank bill did absolutely NOTHING to address the mortgage market. Let's be clear. The mortgage market was that which became leveraged, bet on, and bloated beyond repair, and will cause problems for every homeowner for years to come. The problems will include low home prices, underwater mortgages, and millions of bank owned homes that have been foreclosed upon but not on the market for sale. Banks simply haven't been able to afford taking the huge losses if they sold them short of the mortgage amount. They'll have to let them go little by little, since not everyone can leave by the fire sale exit at the same time. So they hide them and pretend that all is well. Additionally, the two Government Sponsored Enterprises called Freddie Mac and Fannie Mae were not even mentioned in the bill, except that they could still be an investment by the banks under the Volcker Rule. These two monsters had to be taken over by the U.S. government, and are bleeding hundreds of billions in losses that we citizens have paid for. Not only that, they are still plying their craft and underwrite fully 95% of the new mortgages as of year-end 2011. How can a financial reform *not* address the very crux of the problem? Ask Barney and Chris.

Just keep kicking the can

Hopefully, readers can now visualize a clear image of how the massive systemic financial dysfunction of our U.S. fiat dollar is being handled. It's very simply about maintaining the status quo of a flawed system until the bitter end. What is of huge concern is that most of the politicians don't think there will be a bitter end. They just want to get through the next election cycle with the help of the lobbyists on K Street and their campaign bundlers. What about the bankers? Those at the top of the food chain just have to hope and pray (prey) that the system stays glued together until they are safely in retirement or move on to another career with all their ill-gotten cash, bonuses, golden parachutes, and oversized compensation goodies. But we know one thing for sure. The bankers will keep the plates spinning atop the poles as long as possible, because that's all they can do in the system they've devised. The status of *the U.S. financial system is at an extreme juncture.* But the politicians won't give up trying to fix the economy; again, looking at the issue from a completely perverse and incorrect perspective. Let's explore the notion that they can do something to help the economy heal itself via government spending initiatives.

CHAPTER 7
ARE YOU STIMULATED?

Let's throw more money at a stagnated economy

Austrian economic theory would have it that borrowing money to support an economy is a waste of money and exactly the wrong prescription to give to an ailing patient. Now it is time to test this theory with some facts.

President Obama signed the biggest spending bill in the history of the United States in his first month in office on February 17, 2009. This behemoth was called the American Recovery and Reinvestment Act of 2009, which came to be known as the "stimulus" package. This package weighed in at 1100 pages and a planned $787 billion dollars of stimulus. When the dust finally settled, it was determined that the bill actually created expenditures north of $825 billion, not $787 billion as expected, but that shouldn't surprise us. It was billed as about 37% in tax cuts, with an 18% subsidy to the States, and the balance of 45% was designated for Federal programs; all supposedly designed to try to get the country back on track economically. Every penny of this money had to be borrowed, the expense for which was to stretch over three years. Only a small portion of the money was intended to be spent in 2009, with the biggest chunk to be spent in 2010, just in time for the mid-term elections.

Forget patriotism; think politics as usual

When the Gross Domestic Product (GDP) dropped in the third quarter of 2008, the politicians told you that the stimulus bill was needed to kick start the economy. The truth was that the GDP was destined to drop with or without the bill. However, it wouldn't look as bad in the public's eyes if that extra spending got tacked on to the total. But when the money was spent and there was virtually no growth in the GDP as was the case, how did the politicians think it is alright to fund the plan by borrowing? The only growth came in the form of a higher national debt. This was not a smart plan. All that was done under the leadership of House Speaker Nancy Pelosi was to pork-up the first draft at the bill with earmarks and projects that many members of Congress had wanted for years. Now they would have their chance. Both President Obama and the Senate Democrats were appalled by this first version of the bill, and worked night and day to make the changes acceptable enough that 3 Republican Senators agreed to vote in favor of the measure. Let's look at the efficacy of the political solution to our sagging economy.

The bill was so complex and was rushed through Congress so quickly that it is doubtful that any member of Congress even got the chance to study the behemoth before the vote. The buzz on Capitol Hill was that something had to be done, and done quickly. This is a typical line that politicians use to demonstrate their supposed compassion, when in fact they are just fishing for votes. What would have been wrong in opening up a healthy dialogue, taking some time to understand the consequences of some of the spending, and get it right? Well that wouldn't have been politically expedient, now would it? Maybe a little more study could have prevented the measure from getting even bigger after the dust settled and people figured out how much all of the spending would actually cost.

Many politicians, including the President, admitted that some of the stimulus bill may not work as intended. Well, that's no surprise. Couldn't the law have made up for lost time by mandating that more of the money be spent in 2009? Couldn't time have been taken to get more Republican votes? Remember, not one House Republican voted for the bill, and only 3 did so in the Senate. Is this divisiveness in the best interest of the country? Shouldn't everyone get a voice and a chance for debate? Apparently not, as the Democrats so succinctly put it, that "we won". How does that demonstrate patriotism? How does it really help the greatest number of people? It doesn't. Let's dig in to see what we actually got for our money.

The jobs, the jobs!

Mr. Obama assured the American public that the stimulus bill was desperately needed to keep the unemployment rate below 8%, and drive it down to 5.2% within 3 years. After all, the 2009 stimulus bill was supposed to create or save upwards of 3.5 to 4 million jobs. Unfortunately, that promise went by the wayside quickly, as the unemployment rate headed toward 10% by the end of 2009. It is interesting that the job creation target kept expanding as the politicians talked it up. It started at 2.5 million jobs, and escalated from there. Do you have any idea how to measure a saved job? This measurement would simply have to be subjective at best. Maybe if one owns a business and needs a government contract or some stimulus, all he'd have to do is tell somebody in Washington that he'd be laying off 100 people if he doesn't get some financial help. Bingo! He got some help, and low and behold, the government saved 100 jobs!

Caterpillar announced 2500 job cuts only a couple of months after Mr. Obama announced his support for his stimulus bill at the Caterpillar plant in Indiana. The Caterpillar CEO had indicated at that time that he'd be able to save jobs as a result of the government spending intervention via the stimulus package. Oops, maybe it didn't work for Caterpillar after all. But at least its new factory in China would help to generate more employment and more profits for the company!

Did you know that if a person doesn't make enough income to pay taxes, but the government sends him a stimulus rebate check, it is considered a tax cut? Unfortunately, it clearly has the appearance of a socialist transfer payment. These checks were part of the stimulus bill, but what did this do to stimulate the economy? If the person is needy enough, he won't be able to buy an HDTV, but he may be able to pay his electric or gas bill with the rebate. Is this stimulating? Recall that George W. Bush tried the same thing to the tune of $168 billion in early 2008. What did that do for us? Nothing, as the economy still sank. When we are running deficits anyway, why send more borrowed money back to citizens? This is ridiculous, and it has neither any long term wealth building capability, nor creates jobs.

Get the shovel ready!

Part of the bill set aside $45 billion for infrastructure improvements. Clearly this country has plenty of road and bridge repairs that are absolutely necessary. But fixing them does not create wealth or savings. Yes, they'll be in better condition when the projects are completed, but then the jobs go away. There could be some payback if tolls are charged for the new infrastructure, but this obvious capitalist solution would be ignored for the most part. OK, so the projects get built, the money has been spent, and the jobs no longer exist. The net effect on wealth creation is zero. But we have safer roads and bridges, all done with borrowed money that we as a nation have no way to pay back. Nor were there financial provisions to maintain the improved infrastructure once repairs and rebuilds were completed.

To illustrate, the very first construction project to come out of the stimulus bill was for a road project in Maryland. It was a $1.8 million project using upwards of 14 different contractors. This sounds good so far, right? The project in total was to last 142 days with the most time spent by any one of the contractors being 2 months. Then it was over. The

Washington Post interviewed many of the construction workers to see how the work and money would impact them and their families. Most were simply going to pay off old debts rather than to initiate new spending. A common response was quoted:

"The only celebration I had was paying the electric bill."

No permanent job was created. There was no permanent stimulus or wealth creation that could lead to more government revenues.

Another problem with government sponsored construction projects is that they cost just too darn much. This is partly because they take so long, but mostly because the bureaucrats think the more money that's thrown at a project, the better of everyone will be. Here's another of those stories that will frost you over and illustrate the point. On Kauai, Hawaii, massive flooding caused roads and bridges leading to Polihale State Park to be wiped out. Federal stimulus to the rescue! The Feds estimated that it would take $4 million and 2 years to get the necessary repairs done. The locals there felt that they couldn't sustain the business losses in waiting that long, so they decided to do it themselves! It took eight days, and no cost to the Federal Government to get the roads and bridges repaired so the park could re-open! The locals pitched in with in kind donations in materials, equipment, and labor. Now *that* is the American way!

Workers unite!

Speaking of construction jobs, the unions were heavily supportive of Mr. Obama during his 2008 Presidential campaign. Let's not kid ourselves here with fancy Presidential rhetoric. The stimulus bill was payback for these folks. Let's examine a few salient facts. On February 6, 2009, Obama signed an Executive Order mandating that union labor be used for federal construction projects, and this includes those stimulus bill projects. According to Jerry Gorski, the National Chairman of the Associated Builders and Contractors group, 84% of the nation's construction workers are not in a union! This begs the question of how the stimulus bill is geared toward the construction industry as a whole. How does this benefit the wide majority of the construction trade, and thus, spreading out the jobs in as wide a swath as possible? Was it simply designed to pay back the unions for their support? You decide.

But that's not all. The worst part is that undocumented, illegal aliens took a lot of those construction jobs, particularly in California and other southwestern states. It would have been very simple for any potential employer to check the immigration status of any hire they may have considered. A minute spent on the government sponsored E-Verify website would tell an employer whether or not his potential hire is legal. But there was no requirement in the stimulus bill to use this system. In fact, the Democratic Senate voted to do away with the system before the close of the 2009 fiscal year as part of the Omnibus spending bill mentioned below. The action took effect just before the big money part of the stimulus kicked in! This occurred after there were 6.6 million green card checks in 2008, with over 3 million verification checks in the first 3 months of 2009. According to the Center for Immigration Studies, upwards of 15% (or 300,000) illegal aliens could be hired for these supposedly American jobs due to the lack of immigration status checks. And what do the illegal aliens do with the money? Send it back home to the family in another country! How stimulating is that?

Michael Steele, the Republican National Chairman stated:

"President Obama's Executive Order will drive up the cost of government at a time when we should be doing everything possible to save taxpayer dollars. Federal contracts should go to the businesses that offer the taxpayers the best value."

Alms for the poor

As part of the stimulus bill, there was also an increased amount to be sent to the states for the purpose of enhancing unemployment benefits. Giving an unemployed person a little more time on his benefits so he can cover the family bills is valid in a lousy economy. But this isn't a stimulus. From a politician's viewpoint, it helps the family, and makes our GDP look like it doesn't drop quite as much had the family not gotten the money. But for that one little family microcosm of the economy, *the GDP still drops*, very simply because the unemployment benefit is less than the family earnings (and subsequent spending) prior to the unemployment! How does this help to build national savings or wealth? It doesn't. The government bean counters say that we get a "multiplier effect" on the extra stimulus spending, making the GDP go higher. This means is that the money turns over to other people or businesses, and then they can spend it too. But what they never mention was that the faster the money turns over, the more prices escalate! They also don't tell you that as people start to pay off debts and save, the less money is available to spend, and the economy remains listless until the mindset of the consumer changes.

Unfortunately for the states, there is a further problem with these enhanced unemployment benefits, as Governor Bobby Jindal of Louisiana pointed out. Any additional money that came from the stimulus bill which was used for unemployment benefits had to be continued after the stimulus ended. In other words, the Federal government would give all states an additional shot in the unemployment benefit arm, but they were not allowed to lower those benefits when the stimulus money ran out. This shifted the burden onto the state taxpayers after 3 years! So Bobby Jindal turned the money down, and was followed by other governors too. A political move, you say? Probably, but the greater point is that by using the temporary stimulus today, the obligation would become a permanent future problem of the State taxpayer.

Poor and less fortunate citizens should be helped. If they can truly demonstrate the need and a desire to try to dig out of their problems with some help, that is the right thing to do. But it is certainly not stimulating for an economy. The only permanent and valuable type of stimulus *would pay for itself in the form of permanent jobs and permanent tax revenues to government at all levels.* It's called income creation, capital formation, or wealth creation, if you will. This is the way it has to work in our capitalist society. But given that almost half of all Americans are now receiving some form of financial assistance from the government, it has the appearance of socialism!

Former British Prime Minister Margaret Thatcher once said that the big problem with socialism is that you eventually run out of other people's money. It has gotten to the point that this has become true for the United States. The taxpayer is tapped out, the business owners are more stressed than ever under deteriorating business conditions along with more regulations and higher taxes, retirees have had their interest income reduced to nothing, and foreigners are reluctant to fund more of our deficits. But the government continues to grow, and this is a major problem given that all this growth is funded by debt. Has the U.S. evolved from a Republic, to a Democracy, to Socialism? You decide.

Porky pig

There was a bundle of pork barrel spending, oops, earmarks, in the stimulus package, even though there was supposed to be no such thing. The spending was actually to be for "shovel ready" projects, green energy development, and the beginnings of health care reform, along with other porky miscellany. Let's see, first we have the idea of a high speed rail service from Disneyland to Las Vegas. Hey, it's only going to cost a few billion. But can we find solace in the fact that the government has been in the rail business for years, and knows what's what in the business? Certainly you have heard of Amtrak, right? Yes, that's the same Amtrak that has drained the taxpayer for decades, without a single profitable year. A review of the audited financial statements reveals current annual operating deficits in the billion dollar range. Is anyone for government ownership of businesses? OK, so there was $1.3 billion in the bill for more subsidies to Amtrak.

But here's the snag. The U.S. does not have the technology needed to build the high speed rail line. So the technology had to be bought from the Chinese. How stimulating is that? While granting money for a multi-billion dollar project to private and foreign enterprises for the construction of the Vegas rail and others, the bill only set aside a comparatively paltry $750 million for other new U.S. public rail transport systems. You got that right; less than 9% of money for new rail projects went for the benefit of "the people", whereas 91% went into the pockets of political cronies and foreign entrepreneurs for their private benefit. Is this stimulus for the U.S. masses?

Later, Mr. Obama went to the west coast of Florida to present a check for rail improvements there. But the maximum speed of 79 mph on this track certainly isn't exactly what would be considered high speed! But passing the bill for the pork, now that was high speed.

Health care subsidies

The stimulus bill also called for subsidizing up to 65% of 9 months-worth of COBRA health insurance coverage for those who lost their jobs to the tune of almost $25 billion. COBRA maintains the same employer health insurance benefits after an employee job loss, except without the group rate enjoyed by the rest of the employees. This type of coverage is double or more the cost of traditional group plans offered by employers. It is also at least triple the cost of coverage offered by many insurance companies for those who are in between jobs. This is proven by the fact that in 2007, only 10% of those eligible for COBRA actually bought it. These people likely included those with preexisting conditions that may not have been covered otherwise under a new plan if they are not eligible under the HIPPA law, allowing for the movement of people with preexisting conditions to their new plan without a waiting period. The point of this proposed stimulus is that it isn't stimulating. It's just another transfer payment, this time helping to further enrich the insurance companies.

There was also about $20 billion in subsidies for health research and information technology. Part of it is a billion dollars to research the effectiveness of certain healthcare treatments, along with a plan to get doctors to put all medical records on-line into an 'Animal Farm' or '1984' type data base. This has had a good many of citizens crying foul over privacy and socialization concerns. Well, at last something in the monster bill stimulated a response! Here the bill worked as a stimulus! Finally, in the health care related subsidies section of the measure, there was $500 million set aside for health services on Indian reservations. They need and deserve it; but it's doubtful that it is stimulating.

Enhanced education?

Let's talk education now. Improving our educational system seems like a great goal. Within the stimulus package $90 billion was set aside for educational initiatives. There is nothing wrong with the Federal government facilitating a better system for educating the populace from day one. But the oversight needs to reside locally, and with the parents. This is one of the best investments this country could make, if handled properly, and there's the rub. The problem is one of accountability, waste and the fostering of the status quo. As is usual, the government throws money at a problem and assumes that will do the job. But it doesn't.

For instance, $44 billion of the educational subsidies in the stimulus package was for local school districts to prevent layoffs and cutbacks. It saved jobs!! How does this stimulate the economy? It may stop the bleeding for a while, but it is still treading water. It provided no capital formation! It did not guarantee those teaching jobs for the long term. It encouraged no financial, structural change. And how did it provide for *effective* education? Only politicians can think that borrowing money to maintain the existing circumstance is stimulation! The funding was supposed to help to expand school days, reward good teachers, get rid of bad ones, and measure U.S. student performance levels against the worldwide competition. In addition, it was to be used to rehab old school buildings, help prevent layoffs, and educate children from low income families.

Secretary of Education Arne Duncan said he wanted to "encourage" states to adopt tighter standards of measurement for student achievement, as well as make the teacher standards for achieving tenure more rigorous. These are all worthy goals, *but how do we measure success?* And how can we get the unions to yield in protecting marginal performance by some teachers? And where are the standards of performance for a state or local system which receives the added financial help? And how do we hold these entities accountable? And how can we change the curriculum to make it more relevant? And how can we get the parents to help, as we know education starts at home? There are too many holes in the feeding tube, and there was a huge potential for waste, with little to show for it. Education is job one in order to maintain a free and capitalist United States. However, throwing money at it with no debate, forethought, or accountability is not the way to affect real change.

One provision of the educational subsidies that could prove to be worthwhile is an increase in the Pell Grant amounts. Pell Grants provide free money for low income students who want to go to college. Even though the Pell Grant funding was only boosted from $4731 to $5350 per year (costing an additional $15 billion), at least it had the potential of paying itself back in the form of a better educated and more productive college graduate. All the grant recipient had to do was to graduate, find a job, and pay taxes. This could be problematical as we'll see later.

Let's energize

Should the government sponsor energy projects? Part of the stimulus bill called for the expenditure of $50 billion over the next few years to focus on efficient and renewable energy programs. This was simply a down payment on the larger Obama $150 billion, 10 year master plan. About $14 billion of the money was to be dedicated to loans for renewable energy projects. This seemed like a good idea if the American taxpayers were protected. Unfortunately, it was later discovered that the loans were used as an apparent device to make political paybacks. Solyndra, which just happened to be an investment banking client of Goldman Sachs, was the poster child for political payback.

In short, a big fundraiser "bundler" for Mr. Obama was on Solyndra's Board and was a major investor in the company through one of his business entities. The company was put on the fast track for approval by the money handlers in DC, in this case the Department of Energy. Forget the regular bureaucracy and credit due diligence, there was no time for that before the big speech the President was to give at the plant. In fact, the Energy Department had no wherewithal to do any credit due diligence in the first place. The credit work on the loan applications in the stimulus program was farmed out to the Department of Agriculture, since it already had these systems in place. But there was no time to send Solyndra through all that bother. Didn't we just get in to a major bind over not screening credit customers too well? Did we not learn anything, or did politics win over good sense? Sadly, we all know the answer. So the company burned through $535 million in a year or so then needed to have its loan restructured. This means they couldn't make payments as they had originally agreed, so the deal had to be adjusted after the fact. Part of this add on deal was to put the taxpayers in 2nd place for re-payment on their $535 million, behind the original investors like the bundler. Was that what the taxpayers would want? Well, not exactly!

Company production ramped up and their costs of production per piece were too high. The units couldn't be sold at a profit due to less than current technology. Crank up production to get the cost per piece down! Run out of money! Sell grossly bloated inventory back to one of the bundler's companies at a substantial discount. File bankruptcy! Taxpayers lose on the heels of the bundler and his merry gang. Solyndra has been cited because it was so highly publicized due to its preferential treatment prior to its failure. But other bundlers got preferential treatment too, as Peter Schweizer points out in his book 'Throw Them All Out'. Is political payback stimulating?

At the back end of the renewable energy subsidy program, over two and a half years from the time it came on stream, and just the day before it was to shut off all loan activities, the Department of Energy issued well over $4 billion in loans - on the last day! Those guys getting last minute loans must not have rated too highly along the way. But some of the loans at least have the possibility of creating wealth by providing long term savings through the investment in new energy technology. It is better to have government initiatives directed to private, for-profit companies to create the desperately needed long term energy solutions.

The only way the government should provide any money for the financial part of new energy technology is if it gets solid terms, security, and guarantees of repayment for any loan. Then the $14 billion set aside for this may actually bear fruit. Let private enterprise innovate! We'll chalk up Solyndra to experience (not that the politicians will learn anything). Government money (or yes, even borrowed money) could be directed to certain initiatives that satisfy the long term plan being implemented. Here is wealth creation at its best! Grants for energy technology development are scary, simply because the results aren't guaranteed, and the money cannot be effectively tracked. But loans, if done correctly, could yield some good payoffs for all.

Miscellany

Unfortunately, most of the balance of the $50 billion in the stimulus bill for energy went for pork. What about $5 billion for home weatherization projects on modest-income households? This could help low income people save on their heating bills, which is great for them. Saving energy is a good thing, but that one is hard to measure. Newer technology would seem to offer a better long term solution to the savings question rather than plugging holes. Sure, it is a worthy cause, but how does saving the homeowner on some heat bills help with wealth and savings creation? The money saved on the heat bill will have to be spent on increased prices on everything else. The poor will remain poor. And the energy provider will see his revenues drop. So where's the stimulus?

Then we had $6.4 billion to clean up nuclear production sites, and $4.5 billion to make Federal buildings more energy efficient. Or what do you think about $3.4 billion for carbon capture experiments? Add in $15 billion for the beginnings of the installation of an electrical smart grid. And the list goes on. The reader should get the picture. Do any of you believe that these expenses would add to the GDP of our nation on an ongoing basis? Will they help to pay for themselves, to create wealth? You decide.

Under the category we can call "other", we find the following stimuli: $8.8 billion to states to help defray budget reductions, $1.1 billion for added airport security, $650 million for coupons for digital TV conversions for consumers, and $24 million to improve security at the Department of Agriculture. Sure, help the states maintain profligate spending, add more idiots to the rolls of the Transportation Safety Administration (TSA), make sure low income folks can get digital TV, and watch out for those terrorist farmers! This was stimulus at its finest!

No stimulus for business

What did the huge stimulus package do for the formation or growth of new business or technological advancements that could lead to more tax revenues? Nothing! Consider that small business comprises literally 99.7% of all firms with employees, according to the Commerce Department, and that they pay about 45% of all private payrolls. Not only that, these firms created about 2/3 of the new jobs in the past decade. Small business represents the engine of growth in this country, but it was ignored. This is profound when you think about it.

One should also consider the fact that the United States has the highest corporate tax rates in the industrialized world. And how do these taxes get paid? Either the consumer pays them in the form of increased prices, or the production goes to lower wage overseas jobs. That's just the way it is; there's just no denying reality. Consumers must pay the costs of a wanted product or service, and tax is part of the cost. So why not help businesses provide lower prices and innovation to the consumers? Couldn't this ultimately create greater revenues to the federal government by a greater volume of sales due to better product offerings? Wouldn't this spur employment? Of course! If you provide incentives for good old American ingenuity and leave the rest to the risk taking entrepreneurs, more tax revenues would follow!

Didn't Dell, Apple, McDonald's, IBM, Google, Starbucks, Facebook, and hundreds if not thousands of other household names start as small businesses? Don't these firms and others like them provide millions of jobs? Of course they do, and they all had to start from scratch. Even President Obama declared that small business create fully 70% of new jobs in the past decade. The statement was in conjunction with his announcement of a new federal loan package for small business, *a month after* the stimulus bill passed accompanied with a groundswell of criticism from the business community and the Republicans.

The consensus that wasn't

At the time of the stimulus passage, the politicos in Washington DC wanted you to think that all economists agreed on this particular course of action, and that the government was going to spend us out of financial trouble. However, the January 28, 2009 editions of the New York Times and the Wall Street Journal featured a full page ad listing 200 economists who disagreed with the plan. They stated:

"…we the undersigned do not believe that more government spending is a way to improve our economic performance…*To improve the economy, policymakers should focus on reforms that remove impediments to work, savings, investments, and production.*"

The ads went on to say that a reduction in governmental expenses is the best course of action to foster growth. Remember, it's axiomatic that the more borrowed money government spends, the less money is available for the private sector to foster growth and subsequent higher tax revenues to the government. This is not a complicated thought, but the Keynesians don't see it that way.

However, on February 4, 2009 the Congressional Budget Office (CBO) issued a report demonstrating that the stimulus bill would increase employment and output in the short term, but would have a net effect of lowering the GDP and thus tax revenues by 2019, as compared to their baseline projections. CBO Director Douglas Elmendorf said that the long term effect would be to slightly reduce output by crowding out private investment while increasing the public debt. Clearly, not everyone was on the same page.

Not only that, deficit spending will prove to have the effect of eventually causing a rise in interest rates, making the carrying costs to the taxpayer even higher, and taking mortgage and commercial loan rates higher. We know we need sustainable and financially productive activity. But this type of deficit spending isn't going to get us anywhere except onto the hyperinflation highway. The stimulus efforts are a perfect example of yet another new battle in the fight against changing our monetary structure, it's as simple as that. That is a truth not told by the bankers and politicians.

Stimulus two

If the stimulus package weren't enough, Congress quickly followed it up with one of those Omnibus spending bills with another $410 billion of high grade pork, comprised of about 8500 earmarks. And the largess was to be shared along party lines, roughly in proportion to the Congressional representation at the time: 40% Republican, 60% Democratic. Didn't President Obama run on a platform that included the elimination of earmarks? He did, and it's a national issue, not a partisan issue. The wasteful spending coming out of Washington DC must stop, as it's sapping the economy into oblivion and at the same time weakening our financial system.

On March 3, 2009, John McCain reappeared in full glory and outrage on the floor of the Senate for the first time since his failed run for President. He didn't just pick on the Democrats, he railed on the Republicans as well. He used words like "disgraceful", "theft" and "corruption" in his tirade. He thought it was wrong to waste so much money on things like a $950,000 payment to Las Vegas for sustainability, whatever that is. And of course it's very important to give $6.6 million for termite research in New Orleans. Readers and citizens have to really wonder how the heck anyone could justify millions of dollars to study termites. Forget about the cause; just think about the how that money could possibly be spent. Well, you could hire 44 scientists at $150,000 for a year of study, but then what? Have we then solved the termite issue? Is that stimulating or what?

The Stimulus report card – F

On Friday, July 1, 2011, the Obama administration issued a report (the Seventh Quarterly Report) prepared by the White House Counsel of Economic Advisors, which consists of 3 hand-picked economists tapped as Presidential advisors. They used "mainstream estimates of economic multipliers for the effects of fiscal stimulus" to report that the stimulus had created or saved 2.4 million jobs. Readers should know that this is strictly a guess, presumably biased in favor of the President. But we'll just go with their number for purposes of evaluation. Up to that point in time, the cost for these 2.4 million jobs came in at $666 billion. Astute people with calculators can now determine that each job came at a cost of $278,000. Need we go further?

The Obama budgets

President Obama's first budget submitted to Congress called for a first year deficit of 28% of GDP, or about $1.75 trillion, the biggest deficit by 4 times that of George W. Bush, and the largest in U.S. history. Forgetting about the fact that the deficit was actually a bit lower than projected; how can anyone who is thinking clearly think that spending $3.75 trillion on revenues of about $2 trillion is good for the country? That would be like a consumer spending $75,000 on a $40,000 income! But then, add another 12% of GDP to be spent by state and local governments in 2009, and the total government expenses come to a socialist-like 40% of GDP. Hugo Chavez spends that much (actually 41%) in Venezuela!

The projected deficit assumed the start of a recovery later in 2009, which proved to be wrong. It got worse, as there was tremendous growth in the government behemoth packed into the budget. There was so much growth in spending for health care, energy, education, and services for veterans, that more bureaucrats than ever would be needed to administer the initiatives. The Heritage Foundation, a conservative think tank, estimated the job growth at 250,000 bureaucrats! How's that for employment growth? And who gets to pay for it?

In its analysis of the proposed Obama budget, the U.S. Chamber of Commerce weighed in as well. These are the people who speak for the employers of about 90% of the U.S. workforce. The Chamber thought the budget: "...appears to move in the wrong direction. More taxes, heavy-handed regulations, and command and control government will not hasten recovery." It went on to note that: "...you don't build a house by blowing up its foundation."

This referred to the adverse effects on business, the foundation of wealth creation. So it can be stated fairly that the Chamber of Commerce agrees with this very basic principle; if it's bad for business, it's bad for the long term viability of the capitalist system in the United States! When Ben Bernanke testified before the Senate Budget Committee on March 3, 2009, even he was quite reserved in his answer as to whether all the new government spending would have an impact on the overall economy, stating that it would be: "...subject to considerable uncertainty."

Maybe we could take that response as an "I don't know," although it is very telling that the answer wasn't an unequivocal yes. Nonetheless, the added deficit spending deflected attention away from the very source of the problem, the U.S. financial system.

Unfortunately, Mr. Obama's budget projections used pie-in-the-sky growth estimates for GDP and tax revenues in the future. He claimed he'd be able to cut the deficit in half by the end of his first term based on these estimates. He was wrong. But here's the salient point. The President asserted that he wanted to raise taxes on *only* those making $250,000 or more per year and those making less will be raised by "not one dime". That promise went by the wayside within the year with the passage of the Affordable Care Act. However, the public wouldn't catch on to that broken promise until 2013.

Let's understand it like it is. If Obama would have taken 100% of all income from those making more than just $75,000 per year, he would still come up with a deficit under his proposed budget, according to a Wall Street Journal analysis published on February 27, 2009. Plus, doesn't he realize that people change their methods and behavior in order to find ways to avoid taxes whenever they are hit with an increase? This *fact* has been demonstrated over and over again though the years. Further, Obama wanted to raise a tremendous amount of new revenue by charging energy producers for the right to emit greenhouse gases, called the "Cap and Trade" idea. So do you think for one minute that the consumer won't ultimately pay for these new taxes through price increases by the producers to the consumers? Energy producers would have to raise prices to stay in business! This would have been very inflationary, not stimulating, and the consumer would ultimately pay the tab. Thankfully, "Cap and Trade" fell asleep in Congress.

As the President's top aide Rahm Emmanuel said to the Wall Street Journal, he didn't want a good crisis to go to waste! Rather, it could be used to further a big government agenda. Judd Gregg a Republican member of the Senate Budget Committee, and the guy who turned down the Commerce Secretary post under Obama, called the plan:

"...a game plan for an explosive expansion of the size and intrusiveness of the national government based on a belief that bureaucrats can more effectively manage large segments of our economy and our daily lives than the private sector or the individual."

The talk of stimulus for national economic improvement was and is the wrong discussion. Whether it's a tax rebate or some kind of spending initiative, if it has to be borrowed and if it doesn't create financial advantages for the government then it should not be done. Our national debt continues to grow faster than our income. The hole continues to get deeper, yet we keep digging. The borrowing and spending without the ability to repay debt continues to rob the populace of its purchasing power in a big way. Is it a wonder that the politicians point to improving economic numbers as proof that all will be well? Let's take an honest look at the reality of the most popular metrics used to try to maintain citizens' confidence.

CHAPTER 8
THE CON IN CONFIDENCE

**How U.S. government statistics are
massaged for their desired effect**

In their speeches and assurances to the American public, the politicians and bankers continually use the phrase "restore confidence" when talking about our financial crisis. President Bush repeated the mantra over and over during the fall of 2008 as the crisis unfolded. Henry Paulsen, Tim Geithner, Ben Bernanke, Nancy Pelosi, Barney Frank, Harry Reid, and the whole gang of merry bandits in Washington DC have come to love the phrase. Then President Obama picked up on its continued use once he came into office. It is critical that we understand the absolute necessity of our economic and monetary system having that all important ingredient of confidence. *Without confidence, the dollar is worthless*. This is true because nothing else stands behind it other than the good faith and credit of the United States, whatever that means! This is particularly true *outside* of the U.S. for foreign creditors and users of the dollar in oil and other trade transactions.

How could a leader help the populace maintain confidence in not only its leadership, but also in its financial system? One pervasive and consistent ploy emanating from Washington DC is to paint a rosy economic picture in order to manage the expectations and perceptions of citizens. This is the very reason that government reporting of economic statistics has evolved over the years. Because the numbers really are not good enough to sustain spending on prior promises in addition to new initiatives, the politicians have to fudge the metrics. In this chapter we'll take a look at the common reference points used by the bankers and politicians to try to convince us that the economic picture is bright. Unfortunately, when the word "confidence" is used as an adjective, Webster's Dictionary defines it as "swindling or used to swindle". So it would be instructive to delve into this word-play.

Our leaders use a simplified approach to a very complex set of problems, and for the most part the American people have bought in to the deception. Mr. Bernanke and the politicians continue to emphasize the supposedly better unemployment reports as proof of an improving job market. They also emphasize how low the Consumer Price Index has been when they are questioned about inflation concerns. They point to the growth in the Gross Domestic Product as a positive sign. They also claim that the U.S. national debt is OK compared to other countries like Japan, Greece, and others. Painting over the substandard quality of these mileposts is meant to keep you confident and satisfied. If the pretty façade of these commonly used measurements is closely examined, the picture is ugly.

The Bureau of Labored Statistics

Do you think the numbers coming out of the Bureau of Labor Statistics (BLS) are giving us the true picture? John Williams, of the shadowstats.com website, proves the point that much of what comes out of the BLS is BS! He keeps track of inflation and unemployment like it used to be calculated circa 1980 and before. His calculations tell a very different story. Unemployment in the 1930's topped out at about 25%, and if we measure it now how it was measured then we'd see the unemployment rate at, not 8% or so, but over 22%!! Mr. Williams produces several reports a month dealing with most government produced statistics, and delves into the truth behind the numbers. You don't necessarily have to join his website to see for yourself. You can also listen to him or read his blogs on KingWorldNews.com. Further, you can track the "everyday price index" produced regularly by the American Institute for Economic Research. There you will find the price escalations of virtually all categories of consumer items, and it's quite an eye opener. You'll get more on these three websites in the resource guide in the back of the book.

Mr. Williams provides a plethora of free information and insight on his website for non-subscribers. According to Williams, virtually all statistics produced under the U.S. government label are severely fudged! Let's look at a couple of examples of how they doctor the numbers to instill confidence and make the gullible public think all is well with the *jobless recovery*.

The BLS uses fancy tools like seasonal smoothing, surveys, and the birth-death model to determine employment. These tools resulted in the government reporting fully 150,000+ new jobs per month in the first couple of months of 2009 at the time when the job market was absolutely tanking! This was a farce! What's worse, the figures are always revised later when no-one is looking. This happens almost 100% of the time. Any statistician will tell you that seasonal adjustments or other revisions should never happen each and every reporting period (i.e. monthly) like your government does! Why does it matter? It matters because if a high number is over-reported in one month then adjusted downward later when no-one is looking (i.e. the media), the next reporting period starts at a lower point, and then *that* subsequent month will look better!

Instead of relying on the high-profile number picked up by the press every month, look at the government's *broad unemployment* number, which is closer to the real number (but still fudged), and referred to by the BLS as U-6. That number weighed in at a hefty 16% in March, 2009, when the headline unemployment number reported was only 8.1%. Meanwhile, shadowstats.com figured the number at over 20%. Once the supposed recovery kicked in starting in 2010, the BLS headline unemployment number began to drop from almost 10% down to about 8% again in 2012. Meanwhile, the shadowstats.com broad unemployment number still came in at over 22%, while the BLS registered about 15%. Of course, people who have given up looking for work, or those who have taken another job for which they are over-qualified, or even working part time just to earn *some* money are never counted as being unemployed or even underemployed!

One laughable example was the bogus April, 2010 jobs report. The growth of jobs to the tune of 290,000 was highly touted on the business shows after it was used as proof of a budding recovery. How did the BLS arrive at its numbers? The BLS uses a fudge factor called the *birth/death model* for *estimating* the number of businesses that have been created or gone out of business, and from that they derive a new hire number. Readers should know that these jobs numbers are strictly estimates, and not an actual count, and that it is politically correct to err on the high side in new hiring. So the birth/death model provides cover for a big number of bad guesses. In this particular April, 2010 case, that guess was 188,000 new jobs! But even if we discount the accuracy of the optimistic guess on new business hiring, that still left 102,000 actual new jobs created. However, the Census Bureau hiring accounted for 66,000 new jobs (which were gone after the summer of 2010) and then there were another 26,000 non-census jobs that were categorized as temporary. So that accounted for the government version of a fantastic, budding recovery! A critical point was that *during the same monthly reporting period, new unemployment claims were almost 1.8 million people.* These were lost jobs during the same reporting period that we had a great hiring recovery! It was totally misleading, but who was looking?

The fudge factor in the birth/death modifications to the jobs report is almost always positive and virtually never negative. The upward fudge going back to 2004 has been anywhere from 42% to 167%. In fact, from the beginning of 2008 until the beginning of 2010 there was a loss of over 6 million jobs. That's the good news. The bad news is that it would have been much worse had the birth/death model not added 1.6 million jobs to the positive side of the figure! In fact, even the BLS has admitted to the discrepancies in their modeling. In an October 2, 2009 Bloomberg story, Chris Manning of the Bureau of Labor Statistics stated:

"In this period of steep job losses, the birth/death model didn't work as well as it usually does...To the extent that there was an overstatement in the birth/death model that is likely to still be there."

By the way, Bloomberg figured the overstatement for the first quarter of 2009 at about 675,000 non-existent jobs!

Readers should note that the National Federation of Independent Businesses has its own metrics to track small business job growth, and since the onset of the recession, its numbers have been negative. This group does not have a fudge factor for fantasy new business creation, thus the discrepancy!

Another illustration should be more than enough to make a final point. There was great celebration in early December, 2011. The reason was that the unemployment number made a huge jump down, from 9% to 8.6%. John Williams of Shadow Government Statistics put it succinctly:

"The drop in the headline unemployment rate actually signaled ongoing economic collapse, with swelling ranks of 'discouraged' workers..."

By this he was simply pointing out the removal of over 300,000 people from the ranks of those registered with government unemployment offices who had given up looking for work. Once they stopped looking, they were no longer counted as unemployed. This makes the numerator of the unemployment division calculation go down, which makes the unemployment rate go down! Isn't modern math fun? Add this factor to the seasonal Christmas hiring, and you get a miracle! And the miracle recurred in February, 2012, when the headline unemployment number dropped to 8.3%. It's too bad 1.2 million people had their unemployment benefits dry up and therefore would no longer be counted as being unemployed!

The employment situation in America is *much* worse than the politicians would lead you to believe. It's not that no jobs are being created. It's not that companies aren't bringing new products to market. It's not that there is no innovation and added productivity with technological advances. There are all of these things. Unfortunately, it's just not nearly enough to keep up with the growth in our population, and it's certainly not enough to keep up with our high growth/low wage/low tax competitors world-wide. Here's a view of the problem in the form of two graphs produced from the St. Louis Fed:

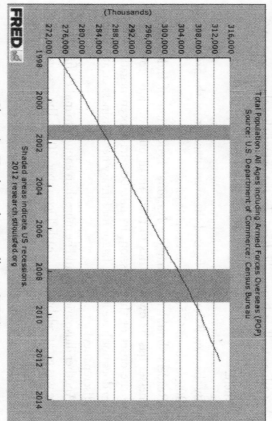

Total Population, All Ages including Armed Forces Overseas (POP)
Source: U.S. Department of Commerce: Census Bureau

Shaded areas indicate US recessions
2012 research.stlouisfed.org

Chart 4 – Total population, all ages (POP):

Chart 4 depicts the growth of the U.S. population since 1998. It has grown by roughly 15% or about 40 million people. Looking from 1998 gives us a perspective in showing that *the labor participation rate* had its high point in the recent past before it started a pronounced decline as illustrated in Chart 5 below. The labor participation rate compares the entire labor force to those with jobs. The labor force consists of people of working age under 65, who are actively employed or seeking employment. Stay at home parents, students, prisoners, and those who have given up looking for work are not counted. Also not counted are those who are employed and working in the underground economy with no reported income to the IRS. This is a much more accurate picture of the employment woes in the U.S. than the purported 8% unemployment numbers you hear from the politicians and the main stream media. As you can see the *percentage* is on a steady downward path while the population continues to *rise*. This indicates a systemic problem, not simply recessionary forces.

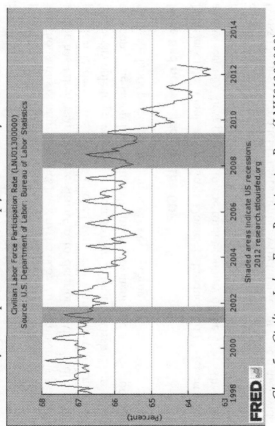

Civilian Labor Force Participation Rate (LNU01300000)
Source: U.S. Department of Labor: Bureau of Labor Statistics

Shaded areas indicate US recessions.
2012 research.stlouisfed.org

Chart 5 – Civilian Labor Force Participation Rate (LNU01300000):

In fact, in accordance with the nonsensical way that the Bureau of Labor Statistics counts unemployment, if the labor participation rate drops in the next 15 years like it has in the prior 15, the U.S. will then have a *zero* unemployment rate (as in 0%) because of all of the discouraged workers having dropped out of the labor force. Therefore, they would not be counted in determining the unemployment percentage! Ah, the power of government statistics! But the fact is that the population is growing, and our economy can't employ them due to any number of factors. Other than the fact that our wages are for the most part far above those in Asia, our tax and regulatory environment is a barrier to attracting new capital, and our superior technology allows companies to produce more, but with fewer people. This is a lethal combination for our economy, and by extension, the funding of our huge government expenses.

The shaded areas in Chart 5 are the officially recognized recessions, but in the supposed good times, employment is still going in the wrong direction. Remember our industrial base has been gutted and sent overseas. If the line above were simply flat, we'd still have more and more people out of work each year because the population continues to grow!

Of course, the baby boomers are coming into retirement and are beginning to die. Many of them will be leaving the workforce if they can afford to do so. But much of the growth in the working population is coming from young adults entering the workforce. The inability of our economy to absorb these people is a pending disaster for the United States and a tragedy for young families. Chart 5 is a graphic of that very problem which will devastate this country if we can't attract thousands and thousands of more factories back to the U.S. This problem is *systemic*, and it has taken years for the situation to deteriorate this badly. Our political leaders have simply ignored this reality and have incentivized businesspeople to go where it is most attractive for these risk takers to set up shop. The lesson here is that the unemployment rate means nothing, while the labor participation rate means everything.

More bad news – fudging the GDP

Now let's take a look at the Gross Domestic Product (GDP) reports that always seem to show growth in the total economy of the U.S. There are many ways this number can be made to look better than it actually is. A couple of those ways include both quality and inflation adjustments. The Gross Domestic Product is that number which represents the nationwide amount of money spent with all transactions in a given reporting period. Is this not a simple calculation? Well, maybe. Is it also subject to fudging? Sure.

One popular fudge factor is the use of *hedonics*. This adjustment is used by the government to account for the differences in quality or quantity of a product sold compared to a prior reporting period. For instance, if you bought a laptop computer last year for $800 and you needed another one this year and it cost you only $700 for one that was faster and with more hard drive storage than last year's model, well the government thinks the GDP should be adjusted. They would say that the computer you bought this year for $700 would have cost you $1000 last year, for example, so we have to add $300 more to this year's GDP, representing the added value of this year's model! That's hedonics! This type of adjustment is used consistently, and is very subjective.

But let's say there was no quality hedonic adjustment. Don't you think that *inflation will automatically take the GDP higher?* Of course! The government recognizes this so it adjusts the GDP downward by the amount of the increase of the Consumer Price Index. This is supposed to keep things "apples to apples" for year over year comparison. But the adjustment is based on the government's already downward fudged inflation factor. So it's axiomatic: the lower the inflation adjustment, the higher the *real* growth of the GDP. By lying about the true rate of inflation, they are able to make the GDP look like it is growing more than it actually is, even if it is actually falling in *true* inflation adjusted dollars! This builds confidence, at least in the eyes of our leaders.

Let's consider the GDP from another angle. Remember, the GDP is a gross number, not a net number. In other words, The GDP is total transaction sales, not profit. Only the politicians care about how much total money is spent. Does money spent equate to tax revenues? Of course not; but profit does, and profit is much lower than sales anywhere and everywhere. The line from Washington is that the deficit spending is necessary to pull the economy up and get it kick-started out of recession. Let's see if the American taxpayer got any bang for his/her borrowed buck with the stimulus spending and all the other normal deficit spending we've gotten accustomed to seeing. We just reviewed the folly of stimulus spending, but now we'll look at two graphics to visually see what happened. Again, the charts are produced from St Louis Fed data.

In Chart 6 below, you can see that between 2009 and 2012, GDP grew from about $13.9 trillion to $15.3 trillion based on the fuzzy math of the government. Using government numbers, the economy as measured by the GDP grew in those 3 years by $1.4 trillion. Did all the stimulus spending and added debt help U.S. to get out of the economic malaise as assured to us by our esteemed leaders in Washington? Well, not exactly.

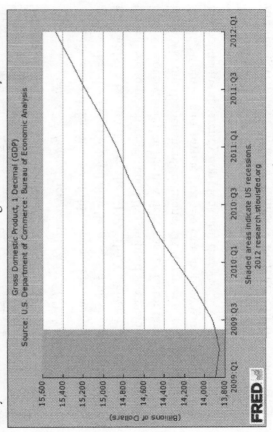

Chart 6 – Gross Domestic Product (GDP):

As you can see in Chart 7 below, the Federal debt went from about $11.1 trillion to $15.5 trillion in the same time-frame. That's an additional $4.4 trillion dollars of government spending of borrowed money to increase the GDP by a measly $1.4 trillion! Does this make sense in your world? Does this indicate a recovery? If we had recovered, why wouldn't the GDP have grown more than the $4.4 trillion that we borrowed? After all, the government gurus claim that the money would turn over and over, adding even more to the GDP. If the multiplier argument is valid, then the GDP should have been a lot higher. But it wasn't because there was never any recovery.

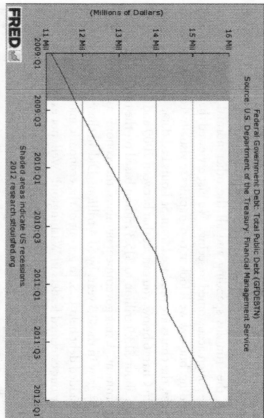

Source: U.S. Department of the Treasury. Financial Management Service
Federal Government Debt: Total Public Debt (GFDEBTN)

Shaded areas indicate US recessions
2012 research.stlouisfed.org

Chart 7 – Federal Government Debt (GFDEBTN):

Let's take a different view of this supposed recovery. We simply must assume that the added Federal debt based spending would most certainly have added a big number to the GDP. That's a given. The point is that the real economy where you and I live dropped in a major way during this jobless recovery, and that the new debt was the factor that made the GDP larger without the benefit of additional tax revenues to pay the interest! It should be obvious to anyone that you can't borrow yourself out of debt. But politicians apparently don't look at it that way!

The Consumer Price Index – the biggest farce of all

Are the government inflation numbers accurate? In this country, we use the Consumer Price Index (CPI) as inflation's measuring stick but it is fudged beyond belief, as documented by shadowstats.com. The government must keep this number low for many reasons. Confidence in the economy is one, but equally important are the CPI adjustments in benefits and salary to all government workers, military personnel, to Social Security Recipients, Medicare, Medicaid, etc. The national debt would be that much worse if the truth were told. People would get their inflation adjustments based on reality instead of lowball fantasy, adding even more to the national debt.

The aforementioned John Williams at shadowstats.com tracks price inflation with methods used prior to 1980. Unfortunately, there has been plenty of tinkering to the formula along the way. After the high rate of price inflation in the late 1970's the politicians certainly had to make sure that didn't happen again, so the formula was massaged under Ronald Reagan. Then, Bill Clinton's oversight of the economy saw yet another set of adjustments. Suffice it to say that a purported 3% official rate for 2011 would actually have come in at over 7% had the government doctor not been watching the patient. Anyone who lives above ground in the U.S. knows that inflation is running much higher than the 3% reported for 2011, and much more than the supposed 2% since the early 2000's.

Politicians like to cite the *core rate of inflation*, telling us that the other factors don't matter, and that prices change too much both up and down to worry about. What do people need and use the most in their lives? Food and gasoline! What don't they count in the core inflation number? Food and gasoline!

Now come the government bureaucrats with yet another new concept, that of the *Chain Weighted Price Index*. In an effort to blunt the adverse effects to the government budget deficit due to CPI increases, yet another device has been put on the table to save money. Without getting to heavy into detail or math here, just know that this *method would make price indexing much less expensive in paying for increases in Social Security benefits, military pay, Medicare payments, etc.* The politicians even admit this fact, which is why it would even be discussed in the first place. This is a big red flag. It's an open admission that the politicians want to take even more purchasing power away from those who rely on cost of living increases to keep up with their personal lifestyle.

Mr. Bernanke has told us how worried he was about deflation taking hold of our economy. So he wanted to target a rate of 2% inflation. Put another way, he wants to steal 2% of your purchasing power per year, instead of seeing prices drop! This concern surfaced after housing and stocks had already taken a severe beating on pricing levels. So if he really wants to target a 2% inflation rate, and 2011 came in at a downwardly fudged 3%, why not shut down the printing presses immediately and raise interest rates to slow down the price inflation? We already know the answer, don't we?

National Debt compared to the GDP: a distraction based on fantasy accounting

Many financial pundits and politicians like to compare the total national debt to the annual GDP as a basis of relative strength to other national economies. The U.S. has surpassed the 100% level, but readers have to realize that this is not a perfect score! The politicos would have you believe that the U.S. is OK so far, compared to countries like Greece (130% debt/GDP) or Japan (about 200% debt/GDP). But we're not, because we don't count all the debt. Plus the GDP is massaged as has already demonstrated. It's a bit like comparing two moving targets, and it makes no sense.

History has shown that once countries ellipse 100% of debt to GDP level, the end is near for that particular economy and financial system. It just can't support that much debt before buyers of the sovereign bonds go on strike and the printing presses have to be used to create the money to pay the bills. Does this sound familiar?

Given that the total U.S. Federal deficit was around $15 Trillion in 2011 against a GDP of about $15 trillion or so, this would indicate a debt/GDP ratio of about 100%. But that's only counting the borrowed money so far; not that which has yet to be borrowed for promises made without any money behind those promises! That adds *at least* an estimated $75 trillion to the ugliness. And this number depends on who can actually figure out what those liabilities will actually cost. Some estimates run as high as $220 trillion. But even at the $75 trillion number, all of a sudden we have a debt/GDP ratio of 600%! This 600% figure would be counting the way a for-profit business has to count under Generally Accepted Accounting Principles (GAAP), not the way a deceptive U.S. government counts! But for now, let's just work with the 100% government admitted number for a debt to GDP, and compare it to a real life situation before we go on to the real problem.

Using government thinking, it would be like telling a businessman that it's OK to have a debt of 100% of annual sales! Why? Because you don't pay your debt with sales volume, you pay it off with income. Income is far less after the expenses incurred in creating that income are deducted. Many, many businesses survive on much less than a 10% profit margin.

Heck, grocery stores and insurance companies have margins of way under 5%, in the 2-4% range! But let's use a 5% profit margin in our example. If a business owner has $1 million in sales with a 5% profit margin, then she can make $50,000 per year, right? Check. If her debt is 100% of sales, then her debt is $1,000,000! Try paying that off with $50,000 of annual income! The interest cost alone would be at about 6%, or $60,000 per year! That would be the same thing as a family situation where the total income is $50,000 per year with $1,000,000 in debts! The U.S. government has this very dilemma.

Unfunded liabilities will cost the U.S. a minimum of $75 trillion on top of the admitted national debt of $15 trillion and counting at year end 2011. So we owe roughly $90 trillion, on income (tax revenues) of about $2 trillion (2011). With no inflation factored in, and with no interest cost factored in, this debt would take about 45 years to pay off; and that assumes that we don't spend any money on anything else! We'd have no money for wars, government salaries, none of the Cabinet Departments, infrastructure improvements, Medicare, etc.; nothing else. Factor in inflation and rising interest costs as the bond market sees the light, and now we're talking well over 100 years to pay off the obligations without expending a dime on any other program or initiative! It can't and won't be done. This is why the lenders to the U.S. have gone on strike! This is why we have to crank up the fiat money printing presses to cover our bills! But the government cannot subvert the laws of economics or financial planning just because it says so. The piper has to be paid, and that point is now upon us. The system is very broken and severe financial dislocation and pain awaits us.

Budget reduction debate–another non solution

After having no budget at all coming out of the Democratic Congress in 2010 or 2011, the newly elected Tea Party folks demanded and got action from the newly elected Republican majority in the House in mid-2011. They attached the looming debt ceiling increase to the debate, and Congressman Paul Ryan led the charge by coming up with a plan to off-load the Medicare expenses to the States accompanied by help from Federal subsidies. The savings of the Ryan plan were purported to be a whopping $2.5 Trillion over a ten year period. Then Mr. Obama chimed in with new-found religion and proposed his own plan to save about the same amount, albeit through the use of foggy accounting. This was curious, particularly after having totally ignored his own Simpson-Bowles

Debt Commission suggestions of the prior December when he put forth a belated 2011 budget half way through the fiscal year, just a month or so prior to his new longer term plan. Unfortunately, this long term plan used growth assumptions for Federal revenues that were, well, embarrassingly ridiculous.

As it became obvious that nothing was going to get done a bipartisan "Gang of Six" Senators from the two parties tried to strike a different deal with no success. When no solution was crafted, Congress dealt the deficit reduction job to a newly formed "Super Committee". This was doomed for failure also, as it was comprised of an equal number of Democrats and Republicans. By the end of 2011, the politicians became worried about American workers losing their 2% discount they had been granted on Social Security withholding. Wouldn't extending the discount exacerbate the underfunding of the program, and by definition, the same for the U.S. government? Of course! So Congress headed for Christmas vacation after extending the 2% discount by an additional 2 months. Now there's some long term planning. While the American public got a two month reprieve for Christmas, the foreign bond buyers were not at all impressed. Unfortunately, all of the budget debates will do nothing to solve the long term insolvency problem of the U.S., since the targeted reduction amounts are grossly inadequate to bring our finances under control.

What if interest rates were to be forced higher by the market place as Bernanke's QE comes to an end or otherwise does not work? This is pretty simple math. Each 1% higher that interest rates go *adds $160 billion to the budget deficit for each year thereafter!* And that's before any additional borrowing due to the debt ceiling being raised again over the $16.4 trillion limit for 2012! Short term rates were over 5% before the crisis, and that means if they get back to where they were it would cost the U.S. another $800 billion per year! That's over $8 trillion over 10 years. Now compare that to the bickering in Washington over a measly $2.5 trillion in budget cuts over that 10 year period. Not only that, because many of the cuts are loaded toward later years, it gives Congress plenty of time to change gears! Actually, the problem is much more acute, as buyers of any government bonds in the future will demand much higher than traditional rates, simply due to the dire financial condition here in the U.S. Even the rating agencies got on board and actually downgraded the quality rating of U.S. government bonds. This is a profound event, and yet another sign of upcoming trouble.

The point is this: the proposed budget cuts are *far* below the massive expense cutting that has to be done, no matter whose plan is used. Please don't be as complacent as the politicians would like you to be when they claim to save those trillions of dollars. It simply is not enough to put even a dinky dent repair into the crashed and totaled auto. Another frightening fact is that the coming expense number does not even include the costs of the new "Obama-care" bill, which again used fantasy assumptions crafted into the law to demonstrate how much money will be saved once the plan was passed. Do you really think the Federal Government can oversee the *additional medical care of 30 million Americans* and save money while doing so? And if Medicare is so far under water financially right now, why can't we fix it with a miracle solution like Mr. Obama's Affordable Care Act?

Just a note on tax increases here, since that is always part of the budget debate. All the blather about tax increases may sound compelling, but it is just political posturing without an iota of a chance of being the end-all solution. Taxes could double for everybody and it still wouldn't solve our longer term insolvency. Do you think the rich people should pay more tax? Maybe so, but the solution rests with a serious reduction of our government profligacy, which will not likely happen. After all, it is now a fact that just about 50% of the U.S. population receives some sort of government help in some fashion. This is obviously unsustainable without serious adjustments to the lifestyle of 99% of Americans.

In his pleas for a debt ceiling increase, Treasury Secretary Geithner wanted everyone to know that the U.S. prints up 80 million checks per month for the benefit of American retirees and families. So the conclusion is simple to understand, but virtually impossible to achieve politically. Everyone will have to sacrifice. The sooner people catch on in their own situation, the better off they'll be!

It would be instructive to give you some alternative indicators that you can track to see if the U.S. economy, and by extension, the financial system is actually headed back from the brink of disaster. That's what the following chapter will do in pictorial form.

CHAPTER 9
PICTURES OF THE REAL WORLD

The long term trend is the key to measuring true economic progress

In this chapter you'll see a few longer term charts on trends that are important gauges to the overall health of the U.S. economy. As mentioned earlier, the United States will always have a lot going for it in terms of innovation and individual opportunity. But our population continues to grow. Our promises to an expanding number of citizens continue to grow, particularly the older ones. But our desperate need for government revenues derived from this growth continue to get siphoned off by our foreign competitors that can produce just as efficiently, but much cheaper. Should we put higher tariffs on imports? If we do, prices to consumers will rise even more, putting heavy pressure on lifestyle choices. Should we continue to encourage unbridled immigration? Maybe, but if so, we have to find a way to support population growth with jobs, opportunity, and a safety net for the less fortunate. Both societal and business regulations continue to grow as well. These regulations may be a great idea to afford rules and protections where they are needed, but it is pretty obvious that the cost of enforcement, along with the destroyed opportunity costs in employment and job creation, become detrimental offsets to the proposed benefits.

The United States has deep structural economic and financial problems which ad hoc, politically acceptable solutions do not adequately address. This is why it is so important for individuals to make their own assessment of progress, and make the adjustments necessary to their own personal situations.

If our economy were actually vibrant and on the up-swing, you would see it in the housing industry with increasing prices and sales, manufacturing employment and factory utilization, increasing commercial and industrial loan activity, strong prices for shipping, more job opportunities for college graduates, more exports rather than more imports (think China), and a reduction in the delinquency levels of consumer loans back to traditional levels. Improvements in all of these measures would indicate progress.

Of course any discussions of our financial system are certainly tied at the hip to U.S. economic activity. So even though our financial system is diseased and dying, looking at some of the patient's symptoms would give us an early clue to its better health in the future. The symptoms reflect the world where you live, work, and invest.

Don't be fooled by a monthly indicator that has just changed direction to the positive. Concentrating on *long term trends*, not one month or even one year positive changes, is the way to go to gauge progress. Indicators go up and down all the time, but by using multi-year time-frames, the big picture direction becomes much clearer. A true trend will take several years or more to establish itself, so you can use these indicators to track progress on your own. Just use Stockcharts.com, Shadowstats.com, or the St. Louis Fed website (research.stlouisfed.org) to find what you'd like to see. Also, since there are thousands of charts of government data that that can be viewed at the St. Louis Fed website, it would be very easy for you to get updates by typing the code in parentheses included with the charts below into the search box on the website.

Housing indicators:

The S&P Case-Shiller Index measures home prices in the top 20 U.S. markets. The chart below from the St. Louis Fed website gives us an idea of the strength of home prices since 2000. Pay attention to this index as the banks start to unload their millions of units of repossessed inventory into the market. What happens when the pent up desire to sell homes by retiring baby boomers and others surfaces? If buy side demand doesn't pick up, more supply coming into the market could put a damper on sale prices for years.

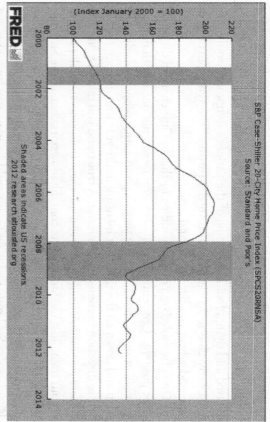

Chart 8 - Case-Shiller 20-City Home Price Index (SPCS20RNSA):

Chart 8 demonstrates that home prices topped out in 2006, just before the start of the crisis, and dropped to 12 year lows by 2012. So where is the strength in sale prices? There is no evidence of recovery yet, but you can watch for progress as we go forward.

New single family home sales are shown below. Even at the drastically reduced prices as measured by Case-Shiller, there is no long term indication of improvement. Certainly pre-owned homes affect the overall price and sales structure of the entire housing market, including new homes. Data from the St. Louis Fed since the early 1960's gives us an idea of the depth of the problem:

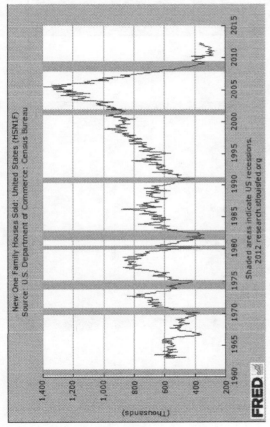

New One Family Houses Sold: United States (HSN1F)
Source: U.S. Department of Commerce: Census Bureau

Shaded areas indicate US recessions.
2012 research.stlouisfed.org

Chart 9 - New One Family Houses Sold (HSN1F):

As you can see in Chart 9 we have experienced the worst sales activity in the 50 years that the Fed has kept data. Take note of the levels of sales after the end of the recessionary periods (in gray). Our current experience is the worst by far since the data has been tracked. The new home sales figures are reflective of a major depression in home sales, regardless of the blather coming out of Washington DC. This is as ugly as it gets, and does not bode well for expanding equity values for homeowners.

Manufacturing:

Manufacturing sector employment is all-important to the needed growth in tax revenues and economic vibrancy. The long term trend has been *down* since the mid – 1980'S. Unfortunately, manufacturing has been driven out of the country for more friendly investment and employment environs. Take a look at Chart 10 below.

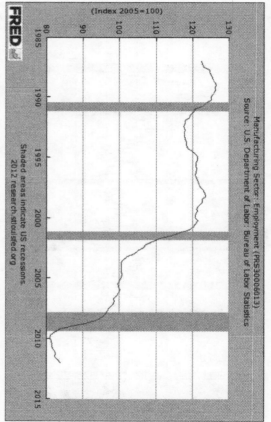

Chart 10 - Manufacturing Sector Employment (PRS30006013):

The Clinton years did not show significant growth despite U.S. population growth, but it has been disastrous ever since. Remember, most wealth is created by manufacturers. How does that jobless recovery look to you at the bottom right? It seems as though we have quite a repair job to do.

Manufacturing capacity utilization illustrated in Chart 11 measures how much a factory is actually producing or being used compared to what it is geared for. A healthy economy would be at 85% or more. It's been a steady bleed since the early 1970's, with lower high points, and lower lows.

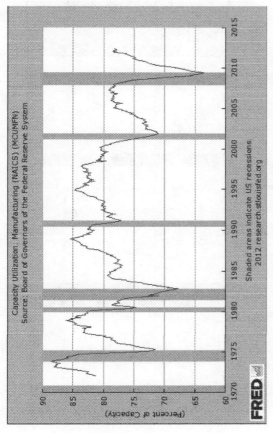

Capacity Utilization: Manufacturing (NAICS) (MCUMFN)
Source: Board of Governors of the Federal Reserve System

Shaded areas indicate US recessions.
2012 research.stlouisfed.org

Chart 11 - Capacity Utilization: Manufacturing (MCUMFN):

This chart data doesn't even reflect the fact that we've *lost* 56,000 manufacturing facilities in the U.S. since 2001, most of which went to oversees labor markets. The chart above from the St Louis Fed indicates steady, long term deterioration on what is actually left. If a factory owner isn't using all he has, what incentive is there for him to expand further? Look at updates on this chart for the first sign of progress, which would be a sustained utilization rate of over 80 percent. Unfortunately, even that won't do much for our desperate structural unemployment picture.

Non-government loan activity indicators:

Commercial and Industrial loans give us an idea of the investment going into the productive elements of the economy. This is where products are created for sale. As loans to entrepreneureal risk takers expand, so does innovation, one of the building blocks for more tax revenues to the government.

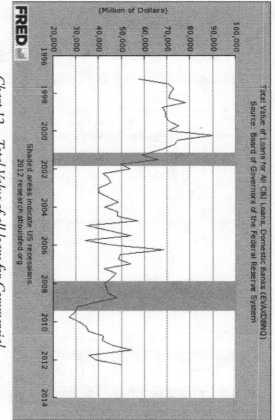

Total Value of Loans for All C&I Loans, Domestic Banks (EVAXDBNQ)
Source: Board of Governors of the Federal Reserve System

(Million of Dollars)

Shaded areas indicate US recessions.
2012 research.stlouisfed.org

Chart 12 – Total Value of all loans for Commercial and Industrial (EVAXDBNQ):

As you can see from Chart 12 above, the overall trend has been down since 2000, with lower peaks and lower lows. This marked the time that China began to dominate the world's growth picture. The peak in 2006 was much lower than it was in 2000. There was never the bubble in Commercial and Industrial loans that there was in real estate lending. Even the so called big recovery in 2011 paled in comparison to prior peaks in loan activity. Remember, this does not even include inflationary factors, so the overall loan volume has been anemic. There is no sign of a long term trend in new investment in this chart.

Delinquencies on consumer loans measure the stress on consumer finances. Looking at Chart 13 below, you can see that the maximum stress lagged the end of the recession (in gray). Even though delinquencies have dropped since their peak in 2010, they are still far higher than they should be in a healthy economy.

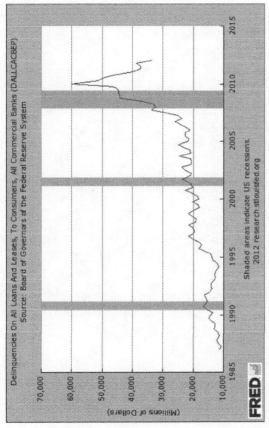

Delinquencies On All Loans And Leases, To Consumers, All Commercial Banks (DALLCACBEP)
Source: Board of Governors of the Federal Reserve System

Shaded areas indicate US recessions.
2012 research.stlouisfed.org

Chart 13 – Consumer Loan Delinquencies (DALLCACBEP):

It isn't actually illustrated in Chart 13, but the fact is that many outright defaults since 2010 have driven the delinquency numbers lower since the loans are no longer delinquent. But the chart still shows no serious recovery up to 2012. Additionally, loan activity to consumers has dropped substantially, so there will obviously be fewer late payments! The delinquency number should get down to about $10 billion or less, as in the mid 1980's and the mid 1990's when the economy was booming.

Shipping:

The Baltic Dry Index is an indication of overseas shipping prices for raw materials. This indicator is important because a big portion of our raw materials here in the U.S. (like oil for instance) are imported via ships. The higher the price index, the more the economy is booming. If worldwide demand for shipping services is high, the prices should reflect that. If it is waning prices will drop.

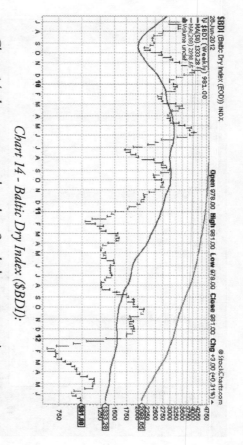

Chart 14 - Baltic Dry Index ($BDI):

Chart 14 above was produced at Stockcharts.com. As you can see, shipping prices have been on a downward slope since mid - 2009. Each individual tick indicates the closing price for that week. The solid down-sloping lines represent the 200 and 50 week moving price averages. No recovery is evident in this chart. Since the recovery was supposed to have started in 2010, one has to wonder why the demand for shipped raw materials is so weak. Is our economy really recovering? This chart would seem to indicate "no".

Jobs for college graduates:

The college grad labor participation rate measures the percentage of college graduates over 25 years of age who are actually working. Chart 15 below uses Bureau of Labor statistics as a source of information. Hopefully it is not fudged in a positive direction.

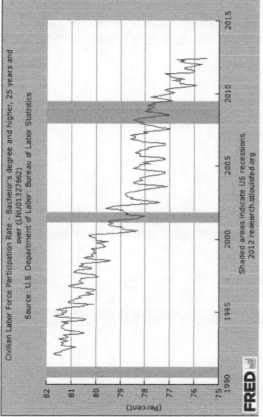

Civilian Labor Force Participation Rate - Bachelor's degree and higher, 25 years and over (LNU01327662)

Source: U.S. Department of Labor: Bureau of Labor Statistics

Shaded areas indicate US recessions.
2012 research.stlouisfed.org

Chart 15 - Labor Participation Rate: Bachelor's degree (LNU01327662):

This illustrates a steady decline from the early 1990's which indicates that there are too many grads for the jobs that are available. Is the cost of college for Junior worth it in your situation? This is tragic. So where is the opportunity for our best and brightest?

Where did all of the U.S. growth actually go?

Check out Chart 16 below to see the explosive growth of Chinese imports into the U.S. since President Clinton gave it "most favored nation" status in the late 1990's. This is indicative of an unhealthy and noncompetitive U.S. manufacturing sector, and it is apparently endorsed by American consumers.

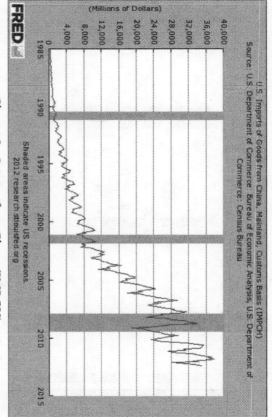

Chart 16 – Imports from China (IMPCH):

Note the recovery in imports after 2009. By the way, this increase also reflects *increasing prices* from Chinese imports, which costs U.S. consumers more. For a better economic prognosis, it would be desirable to have a major upturn in the manufacturing employment and utilization charts (above) in the U.S. in conjunction with a long term downturn in imports from China.

Measuring the disparities in the CPI and GDP

The Shadow Government Statistics website compiles data the old fashioned way. Two charts of interest are presented here. Many thanks go to John Williams for allowing the publication of these charts from his website. Chart 17 demonstrates the rate of consumer price inflation since 1980 as it would have been compiled had the government not juggled their formulas. Basically, it calculates a fixed standard of living, instead of having that standard change to reflect a degraded lifestyle.

Annual Consumer Inflation - Official vs SGS (1980-Based) Alternate

Year to Year Change. Through May 2012.   (BLS, SGS)

—— SGS Alternate CPI, 1980-Based   —— CPI-U

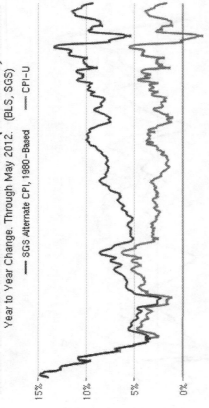

1982 1984 1986 1988 1990 1992 1994 1996 1998 2000 2002 2004 2006 2008 2010 2012
Published June 14, 2012   shadowstats.com

Chart 17 – Annual Consumer Inflation – Official vs. SGS:

One can easily see the wide discrepancies, which really kicked in during the Clinton years. Overall, it appears as though the current rate is fudged by about 7% per year. But it is instructive to note that the above chart is a simple year to year calculation. On a *compounded* basis, this picture gives us a real cause for concern, as the true price accelerations are *much higher* than depicted above. By compounding the discrepancy, the true rate of inflation would be about *100% higher* than the government has reported over the last 10 years. But you know that without even looking at the above chart.

The next shadowstats.com chart is that of the U.S. Gross Domestic Product. As quoted from the website, "The SGS-Alternate GDP reflects the inflation-adjusted, or real, GDP year-to-year change, adjusted for distortions in government inflation usage and methodological changes that have resulted in a built-in upside bias to official reporting."

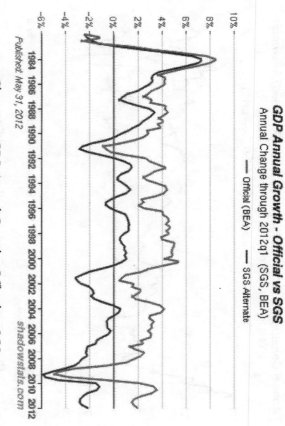

GDP Annual Growth - Official vs SGS
Annual Change through 2012q1 (SGS, BEA)

—— Official (BEA)   —— SGS Alternate

10%
8%
6%
4%
2%
0%
-2%
-4%
-6%

1984 1986 1988 1990 1992 1994 1996 1998 2000 2002 2004 2006 2008 2010 2012

Published: May 31, 2012   shadowstats.com

Chart 18 – GDP Annual Growth - Official vs. SGS:

As you can see in Chart 18, there has been a steady degradation in the data series since 1984. This means that business volume in the U.S. is dropping on an after-inflation basis. It also partially explains the budget deficit, in that less business means an insufficient tax base to support profligate government spending. For 2012, it appears as though the government figures are fudged upward by about 4%. Again, compounding makes the situation much worse than appears on the chart.

Now what?

Now it's time for the good news! There are ways to not only cope for each and every individual, but also to thrive in the coming hyperinflationary dilemma. It appears as though the bankers and politicians will not do the right things for the country, even if they had the time and inclination to do so. We are so far down the insolvency road that solutions are few, and the misery those solutions would cause would very likely destroy an unprepared middle class. Unfortunately, if the bankers and politicians continue on the existing path, these same unprepared citizens will suffer unimagined turmoil and financial destruction. The takeaway is that middle class citizens are in extreme jeopardy regardless of the path chosen from here by our leaders.

Now is the time to understand what hyperinflation would do to you, so the quest for defeating that hyperinflation on your own terms starts now. Chapter 10 uses history as a guide to self-discovery of financial survival tactics, needs, potential problems and methods for daily living in an economy experiencing monetary disruptions. Just know that financial survival is very much an individual endeavor. No one else is going to do it for you. We'll now frame the issues and problems in a deteriorating fiat currency regime. Then we'll get on with some financial defense tactics.

CHAPTER 10

TRAVELING THE ROAD TO PERDITION

Look to the past for clues to your future

Currency collapses are not new or unusual. Every debased fiat currency in history has eventually experienced failure. The default on government debt and other promises, as well as the annihilation of the lifestyle of unprepared middle and working class citizens is always the result. But what is of particular concern in the case of the U.S. dollar is that it has been used world-wide for 40 years as a trade settlement medium with nothing backing it other than confidence of the users and the lack of better alternatives. Let's look at it in another way: *prior to 1971, never before in world history has every developed country on earth conducted its foreign trade on hope and a prayer. It has always been transacted with gold or silver backing the promise of payment behind every sale.* If you think about it, you have to be surprised that the scheme of the U.S. dollar as a reserve has actually lasted for as long as it has!

Industrialized countries can't keep printing money without dramatic consequences, especially the issuer of the reserve currency. When users discover the game of debasement and how it affects them, their repudiation of the non-trusted medium happens fairly quickly. This time will be no different, as demonstrated earlier in 'Theft of the American Dream.' Unfortunately, the American public will likely be the last to catch on. Why is that? The possible reasons are varied. It might be that most uninformed Americans believe for some reason that our country and society are too special and privileged to have it happen in the United States. It could be because most of the populace doesn't have the base of knowledge to put the pieces of the currency repudiation puzzle together. It's possible that most Americans are too distracted in their work-a-day lives to delve into what is really happening. For many, it might be that they trust the politicians to do the right things so they don't have to worry. And finally, it would be because the media does not present the true problem in context to the American public, whether innocently or not. After all, who wants to listen to all the negatives? So it is the naively uninformed citizens who will suffer the most at the end of the fiat currency regime.

Inflationary forces converge

Inflation of consumer prices won't just happen overnight in the U.S. In the case of excess money printing as the chosen method of government debt default, it will likely ramp up from an extended period of rising prices that eventually really dig into the finances of the consumer, as in Weimar Germany. Food and fuel prices are the first indication of trouble, because these are must have items for everybody. There is never a lack of demand for food and fuel, even though changes to driving and eating habits will tend to mitigate the problem a bit until it gets unwieldy.

Price inflation in the U.S. can result from any or all of several factors. Unfortunately, all of these forces will converge soon to force most consumer prices to an extremely high level. The consequences to your lifestyle and its needed changes will become very obvious. But anticipating *when* consumer confidence is broken, and to what degree it will happen is a tough call. It all depends on the psychological fear factor of the people, which could result from the unintended consequences of more global attempts to fix the free market economy by the bankers and politicians. Unfortunately, high inflation will ensue, as the forces are in place and building. A brief look at the forces for extreme price inflation would help the populace to better prepare.

There are several sources of price inflation and they will eventually reinforce one another. First there is *cost-push inflation*. This means that producers of products have experienced increases in the prices of the building block materials they use to make something. Those building block assets are typically where the smart money invests while the rest of the world is sleeping. They can deploy both newly created money and saved money for their venture into commodities. Then, by hoarding the commodities, they can force prices higher. This is why China is building its base of materials for the next 100 years. It has bought and continues to buy on the cheap. In fact, it even cleaned out the United States of its scrap iron at one point, and is still combing the world to make deals to lock in its long term supply chains. This includes gold mining operations and the purchase of the London Metals Exchange!

There is also *demand driven price inflation*. This is where supply and demand forces level out the consumer playing field, and the more demand on a product, the more the tendency to have its price rise accordingly depending on the available supply. In a scenario of lost consumer confidence in the purchasing power of the currency, it causes both inflationary spirals and severe shortages of many consumer staples and other products.

The third way prices can increase in the world economy based on fiat money is through *currency exchange rate fluctuations*. This is why Mr. Obama proposed having the dollar to drop against other currencies. It would make U.S. produced goods cheaper for foreigners to buy. Unfortunately, the opposite is true. Even though a devaluing dollar may help to create more foreign demand on U.S. made goods, it also puts tremendous upward pressure on prices of goods coming into the United States. Go to Wal-Mart and see how most of its shelves are bloated with Chinese goods, and then you'll get a feel for the potential for widespread higher prices if the value of the dollar drops. This is one reason that the trade deficit matters. U.S. citizens have become too dependent on imports for a high standard of living. Consequently, we have become hostages to increasing prices due to our currency debasement at home.

With exponentially more money having been created world-wide since 2008, all tangible assets will be re-priced. As the money creation phenomenon continues, so will the price escalations. Of course supply and demand factors account for price movements, both up and down. But price is also contingent on the additional supply of money being created to buy the resource. It has to be, since it costs far more to find and produce a tangible commodity than it does to manufacture more fiat money with the click of a mouse. Therefore, for building block materials, business assets, and final consumer goods, the world-wide supply of money is a big factor in determining what the cost will be for any given tangible item. Price increases will surely and steadily move into all products and services for consumers, business, and government.

It is only when the inflation is widely regarded as pervasive that the trouble *really* starts. This is the reason that the government must fudge the cost of living numbers. It is all about confidence and if that confidence is lost, it is *the changed psychology of the populace that causes the hyperinflation of prices*. When people are genuinely squeezed out of their comfort zone and prior living style, it initiates a major mental change. This is when the unprepared folks realize that the only defense mechanism they have is to get rid of their money quickly in favor of the goods they know they'll need in the future. This is when they attempt to preserve their savings by holding that value in tangible assets instead of paper or digital money. The added demand puts upward pressure on prices for these favored assets, as does the resulting shortages in the most popular and needed items. Then, the faster the money is spent (called increasing velocity by the academics), the faster prices are forced up even more, and the more shortages develop. It becomes a self-feeding and self-fulfilling prophecy until the end. When the paper money is soundly rejected in all consumer and investment quarters, it will be time for a new money regime. Again, history shows us that the ramp-up takes some time. But, because the Western governments, led by the United States, continue to pay bills and cover losses with fresh new fiat money, this episode will not be any different. Only the timing is in question.

The Inflation / Deflation debate

For this particular section, we'll define inflation as *price* increases. As we know, adding monetary fuel to the fire of money creation is the very definition of inflation, which can and ultimately does lead to price increases. But for this section we'll go with what Professor Bernanke describes inflation to be for the gullible U.S. public, and that is an increase in consumer and asset prices.

Mr. Bernanke assures us that inflation would be good for the U.S. economy, and that deflation has to be avoided at all costs. Naturally, he uses this intellectually dishonest debate tactic while referring to prices, not to the available supply of money. Bernanke is worried because he knows that deflation destroys bank assets. Deflation hurts banks, since bank assets consist of loans and forms of side bets; and as loans go bad, banks lose their assets! They deflate! This is actually what concerns Bernanke. He wants to protect his job and high profile status by protecting his employers.

Will the Fed's efforts to inflate prices help the general population? It is doubtful. Most of the U.S. middle class has taken a big hit to their net worth (difference between what is owned and what is owed) since 2007 to the tune of about 40 percent. Real estate and stock values have gone down. Bernanke thinks lower interest rates will put an upward charge into real estate prices. He has been proven very wrong due to factors beyond his control. The Fed has had several programs meant to boost stock prices, none of which have had a permanent reversal effect on the overall trend, which is down, particularly when measured against monetary inflation. More money is out there than ever before, but the good Professor cannot control how that new money is utilized. He is trying to control both human psychology and the supply/demand dynamic to affect his desired economic outcome, and it just won't work. It won't work because it can't work. What he can do, for at least a while, is to keep the insolvent banks on life support by loaning them money for virtually nothing so that they can speculate for a profit. Plus, he can be the buyer of last resort for new U.S. government bond issues with newly created dollars.

Assets that deflate the most in price are typically those which have been pumped up by borrowed or misallocated money in the first place. What is meant by "misallocated"? It means that the money was invested at the top of the cycle for that particular idea, product, asset, stock or bond. If you are a businessman who develops a new product because it has been hot and you get in too late, that is misallocation. If you are an investor who watches the government bond market go up for 30 years before you get in, that is a misallocation of funds on your part! People who bought at much lower prices might see some, or even all, of their wealth go south when the last surge of buying comes to an end. Then, on balance selling begins to erode prices and profits. This type of price deflation can really sting investors who didn't buy right. The back end investors who are the last to the party have bought from the smarter money, just as the Fed is now doing after a 32 year bull market in U.S. government bonds! This is misallocation at its finest, and it will definitely end badly.

Going forward, your job is to be much smarter about your investments so you won't experience this type of deflation. The debate over "inflation versus deflation" is actually misunderstood. *We have both, and will continue to have both* until the losses are washed out, assets are sold at lower prices, and bad debt is written off. Only then can a fresh cycle of new cash allocation and subsequent appreciation begin.

Housing values experienced deflating prices to the tune of $8 trillion of lost value to the American public by 2012, while at the same time the cost of most consumer goods has risen dramatically. However, the falling prices in some sectors are due to demand destruction by the dire financial condition of consumers and banks, not due to the fact that there's not enough fiat currency floating around. Even the bogus CPI demonstrates this, showing only a 1 to 3 percent annual inflation rate since 2008. But check out the price increases in a huge number of building block commodities in 2010. These commodities include wheat (+74%), Oats (+68%), heating oil (+29%), gas (+25%), pork (+60%), sugar (+44%), cotton (+66%), copper (+37%), silver (+36%), and of course gold (+31%). The list goes on and on. These prices reflect increases on a year to year basis from October 2009 to October 2010. And what, you might ask, was the Consumer Price Index during this period? Try 1.1% on for size! Although the prices in building block commodities leveled off in 2011, they started to accelerate to the upside again in 2012.

The cost of raw materials to producers is escalating rapidly, which is reflective of cost push inflation. Due to increasing costs of raw materials, the producers will attempt to reduce their other expenses first, such as trimming jobs. Then they'll try to keep their pricing in line with their competitors by reducing profit margins, which they will absorb if they have no pricing power (excess demand) to raise their price. Then, when the pain gets so bad that they can't produce without losing money, they'll have to raise their prices just to try to stay in business. This is where you, the consumer enters the picture.

If you are a consumer or business with money to spend, there is nothing wrong with decreasing prices! But as far as consumer goods are concerned, price inflation is tricky. It doesn't always affect the prices of what we want to buy in the same way. Some prices escalate a little, some a lot, while others do not immediately go up. The consumer is in the dark as to what is actually happening, because it does not appear to him that there is a systemic inflationary problem. It seems isolated, and manageable. Consumers may wait to buy what they really want until prices come down, or switch to suitable alternatives. But eventually, once the vast money expansion begins to show itself in the economy, both business owners and consumers do a double take and realize that this inflation thing is getting serious.

If you are a buyer with cash, you would love lower prices, right? Why do non-financial U.S. companies sit on so much cash (over $1.75 trillion by mid 2012)? Why are wealthy countries sitting on so much cash (think China with $3 trillion+)? Why do savvy investors hoard cash in times of economic stress? To buy at lower prices, that's why! Check out Chart 19 below, produced from St. Louis Fed data:

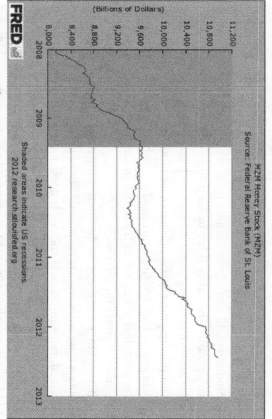

Chart 19 – *Money Stock, zero maturity (MZM)*:

What you see is an *increase* of 2.8 trillion dollars in bank deposits by their customers (you) held in the United States from 2008 to the first quarter of 2012. This represents a 35 percent increase! U.S. citizens and businesses now have a *huge* hoard of cash waiting to be spent.

Just as the chart of the monetary base presented in the preface was showing bank ammo for hyperinflation, so too is this chart in an equally dramatic way. What you see is the accumulation of low yielding money waiting to be deployed. It consists of checking, savings, and CD money of the United States populace, and it has grown by an astounding $2.8 trillion since the start of the crisis in 2008. When people and businesses catch on to the inflationary wave that approaches, this money will charge into tangible goods and other real assets, forcing prices *much* higher!

When (not if) confidence is lost in the purchasing power prospects for these dollars, the breakdown in the currency function happens. People rush to unload their money so they can stock up on real goods. Hoarding starts, not because there is some necessity that this family just has to have today, but rather because the items they buy represent real value in their eyes, and they are convinced that those items will cost more next time they go to buy. This phenomenon happened with the Continental currency toward the end of the Revolutionary War in 1781, and it happened with both the Northern Greenback and Confederate Grayback currencies during the Civil War. These are just two episodes in U.S. history, but the list goes on throughout world history. Fiat currencies get inflated away, albeit some faster than others. The crack-up boom lives!

Consumers should not be deceived, because some prices can and do drop in an inflationary environment. Prices will deflate in those assets which experience less demand, as some corporate profits stagnate in such an environment. Meanwhile, prices will escalate in tangible assets which look undervalued in the eyes of the buyer, and companies producing these items will see expanding profits. This phenomenon was called *stagflation* in the 1970's.

Unfortunately, the money system has become so dysfunctional due to the fiddling of the bankers and politicians all over the world that this time it will most certainly lead to a hyperinflationary depression here in the U.S. It will likely be a super-charged version of stagflation. The die has already been cast. There will be no exit strategy by which the good Professor Bernanke claims he can drain cash out of the U.S. economy to avoid inflation. He even deceptively fails to mention the vast quantities of money being created all over the globe, as demonstrated earlier, that can drive prices through the roof in any and every country.

Repatriation of U.S. liquid dollar assets spells big trouble

China was the first to start the grumbling in 2009. It was very concerned that the U.S. chose an inflationary path to cover its expenses at home and internationally when the budget deficit exploded. As we have already seen, it started to make deals internationally for both barter and trade in the currencies of its trading partners instead of the U.S. dollar. Throughout 2010 and 2011 it continued. Meanwhile, other prosperous and growing countries caught on and started to do the same. Finally, the great Congressional budget debate in the summer of 2011 signaled no end in sight for U.S. money printing. The trickle of international deals to settle in currencies other than the dollar became a torrent by the beginning of 2012. Many economically developed countries went into a full retreat mode to protect their purchasing power. This is an absolute death blow to the international value of the U.S. dollar, and concomitantly a death blow to U.S. family finances.

World leadership is about economic might, which is how the U.S. got the honor of having its currency used for international trade settlements. But things have changed dramatically since World War II. We have sent vast swaths of our manufacturing base overseas, and they will not return anytime soon. Modern factories have been built elsewhere; think

China, Mexico, Brazil, India, Russia, Southeast Asia, and Canada. Do you remember when Ross Perot warned us of "that giant sucking sound" of jobs leaving the U.S. in 1992, referring to the passage of the North American Free Trade Agreement (NAFTA)? Well, it happened. President Clinton's endorsement of *most favored nation (MFN)* status for China and entering the World Trade Organization was probably the last nail in the coffin. Now we have to continue to import the very most basic needs for our modern way of living, and this will prove to be big problem as international settlements in other currencies become more pronounced the world over. It is happening now as astute observers can see. There has been a steady stream of new deals reported in international media news stories while the U.S. reporting goes lacking. *The era of U.S. dollar dominance is over* and this fact could cost you dearly if you aren't prepared.

Since 1944, countries and their respective central banks needed to accumulate green cash U.S. dollars, T-bills, and T-bonds, and U.S. government agency bonds as a reserve against future dollar obligations. This gave the U.S. the buyer's market it needed so that it could incur more debt and print more money. By 2012, the amount of this reserve money in foreign sovereign funds was over $7 trillion. But now things have changed, as the dollar has two major forces working against its ability to maintain its value. *International dollar accumulators are fleeing in droves at the same time that the U.S. is manufacturing dramatically more of those dollars! And the fewer buyers we have for our new debt, the more dollars need to be printed.* As more dollars are printed, the more foreigners will lose confidence in the viability of the dollars they hold. This means that the $7 trillion of foreign held Treasury bills, notes, bond, and other government agency instruments held will be unloaded in the place where they will still buy the most: the good 'ole USA! Additionally, there is another $5 trillion of overseas dollar denominated investments which have the potential for repatriation too. So, the threat of upwards of a total of $12 trillion dollars coming back in to the U.S. will add to the woes of the American consumers and force prices much higher across the board. This means big trouble for those who are not prepared.

We know that the Dollar Index is a flawed device to determine its comparative value. Countries with vast natural resources, a burgeoning production capacity, and the ability to invest their wealth know this. They can measure relative value in their resources, in their production, and in the value of the international financial medium of last resort - gold. They don't need the U.S. Fed and the U.S. politicians determining the value of their own wealth, so they now are running away from the dollar as a measurement. If a deal is struck in dollar terms, it is *they* who will decide the value of the dollar payment, not the Fed. So if a resource, such as OPEC oil, produced in a foreign country used to trade at let's say $30 per barrel several years ago, price fluctuations after the crisis surfaced demonstrate that the price can go to $100 per barrel or more without even considering that the Dollar Index was roughly the same as it was at $30 oil. This is how the international value of the dollar can drop. Imported products get re-priced, even as demand wanes! In fact in oil terms, the dollar has depreciated by 98 percent since 1971. This is not entirely due to demand factors, but rather currency depreciation factors!

Even though imported goods will come into the U.S. at *much* higher prices as the dollar loses its reserve status, domestically produced goods may well not experience such a dramatic increase right away. Money created to cover the added national debt could go into stocks, bonds and tangible assets first before it eventually gets into the hands of the public. Just as increased borrowing from rising home equity fueled consumer spending and higher prices throughout the U.S. economy in the 2000's, so too will the next surge in stocks and tangible assets. If stocks go higher as the budgets of the populace get squeezed by higher consumer prices, consumers are likely to use that new found wealth to try to maintain their lifestyles. But that is a big "if". The new wealth in stocks will still be a depleting asset as inflation erodes it faster than it can grow. When that money hits the street, even more inflation will ensue. And all this price inflation can now be generated electronically, without having to spend actual physical green currency.

Additionally, the paper U.S. greenback (cash) has been used all over the world for consumer transactions. Anyone who has traveled outside of the U.S. knows this. Small time business owners in most countries have readily accepted those paper dollars. In fact, more than half of the U.S. currency in circulation is outside of the U.S., and it is not a small number. It is estimated that about $500 billion ($5000 million) is floating around out there, and that doesn't include counterfeits. The counterfeits are a big problem, which accentuates the potential for trouble here at home.

Unfortunately, many exchange windows at foreign banks will no longer accept U.S. $100 dollar bills. This is due to the explosion of counterfeits world-wide. If this isn't a big warning signal of the coming repudiation of U.S. currency in foreign countries, nothing is. So now we have two forces working against our paper currency as well. As holders of the dollars overseas find that they have become worth far less than previously, they'll look to off-load them where they will be worth the most. The other negative factor is the eventual refusal of those small business owners to take the U.S. dollars at all, or otherwise charge a stiff premium for their acceptance. So where will all that excess currency go? It will eventually head to where it retains the best value; back to the U.S. for U.S. based assets and produced goods. As mentioned, price increases of stuff made in the U.S. will likely lag in relative terms to the price increases of imported products. So this is yet another inflationary force in play. More currency will chase a relatively fixed asset or product base at home in the U.S. The translation is simple. There will be even more price hikes for the things we want to buy.

Finally, after an extended period of severe U.S. dollar debasement, there will be certain foreign currencies that become very strongly valued against the flagging value of the U.S. dollar. This is yet another piece of kindling for the fires of hyperinflation. By definition and the laws of economics, strong currencies will exist alongside weaker ones. That's how it works, and it's axiomatic. The strong currencies would likely be those whose national financial policies are the most solid and respected worldwide, or maybe ones that come up with some commodity backing for their paper money. Think resource rich countries with solid finances. *These super strong currencies will then be converted to U.S. dollars for purchase inside the U.S., adding even more fuel to the inflationary fire.* There is an absolutely huge pile of ammo world-wide with which to bombard the U.S. economy with higher prices. The good news is that investments in tangible assets bought in the U.S. will definitely have price escalations as well. Not only that, selected foreign stocks can also make astute U.S. investors very wealthy!

Two studies for clues to necessary action

What should consumers expect to experience as they go down the road into the perdition of hyperinflation? Some of the possible consequences for the populace can be based on the study of prior incidents. The vignettes below describing two episodes of hyperinflation are very important because many of the same consequences will be felt here in the U.S. We can all benefit by having a clear understanding of the consequences of a currency failure before it happens. The wise will be those who begin preparations now!

Readers should know that individual endeavors to prepare will not be an exact science. They can't be. One cannot know exactly to what extent, how, or even when events will transpire. One cannot know what further actions the bankers and politicians will try in order to avert disaster. We do know that so far none of the tools or policies used to fight the crisis has worked. The *end result* is knowable, and it *is assured* at this point. What the currency failure means to you and what preparations, sacrifices or lifestyle changes will be tolerable for you is a personal decision.

One of the most famous incidents of hyperinflation was Weimar Germany in 1923. Anyone interested in some detail about it may want to read 'When Money Dies' by Adam Fergusson. The book offers good insights into the phenomenon of hyperinflation and its consequences, and some of those by-product circumstances are pointed out below. Another good resource is 'Weimar Germany: Promise and Change' by Eric D. Weitz. Of course, if you use the search engine Google.com, you'll be rewarded with many resources you can use to understand hyperinflationary issues and to prepare yourself accordingly.

In the case of post World War I Germany, it tried to print itself out of its mandated war reparations bills, even though it had already inflated the currency consistently to pay the ongoing tab of the Great War (WWI). The devaluation evolved over a 9 year period, but really ramped up after the war, and went exponential in 1923. The process provides us valuable insight, as the U.S. is now following the same path.

Another book based on a more recent incident of currency destruction is a first-hand study of the Argentine debt default and resulting hyperinflation of 2001 entitled 'Surviving the Economic Collapse' by Fernando Aguirre. The author lived through the entire ordeal and has a lot to say about his tactics for both economic survival and personal safety, some of which are reviewed below. And again, there are plenty of resources found on Google. com that you can read to understand how people coped (or not) when the value of their money was dramatically reduced.

In the case of Argentina, its Peso was devalued with the stroke of a pen from 1:1 with the dollar to 1:3, and with it a de-facto government debt default. On the street, cash traded at 1:4. Put in easier terms, before the devaluation, one could give 1 peso to get 1 U.S. dollar. But after the devaluation people would have to give 3 or 4 pesos to get that same dollar. In this experience, there was a direct default rather than an indirect default such as the money printing of Weimar Germany. But the end result was the same in both instances. The unprepared middle class got wiped out due to hyper-inflating consumer prices.

What happened in Weimar Germany?

Here is a telling quote from 'When Money Dies', page 201-2:

"Inflation is the ally of political extremism, and the antithesis of order...the inflationary policy was the consequence of financial ignorance, of industrial greed and, to some extent, of political cowardice."

Does this sound familiar to you? It could have been written today, referring to the post 2008 experience in the United States. Massive social and financial disruptions await the United States. A short synopsis of some of the chaos experienced by the Germans may give us some clues to our own future:

Before 1914, the German Mark was gold backed. When the war started, Germany went off the gold standard, and prices doubled from 1914 to the end of the war in 1919.

Government had to cut expenses in many areas. Tax revenues dropped due to a burgeoning underground economy while rising prices adversely affected government services. It got to the point that the government had to make choices about where to spend its tax money. *Not all promises could possibly be kept.* This was particularly true for local and state governments. Services had to be curtailed. Police, fire, safety, maintenance, and yes, even bureaucracy was ripe for cuts. Corruption was the norm, as bribes became the way to get what you wanted. In fact, some cities and states began to issue their own money.

The *government had to pay gold for its foreign purchases of food and fuel,* depleting its supply as prices escalated.

After the June, 1922 assassination of the German Foreign Minister (who had negotiated the Treaty of Versailles) *well-to-do citizens lost confidence and began to unload their money for tangible assets* such as diamonds, antiques, art and real estate.

In January of 1923, Belgium and French troops occupied the German Ruhr manufacturing area, in order to get their reparations in finished goods and resources. *Products became money.*

As inflation progressed over the 9+ years ending in total failure in 1923, the *government cooked the books as to the true level of its inflation index;* but the populace eventually figured it out at the grocery store, and the surge for goods was on as it lost confidence in the system.

Foreign sources of *loan money to the government became virtually impossible to find.* The debasement of the currency scared off creditors who would have demanded onerous terms if they would even consider making any loans to the German government.

Higher valued *foreign capital came in* to buy up factories, businesses, land, rental real estate and all sorts of tangible assets, driving prices even higher. Meanwhile, German investment capital flowed out of the country where it could get a better, protected return in another currency.

Tradesmen would not take paper Marks for their services. They would however trade their time and generally accepted many sorts and forms of tangible assets as payment.

Not only that, *shopkeepers tried to get foreign currency* from consumers for payment for their products. This way they could maintain purchasing power when they went to replenish the goods from their suppliers, who also wanted the foreign money.

Foreigners who lived in nearby towns across the border *became frequent customers* to many restaurants. They had the desired foreign currencies to pay for the meals, and the price was very inexpensive compared to their home countries. But restaurant owners didn't even print menus due to ever increasing prices.

Hoarding, even though it was illegal, was a widespread practice, and was felt to be a common sense way to diffuse the effects of price increases. Many who could afford to do so borrowed money to buy up goods for barter, which exacerbated the inflationary forces. The rate of price inflation exceeded the volume of money printing, as the velocity picked up.

People *grew more produce at home,* while farmers withheld their crops from the market. Farmers felt that the toil to produce the crops was too great to sacrifice their harvests for lower prices today than they could get next week. They held on to them as a store of value, and when they did decide to sell, they were accused of price gauging for milk and grains.

As the crisis progressed, townspeople would go out to the country *to steal the crops of the offending "profiteers".*

There was a *huge increase in petty crime* as the problem worsened. There was a marked increase in burglaries. Metals such as copper and brass were stolen and fuel was siphoned. In fact, metals and fuel became forms of currency for barter. A portion of otherwise upstanding middle class citizens turned to crime in order to provide for their families. Mothers routinely dug through trash cans for food and anything of value. Famine was widespread. Many militia organizations were formed by the middle class to protect themselves.

Food riots began in Berlin as early as 1921, two years before the hyperinflation kicked in to overdrive. This was because of shortages due to hoarding because of rising prices, *two years before the end!*

Home *possessions were sold* for gold, many times to foreigners. Family heirlooms had to be sold too. The gold was used a store of value until it had to be spent for necessities.

Speculation in stocks was rampant throughout the population. Indeed, the stock index escalated handsomely (1300%) from 1914 to 1923. Unfortunately, it did not even come close to making up for the destruction of the buying power of the Mark, which withered by a factor of ten against stock gains. Winners in the stock market still lost 90% of their purchasing power.

Speculation in foreign currencies became fashionable. With the devaluation of the Mark, the arbitrage opporunities were widespread, and the money changers thrived. It also became fashionable and profitable to invest on foreign stock exchanges.

There were large numbers of unemployed, who participated in severe civil unrest. Jealousy and envy were pervasive. *Class warfare* was obvious and ill-tempered. Proportionally, the middle class suffered the most, as their savings was wiped out. The poor had to burn anything they could find to stay warm in the winter.

"It was natural that a people in the grip of raging inflation should look about for someone to blame. They picked upon other classes, other races, other political parties, and other nations." ('When Money Dies', page 69.)

The Nazi Party arose from the mal-content of the middle class, many of whom blamed the Jews for the economic ills. They perceived that it was the Jews who were doing much of the buying as middle class homeowners sold their possessions in order to provide for their families.

Initially, the working class was able to win wage concessions to try to keep up with inflating prices. Early on it looked as though they would survive the ravages of inflation compared to other segments of the middle class. Eventually however, the wages fell way behind and the factory workforce became destitute. Union leaders lost control. By then, some companies paid in coupons redeemable at certain shops and stores.

Professionals got crushed. Their earnings simply could not keep up with the dearth of clients and patients. They had no ability to raise fees. Civil litigation was thought of as a luxury. Book sales dropped. Architects were out of work. The arts became a luxury most could not afford. Tuition was unaffordable. No elective medical care was affordable. The more educated class got even more hostile toward the government than did the working class.

Charitable donations dried up. Some hospitals, religious, artistic, and other charitable organizations shuttered due to a lack of funding. This is understandable, as almost all prior benefactors themselves were affected by exploding prices.

Taxes on the wealthy escalated tremendously. Anyone or any activity that was seen to benefit from the inflation was taxed accordingly. Unfortunately for the government, tax cheating and avoidance was rampant, while enforcement could not keep up.

One benefit of an extremely *weak Mark* in international markets was that it *bolstered international sales* (exports) while inflation raged at home;

"The apparent health of industry was one of the factors which most effectively confused the inflation issue." ('When Money Dies', page 32)

But as well as the industrial sector was doing, it could no longer afford to sit on cash. Instead, it built up credits abroad to avoid the income tax at home and *invested any excess cash in all sorts of real and fixed assets for* future use.

Many businesses had to resort to *gliding clauses* in their contracts. This provided for price escalations depending on the timing and delivery in the fulfillment of the agreement.

Small businessmen found it difficult to compete against the big corporations. Big business was reviled by many for being tough competition and more easily able to fund acquisitions for future business growth and production.

The central bank made loans to business while the private banks would not. The *private banks* rationed check cashing for customers because they lacked the cash, as many customers had fled with their money. Those holding their un-cashed checks saw the value depreciate before they could even cash them!

Bankers *sent money out of Germany* and converted it to foreign currencies in an effort to protect its value. Even they had lost confidence in the money system, and it made the banks totally dysfunctional for citizens.

Even as early as 1921, the *German Central Bank began to buy up foreign currencies* with its reserves. Talk about a smoking gun! In fact, it sold gold and re-bought Marks on foreign exchanges a year later as a way to contain the damage to the Mark. But by 1923 that didn't work to keep the floor from caving in on the Mark. And it even gave currency speculators easy profits in that they could buy on the very temporary dips in prices of their targeted currencies.

By 1923, the government passed a law enabling it to *seize gold, silver, and foreign currencies* in exchange for "gold loan scrip", which were IOU promises to pay people back. And part of the *constitution was suspended* with regard to personal rights and privacy, even within one's own home.

The possibility of a civil war became a common theme in the press, as the government denied its credibility. *Riots and looting* became commonplace, as public open air meetings were prohibited in Berlin; but demonstrations occurred in other cities. Martial law was declared in Bavaria. Young people were the most troublesome and vocal:

Despair consumed the public as their national sense of pride disappeared. It was accompanied by a surge in fear, greed, immorality, illegality, demoralization, dishonor, disdain for the perceived survivors, back-stabbing, and family disintegration. By 1924, the hyperinflation was dead. It had done its work.

"...revolution and youth ran together" (Weimar Germany: Promise and Tragedy" page 24)

Argentine devaluation, 2001

Argentina was quite the first world country in the 1990's. It had all the trappings of a modern world economy, a high standard of living, a big middle class, a thriving agricultural sector and a growing industrial base. Soon after it became democratic in 1983, it had a bout with hyperinflation. By 1991, the value of the peso became tied to the dollar, guaranteeing convertibility. This immediately stopped the inflation, and the country thrived, as did much of the citizenry. Foreign capital was attracted by companies that the government had privatized. Imports became very cheap, particularly U.S. goods. In fact, the dollar was so cheap compared to the peso that Argentines regularly traveled to the U.S. to buy "stuff", crowding the malls and jewelry stores to spend their money in South Florida and Texas. They were seen as the rich folks of the world during these forays. The problem was that the Argentine government continued to incur more debt than it could carry, while at the same time tax revenues could not possibly keep up.

Because of a faulty peg to the U.S. dollar, Argentina evolved into non-competitiveness. More money began to leave the country than was coming in. It became much cheaper to import products than to produce them in Argentina. It had a large, unsustainable trade deficit. Does this sound familiar? Its unemployment rate topped out at 25%, while overall real estate prices dropped about 30%. The stock market dropped by 45% at one point. With the severe hit to asset values, the banking system became far too leveraged, and this made depositors nervous.

Meanwhile, the country tried to reschedule its debts. That meant they couldn't make the payments. There was plenty of uncertainty (loss of confidence) among the citizens, and a bank run started in November, 2001. People demanded, and got, their U.S. dollars, and sent most of them out of the country. By the end of December, government took action and the hyperinflation was set to begin.

Argentina had been borrowing money from the International Monetary Fund (IMF) for years, even though the government was continually in financial difficulty and unable to repay its debts. Finally, it had to affect a devaluation of the Peso so the debt load would be easier to manage and repay. It was done by de-pegging from the dollar and letting it find its own level. Within a few weeks, the peso dropped by almost 70%. This meant that officially, only 30% of the debt would be made good. It also meant that citizens would now only have 30% of the purchasing power they had previously.

The difference between what Argentina did compared to Weimar Germany and the United States was that they decided to default by a stroke of a pen, instead of re-inking the printing presses time after time. The inflationary impact was about what would have been expected, but it happened much faster, as did the subsequent healing!

Once the devaluation was complete, imports crashed due to their high expense for Argentine citizens. Conversely, it would then be much cheaper to produce those goods at home, and a business boom ensued. Unemployment dropped dramatically, and tax revenues soared. The government began to run a surplus! Even though it took a few years to get to that point, it is instructive to see what happened during the intervening devaluation period. We'll start with a quote from Argentine citizen Fernando Aguirre, the author of 'Surviving the Economic Collapse',

"I don't think anyone expected things to turn out the way they did, or how the economic crisis transformed everyone's lives. The crime, inflation, corruption, generalized degradation of our cultural standards and way of life." ('Surviving the Economic Collapse', page 13)

Banks became insolvent. Many held a significant portfolio of government bonds, effectively crowding out the loan needs of citizens and business owners. When citizens got wind of a potential devaluation, they began to withdraw their money. So it was double trouble for the Argentine banking system. Banks closed and deposit assets were frozen. *ATM's ran dry of needed cash for citizens.*

There was a thriving business on the streets for *money brokers,* who dealt in exchanges in foreign currency, particularly the U.S. dollar. Most people wanted to spend their pesos as fast as possible before consumer prices rose even further.

Paper money still held some value after the collapse, as banks limited cash withdrawals to 300 pesos per week. No U.S. dollar withdrawals were allowed. Even though the pesos would not buy much, the cash *money was still desperately needed and desirable, as was gold.*

Hyperinflation did not happen immediately, as it took a few weeks for the devaluation effects to kick in. But *hoarding and shortages appeared* soon after the devaluation, forcing prices higher. The economy completely collapsed in December, 2001 while the 2002 economy was frozen as consumer prices continued to escalate. People had to pick and choose carefully as to their purchases, since they could no longer afford everything they wanted.

Most shop owners and other *businesses would not accept plastic,* either debit or credit. They wanted cash, barter items, or silver and gold. People resorted to using links of gold chains for payments of consumer items.

Food prices escalated 200% to 300%, while prices on other desirable items rose as much as 600%. *Bartering clubs soon appeared,* although it was still difficult to find many needed items. Many evolved into black market operations, and many deals were struck in foreign currencies. Cigars, liquor and cosmetics were popular barter items, as were precious metals.

Haggling at stores was commonplace, depending on the circumstances. Smaller stores had less pricing power for reductions, but would work a deal if possible. The bigger stores would not offer any deals. Many purchases were actually done on the street in black market fashion.

Gasoline had to be paid for with cash only. This was a major problem for most people.

Professionals got hit hard with lack of clients and payments. Bodyguards, private security services, emergency medical technicians, private transportation services, and the military were where much of the growth in employment occurred during the depth of the crisis.

Even though both local and national *government* had to cut back on services, they still made more laws; they *became more authoritarian.*

As the prices rose, *social unrest and crime accelerated.* Looting was commonplace. People in the cities were hit hard by crime, but those in the rural areas were even bigger targets. The lack of nearby neighbors made these folks appealing to thieves.

As to crime enforcement, it was not so much that police were laid off as it was the explosive growth in crime. There were just not enough enforcement officers to deal with the *rampant robberies.*

Poor people went from home to home asking for handouts. These were the more honorable of the *starving crowds.* Others simply stole what they needed. Women became involved in many more robberies than had been prior Argentine experience. Children even got in on the theft. And almost half of the get-away tactics utilized motorcycles. Purse and gold chain snatching were commonplace.

Organizations that counted on government support went lacking. Some hospitals, schools, and public transporation systems collapsed.

Public *infrastructure went unattended,* and came into disrepair.

Bribes became commonplace with public employees of all kinds, and at all levels of government where none had existed before, particularly at the local level.

The *rich folks left the big cities with suitcases full of cash,* which they had accumulated before the collapse.

Foreigners left with their money, and *investment capital stopped coming into the country.*

Most folks considered to be *middle class before the crisis became poor.* The poor before the crisis became destitute. Shanty towns were prevalent, and squatters occupied vacant homes, factories and other buildings.

Jewelry stores became bigger robbery targets than the banks.

Civility and good faith degraded significantly, even among families. Multi-generational living arrangements became commonplace. Prior friendly acquaintances were lost, as "every man for himself" became the norm in a survival of the fittest type of attitude.

Farmers hoarded their harvested grain in silos as a substitute for holding cash, and as a hedge against price inflation and further peso devaluation.

Grain contracts were priced in dollars, but were routinely exchanged for other big ticket items when cash wasn't available. Cars, trucks, and farm equipment were used in barter.

The *government economic statistics became fudged on a regular basis*, so much so that no-one believed them. But it was not just the unemployment and inflation numbers that were fudged, but also the crime statistics. Government bureaucrats thought it was more patriotic to have rosier reporting, no matter what the truth.

Censorship was common, starting at the office of the President. Threatening calls were regularly made to the news media.

Phone tapping and email surveillance were the norm.

The *legal system* became overloaded and crippled. Many brutal criminals were simply sent home on a house arrest type of pass.

After the default by the Argentine government via devaluation, the pain lasted for 2 years before the economy turned around. After 2002, its GDP averaged over 8.5% annual growth! That's the good news coming out of a snap-of-the-fingers default! Such was the recent experience in Argentina, with many of the same attributes as were experienced in Germany in the early 1920's. In fact, if you study additional instances of hyperinflation cited below, you would discover the same types of problems and public coping mechanisms.

There are many parallels between pre-2002 Argentina and the U.S. today. After our pending crisis washes itself out, we should expect foreign money to flood the U.S. in search of businesses, real estate, and other gems that will seem very cheap to foreigners. This will drive prices through the roof. But prior to that time, we will have serious adjustments to make to our individual thoughts and actions. One of the most important factors to consider is how to get the most out of our money right now, before the currency failure and concomitant inflationary price increases.

Hyperinflation happens all the time

There have been numerous examples of hyperinflation in world history, all caused by profligate money creation far in excess of the productivity growth of the subject countries. A few examples with the ending and worst years are: Brazil in 1994, China in 1949, France in 1803, Greece in 1953,

Israel in 1984, Japan 1946, Mexico in 1993, Peru in 1985, twice in Russia in 1922 and 1992, twice in the U.S. in 1781 and 1865, and Zimbabwe in 2009. Both the Roman Empire and the Byzantine Empire declines were accompanied by debased money. Anyone who wishes to delve into the causes, consequences, end results and social upheaval of these situations will find many similar ingredients, and many of the same survival tactics of the masses. This should give you some of your own ideas of what you'll have to do to prepare, in addition to the ideas presented in the next section of 'Theft of the American Dream'.

The trigger is not predictable

An event will happen that finally wakes up the public here in the United States, and a run on the banks will commence as they lose confidence in the money they are holding. Cash will become more important and valuable than checks or credit and debit cards. The price surges due to the rush into tangible assets and products will go ballistic. The trigger event and timing is not predictable. But it will happen because of the path our politicians and bankers have chosen. All the ingredients and symptoms are there.

Don't be surprised if the trigger comes from overseas, because most modern banking systems are intertwined with derivatives and cross border loans. Unanticipated runs on European banks by customers have already occurred in several countries, and this is significant. Because of the interbank relationships, all Western banking systems are tied at the hip. What happens in one can easily affect others. If a country or large banks fail, it will cause a chain reaction. If an interest rate swap triggering event occurs, that could be the key factor. If the U.S. debt gets downgraded again, that could do it.

U.S. debt has been nothing less than AAA since it was first rated, but now that has changed for the worse. In fact, on March 15, 2012, S&P indicated that their outlook remains negative regardless of perceived economic progress. If Spain, Italy, Greece or Portugal needs further bail outs or are forced to leave the Euro currency that could set things in motion because it would cause severe stress on U.S. banks. If U.S. banks begin to sell their portfolio of U.S. government debt, that could usher in the next phase of the crisis. If the French banks with their 80:1 leverage have to default, that could be the beginning of the end for many U.S. banks. Any exogenous event anywhere could start the house of debt cards to cascade. Remember, we are talking about *confidence*. One cannot predict what will take confidence away from the American people, or when. Nor can one predict the effects or the unintended consequences of the untidy and untimely fiddling with the economy and financial system by politicians and bankers. Just know that an inevitable financial disaster awaits us.

Start with the basics

Now we have to act on what we know, and those actions will be a very different experience. You shouldn't be afraid, nor should you panic. Rather, you should act now. This will be an *individual endeavor* based on your own financial situation, income, savings, expenses now and in the future, job or career goals, time management, debt load, health, family issues, likes, dislikes and other biases. So the problems and solutions to your own financial defense lie within your own head. Just realize that many of the solutions are very radical from the old school way of thinking, and you have to be able to embrace these new ideas and strategies. Your thinking must allow for going against the traditionally suggested solutions if you expect to survive hyperinflation. You job is to pick those ideas which you can best adapt into your life and mindset. What will be presented next are go-to ideas that you can customize into your own situation.

Before we get deeper into solutions and survival techniques, here are some basics:

Saving time can be your best friend, while wasted time is your enemy. You'll need to nurture your time, and keep it as close as you would your most cherished loved one. It is your best asset for financial survival.

A lifestyle change is coming for most of the U.S. populace. You have time to adapt to the changes now. The longer you wait the more difficult it will become, and the less options there will be. The time for fashioning your personal new world order is now.

A mindset change is in order. Things will be different going forward. The best thing to know is to understand what happened to the citizens in other inflationary events, and extrapolate them into your own situation. Be creative. In fact, if you put more time into studying hyperinflation phenomena, you can pick up even more ideas that would work for you.

The first step is self assessment of where you are with your financial and personal security. Examine your strengths and your vulnerabilities. Then act continuously on this assessment. It will be a long term process that you can't put in the closet or consistently ignore.

You'll have to be far more independent that you likely have been in the past. Those who adopt more of an entrepreneurial approach to their lives will have the best chance of survival. Self sufficiency will be critical.

Your ongoing financial and political education is an absolute must.

You'll need to continue to work, and take steps to protect your income. You will likely have to postpone your retirement to a much later date. In fact, starting now you will have to put in more hours in your spare time for your own financial defense.

You'll have to prepare now for using different forms of money. This doesn't have to cost you anything other than time. In fact, the sooner you convert a goodly portion of your paper assets to tangible assets, the better off you'll be. This does not mean you won't need paper money in the future; you will need cash. But that cash does not necessarily mean U.S. dollars. In terms of paper money, it could mean Canadian dollars for those near the border, for instance.

Having alternate forms of transportation could be a good idea. The storage of extra fuel could be a good idea. Having a generator at home along with something to power it could be a good idea. Even becoming a proficient gardener could be a good idea for some folks.

Debt management is all important. Using debt wisely could help you to overcome severe inflationary effects.

Your view on investing in stocks has to be different now. No longer will you be able to throw money at any old mutual fund and expect to retain your purchasing power, even if it looks like it is growing in nominal (non-inflation adjusted) terms.

If you are *wealthy*, you'll need to store some of that wealth in gold. You'll also need to investigate the many ways you can protect your purchasing power with tangible asset investing, both inside and outside of the U.S. Become familiar with foreign currencies and the financial stability of the countries producing them. You may find that securing some of your savings in other than U.S. dollars in the U.S. would be wise. You'll also need to take steps to provide for your personal security.

If you are not so wealthy but have some savings (*middle class?*) you'll need to consider getting some silver and other items for barter, start to lay in supplies of your most wanted or needed items, and put some of your longer term savings into gold. You'll also need a green cash stash (or cache).

If you can save no money because you *live paycheck to paycheck*, you'll have to begin hoarding those items that you need the most. You are very vulnerable, so you'll need time to educate yourself on financial defense mechanisms. No-one will do this for you. You are the one who could benefit most by being much more independent, self sufficient, and entrepreneurial.

Now let's get more specific on what to do and how to do it. Part 2 of 'Theft of the American Dream' will give you plenty of guidelines, while Part 3 will give you resources with which to mold those guidelines into your personal action plan.

PART II

PART II

CHAPTER 11

CHANGE YOUR THINKING AND YOUR BEHAVIOR

The first step is to invest in you

After having read Part I of 'Theft of the American Dream' you can now see how dire our financial situation in the U.S. *really* is. *Now* is your time for action. The more prepared you are for the inevitable, the better off you'll be. Make no mistake: the purchasing power of your dollars is definitely going to drop dramatically, meaning that you'll experience a breathtaking rise in consumer prices. The U.S. probably won't directly default on its Treasury debt. It is extremely unlikely that the politicians will directly renege on Medicare and Social Security. The Fed can't raise interest rates, although the free market certainly can. The U.S. doesn't have the manufacturing and resulting tax base to support its planned promises and initiatives. You now have a perfect picture of the box we are in. Even though money creation has been the strategy of choice to try to cover over our national insolvency issues, the end of that road is very ugly for citizens, so advance preparation is the key to survival.

In this section of the book, there will not be cookie cutter solutions or investment recommendations for the masses. That won't work. Facing a radical problem dictates the use of radical measures to avoid personal financial destruction. Following time tested investment principles will help, so we'll concentrate on some that will be quite useful. There are many ways to get through the minefield of currency destruction, and they are going to be based on your own individual situation, risk tolerance, areas of interest, time allotment, funds for investment (or lack thereof), income, personal interests and biases, family situations and needs, and many other factors.

Radical change for human beings is very difficult; but it isn't impossible. To make the changes necessary for financial survival, most folks will need a new mode of analytical thinking and acting. The best overall suggestion to get started is to *alter your modus operandi in your personal life and lifestyle, and change the methods you use in dealing with your income, expenses, and investments.* Simply stated, you must now be more proactive than ever in dealing with your employment or business, lifestyle, and investment decisions no matter what they are and no matter how much money you have. Floating along with the status quo could prove to be extremely destructive to the finances of a wide swath of the American middle class who think it can't happen to them. That approach will be a losing proposition for sure.

Starting now, you'll have to *re-invent an approach to a new way of living, working, and investing*. The solutions are different for each individual or family. You will need to *think like an entrepreneur*, even if you are employed by someone else. This doesn't mean you should quit your job! Those who are already self-employed or own a small business should already be used to risk, change, and adaptation, so that's a plus for them. And those who are skilled in a trade are in a good position relative to those who are not. Many folks will feel a bit of trepidation about going it alone when it comes to delving into investment strategies and lifestyle changes. Even though you don't actually have to go it alone, your mindset has be that of more independence than you may be used to. But you must believe that financial survival for the next decade and beyond will be possible by devising and implementing your own strategies.

If you believe that a total wipeout of your purchasing power can't happen in the U.S., think again. It can, it has, and it will once again. Leaning on your financial planner, accountant, insurance man, lawyer, or stock broker simply *will not save you*. Yes, it would certainly help if they themselves are of a similar mindset and acting on their own behalf for financial survival while you tag along. But for the most part, *the preservation of the purchasing power of your income and investable assets or savings is strictly an individual endeavor*. That means you'll have to learn things you and your advisors don't know. That means you'll have to act differently in your non-working hours. That means that you'll be seeking to mitigate your risks through self-education, which takes time.

Self-reliance is the best and surest way to protect yourself, since it's likely that most of your advisors are well behind the curve. In the past 30 years, too much incompetence by advisors was covered over by rising markets. Heck, a donkey could have made money in the three decades preceding the crisis. This does *not* mean that you should dump your trusted advisors. Rather, *you must take the lead*. But don't be surprised if you encounter some resistance to your ideas on their part. It is more than likely your advisors aren't ready for the currency destruction ahead.

If they are, you will be ahead of the pack. You have to be your own judge on that score.

There is no living U.S. citizen who has personally encountered our existing dilemma before. It's certain that our current financial situation is so different, and the moves by the Fed have been so radical, that the consequences will be unique to our lifetimes. We can't predict all of the consequences, but the ones that are predictable are the ones we need to be most defensive about.

It's understandable that right now you could lack the confidence to charge ahead. But this is a *process*, not a one-time exercise. The key to confidence is knowledge. The key to reducing risk is knowledge. The key to your success and financial survival is knowledge. These are the reasons that the resource guide at the end of the book is so critical. It's an absolute gold mine of information, and will give you a roadmap for your chosen direction. To better cope with those consequences that we can't predict, education, preparation, and the ability to quickly adapt are all important. And how does one prepare and adapt? Change the way you think!

Change the way you think!

Before your behavior can change, your mindset has to change. You have to be confident in the knowledge that you can make a big difference by acting on your own. There is absolutely no doubt that you *can* self-improve your situation by not relying solely on one or more advisors. Take it from someone who has been on both sides of that fence. Americans have been living the dream for over 40 years. But that's the problem; it was a dream based on borrowed money combined with friendly markets, and for the most part, comparatively benign price inflation to what lies ahead.

It is shocking to think that many professionals, business owners and other well-off individuals became so short sighted in the friendly investment climate of the past. They just became too complacent. But worse than that, they got away with their complacency! It didn't cost them anything, since it was almost a no-brainer to make money in the stock and bond market, at least until the dot-com boom busted and the NASDAQ went south. You can no longer assume that your income, investments, or plans for the future are safe. You must look for creative ways to protect them, no matter what your avocation, and that requires changing your mindset.

Job one is to understand how an entrepreneur thinks, particularly in terms of self reliance. This means that you have to rely on your own talents and interests to find successful investments. This is very different, in that most successful people have become accustomed to leaning on the advice of their financial advisor. But most successful financial advisors have way too many clients to do an adequate job in this unique financial environment we now face. Not only that the markets and laws change so fast that it's difficult for them to be on the cutting edge. Of course most are mandated to taking continuing education courses, but this is like driving a car by only looking out the rear view mirror. It just doesn't teach what needs to be learned to survive the ravages of hyperinflation.

It is very different to *invest for the enhancement of your purchasing power*. Now it is critical to forget about nominal returns. Measuring your inflation adjusted returns terms is what really counts. In doing so, you must simply ignore the Consumer Price Index. You must consult other sources for the real purchasing power picture. People who had money in the bank earned virtually nothing in interest in 2011, yet true inflation ran at about 7%. So, that $1,000 in your bank account designated for consumer purchases to start 2011 would have bought only $930 worth of the same goods by the start of 2012. This is profound, and is about to get far worse. Everything you do in any investment has to have *increasing purchasing power* as the number one concern. This can be done with time, education, patience, and a different mindset.

Let's frame some general principles needed to save yourself as best you can. We know that everyone will be affected by the profligate deficit spending coming out of Washington, D.C. in the coming months and years. Everyone will suffer from the necessity of the politicians to keep their promises by using the printing presses. Remember, even if by remote chance we get to a balanced budget, it really won't be balanced due to the high costs of Social Security, Medicare, and a plethora of other giveaways that are "off budget". If you have something to lose, you should consider it to be more at risk now than ever before. There is hope, but the winning strategy will be based on adherence to your own set of principles that you yourself can establish with a little thought and practice.

It's not as much about the amount of money you have, it's about what that money will buy, and when. It's about trying to maintain some semblance of the standard of living you've been used to. There will be sacrifices to be made for most folks, even the very rich. Just know that the winners will get to pick their own sacrifices, while the losers will have those decisions made for them.

Invest in yourself

The most important aspect of this investment is that you already have the wherewithal to do it! You don't need much money to start. All you need is time. We know that time is the most precious commodity that human beings have, so embrace that fact and find more productive time in your own life. It is so much more precious than money. You might be able to make up for an investment loss, but you can never recoup lost or squandered time. So you must treat it with the utmost of care. By saving and subsequently investing that time, you can make a *huge* difference in your financial situation. Of this there is no doubt.

Time is a wasting asset, depreciating as we go forward. However, time can not only retain its value, but can become that much more valuable if you use it wisely. Even if you have very little disposable income to invest right now, the correct and effective use of your discretionary time will pay off handsomely! And the beauty of this resource is that most individuals can create more of it for themselves to redirect into other arenas.

But there is a potential problem here, and that problem could be you, the individual! You could be your own worst enemy. It could be that you are currently into a certain mode of behavior that may not maximize your financial health. This means that many people waste a tremendous amount of time. In the run-up to and during the hyperinflationary scenario, the time you may have squandered could cost you in a big way. Think about this in your own situation.

Many readers may say they just don't have the time to devote to financially plan for the future. This is silly. There may be exceptions, but they would be very limited. Or maybe there are people out there who consciously ignore financial planning their own specific reasons and that's OK. However, for the vast majority of the people, anyone who doesn't think he or she can find extra time has a conceptual deficit. If you are running in place to maintain that comfortable income without attending to what is left over after satisfying your lifestyle, you are making a mistake. Spinning wheels to preserve the status quo will be a loser's game, guaranteed. That goes for both individuals and businesses.

The best investment you can make to save yourself is to craft a way to save time, which can then be devoted to getting a substantial return on your savings dollars well in excess of the true rate of inflation. But how can you save time? Think like an entrepreneur and change the way you go about your daily existence. Everyone can do it for little or no cost at all.

It only takes a bit of thought. Think self-sufficiency and act accordingly. Let's explore this notion.

Change your lifestyle

No-one can or should make suggestions on how to live your life. But by taking a close look at your lifestyle, and then making adjustments, you could yield fantastic benefits in time and subsequently, money. I know: this is very difficult. Most folks work hard during the day and enjoy their own brand of downtime on their time away from work. This downtime may or may not include spending money on feel good items and activities. But to gain maximum advantage of the upcoming suggestions in 'Theft of the American Dream' you'll need some time, some disposable income or savings, and a desire to improve your financial well-being. So where does the extra time and money come from? That's where you come in, and that's what you have to decide for yourself. A good place to start is having a clear understanding of where your discretionary time and spending actually goes!

Lifestyle is all about time and expenses. How you use your time has everything to do with your financial success. If you can save time outside of your normal workweek, this could reap tremendous benefits. If you could downsize your expenses, this would yield yet further benefits and add to your security in the future. 'Theft of the American Dream' is about to suggest ways to spend that extra time toward the betterment of your financial future, and what to do with your investible dollars. Of course, if you are living paycheck to paycheck, and have no money to invest, you'll have to concentrate on hoarding and bartering. But even that requires self-education and time.

The first suggestion in this regard is to *truthfully analyze your daily schedule*. This is not an exercise that needs anyone else's approval or inspection. This is about introspection of your own way of life, and being honest with yourself as to the time you waste. Make a daily log for at least a month of where all of your time goes. At the end of that month, your assessment should be very clear. If you can find even an hour or two a day, it could reap tremendous rewards. If you honestly can't find even a half an hour per day to dedicate to your own financial well-being, look to the weekends. What do you see? Where are your biggest gaps of wasted or unproductive time? Most people only work 8 or 10 hours a day and maybe sleep 6 to 8 hours. This leaves a lot of time for family, recreation, being a couch potato, or whatever. Just be honest with yourself, and you'll find that daily hour or so to work for the benefit of your financial well-being. But you have to want to do it, and *motivation is the most critical ingredient to your success.* Only you can provide that ongoing self-motivation.

Another suggestion is to *log all of your expenses* for as long a time period necessary to get a firm grip on where your income goes. Presumably this would be at least a 3 month exercise, but preferably longer. Include everything, even taxes. If you use credit cards, log all the individual expenses into categories. Your logs will very likely reveal several areas for savings. Remember, discretionary spending is just that. The point here is that it really doesn't matter what your level of income or current investments are. There *is* room for improvement, and it is your task to find the ways to save dollars and invest them wisely in ways that fit into your desired minimum lifestyle and time constraints.

Make sure you are computer literate

For the complete neophyte to investing or financial survival, *job number one is to learn the internet and how to use the search engine Google.com.* Even if you have never touched a computer in your life, you could likely master this basic skill in less than an hour. Remember, Apple, Dell, Facebook and Microsoft didn't become household names by making it difficult for those households to use their products. Computers may be very scary for some, but they are made for everybody to easily understand and use. You don't have to be a nerd, just a person who can hunt and peck on a keyboard! So get on the band wagon and get on-line. The world is waiting and your financial survival is in the balance.

The fact is that in today's world, if you are not at least a little internet savvy, you'll be left in the dust. This is particularly true as far as the necessity of digging beneath the surface in order to profit from the coming suggestions in 'Theft of the American Dream'. The resource guide in Part III is all about using, learning and planning from the vast resources on the internet. Even though young adults and most baby boomers are internet literate, many retirees are not.

If you're a retiree who is not on the net you are setting yourself up for disaster. The first reason is that you're likely on a fixed income; problem. The next issue is that you may be stuck with very low yielding investments like CDs and annuities; problem. The third reason is that you simply can't afford to assume the risk of seeking out higher yields or growth opportunities without the requisite knowledge; problem. First and foremost folks, get educated about the internet. You have the time, so go to your local library and sign up for classes using the library computers. Then, find a way to spend time each day on the computer so it becomes second nature to you.

Protecting your income as an entrepreneur, business owner or self-employed individual

If you happen to be an *entrepreneur, self-employed, or a business owner,* you had better be prepared for extreme business conditions. It will be imperative to add the greatest value to your product or service than you ever have before. Now is the time that you'll have to run faster just to keep up with your competition. To get ahead and actually grow, you'll probably have to change your M.O. Most of you have been through plenty of ups and downs in the past, but this time really is different. Salespeople and business owners are used to good months and bad months, or good years and bad years. Many have learned how to handle the uncertainties, and the ebb and flow of their stream of income. They undoubtedly have certain policies and practices that have worked for them in the past. That's good, but it's no longer enough.

Now you'll have to act more aggressively toward your financial self-preservation. This may even mean that your business philosophy will have to change. Most business owners try to be as efficient as possible, and that's what is necessary to maximize the bottom line. But now you'll have to do even more. Now you'll have to step outside of your comfort zone. Trim your costs to the bone, while adding more quality and service. I know, you've always tried to do that, but your survival is now in the balance. You'll need to run through the exercise of re-building your business from the ground up. Get rid of the old notions that have worked for years. Assume that you are starting over, and be innovative in your approach. Embrace the internet if you haven't already done so. If you don't think that pertains to your business, think again. Your competitors are passing you by if you aren't active in both on-line sales and service.

For entrepreneurs, innovation and added value are now critical for your survival. If you are not innovating or adding value for the customer, you won't make it. Consumers will become more and more discriminating, so you'd better be ready. Take another look at the range of products and services you provide. Break them down and concentrate on the most profitable. Many business owners accept marginally profitable business practices just to keep the cash flowing. This allows them the ability to keep some of their long-time marginal employees, or simply continue to pay the bills. That's fine for the short term, and there is some logic in this. But wise business owners and self employed people need to get ahead of the curve and plan for the toughest business conditions of their lifetime. Treading water won't make it, as inflationary forces are going to take over. The faster you recognize this fact, the better off you'll be. So look to potentially profitable new products or services to add to your offerings and dump your laggards. If this also means dumping marginally productive people that you've coddled for years, then so be it. It's all about the protection of your source of income.

Business owners should go to their customers. Don't simply rely on your sales force to do this. If customers are important enough, they need to know that from the top, and that would be the *person* at the top. Become more visible to them, and understand their situation from *their* perspective, not yours. Ask for immediate and candid feedback. Put it all on the table; the good, the bad, and the ugly. In being proactive like this, you should be happy with negative feedback. If the customer cares enough to criticize a product or service you are giving them, at least you have a chance. Both sides can make necessary adjustments, whether it is regarding price, service, quality, or anything else. If you don't hear any criticism, beware, as something isn't right. There is *always* room for improvement, and you simply must seek out candid criticism, even if you lead in the talking points yourself! Remember, the person with whom you are having this frank conversation is likely having business or financial concerns of his own. What that means is that *you* could be part of that concern, whether you realize it or not. You must solicit his help so that you can work together for the benefit of both. Work to keep his business.

Finally, remember that customers or consumers will support their own values, needs and biases by purchasing those products and services that best matches those attributes. So the entrepreneur, business owner or salesperson has to sell to those biases, needs, and values. You must *listen*, and then adapt your product or service accordingly if you can. Remember you can't learn a darn thing by talking. Then sell the *benefits* of your company or products and services, not the features! This one basic tenet of customer satisfaction is far more effective than volumes of slick sales brochures.

You must *go to your suppliers* as well. Now you get to play customer, and face to face meetings work best. If you have the ability to video conference, this is OK, but personal meetings are better. Simply using the telephone won't do. You don't have to a body language expert or psychologist to know when something is amiss with a business proposal or other candid conversations. You just know something is being left unsaid, or otherwise isn't right. And since you'll likely be asking for some price or service concessions, like everyone else, you'll want to do this in person. Calling someone for a discount is less likely to work, particularly when everyone else is doing the same thing. You have to have an edge so your request is received more readily than others.

Be ready to bring something to the table for the supplier as well. Maybe you have more than one supplier. Be ready to give a guy more business. What he can't get in margin, perhaps he can make up in volume. Getting the suppliers out of their own environment is good too. Take them to lunch. This avoids all the normal interruptions, and leads to a more focused discussion. Loosen up, and try to get to *know the person behind the business deal.* You'll find that he's got the same type of concerns as you do, so compare notes and see what adjustments can be made for the benefit of both of you. Remember, a good deal is good for both parties.

Have alternatives in your pocket! In your discussions, try to frame the answer or solution to an issue as *either/or,* and not as a *yes or no.* This either/or solution is not to threaten, but rather to give choices, both of which would be of benefit to you. With this type of approach, you can more easily come up with a positive result no matter what the supplier decides. But with a yes or no scenario, only 50% will be in your favor! Be positive without being threatening, while at the same time being truthful. Most importantly, *don't BS people.* You may think what you are saying has credibility, but most of the time the other party picks up signals that not all the facts are as they appear. So don't make that mistake. Just tell it like it is in a non-threatening way, as it'll save you time and energy, and it will build trust. In inflationary times, successful business dealings will be built on trust and a more favorable cost/value relationship. So exploit that fact. If you are simply selling "price", beware! You are training your client or customer to leave you for a better price. You must sell trust, benefits, and value!

We've been examining relationships between existing customers and suppliers, but what about new ones? If you need more sales, now is the time to be looking. Many businesses are doing the same re-evaluation as you should be doing, and this affords opportunity. This is why it is so critical to concentrate on your most profitable product or service. You'll need to be as competitive as possible, so this means you have to concentrate on the avenues where you have the most efficiencies and pricing wiggle room. *Salespeople* beware! If times have been good in the past and you have become complacent, watch out. More activity is the key here. The more "no's" you hear, the better. That means you are getting that much closer to the "yes's", and you need more prospects saying "yes". Are your sales concentrated with just a few customers? If so, this could be a major problem for you going forward. Get off the sofa or the golf course, and get back out on the street. The competition will become stronger than ever, so forget the old ways. Re-invent yourself. Not satisfied with the product line you represent? Can't find a new line? Concentrate on the ones you know well.

It is critical to remember that *people buy from people*. Of course they buy products or services, but in competitive situations, the person who is more liked has an edge. Use that edge. Your job is to get your face in front of the customer and be a person. Are you in a situation where the commission is variable, based on profit of your company, or simply at your discretion? Get ready to concede some commission, which you can make up with higher volume. Remember, for a sales person, by definition, higher activity leads to higher volume. So be more aggressive and more active than in the past, and think of new ways to approach the old customer needs, problems or concerns. Add value, and you'll make more sales.

Employees also have to think like an entrepreneur

Most employed individuals spend a lot of time at work, so how can they treat that mandatory or non-discretionary period of every day to help themselves? Let's take one thing at a time here, and of primary concern, of utmost importance, is your income. No matter what, you must protect your income. Without it your choices are limited, right? So let's look at a few basics first which are more philosophical than economic. This goes along with the premise that you'll need to change the way you think, and then act differently. It means that you'll have to work harder, and think smarter. *Think and act like an entrepreneur, even if you aren't!* This basic tenet is all important to your job security.

If you're an employee just about anywhere, in any type of business in the United States, you should be concerned. Re-read what was just presented above regarding potential strategies of your employer and think about it. Maybe you can't actually think exactly like your employer, but you *do* have to understand what is going through his mind. This will help you in your plan of attack to help save yourself from the roles of the unemployed. Remember, finding another job in this environment would not be simple. Companies across the spectrum of manufacturing and service industries are cutting back, and when hyperinflation kicks in, employment prospects will get worse in most (but not all) sectors of the economy. Even though you can't do a lot about that, what you can do is *add value for your employer*. That means you'll have to do more without demanding more pay. Be more efficient with your time at work, and make it work to your benefit.

You know what your job is, so not only should you do it better, faster, and with a smile, but you had better *assume more responsibility*. Don't wait to be asked; anticipate and just do it. Your employer does not owe you for the job well done in the past. That is faulty thinking. That was then. We have entered a new paradigm whereby value judgments will constantly need to be made across the board by managers and business owners, and it is *your job to make yourself more valuable*. This would be particularly true for middle management types. That's where most owners or CEO's look, to cut first. After all, that's where a lot of the responsibility lies that may be taken on by some of the higher echelon managers, or even moved down the ladder to underlings.

This is not to say that the lowest echelon workers are safe. Of course, they aren't. This added value concept goes from the bottom rung of the ladder to the top. All levels of employees should be looking to assume more responsibility, and they should be looking to do it sooner rather than later. Show some initiative. Those employees associated with marginal product lines or services should be concerned. Do you know how you fit into that type of picture? You must assume more responsibility, and that means that you may have to re-educate yourself as best you can about other aspects of your employer's business. Volunteer for more work, even if it takes more of your personal time. Remember, we're talking about protecting your income. What better way to do so than to make yourself more valuable to the person signing your paycheck?

If you do find yourself among the ranks of the unemployed, *consider a free trial period for a potential new employer*. Offer to work for free for some period of time to prove your worth. Only you can decide what that period of time could be, but take note that it should be significant enough to give the new employer enough time to make a decent evaluation of your attitude, knowledge, skill-set, and work ethic. Put your pride aside. No-one wants to work for free, but consider the alternative. If your unemployment benefits run out, then you would experience an even bigger problem in taking care of yourself and your family. Think about it! Most importantly, if you are on unemployment benefits, please don't sit around, assuming there are no job prospects. Use the time to reeducate yourself. Investigate and act on learning a new skill. Take a different approach to your life, and you may be surprised. Use internet search engines creatively. Call up 'Video Professor', which offers computer learning CD's on any number of skill-sets! This is not a paid ad, but a just a viable suggestion. The point is that losing your job should not be the end of your world. Adjust your thinking and actions for your own future benefit. In fact, try something entrepreneurial!

Professionals will not have pricing power

Professionals are also at risk of reduced income. As your clients are squeezed by rising prices elsewhere, you may not get the volume of business you're accustomed to. Indeed, attempting to raise your own fees to keep up with rising price inflation could dampen the enthusiasm of your existing clients to continue with your services! Don't assume that your fees can continue to go up without a dramatic drop in patient or client volume. Of particular concern will be the slower paying clients. Either get used to it, or try to transform to a higher income group of clientele. If a long time client continues to get further and further behind, chances are that he/she will never catch up. Beware of these types of situations and be preemptive. You cannot continue to work for people who can't pay your bill. This takes valuable time away from those who *can* pay the bill, whether they are your client or not! Seek out only those who have the resources to pay for your services!

Many professionals are either self-employed or entrepreneurs, but some are simply employees of larger firms. Therefore, much of the above discussion can apply to you, no matter what your particular situation. Unfortunately, many professionals are lacking in business acumen. What about you? Of course you know your particular skill or avocation. But if you expect to maintain a certain lifestyle, some planning is most definitely warranted, and you should not blindly nor solely rely on your financial advisors. You simply *must* assume control of your own financial well-being, and one way to do that in a hyperinflationary environment is to work smarter and harder at your avocation, while at the same time educating yourself on money matters.

Employees of non-profit organizations

If you are an employee of a non-profit organization, you should be acutely concerned. Grant money may well dry up, and cuts within your organization will need to be made. The same concept of adding value as noted above would be important, but it may not have the impact as it would in a for-profit firm. If your employer has its own internal income source, work toward making that income source more secure for the benefit of the organization, if possible. Remember, the more you can bring into the picture as to the value of your work ethic and service to the company, the better. If you are a full time executive director, watch for a potential cut to part time. Executive directors should look to have meetings with funders to see where your organization stands in terms of future funding prospects. Also remember that part of the deficit reduction talks in Washington include plans calling for decreased income tax deductions to wealthy philanthropists who fund most of the $4 billion of annual charitable donations across the country. Whether it is this Congress or one in the future, you must keep up with what is happening in Washington DC! Surprises are not the way to go. You must anticipate. Therefore, you'll need to do some strategic thinking so your income doesn't take a drastic hit. You may find that your best course of action is to look elsewhere for employment. Just remember to add value to the greatest possible extent.

Retirees are at maximum risk

Retirees are probably more vulnerable to the financial crisis than any other segment of the U.S. middle class population. Aside from the fact that many of you are on a fixed income, the income or return from your savings and investments is certainly not fixed, and most of these investments are headed in the wrong direction. Thank the zero interest rate policy of the Fed for that. When you factor in the TRUE rate of inflation, you could be at severe risk if you aren't a millionaire. But you do have the one resource that is that can help to mitigate your income loss, and that is time. If your health is decent, you have the luxury of being able to use your time wisely. Take note of my comments above on getting computer literate! I know; this could be the hardest psychological barrier you've ever tried to overcome, but it is absolutely critical to your financial defense and survival.

Most of you may have no idea how to recoup your stock portfolio or home equity losses, short of going back into the workforce in the worst of economic conditions. You will definitely benefit from the investment recommendations in this book, as difficult as that may appear when you first read them. You will also need to take a close look at actually using the equity in your home to grow your purchasing power. Investment advisors up to this point have necessarily suggested more conservative investments such as bonds, CD's or annuities for retirees. But in your attempt to grow the purchasing power of your savings in times of serious inflation, these types of fixed investments will certainly not do the job for you. In fact, they could quickly lead you to the poorhouse.

Retirees must now become entrepreneurial! One thing the retiree could do is to develop a skill that he or she can perform at home for a fee. No-one can say what would be best for you, but you are only limited by your creativity. One web site called 'Liveperson.com' sells expertise on line. You actually talk to people and advise them on practically any subject. The site has thousands advisors who do this work right from home. For a fee by the minute, you can lend a hand from your area of expertise to someone needing inexpensive help, and you can do so at your convenience while sitting in your EZ-Boy. Use your imagination when you look for ways to earn money at home. The possibilities are there for the picking, but you have to be willing to investigate those possibilities and act on your ideas.

Clearly there will be more hours worked by those families who do have jobs, so perhaps some retirees could pick up the slack on tasks that those folks just can't get done during the day. This issue has become particularly important, primarily because your opportunity for work may be limited, and your health could be more of an issue as time moves along. But modern medical technology will keep you alive much longer than your parents, and you've got to make sure that you don't outlive your income and savings.

If you find the need to enter a nursing home or assisted living facility, this will drain your resources *much* faster than the rate of the understated BLS inflation rate. Once your savings are depleted, Medicaid may or may not be available; under existing laws, you might have to be poor for 5 years before you would even qualify. Aside from this fact, the finances of the U.S. may preclude future participation in Medicaid except in the most extreme circumstances, if the program even survives in its current form. So you must take steps *now* to protect your purchasing power, and you likely have some discretionary time to do so. But personal motivation is the key, and that is something that only you can control.

Government workers

If you're a Federal government worker or politician, then maybe your income will be safe, unless you get dumped by the voters or downsized out of your job. The Federal government seems to be the only thing that continues to grow, as has been demonstrated on a daily, yearly, and generational basis. Even though that is precisely the source of the problem, money continues to flow inside the Beltway. So if you need a job, check it out! Will the spending profligacy change with the new religion of both political parties talking about cutting deficit spending? Maybe, but it looks as though there are not enough willing politicians of either party to affect real change right now. Half of the citizenry depending on some kind of government help (49.1% as of 2012) probably wouldn't like the idea anyway. Typically, most folks want cuts, but not out of their particular pie. Think about it. Would the boomers put up with massive cuts to Social Security or Medicare? That is doubtful!

Finally if you are a *state, county or local employee*, you had better watch out. Revenues are falling in most cities and states and higher taxes are not a solution. Spending less is the solution, as the Federal government can't prop them up forever with stimulus money or Block Grants. Federal stimulus funding only prolonged the inevitable, in that most state governments ran serious deficits by 2011, and they have no way to print up money to cover the excess spending. Fully 44 state governments went into the red by the end of 2010, and most have no easy way out of the problem. If cuts are to be made, who goes? If you are a public employee of any sort, you should be concerned. Adding value to your employer as discussed above would certainly help, but there is always the political angle that could doom your job retention! Just think, now you may have to change party affiliation or start making donations! Whatever it takes, protect your income.

Will you be able to make changes necessary to defend your financial future?

The time has come to completely re-arrange your thinking patterns and actions in terms of securing your income and investing your savings. Your financial future is at stake, and changing your mental approach should be top priority. Believe in the premise that this time is very different. Face the truth. Confront your fears. Believe in yourself. As hard as it may be to change your thinking, it's *the necessary first step* to your financial survival. It will allow you a genuine opportunity to act in new and profitable ways. Try it, you'll like it!

CHAPTER 12
INVESTMENT PRINCIPLES TO THRIVE BY

Ignore these guidelines at your own risk

Now that you've decided to change your perspective at work and at home, let's get down to business. Remember, the game is to beat inflation so that your purchasing power grows. It doesn't really matter if you have $10 or $10 thousand or $10 million dollars. The assumption is that you'll want to get the most out of it when you invest or spend it. Below are some general thoughts on investing that you may not hear from your financial advisors. If you have heard some or all of them before, have you heeded the advice? Some of the points seem so *obvious*, but equally obvious is that most investors have ignored these tenets for years. The key to investing for the growth of your purchasing power means that you'll need to build on some basics. The more you heed these basics, the more successful you'll be. The following suggestions pertain to any investment you make.

Invest only in what you understand very well.

The basic premise for this section is that *if you personally don't have a good grasp on an investment, don't make it!* The importance of this guideline is ultra-critical. This is the very foundation of your financial defense. There are hundreds of investment classes to choose from, and many paper assets such as stocks and bonds are fraught with peril. If you ignore all other suggestions and ideas in 'Theft of the American Dream', don't ignore this one. Your financial future depends on it.

Stockbrokers are notorious for wearing rose-colored glasses and are solidly bullish no matter what, as that is basically mandated by their employers. Plus, stockbrokers are only allowed to recommend those issues which are on the firm's approved list, which makes one wonder the real reason a company is included on the broker's buy list in the first place. Is it that the brokerage house really thinks the stock is a good investment, or is it that they have too much in their own portfolio they need to dump, or is it that they are actually shorting that which you are buying? It's hard to know for certain, but all of the above scenarios are common. Unfortunately, two of them do not work in your favor. The fact is that the retail investing public is to whom the professionals and big money interests sell. This notion is not meant to be cynical, just factual.

Financial advisors, such as Certified Financial Planners (CFP's) or Chartered Life Underwriters (CLU's) need to earn money too. Do not assume that just because you paid a fee for service you will receive either educated or unbiased investment advice! This is so very wrong. If you are investing money with a fee based financial advisor, his product recommendations will not be unbiased. Whether it is due to his own corporate compliance rules, his own lack of due diligence, his own personal philosophies or other reasons, it's simply human nature to lean toward personal bias in an investment recommendation. You must realize that there is probably something behind the recommendation that you don't know. Or, if you pay the advisor by the sale of some product on which he or she earns a commission, it automatically comes with some an agenda, no matter how sincere the advisor seems to be! Many times the agenda will work against your best interests. For this reason, ideas should come from your own curiosity, ideas, and self-study.

And if you think your accountant or attorney can advise you on an investment, think again. Paying those folks to peruse the prospectus or look at the numbers *should only be done after you do your own due diligence, and to double check your work.* Know your investment well!

Get help from like-minded people in your efforts to search out ideas

Listed in the resource guide are numerous investment advisors who have web sites and newsletters. They have proven their efficacy over the years. They are on target with the issues covered in this book, and they have stood up to scrutiny as to their investment ideas and specific recommendations. Having said that, *nobody is perfect*, so don't expect miracles. Most of them have a fee for services, but also write frequent essays which can be read and reviewed at no cost at numerous websites, some of which are listed in the resource guide. These essays are a great place to start for the novice investor.

One viable idea is for you to *start or join an investment club* comprised of people who are genuinely concerned about their savings and purchasing power, and are worried that they have a lot to lose. You'll want to *associate with like-minded people* because the investment environment we face is so different than in the past; and the tired old way of looking at things and bygone assumptions won't likely work this time around. By being in a club, members could each agree to join a different investment newsletter service and compare notes at regular meetings. When you come up with an idea worthy of merit, research work could be meted out to the folks in the club for a better understanding of the target's business and future prospects. This is the kind of approach that can pay big rewards. Remember, the idea is not limited to only the discussion of stocks. In fact, it should be much wider than that. You will need to go for the investments with the highest possibilities of a superb return, so mitigate your risk with as much knowledge as you can muster.

Hone in on specific targets

Aside from *educating yourself in that which interests you*, make sure to *focus on a small segment* of that area of interest. This approach will make your time much more fun and profitable. This could apply to stocks, rental properties, pocket watches, rare coins, old bicycles, agricultural land, livestock, oil, or anything else. But the two key ingredients are that you should be *highly motivated and interested* in the subject matter. With the internet at your fingertips, this becomes far easier than it would have been in years past. In the case of tangible assets, you must particularly understand your pet market better than the seller. And don't assume you couldn't possibly know more than the seller. That simply is not the case.

For instance, many very knowledgeable people collect rare coins. Anyone can go to coin shows or coin dealers to find them. Many times the dealer has so many types of coins that he simply can't be an expert on all types. If a buyer knows more than the dealer on some *specific and tiny segment* of the coin market, he will be able to stumble upon some superb buys. The buyer is in position to identify a super deal because of his knowledge in just a sliver of an otherwise huge market. But let's look at another more common example here that goes hand in hand with achieving superior knowledge in a dinky segment of a huge market.

Market awareness

Honing in on specific segments of your target market requires market awareness. Take real estate as an example. This is not to suggest that you go out to buy real estate right away. Rather, it is to elucidate the point of being aware of your market. In real estate, we all know that the location of a real estate buy is all important, but equally if not more important is market awareness. Pick a certain segment of your targeted area or type of land or structure, and learn everything about it. You can easily become more familiar with it than any agent, because in theory you've put a major focus on just that particular market segment in a more specific area or neighborhood. Just looking at a specific neighborhood is the way to go. Your target area needs to be as *small as possible* so you can easily compare and contrast. Check out *all* properties of your target type before making any offers. Don't just look at those that are listed for sale, look at those listed for rent too. Look at past sales. Analyze dates and sale prices. Look for price trends. Look at amenities. Look at rents. Look at condition. Look at everything. Most agents are pretty generalized, and will try to sell anything to anyone. You don't have to be that anyone. By being focused and super educated, you will easily be able to identify a good deal when you see it. But without market awareness, your purchase could be a game of chance. You do not want to leave your success to chance.

Pay only for what is, not what could be

Many sharp sellers of any number of investment classes like to site what wonderful possibilities this or that purchase could offer. Yes, you are looking for good prospects in your investment, but that doesn't mean you should pay up for something that doesn't currently exist. Only buy what exists when you are buying, not what could be after your effort and money is applied. If an investment has potential for greater profits later, that's great! That's what you want. But it will likely take some initiative to get there that the seller has chosen not to undertake. Instead, the seller wants you to buy into an idea which has yet to be realized. Ideas are cheap, while implementation is dear. The successful investor puts an idea into action, and subsequently profits by it. So don't let the seller in on any of those profits! Again, *don't be conned into paying for what could be, pay only for what is.* If the price in any way reflects what could be, have the discipline to walk away. This pertains to any investment you make.

When diversifying, don't spread yourself too thin

Investment diversity is a good thing, but *too much diversification or asset allocation can cost you dearly.* In the above section on educating yourself on your targeted market, *focus* was the emphasis. Focus will reap great rewards for the educated investor. But that doesn't mean you have to focus on just one kind of investment. In fact, it is good to have more than one asset class, but it is equally bad or even worse to have too many. Many financial planners like to see their clients have a wide variety of not only asset classes, but also individual investments within those asset classes. They think this will mitigate risk within the overall portfolio. In an inflationary economic environment, this is wrong. What it actually does is increase your risk of purchasing power destruction, mire your portfolio of investments in mediocrity, and limit your overall return due to the duds in your allocation model.

In the inflationary environment of your new investment paradigm, the more you diversify, the more you will put severe limitations on a superb return on your invested dollars. The emphasis must be on *getting a superb return, not just an acceptable one*. This is why do-it-yourself education is so important. If you take the time to learn about something, then you can certainly afford to invest a higher than normal percentage of your portfolio into that idea. Why wouldn't you? Actually, you *must* take this approach. It is the only way that your investments can far outperform inflationary forces over time. And it's the only way that you'll achieve a payoff for the time you have spent researching your subject matter.

Most financial advisors think in *nominal* rates of return, not inflation adjusted returns. And when they do consider inflation, most of them cite government statistics. This is absolutely the wrong approach, and the emphasis of the advisor on nominal returns does you a major disservice. You have to *think in true inflation adjusted terms* if you expect your investments to exceed the true rate of inflation, not the baloney doled out by government accounting! Be aware of this fact, and educate yourself enough to be confident in paring back some of the diversification that you previously thought was a good way to avoid risk. It isn't.

Let's look deeper into the diversification picture. Forgetting for the moment that you have investments in other asset classes, let's say you have $100,000 in growth stocks. Conventional wisdom would have it that you could have upwards of 20 different stocks. This is not the correct approach. It would be better to hone in on say, 4 or 5 of your best picks and watch them like a newborn baby. If a stock is good enough to hold, it had better be good enough to provide a safe and superior return in the form of dividends and/or capital gains. And if it provides a safe and superior return, you should own a sizable position. Attend to the defense of your purchasing power by *applying education and concentration*. Of course, this same principle particularly applies to an overall portfolio of multiple investment classes. Use superior knowledge and concentration for a far better return.

Dump your losers.

This principle requires some thought along with education. If you don't really understand your market or why the price has dropped in your beloved investment, sell it. But you might say, *"I just want to get out even!"* Forget it! This is one of the worst mistakes you can make. Do you actually think that your underperforming pet investment will outperform a better one that you could buy on the cheap? This is virtually impossible. Take your losses. Write it off to experience, and now you'll have cash for something that will actually work in your favor if you do your homework. Here's a test: if you can honestly say to yourself that you know everything about your investment and are convinced that this thing will be your best shot at not only recouping your existing loss but also exceeding inflation, then double down or average down; buy more. In most cases this would not apply. But in your special case, if it's good enough to hold, then it's good enough to buy more. Simply, your understanding of it had better be crystal clear and not cluttered with emotion. If you don't understand it, aren't sure what will make its price go back up, or simply have lost interest due to underperformance, then sell now. Raise the cash to go on to something that you understand and that you can get for a relative song. If you are holding something that you would not want to buy again, even at the current depressed price, sell it. This rationale is simple really, and very effective. Don't let your emotions get in the way. Virtually every investment market or sector is driven by emotion, which brings up another principle.

Control and use your fear and greed.

It seems counterintuitive, but the best investment results from a price appreciation standpoint come when you are scared to death to make the investment in the first place. This is particularly true when investing in stocks, but it could pertain to any market that has dropped dramatically. Many times, this fear is due to the fact that nobody you know has done or would do what you want to do. Actually, this is a perfect indicator that you are likely on the right track. Now, assuming you have educated yourself prior to buying, *fear is a good thing.* It will keep you humble, and it will make you money. Fear causes you to be very analytical about what you are doing and it *makes you feel lonely,* which is perfect.

You don't want to be investing in things that your uninformed friends are buying. You want to be investing in what the financial elite have done on the sly and which the unobservant public is not aware. If you want to make the big bucks, you'll have to be lonely and fearful by doing so. Climbing that "wall of worry" by owning an asset as prices appreciate, that none of your friends like or understand is the way to go. If you are investing with the rest of the ignorant public, you may feel better, but that probably won't make you much money. You might even lose money. For the most part, you'll want to avoid doing what the rest of the retail investment public is doing. Remember, these are the people to whom the knowledgeable insiders and big money players sell.

If you hear about the next hot investment thing at a cocktail party or from a hair stylist or cabbie, the chances are good that it's not a good time to buy. In that case, look for a way to sell it, not buy it. You'll almost always be on the winning side of the transaction. By now you should know that *you should not follow the masses with investments, as this is a symptom of greed. They are there for selling to, not buying with or buying from.* When they appear to be getting greedy it's time to sell. When they are scared to death, buy from them. This is what the smart money does. Follow the smart money, the big, elite money for investment ideas and strategies. They take the emotion out of their decision making!

Greed will typically lose you money, or at the very least make you give up some of your prior profits. As prices escalate, the temptation is to ride the wave, or even invest in more of the same. This is generally just the opposite of what you should be doing. The best move would be to lighten up as prices go higher. At a minimum, consider taking your initial investment off the table, and ride your profits until the eventual correction displays itself.

Either way, education will help you to control your feelings of fear and greed, and then you can more easily act with confidence. Overcoming your emotions isn't simple. Every human is subject to emotion. But leaving emotions out of the investment equation is absolutely the right thing to do. The more confident you are with the homework that you've done, the easier it will be to control your emotions. Fortunately, you can practice emotional control with just a small investment before you go all in. Let the rest of your cash sit on the sidelines, ready to deploy at the right time. This brings us to yet another investing principle.

Sitting on cash is good, not bad

With today's interest rates at the bottom of the fish tank, most people are desperate to look for higher returns. The problem is that most of the folks who have their "savings" in a bank or insurance company have no business dumping money into something they don't understand to try to achieve a higher return. This could be a retiree who really doesn't understand stocks and bonds who buys something recommended by a trusted advisor. Or it could be a middle class family who wants to do the right thing for that college fund for sonny boy. Examples abound. This has everything to do with your thought process and self-education.

If you buy into the premise that self-education and research are the way to super investment ideas, then *sitting on cash at virtually no interest is smart*. It's just what the money elite do. The reason is that an informed investment decision you later decide to make will far and away make up for some measly 1 or 2 percent interest rate at the bank or insurance company. All they are really providing you is a guaranteed confiscation of your purchasing power. So think of the bank as a convenient parking place for your investible funds while you are doing your homework. The payoff could be outstanding in doing so. For example, let's say you have identified something that you'd like to buy, but the price just isn't right. Sitting on cash at no interest isn't so bad if you're able to buy your idea for much cheaper simply by waiting. You've made money by waiting! It wouldn't even matter if it took a year or two for you to finally buy, because you've gotten a substantial discount by not acting rashly!

Along the same line of thinking, it is also not bad to hold some green cash (currency) outside of the banking system. It's quite likely that when the bank holiday hits (and it will), you will be restricted on how much cash you'll be able to withdraw from the bank at one time. So build up an at home stash of cash for future contingencies. This does not mean that you should hold all of your investible money in green cash. This suggestion is for consumer convenience. Holding enough greenbacks to provide 60 to 90 days of expenses would probably be fine. How much interest do you think this insurance would cost? Virtually nothing, so go for it. By the way, you don't need to broadcast the existence of your stash to your friends. One trusted person, and only one person needs to know in case of some unforeseen circumstance or emergency.

Seek out supreme value.

Don't try to get a fair deal on your investment ideas. Don't try to get a good deal. You need to get a fantastic deal. Since you have spent the time educating yourself, you deserve a sizable return. Remember, a significant part of the return that you will ultimately realize will come from your deeply discounted price under the prevailing market at the time of purchase. Go for it! Let's say you've spent the time and effort analyzing an investment idea, but you just can't find an outstanding value. If that's the case, don't buy! Hold your fire on investing until you are absolutely convinced that you are buying at a deep discount to the true value. If you buy something that is a fair deal, it will be far less liquid when you go to sell it. You may even take a loss in trying to unload it to raise cash for something else. Buying at deep discounts provides superior liquidity, in that it allows you that extra wiggle room in the future sales price to your buyer.

If you have made a fabulous buy, you have a profit from day one if you ever need to sell in a hurry! As a reference point, watch 'American Pickers' or 'Pawn Stars' on History Channel. These people make money by buying substantially under the market, and the only way to do it is to be educated in that market. Please note that this is not to suggest that you dig through barns for antiques, or open your own pawn shop. The point is to use the principles that those people use, and that is to buy into a deep, deep discount. This is not immoral, or unethical, because the seller is a willing participant in the transaction. In fact, time after time on the 'Pawn Stars' show, an expert will tell the seller what the retail value of his item is, and he'll still sell it at a 50% discount, or even more, to the buyers. Remember, many times you just have to walk away from something that catches your eye. Save your money for legalized theft in the form of deep discounting. You'll be glad you did.

Don't buy just because the price has dropped.

It could be a big mistake to let the market do your work for you. Don't fall in to this trap. Investments go up, and yes, investments can go down. *Don't buy into a falling market.* Seek out evidence that your particular pet investment has actually bottomed out and is headed back up with stronger prices. Most of the time you will want to buy into a rising market. If you expect to garner a future profit, don't try to catch a falling knife. Wait until you are convinced the price bottom is in. There is nothing worse than thinking you got a good deal because the price is low, only later to find out that the item is now even lower. This is why a clear understanding of your targeted market and price direction is all important. You can more easily make money by waiting. Not only that, if the market prices are now going up after having been dropping or depressed for a while, you have not necessarily missed your chance. After the initial market surge in price which can accompany a reversal to the upside, there is inevitably a resting period when prices soften again. That's when you should buy. The bottom line here is that *you should never expect to catch 100% of a price move*. If you get 80% of the move, you'll be doing fantastic. So be sure that the price is going in your desired direction, and seek out confirmation of that fact. It is only then that you should plunk down your cash.

Learn to hoard and barter

Readers should not confuse this investment principle with normal consumer purchases. In a super inflationary environment, you have to have a hoarding mindset. This means that you have to kick in the overdrive when you go to the store to buy food and staples. You know what a good price is. Change your spending habits to buy *only* that which is on sale and buy more of those items to boot. If it isn't on sale, don't buy it! But you may say that won't work because you need what you need! Do you need it, or is it more of a want? Taking this hoarding approach to consumer purchases takes time, because you have to build up your inventory. Of course you would act wisely in this regard. If prices for your items have been consistently dropping, then obviously you don't want to hoard them. If you're not a good shopper, you may want to take the time to learn. If you don't, you'll be poorer as time passes for the lack of effort. Not only that, shortages will take your choices away from you. Then, if you really need something you'll have to find a way to pay a potentially hefty price.

Most traditional hoarders do not off-load their stuff. But that's not what we're referring to. You have both buy *and* sell or trade. If some or even all your financial defense is to hoard consumer goods, which may work for certain people, it is best that you find like-minded people with whom to trade. Start a club for this purpose if you need to so you can coordinate who buys what, and then set up a system for trade.

Not too many folks are barter experts, but all currency failures feature a vibrant bartering marketplace. Waiting until a real crisis unfolds is not recommended. As with anything else, education and practice are important. This means that you'll need to start now if you hope to survive by bartering. Consumers with families or modest incomes should embrace this concept. But be aware, as Fernando Aguirre of Argentina makes very clear in his previously referenced book, bartering goods is not that simple. It could be difficult not only to procure items that you need, but also to find the person who will take what you have to trade. There are plenty of websites to visit to get you started, and they can be accessed through Google.com. One place to start is BarterQuest.com.

As good as bartering sounds, it certainly isn't a panacea. You'll need cash and silver for smaller consumables, and possibly gold for the bigger ticket items. People who don't want to bother with trying to barter may be paying with gold or silver for purchases if the masses start running away from dollars as a payment medium.

A recommendation to hoard doesn't bring much comfort. But it will become the right thing to do, and empty store shelves on the most desired products will demonstrate this fact. Everyone would feel compassion for a family that can't get what it needs due to others hoarding those necessary goods. But we have to deal with reality, and that is that hoarding will be viewed as a self-defense mechanism by most of the populace as we get into hyperinflation. So the time to start the process, particularly for those who find it difficult to save a lot for investing, is right now.

Time bank co-ops

Setting up or joining a time bank is also a viable idea. This means that you can establish or join a club or network whereby you trade your particular skill for someone else's. Trading time would be valued by prior agreement of the network members depending on the discipline involved. For instance, a plumber's time would not necessarily be valued the same as an accountant's, so a system of time credits would need to be established with pre-agreement of the members of the network. When hyperinflationary forces reduce most of the middle class to paupers, a time bank will allow you to have some semblance of pricing power for your skill sets. You are only limited by your own creativity and necessity in this regard! And now is the time to solidify your friendship or business relationship with as many professionals as possible: before the crisis hits hard. They may be very valuable to you for services needed that could require something other than traditional payment methods.

Forget the CPI, make your own index!

We know the government fudges the Consumer Price Index beyond credibility. We know that John Williams at shadowstats.com keeps the real numbers. But that does not necessarily have anything to do with your particular lifestyle and its spending habits and its related price increases. In an age of ever increasing consumer prices, you need a way to make sure that you're actually increasing your own individual purchasing power with your invested assets. So, a viable suggestion is to keep your own price index. You may be able to use the American Institute for Economic Research website (check the resource guide) to help you in the effort.

This doesn't have to be hard. And if you aren't comfortable with the math, seek out the help of someone who is. Basically, the suggestion is that of keeping track of either quarterly or annual prices of the things you spend money on. Just make a chart of your own categories of expenses (including taxes) and post the numbers as frequently as you can. This way, *you can actually quantify what and where and how much the price inflation is in your own personal living style.* For instance, if your medical insurance costs $400 per month this policy year, but next year the premium goes to $500 for the same benefits, that's a 20% increase. If you favorite cut of meat is $10 per pound this year, and $13 next year, that's a 30% increase. Keep track of all your daily living expenses in this fashion and you may be surprised at the erosion of the purchasing power of your dollars. You can keep it very simple as illustrated above, or get as sophisticated as you'd like by using weighted averages, accounting for substitutions because your normal purchase has gotten too high priced, etc. You'll also be able to easily identify any prices that have actually dropped, which is possible. Now compare these numbers to both your income and also to the return on your invested assets. It should be pretty clear whether you are getting ahead or falling behind. Then make necessary adjustments.

One area that could be messy is trying to track increases in durable goods. These are things like refrigerators and other stuff that is supposed to last for a while and that you wouldn't buy on a regular basis. The answer for tracking these items is to anticipate what those future purchases will be, and get an early start on your saving, watching and waiting.

Now that we've looked at important principles of investing for hyperinflation, let's get on to how you can actually protect your purchasing power by converting your dollars to other kinds of money. They are called gold and silver.

CHAPTER 13

THE BEDROCK OF YOUR
INFLATION DEFENSE

How to buy gold and silver related investments

Your new portfolio of inflation fighting tangible assets should begin with gold and silver at the foundation. *Gold* is a long term store of value, and is a *must have* for those who have plenty of savings dollars at risk of depreciation. The price of silver tends to be more volatile than gold, since its price is highly manipulated as both an industrial metal and a form of money. Even so, you will find it most helpful as a medium for barter with outstanding appreciation potential. Simply stated though, the two precious metals are not so much investments as they are *money*. If you are not convinced that something is very wrong with our fiat money system, just look at what the big money is doing. Big money is hoarding gold and silver. Let's review some basics before getting into various ways to participate in the dollar price appreciation in the precious metals markets.

Prices have been "managed" for years: a retrospective

We know that gold and silver prices have been suppressed for more than 45 years, going back to the 1960's. Then, keeping the price of gold at $35 per ounce was a tricky proposition as many central banks inflated their currencies, led by the U.S. Fed. Price management was no problem in the U.S., because there was no market for gold, as holding it by citizens was outlawed in 1933. But the world-wide free market price still had to be controlled. So in 1962, a consortium of 10 nations established the London Gold Pool for that very purpose. It used open market interventions to keep the price of gold stable. If the price went too high, the Gold Pool could sell its gold into the open market, and as the price dropped back down, it would buy it back. That worked until March, 1968 when an international run on gold finally destroyed the Gold Pool. The free market price was to be forever higher than the agreed upon $35 per ounce established by the participating governments under the Bretton Woods agreement (1944). Now the price of gold would be able to seek its free market level while at the same time the U.S. kept its official exchange value to the international community at $35. It was clear that this could not work long term, and it didn't!

Once President Nixon cut off gold exchange rights to the international holders of dollars on August 15, 1971, Keynesian economists claimed that gold would fall by the wayside and fade out of favor as a monetary instrument. They just knew the price would then drop well below the long established $35 dollar benchmark. After all, the U.S. dollar was still king of the hill as the world's reserve currency. The Keynesian pundits were wrong, as the price of gold then began to rise in the free market. Meanwhile, Nixon led the charge with 'The Smithsonian Agreement' in December, 1971. This obligated participating countries to maintain fixed currency exchange rates, without gold as a policeman of value measurement. By March of 1973, the gold price had escalated to over $200 per ounce, and the Smithsonian Agreement fell apart. Pure fiat money was now the way for the entire world, leading to the most profligate un-backed money printing the world had ever seen.

When the U.S. bankers and politicians lost control of consumer prices in the late 1970's, the next trick was to contain the inflation by dramatically raising interest rates. Gold topped out at $875 per ounce, and then proceeded to go into a 20 year slumber, finally bottoming our at about $250 per ounce in 1999.

Readers may recall the *strong dollar policy* espoused during the Clinton Administration. During this time, the U.S. economy appeared to be pretty strong, with plenty of job growth, and a balanced budget that became balanced as only Washington DC could conjure. For now we'll ignore all the lost jobs to Mexico due to NAFTA and all of the unfunded liabilities. The emphasis on the Dollar Index was the favored ruse to deceive the public. Amid continued money printing, the index did not drop. We've already been through the explanation of that phenomenon. If all the countries measured against the index printed money, and gold was seen to be stable, the index would look good, right? The fact was that there was a coordinated effort by western central banks not only to print money but also to *lease* out their gold. Robert Rubin, the Secretary of the Treasury at the time, and former head of Goldman Sachs, sacked the U.S. gold stash by leasing it out. Do you wonder why Ron Paul has been stonewalled all the way in his effort to get our supposed gold stash at Fort Knox audited and assayed?

When gold is leased into the market place (to bullion banks such as JP Morgan, Barclays, HSBC, etc.) for a pittance, the lessees certainly have no reason to hold it for appreciation, so they sell it with the intent of buying it back later to return it to the leasers. That way they can use the proceeds to invest in more profitable ventures. In doing this, of course the dollar would look strong against its only true measure: the measure of the gold price. When all these tons of gold got sold into the marketplace, particularly on low volume days, the price drops were dramatic, and this price action had a tendency to put a damper on the enthusiasm of other would-be buyers.

By the end of the 1990's the central bankers were becoming a bit concerned. Their efforts in gold leasing had to come to an end. After all, its supply was limited and the leasers were reaching those limits. Anyone who wants to check out the facts regarding the gold leasing scheme of the 1990's can go to www.gata.org/node/4279 for the documentation, and even quotes by the bankers. Of course it was very hush-hush at the time, but the facts have since come out. Given the limited supply of gold availability, a new strategy had to be devised to contain its price.

'*The Washington Agreement*' (officially named the Central Bank Gold Agreement) came at the annual meeting of the International Monetary Fund (IMF) on September 26, 1999, and actually it was perfectly timed to its cover story. Fed Chairman Alan Greenspan was in attendance. This was during the same time frame that Britain's Gordon Brown (Chancellor of the Exchequer then, not Prime Minister) announced to the world in advance his intention to sell 58% of Britain's gold stash. Who in their right mind would make such an announcement in the face of 25 year lows in the price of gold? Most countries which would have intended to sell their gold would do so with stealth and even sell in baby steps so as to get the best prices on the sale, right? Do you think Brown *wanted* lower gold prices? Yes!

The Agreement called for central banks to sell a combined total of *only* 400 tons per year for the five years ending on September 2004. It was subsequently renewed for another 5 years into 2009 at the same 400 tons per year. Participants to the agreement were the European Central Bank, the U.S. Fed, the Bank of England, and the Swiss Central Bank. So, on the surface, it looked to the rest of the world that gold was a "sell" because so much supply was coming into the market. It was actually just the opposite, as that was when gold entered its bull market after 20 years of price stagnation. But how could this possibly be in the face of so much supply coming into the market? Because the new supply never came into the market!

The Washington Agreement was a coordinated effort to deal with the previously leased gold, to the tune of at least 4000 tons! The lessees would have driven the price of gold skyward if they had to go into the marketplace to buy the gold to return it to the central banks from whence it came in the 1990's! So instead of the central banks demanding the return of their leased gold, they allowed the lessees to buy it. No gold had to change hands. No gold had to be bought back from the market. It was actually a seamless way to continue the price suppression. What was supposed to look like a very negative event for gold prices actually had just the opposite effect. Proof is in the fact that the gold price escalated for 11 straight years and counting after the deal was struck, to the disappointment of the western central banks involved.

Finally, one has to look at one simple statement from the Washington Agreement, which emphasizes the real point: *"Gold will remain an important element of global monetary reserves."* And why would that be? Because gold is money--real money!

More recently, the prices of both gold and silver have been proven to be controlled by several big money center banks both on the U.S. COMEX (Chicago Mercantile Exchange) and the London Metals Exchange (LME). These organizations work in concert with the U.S. government and the U.S. Treasury Department's Exchange Stabilization Fund, yet the world-wide demand is such that the price keeps rising. That's because the western debtor countries keep printing more money while eastern central banks continue to buy gold. It's very simply a struggle for economic supremacy, and it is happening right now.

If you aren't convinced, just delve into the proof positive at the Gata. org website, as noted above. Further, you can check the archives of King World News and the interviews of one Andrew McGuire, a London trader at the scene. A whole book could be written on the subject, but that's not our purpose here. At this point however, it's not so much that the western central banks and governments want to drive down the price of the precious metals; it is actually more an effort to contain the upside moves to a slow rise instead of an exponential liftoff. It's a fight between fiat money and commodity money. Commodity money has always won these battles, and it will do so this time too. The explosive price movement higher will happen to the extent that the money creation continues, which it must.

Gold as money

In an interview published by Bloomberg on August 23, 2011, former Fed Chairman Alan Greenspan was asked to comment on gold, since it had just hit the $1900 per ounce milestone. His answer was reminiscent of the Greenspan of the 1960's. Not only did he state that he didn't think gold was in a bubble, he also said:

"Gold, unlike other commodities, is a currency...And the major thrust in the demand for gold is not for jewelry. It's not for anything other than an escape from what is perceived to be a fiat money system, paper money that seems to be deteriorating."

The Maestro has spoken!

Greenspan had always been a member of the intellectual sphere and beliefs of Ayn Rand. Rand was a Russian objectivist who applied her thoughts to both economics and politics. In fact, Greenspan wrote an essay in Rand's 1967 book 'Capitalism, the Unknown Ideal'. Greenspan's essay, entitled 'Gold and Economic Freedom,' argued for a gold standard and against the follies of the elastic fiat reserves created by a central banking system. Indeed, in explaining the Federal Reserve monetary policy of the late 1920's Greenspan stated:

"The excess credit which the Fed pumped into the economy spilled over into the stock market – triggering a fantastic speculative boom."

Do you really believe that Greenspan didn't know he was creating bubbles in the financial markets with his easy money throughout the late 1990's and early 2000's? Here's another quote from that same essay:

"In the absence of the gold standard, there is no way to protect savings from confiscation through inflation...Deficit spending is simply a scheme for the confiscation of wealth. Gold stands in the way of this insidious process."

The sainted Mr. Greenspan's statement could not be more instructive and succinct.

Given the above, one can only conclude that we had witnessed the sellout of the "The Maestro" to the politicians. How sad that a man with such a voice before Congress for so many years could not use that voice for the benefit of the ordinary citizen; instead he favored the bankers and politicians to maintain his power and ego. He inflated the system for 18 years. Yet another key Greenspan quote on gold came in a House Banking Committee testimony on May 20, 1999:

"…gold still represents the ultimate form of payment in the world. Germany in 1944 could buy materials during the war only with gold. Fiat money in extremis is accepted by nobody. Gold is always accepted."

Our current experience is fiat money in extremis! Revisit the charts on our monetary base for reinforcement!

Had the more recent games of price suppression not been played for the past 20 years, the price of gold would likely have been substantially higher by now. Manipulative forces can temporarily hold back the price levels in virtually any market. But they can't overcome a powerful world bull market in the precious metals; there is just not enough money available to do it. This is particularly true when we now know that both Asian central banks and other big money players are stockpiling it.

Meanwhile, the investing public of the West sleeps, as less than ½ of 1 percent have any exposure to gold in their portfolios! Even though gold has gone from a low of $256 in 1999, it had closed out 2011 at over $1500. It has had positive returns for 11 years running (and counting). In the crisis year of 2008, it was one of the very few asset classes that actually went up once the crisis seemed to be swirling toward financial Armageddon. But again, it isn't that the price of gold has risen, so much as the price of paper money has fallen. Gold is a simple barometer and a store of wealth.

The new gold rush

International attitudes toward gold began to change toward aggressive accumulation in 2010. The GFMS (formerly Gold Fields Mineral Services) reports that 77 tons of gold were purchased by central banks in 2010. And the number for 2011 came in at an astounding 430 tons! This was the highest amount purchased since 1964! Why are they buyers now? They'd like to preserve their wealth as well as to participate in the guaranteed price appreciation as the world catches on to the outrageous money printing and drives the price much higher. And more importantly, they'll need it for a newer, more stable currency regime which will somehow be hinged to physical gold after western central bank fiat currencies collapse. After all, with the broken promises and degradation in value of a fiat money regime, how could it be replaced with another fiat regime? It won't! Which central banks are doing most of the buying? Think Russia and China as the biggest players, along with *many* others to a lesser degree. The biggest buyers are those which have vast money and natural resource stockpiles and fast growing economies. This is the smart money. Watch what they do, and act accordingly!

Further, when politics over nuclear weapons heated up with Iran in January of 2012, the European Union banned all gold and silver trade with Iran. It was reported earlier by the Financial Times that Iran had been adding to their gold reserves in 2011, with a total war chest of 168 tons. Now why do you think both sides would take the actions they did? Very simply, because *gold and silver are real money* and the U.S. and its allies wanted to wage financial war with Iran. Speaking of Iran, you should also note that on January 23, 2012 India announced that it would begin to pay Iran *in gold* for some of its oil! India is Iran's second biggest oil customer after China. This is extremely ominous for the dollar, and hugely bullish for gold.

There are a few other very simple indications here and now to consider as a final sales pitch for ownership of the two precious metals, and their use as money. With a negative real return (after inflation) on government bonds, the financial elite may as well keep their wealth in gold, and that is exactly what they are doing. In fact, U.S. government bonds are a losing proposition. With 10 year yields under 1.6%, and with government reported inflation (CPI) around 2 to 3 percent, holding bonds looks like a losing proposition to the smartest investors in the world. Smart money wants to preserve the purchasing power of its wealth, and in a hyper-inflationary financial environment, this becomes critical. Therefore, it is logical and savvy to *park wealth in gold and other tangible assets* before fiat money depreciates even further!

Additionally, China has encouraged its citizens to buy gold and silver for their savings needs, and the biggest national population in the world has taken heed. These people are not forced into the purchase, but they have found the rationale in doing so. Also, China is a huge force in metals mining, and they have disallowed the mines to sell to foreigners. All the gold and silver mined in China is to stay in China, and much of it is purchased by the Chinese government. There is a very good reason for China's actions. The Chinese are most distressed by the U.S. dollar money creation and the depreciation of their U.S. dollar holdings in the form of Treasuries. So they have been busy taking every step to position the Yuan for international acceptance. If the Yuan is backed by gold, the Chinese will dominate the 21st century.

Finally, in India gold has been used as a store of wealth for generations. The huge population of citizens love gold, and as India becomes more of a force in the world as one of the top growth economies, the middle class there continues to burgeon. Indians don't save paper money, they save gold. The dowries consist of gold when the women get married!

As the dollar gets rejected on a mass scale throughout the world, the most natural home for that money will be precious metals and other U.S. based tangible assets. And prices will absolutely skyrocket. Hello hyperinflation. Intelligent U.S. citizens should *follow the big money into gold and silver.* Your financial survival depends on it!

There is a vast array of investment products and approaches you can use in the precious metals complex, and we'll review some of them here. Precious metals prices can be very volatile, so the one basic premise that can tack on many percentage points to your overall return is to buy right. That means wait for price corrections or retracements. These soft patches appear often as the schemers do their work, so look for them and take advantage. And when selling, do not panic into dumping into price weakness. This is when the pros pick the pockets of the weaklings. You simply must sell into increasing prices. The best suggestion for looking into the most advantageous times to buy and sell is to look at the charts of the Exchange Traded Funds (ETF's), as we'll review in the chapter on stocks. Don't buy or sell blindly. Look at a picture of where you are in the price cycle and act accordingly.

The best way to participate – get physical

First and foremost, you must *buy the physical metal and keep at least some of it in your possession.* If your wealth precludes you from being comfortable with self-storage, there are a couple of other alternatives to storage listed below. But for the majority of the middle class, you want to be able to access the physical metal at a moment's notice. You need to possess it! This means that you should *not* solely rely on a paper certificate that says you own some amount of a precious metal designated just for you in a vault somewhere. Another critical rule is that you *do not buy precious metals with borrowed money.* The price action is just too volatile sometimes, and you don't want to be forced out of your position if your loan is called in or you have to post more collateral for a margin account. So using leverage is a big no-no. But you say, I don't have any savings but I have home equity, so wouldn't that be OK? No it wouldn't. As you'll discover later, borrowing money for certain investment activities is a good idea, but not with gold or silver, period. Thirdly, you should consider instituting a regular buying program of both gold and silver. Don't just plunk down all your savings at once and forget it. You need to *buy regularly on price dips, and hold on for the longer term*. A quick glance at a price chart will show you that you'll have plenty of time to buy when the prices of precious metals are soft. Physical gold and silver are not for trading regularly. Forget that. Just establish a regimen of regular purchases that won't cause you to lose any sleep. The time to sell will be years away.

Where can you buy? *Go to coin shows for smaller amounts*, which happen often, and everywhere. Just use Google.com to investigate where the shows are nearest to your location. Unless you are in an extremely rural area, you should be able to find multiple shows per year close to home. In this type of venue, anonymity is a plus. And coin shows generally have the most favorable prices, mostly because you are dealing with many Mom and Pop operations as well as wholesalers. This means purchases are very negotiable. They become even more compelling if you are dealing with green cash on hand. Sometimes personal checks won't work, but many times debit or credit cards will. But cash is usually king in these venues. Just see what you can negotiate, and don't be timid. You can be assured of finding a deal to your liking if you spend the time going from booth to booth. Even though going in toward the end of the show might offer lesser inventory, prices are softer then. This is particularly true if the dealer has excess inventory and needs to put his sales over the top for that weekend. However, if you are buying silver, you'd better go early, as there is an acute shortage.

You can also *go to your local coins shops*, but their prices may not be as compelling. After all, they have overhead to pay, and many can't offer the best pricing. Overall, person to person buying would be best for most folks. That way, you pay your money and you get your product. Finally, try to develop relationships with a few dealers. In the short run it may not help, but in the long run it will work in your favor for preferred pricing on both the buy and sell side.

Many folks may be tempted to buy their gold from TV shopping shows. Forget it! It's not that they are not reputable it's just that most of the premiums are through the roof. The hawkers make it sound so good and that you only have 3 ½ minutes left to act, but don't be tempted. Even their purported sale of a lifetime is way too high priced. After all, they have to pay for the air time! Go to coin shows for the best pricing.

By the way, *never* pay more than a 5% premium for your gold purchase or silver purchase. Generally lower premiums are common at coin shows, or even flea markets if you can find the volume you are looking for. In fact, many times you can actually buy *under the spot price* at coins shows! Spot price refers to the price here and now, with no premium for time purchases or profit margins. It is the price quoted in the newspaper and on internet web sites, so be sure to check before you buy. Even though you could get fabulous bargains at flea markets, they are typically not the venues for sizable purchases.

For larger purchase amounts, you can buy from trusted dealers which you can find on-line and then order by telephone. Some reputable ones include Kitco, International Precious Metals, and Blanchard, but there are many more, many of which advertise on Fox News Channel. However, ordering on-line may not be the best method for some people. You may want to deal with a live person and the telephone offers advantages, including better confidentiality and security than does the internet. There are many reputable nationwide dealers who have stood the test of time. In buying from the big time dealers, the best approach is to call several of them in succession right before you buy. Believe it or not, many offer specials with lower premiums or other incentives, so you just have to shop around.

This is critical: *do not pay an added premium for graded and certified modern bullion coins*, such as silver or gold Eagles produced by the U.S. government. The certification and near perfect condition of U.S. Eagles for example have a tremendous amount of "air" between the actual spot price of the metal and the price these dealers want to charge. Yes, these coins have appreciated more than the metal, but only because of promotion, not because of value. You want value. This doesn't mean that you shouldn't buy U.S. gold or silver Eagles. It just means that you should not pay more for their purported rarity or exceptional condition. For most people, you simply want to buy the metal, and that's all you should pay for. Again, do not be suckered into paying more for the MS69 or MS 70 grading and the supposed rarity of these coins. They are not rare! Do not treat these purchases as collectibles; rather treat them as money.

Also, you may want to search out and ask for your own references when dealing with anyone new over the phone. But don't expect the dealers to give you references from their other customers. Think about it; would you want your name given to someone who has purchased from that company? That will not likely happen. Instead, you'll need to find someone you know or a trustworthy dealer at a show to give you some guidance or help as to where to buy. This is important because there will definitely be a waiting period between the time you remit your payment and actually receiving your purchase. This may make some people uncomfortable, which is why you may want some assurances or hand-holding if it is your first time to purchase. But if you stick to the national names that have been around for years, you should be fine. Also, please note that most dealers will lock in your price when you make the verbal commitment to buy, and then give you a certain amount of time to remit payment before they pull the offer. This way you can easily buy on price weakness without having to worry about any time lags.

What are some of the choices in buying gold bullion coins? You may prefer coins such as 1 ounce U.S. Gold Eagles, U.S. Buffalos, Canadian Maple Leafs, South African Krugerrands, or even Austrian Philharmonics. Krugerrands offer the lowest premiums over the spot price, but are somewhat ugly. The other ones mentioned above are prettier. Even smaller gold bars would be OK, but you'll need to make sure they are certified and numbered. For most folks, smaller denominations in your gold holdings would be best because they would be easier to sell quickly or use for barter if you need to do so. You may not find too many buyers to take a kilo bar off your hands if you need some paper money or want to use bullion for barter! Plus, you need to be aware that there have been numerous discoveries of tungsten filled gold bars recently. Crooks use tungsten because it is the same weight as gold. So if you are wealthy and want to buy in the bigger sized bars, see a couple of the suggestions below. If you are a neophyte at a coin show buying and want a bit of comfort, take a magnet with you to the show. Gold is non-ferrous, and will not be attracted to a magnet. Nor will silver. But note that there is no evidence to date of counterfeit or tungsten filled U.S. Eagles, or any other of the smaller weighted forms. Just as in counterfeit money, the crooks appear more likely to go after the big kill, not the little pilfering.

For those with a bit less wealth to store, physical silver is best, although much more volatile in price. For future bartering as well as price appreciation possibilities, *pre-1965 U.S. circulated half dollars, quarters and dimes* - sometimes referred to in the industry as *junk silver* - is the way to go. Each of these coins is 90% silver by weight. Also, the Kennedy half dollars contained 40% silver until 1970 and are another way to hold silver for barter. U.S. Silver Eagles are also OK because they are so recognizable and negotiable, but they usually come with a much higher premium than do the circulated coins, which you can often find at the spot price or even less. These silver holdings will allow you to use them for trade and barter when the paper currency fails or becomes worth much less in buying the goods and services you need. They are quite recognizable to anyone who used to use them as money! Just wait and watch as you'll be able to negotiate good discounts using silver instead of paper money in the future. Now that nations have begun to announce barter of oil for food, or gold for oil, or crops for silver, you can be sure that the notion will spread to the masses. The best time to get prepared for such an eventuality is while the prices for the metals are relatively low. The one drawback to a large position of silver in any physical form is its weight compared to its value. As an example, at say $36 per ounce, it would take about 174 pounds of the stuff to have a value of $100,000. This can become unwieldy, for sure. But, that same $100,000 could be in the form of only about 3 ½ pounds of gold at $1700 per ounce. That's more like it!

Storage considerations

An important aspect of holding physical precious metals is storage. *Do not* use a bank safety deposit box. There are just too many issues with doing so. Aside from the fact that they are not instantly accessible, the Patriot Act would allow the Department of Homeland Security (DHS) to inspect contents of any safety deposit box without a warrant or provocation. Not that that's necessarily offensive to most people, it's just the confidentiality and hassle factor. Further, if you have a judgment against you, the contents of your box could be seized. Finally, in the event of a bank holiday, you'd not have access. There are a couple of links on this subject in the resource guide.

You'll need to be creative on where and how to store your valuables, including precious metals. So here are a couple of guidelines. First, tell *one person* and one person only where your gold and silver are stored. It's pretty obvious that the one person would be a close and trusted friend or family member. Because you may be having your wealth stored close at hand, you don't want the word to spread that you are doing so. In fact, you should not even tell anyone you have even made any precious metals purchases. An innocent or off-hand comment to a friend or family member could lead to an off-hand comment by them to another. Then that person mentions it later to someone else, and eventually the rumor could easily float into the wrong ears. So be excruciatingly private about your gold and silver holdings.

Also, the more of your precious metals assets that are held by you personally, the more you should split them up. Find multiple hiding places. That way, if you do get ripped off, the damage will be minimized. Large fire-proof safes that bolt down from the inside of the safe to a concrete floor are a great idea. If the safe can be hidden, that's even better. And a decoy safe that would be easier to find by a thief with a few things in it is a good ploy. You can even bury the metals in a moisture proof container somewhere in the garden or yard. But watch out for nosy neighbors when doing so! Since metal detectors could theoretically be used to locate your stash, bury old metal cans, pipes, or other junk around your hiding place too, so if someone digs, they'll find the cans, before they'll even consider digging deeper for the real thing! Another idea is to hide your stash in plain sight. You can be creative in doing so. Maybe you use a can in the pantry, or hide coins in a metal lamp, etc. You are only limited by your creativity here, so give it some thought and go for it. Just remember to use plenty of "decoys" to frustrate those with metal detectors.

But that's not all...

For many, holding physical metals nearby may not be practical or desirable. The wealthy will become bigger and bigger targets as the crisis unfolds, so they may seek out better ways to hold their wealth with precious metals. There are just a few suggestions worthy of merit. The first and foremost is *Perth Mint certificates for both gold and silver.* Check out perthmint.com. au. The mint also has a platinum storage program for those of you who want more diversification. The Perth Mint is in Australia, and is owned by the state of Western Australia. This method of storage of your very own gold has been tested and audited in many ways. It has stood up to the utmost scrutiny, and it is acceptable for those with more than run of the mill wealth. Investigate it, and have your most trusted advisors double check your work. This is the real thing, and it is worthy of your study and consideration.

Another way to store gold and even hold it outside of the U.S. is to do so in electronic transactions. James Turk runs *Goldmoney.com* and he and his company are top notch. With this service, you will actually own your own gold; numbered, certified and titled to you. Turk has stood up to the utmost scrutiny and his system works well. For Goldmoney.com, you would wire money into your account, and then at your discretion you can buy and sell gold on-line. It's your money, and it's your gold that is stored in the Goldmoney.com vaults in any of several politically friendly international locations. Readers should know that there is a small fee for the service. After all, you do get the benefits of their storage and security services. Check out Goldmoney.com more closely and see if it suits you.

The third recommendation for storage of your gold or silver position is *SilverSaver.com*. For those of you who like silver's investment potential, this may the way to go for larger purchases. The company offers convenience, security, good pricing, and flexibility. The storage facility is in Maryland at one of the largest *non-bank* facilities in the United States. The non-bank feature is certainly attractive! You would have all the convenience of online banking, with no transaction fees for U.S. investors. Plus, you can set up regular *dollar cost averaging* plans to smooth out the price volatility of your various purchases. Go to the website for an education!

Other considerations

Do not buy into a "pooled" account. This is a situation where your precious metal is co-mingled with other peoples' supposed holdings. This type of situation does not offer much comfort to those who understand how many of the operators of these accounts work. Think of these as goldsmiths of old. Don't get into a fractional reserve gold or silver program unwittingly. There are likely reputable facilities out there for such investing, but you don't need the worry. In a pooled account, you are simply a creditor with un-allocated metals, a fact that should not give you comfort.

One thing you must know is that there are a few *exchange traded funds (ETF's)* that have become very popular in recent years, which include those with the trading symbols SLV and GLD. The gold and silver for these funds are held by JP Morgan and Barclay's. The hype on these two investments is that each share is backed by 1/10th ounce of gold or silver, and that you could cash in your shares (there are minimums for this privilege) for the metal. If all of the metal were actually on hand, the funds would not be selling at a discount to the actual price of the metal. Investors should be aware of this fact. You may decide that you'd just want to use them to catch a move in the price of the underlying metal, but it is not recommend. At some point in time, if various factors preclude them from delivering on the promises in the prospectus, the whole structure could tumble in efficacy and price. There are just too many shenanigans that could be going on behind the scenes that are allowable by the prospectus. This could include short sales of the underlying metal or the shares, or even fractional ownership. No offense to JPMorgan or Barclays (custodians of the metals), but we are talking about owning physical metal here. Owning

GLD and SLV is not holding the physical product, period. Avoid these as long term investments. If you want to speculate on price swings, fine; buy and sell at will. Just know that you may not be able to count on them for owning and holding the requisite silver or gold for redemptions of all of the shares outstanding, which means that you may not end up with it in your possession if you wanted to cash in your shares for the metal in a time of crisis. And the share price could drop below the physical metal price if the custodial inventory is lacking!

A set of ETF's that appear to be the real deal and that actually would redeem your shares in physical silver is *PSLV*, and for gold, *PHYS*. These are run by the respectable billionaire Eric Sprott and are newer than the others mentioned above. Sprott made a big splash in the investment circles by going directly to the silver miners to buy his metal, as he was precluded from doing so on the COMEX. By early 2012, he added millions more ounces to his portfolio in order to issue more shares. However, and it's a big however; because he actually does have all the metal he says he has, his ETF's generally sell at a premium to the spot price of the physical metal, as opposed to a discount for the GLD or SLV mentioned above. This reflects the fact that when one wants to redeem shares for the physical product in hand, premiums have to be paid.

Never pay too high a premium for the Sprott ETF's. This means that you have to check your price charts and the premiums built into the prices of the shares prior to buying. And again, just because you read about PSLV and PHYS in a book doesn't mean they are right for you. You'll want to review the technicalities of the investment before you dive in. By the way, for those readers who don't know, premiums on this type of investment vary on a daily basis. This means that you could have a big move in either direction in the price of physical metal, but that same percentage move may not be reflected in that day's ETF price action. This gives you a chance to pick off the shares at a discount to recently experienced higher premiums. You just have to wait and watch.

A critical rule: be an investor, not a trader

Consider holding the physical metal as a different form of money. Again, *you should not trade in and out of the market with your physical metals*. Buy and hold for much higher prices as the dollar and other fiat currencies self-destruct. Do not be scared out due to the volatility. That's just what the price manipulators need and want you to do. Establish a regular accumulation program, and then sit. Just know that because the price managers have consistently driven the short term prices down for years, there will regularly be plenty of opportunities to buy right. The bottom line is that the precious metals will continue to go up in price on a long term basis as long as the money presses continue to crank out their paper. When the extensive bull market in gold finally ends, the downside risk at that time will likely be limited. By then, most central banks and gold accumulators will not be in the mood to unload their real money in favor of more paper money that is un-backed. And if it is backed, that affords another reason for price stability in the precious metal at substantially higher prices.

Another way to participate in the bull market in precious metals...

In the 1930's *gold and silver mining stocks* were up on average about 1500%. The same phenomenon occurred in the late 1970's, as the price of precious metals soared. In today's crisis, many gold and silver stocks soared upwards of 1000% after the stock market bloodletting of 2008 and 2009. But many of them remained depressed for any number of temporary factors, while others have corrected a huge portion of their previous move up, and were as undervalued in 2012 as they have been for this entire gold bull market cycle. They are undervalued because the stock prices have not moved nearly as much in percentage terms as the physical metals have, and many of the miners are raking in an absolute fortune which has not been priced in to the stock. Not only that, the big producers, the junior producers, and the explorers have money in the bank in the form of gold reserves still in the ground!

Let's delve into the rationale for investing in this sector of the stock market for a minute. If it takes a miner say, $600 per ounce to get the gold out of the ground, process it, and take it to market when the price of gold is say $1200 per ounce, that miner's profit margin is 100%. But if gold goes to say $1800, then the miner shows a much higher profit margin, because his costs certainly don't double. Yes, they may go up due to the rising cost of fuel and labor and other factors, but they sure wouldn't double. The miners don't have to do anything different other than to re-price their product to the current market! But if the stock price hasn't budged due to the increase in profit margin, the stock becomes substantially undervalued. This is where the sector was in the summer of 2012. A large majority of these companies had become grossly undervalued. And further, many of the company stock prices became super low due to naked (illegal) short selling by the big money interests. It goes hand in hand with the price suppression of the metal prices. The same goes for many of the stocks. But that should not deter you, because when these companies start to move to the upside, the appreciation is breathtaking. Investors should be heartened by the fact that the more these companies discover new reserves in the ground, and the higher gold and silver prices are, the more "money in the bank" the miners have!

So, one way to get potentially super leverage to further escalation in the price of gold is to make investments in the miners. You could go with the mature producers, some of which are increasing dividends substantially as their profits soar. Many of these major producers are actually running out of easily accessible gold in the ground, so they need to increase their reserves. They could explore for them, which would take a lot of money and time, or they could buy them. Buying the reserves is an attractive alternative, and this is where the *junior producers and explorers* come into play. They have become and will continue to be *takeover targets* for years to come. Your job is to seek them out and invest in them. You could begin your search for the gems on websites such as Kitco.com, which has regular contributed commentaries on this very subject, including all of the facts and figures. Another website to check would be gold-eagle.com.

Mining is not a simple business. From discovery of a new gold find to actually pulling that gold out of the ground could take upwards of ten years. There are so many risks involved that the barrier to entry into the business is a very tough road. Not only that, as the gold price rises along with the profits of the miners, the risk of some countries taking over (nationalizing) the mines becomes a real concern. Just know that the miners have plenty of risk, which has proven to be compensated in the form of huge stock price escalations.

Another idea for your consideration would be investing in the stock of *gold and silver royalty companies.* These companies don't need to bother with the mining hassles. All they do is to cut deals with the miners to buy the end product before it is ever mined. They collect profits without all the risks of doing the digging. They are like gold and silver mining gatekeepers, and they can reap fabulous profits when they make the right deals as the metals prices escalate. Investors should definitely check out some of the business plans of royalty companies and evaluate them for investment, such as Silver Wheaton (SLW), Franco-Nevada (FNV), and Tanzanian Royalty Exploration (TRX). It just happens that TRX is run by "Mr. Gold" himself, Jim Sinclair; but that doesn't mean this is the investment for you. Nor is this to suggest that you invest in any of these names because you read it in a book. Do your homework. Check business plans, profit pictures, and the price charts before you make any decisions. The point here is that royalty companies should be investigated as yet another way to participate in rising precious metals prices.

By the way, it's OK and in fact desirable to trade in and out of at least some portion of your mining stocks to lock in profits and to have ammo for lower prices later. This is actually just the opposite of the advice for not trading the physical metals. But nonetheless, it's a good practice. Check the next chapter for advice on technical and fundamental analysis on buying and selling stocks, including the miners.

Numismatics

Simply, numismatics deals with the study and collection of rare coins, paper money and the like. Many people collect rare gold and silver U.S. and world coins. For 99% (or more) of the populace, this would not be a top recommendation. The novice would be a very easy target, and could easily lose money. The reason is that there is just too much wiggle room (or air, if you will) in rare coin pricing and the novice would do all of the wiggling. The price disparities between even the smallest differences in the grading could be huge. Even though it's fun to find a rare coin at a flea market for a song, it's just not as easy and exotic as it sounds. For those of you with more dollars than sense and want to give it a try, the best way to start is to pick a tiny sliver of the coin market in which you can become super knowledgeable. We've already covered this technique. Plus, you have to decide whether to be a trader or a collector. Traders seek income, while collectors don't.

If you do decide to delve into the rare coin market as a novice, start by buying just a few certified and graded coins by ONLY either Professional Coin Grading Service (*PCGS*) or Numismatic Guarantee Corporation (*NGC*). Buy only the best grades you can afford, most of which should be *uncirculated*. Get an eye piece magnifier so you can see the minute scratches and imperfections on the surface of the certified coins you buy. And buy a guide book to grading so you clearly understand why your coins are graded as they are. Google.com can help with your efforts. After you do this, you are then ready to go to shows to look for *ungraded* coins that could be grossly undervalued. Is it easy? No. Is it the road to riches? Not necessarily. But it can be fun and profitable if you exercise discipline after getting educated on your particular segment of interest in that huge market.

Your future is not in futures

Do not try to make a killing in the futures market for any commodity, particularly gold and silver. This is the venue for sharks and price managers, and they'll eat your money for lunch every time. No novice has ever made consistent profits out of the futures pit. Novices are for fleecing by the masters, who have more money, more computing power, and more knowledge of order flows than you ever could hope for. The margin requirements can change at anytime, forcing you to the exit doors, likely with big losses. Not only that, if you are a big buyer who wants to lock in a price for a gold or silver purchase in the near future, it does not mean that you will get delivery when the time comes. Even if you stand for delivery with all of the necessary funding, the exchange may offer you a premium in order to dissuade you from taking actual delivery of the physical metal, as they are far short in supply compared to their paper commitments. Sure, you may end up with a few more dollars in your pocket, but don't count on getting the physical metal. And finally, if you want the biggest reason for avoiding this market, check behind the scenes of the MF Global disaster, and you'll see how your money can be legally hypothecated or re-hypothecated away (put up as collateral for someone else's bet), never to be seen again. There is a reason that the customer money held by MF Global disappeared without any management prosecutions, and that reason is re-hypothecation. You need to have the physical metal in your possession, and the futures market will not guarantee you this result.

CHAPTER 14

BUYING OTHER TANGIBLE ASSETS

Here are more ways to defeat hyperinflation

In a period of hyperinflation, tangible assets hold their purchasing power much better than paper money or paper investments. The best time to accumulate any tangible asset class is before the masses get interested. Remember, these are the folks to whom you'll eventually sell. What is a tangible asset? It is something that is physical that you can see, feel, and touch; but we're not talking about a stock or bond certificate. We're talking about an actual object of some sort. Yes, it could be a factory, land, art, gemstones, commodities, rental real estate, or collectibles such antique guns, pocket watches, old toys, and hundreds of other items. Some tangible assets are easy to sell, while others are not. Some tangible assets produce an income stream and capital gains, while others are held simply for their appreciation potential.

If you are a working person with little or no disposable income after you pay the monthly bills, then a tangible asset could be as simple as stocking up on staples at discount prices when you can. After all, even toilet paper on sale could represent a great buy on a tangible asset!

For investors, part of your portfolio should be dedicated to those tangible assets which are easy to sell, meaning that they are liquid. Other tangible assets could be used for holding longer term for a capital gain or income production. In terms of collectibles, you could buy and sell old bicycles, rare books, or old glass table pieces, it really doesn't matter. But the area of your interest needs to be something that somebody else would like to own, and those potential buyers should be easy to find. For purposes of this chapter, we'll discuss a few general suggestions regarding the purchase and sale of collectible tangible assets you purchase with hopes for a gain, before we get to more specific recommendations on assets with income potential.

Be passionate

The best way to profit in collectibles is to *invest in the tangible assets that hold some interest to you*. It could include any type of item that enjoys a thriving market for buying and selling, and that is all important. We are not referring to collecting as a hobby, but rather a profit center arising from your own specific knowledge, curiosity and effort. You only need some creative thinking, spare time, and some investable dollars to get started. The key is to have a deep desire to learn about your subject matter, and to *be passionate about it.* That passion doesn't come just from the desire to learn more, but also to profit in the process. *Passion is the key ingredient to success.* The more you learn the more profits you'll realize. Remember, this is exactly what Warren Buffet does. Of course his company, Berkshire Hathaway, is a stock. But Warren Buffet is the tangible asset buyer behind that stock. He buys tangible businesses. He has proven that there is big money to be made in deriving cash flow and capital gains by buying and selling tangible assets! You can do this too on a smaller scale.

It's about the market, not the product!

For the average citizen, investing in collectibles and other tangible assets requires *a vibrant market for buying and selling,* and this is *critical to your long term success.* Many people go to estate or garage sales and flea markets and absolutely steal items of their choice. No, they don't actually steal them, but since they know far more than the seller about certain items, they can get fabulous bargains. You could be talking about pennies on the dollar here. The seller simply does not know what he has, and that works very much to the advantage of the knowledgeable buyer. The only price you'll pay for your specialized knowledge is an investment in time. Remember, you make your best profits on the buy side, and you realize that profit when you sell. Do not pay too much for any collectible; and know where, how and at what price you could sell it if you wanted to, *before you buy.* This principle bears repeating: *know where you're going to sell the items, and for roughly how much, before you ever buy them.* This is rule number one and it is critical. If you don't have the answers to these questions, don't buy.

So before springing into action, study what you like. Where are these things bought and sold? Are there trade shows, dealer conventions, or regular auctions? Is there a market on the internet? Can you see price histories on your targeted investments? Tracking prices is very important, as this will be the only way for you to measure your success. Make it a fun and profitable enterprise, and become an expert at it. Watch, anticipate, and jump on an undervalued asset. Only you, as your own expert, can be the judge of that item's value. Most importantly, *you must both buy and sell. Do not just buy and hold.* That's what collectors do. For the most part, you won't want you to be a collector, but rather an investor. This is not a hobby suggestion, this is a business proposition.

Top quality pays off

Another tenet to heed is that *you must buy the highest quality* you can afford. That's where the buying and selling activities become all important. The increased value that you realize on a tangible asset investment can then be used to upgrade to a similar item of higher quality. This means that you should always be looking for opportunities to *trade up*. In every collectible market, the highest and best price appreciation occurs on the highest quality items. So try to avoid buying on the low end of the quality scale. If you can't afford the higher quality item now, think twice about jumping on the lower priced one. Instead, look for ways to trade into higher quality. This is critical, and you will be amazed at the profit potential even before we have super-inflationary times.

Another guideline for success is that *you must leave some available profit for the next guy*. This is another reason that it is so critical to buy right. The buying right strategy will work 100% of the time if you do it with discipline. If you know enough, and you see that the buy price isn't right, you can walk away at no cost! This is beautiful. Nobody can twist your arm to make a bad deal. Don't be afraid to throw out lowball offers. If you throw out enough of them, at least a few will score, and you'll be on the profitable side from the first minute. Also don't be afraid to tell the seller you are paying in green cash. This gives some folks added incentive. They might be able to turn that cash over in the same venue, same day for something they want. Getting your collectible for a super low price gives you plenty of wiggle room in setting your price when you want to sell. *The more profit your buyer can make on his eventual sale, the more liquid your item will be!* Think about this. The market is a two way process. You'll want to be on both sides of it, and you don't want to be stuck with stuff you can't sell. Just know that there still has to be "meat on the bone" when you sell it, meaning you have to buy right.

Diversify among markets

One of the biggest forces for price deflation in the world today is the E-Bay web site. Using E-Bay for buying and selling is great. But collectible dealers have to beware. Why do millions of people use it? Because it is so easy to sell stuff, right? Yes! And you can buy at low prices, right? Yes, and that is precisely the problem! Before you decide that your first place to try to sell something is E-Bay, check your particular type of collectible on the site. If in your informed opinion there are screaming good deals on your type of stuff, go ahead and buy! But don't even think you can both *consistently* buy and sell the same type of tangible asset on E-Bay and make big bucks. It will not likely happen on a regular basis. This principle does not just apply to E-Bay. It applies to any venue for buying and selling. If you have a favorite flea market you like to visit, what makes you think you can both buy and sell the same items at a decent profit in the same place? It is most likely that you cannot. The best solution to this issue is to *have multiple outlets for buying and selling*. Remember, *it's about the market, not the product.*

Look for arbitrage opportunities

This means to *look for price disparities in the various market places that interest you.* It means that, in theory, you could buy and sell in a very short time span and make a profit by doing so. This is why it is so critical to understand your market, and where the purchase and sales opportunities are. You have to mix and match your markets in order to profit. Remember, sitting on cash until you find a super price is OK!

Yet another way to profit is to *add value to your product.* If you buy it on the cheap, but would have difficulty selling it at a decent profit, try to improve on it in some way to make it a better value for your buyer. For instance, in collecting rare coins, some people try to buy ungraded and uncertified coins on the cheap, and then get them graded and certified for a profit. If they are smart enough about their target market, this method will work more often than not. Look for ways to add value and you will be guaranteed a profit. Sometimes, something as simple as cleaning your purchase could reap big profits upon sale. But before you start cleaning many types of antiques, you had better be careful! Rubbing off the patina on many items is a good way to destroy its value. So, understand *how you will add that value for resale before you buy!*

Understand the price cycles

Finally, you have to realize that even collectibles have their price cycles. Sometimes the market gets softer than others, affecting price. Research the price cycles, and look for the soft patches. Be ready to buy, but not over-anxious. Conversely, collectible markets get frothy too. Sell into the froth when you get the chance. All markets breathe. You need to buy when your market exhales forcing prices lower, and sell when it inhales the money. This is why it's so important to understand your market, how prices run, and how many buyers actually exist when you decide to cash out. This is where your passion for your pet items comes into play. You have to be an expert. It's all well and good to get a great buy on something, but if you have no way to cash in, you'll be prevented from obtaining what could be a more productive use of those funds. Know your market; know your market; know your market! Then buy and sell.

Think agricultural land and related commodities

World famous investor Jim Rogers thinks commodities are the way to go for the next 15 years or so, and that's hard to dispute. When hyperinflation begins, it will begin in the goods that people need the most. What do people need the most? Food and energy! What does the government leave out of the core inflation calculations? You know the answer: food and energy. We don't believe the phony Consumer Price Index (CPI) numbers, and we know when prices rise. But we also know what a good deal is at the grocery store, discount mart or dollar store. Remember, both consumers and producers will begin to stockpile and hoard when they think they can save money by doing so. And what is the most needed commodity class? Food! And where does the food come from? Farms!

For those readers who can afford to do so, a top suggestion is to invest in farmland that can actually produce. That land should always be purchased for cash. Don't use borrowed money, even if you could get it. Land is illiquid, but could produce a great income stream. Through the crisis, some agricultural land pricing is still depressed in many areas, even in some of the best growing regions of the country. Watch how foreigners come into the country to swoop up prime farmland in the Midwest. Think China in that regard. This is a huge sign of things to come. The big money will not be sitting idle with this farmland, they'll make it produce. And it will produce big profits. The population is growing, crop and livestock needs are growing, the need for pastureland is growing, the need for fertilizer is growing, and the need for water is growing. Do you think there is investment potential in food commodities and other related items? Absolutely, so try to exploit that fact.

It makes sense that most of you wouldn't want the risk or workload of being a farmer. So why not lease your land to someone who is, with a possible share of the production, either in cash or in crops? Search out nearby farmers or the bigger corporate producers. The beauty of having a portfolio including farmland and crops is the possibility of ever increasing cash flow. If food prices go up, so do your revenues, and so does the value of your now productive land. When searching out possibilities, don't forget about *conversions*. That means you might be able to find land that is arable, but not currently productive. Pay for what is, then make it what could be!

Act like a sheik - with oil

When oil prices started a dramatic rise in 2011, President Obama assured the American public that production was up under his watch, which was true. But what he did not say was that all of the increase came from private land, and not government controlled territories, on which the production had actually dropped. Americans need oil, and are stuck paying higher prices because of our supply deficit. So, *invest in oil as a direct partner*. This means that you should *not* buy into pre-packaged partnerships put together by the financial crowd. You should be very skeptical about them, as there are too many things that could work against you. Rather, direct investment is the way to go. If you own land, check for drilling prospects. If you don't, check out land leases for that purpose, or tag on to someone who can do it for you with your backing.

Many cities, counties and states are oil drilling friendly, regardless of the environmental concerns you may have heard on the news. In fact, due to the dire public financial condition many local communities are suffering, there are many cities and towns that already own land that could be used for drilling. Your job is to find those local officials who would work with you for a cut of the royalties. Does this require work, risks, and political hassles? Of course! But if you expect super returns, no-one will simply hand over the cash. You have to assume the role of entrepreneur and get rewarded accordingly. You could even bring in an experienced driller for a cut of the profits after you have done all of the groundwork.

If you like the idea of collecting royalties but don't have the bucks to put up for drilling, put a land package together that meets the local requirements for the proposed drilling site. This could involve getting numerous parcels with different owners together, and you'd be the go-to person and coordinator. Or, if you do get a land package together with all the homework in place for a turnkey site, sell the package to a driller. The beauty of this concept is that you can do it in your spare time.

This suggestion clearly isn't for everyone, but for those with the financial wherewithal and/or time to do so this is an excellent strategy to beat hyperinflation. All the investment principles previously discussed apply. Do your homework to mitigate your risk. When you come up with a solid idea, get your advisors involved.

Finally, there are ETF's that trade on the stock exchanges that are supposed to emulate the price movement of oil. These should not be considered direct investments, but could be used for speculative purposes to catch some profits on the price movement of crude oil. We have seen quite a lot of volatility since 2008, and it could continue. From a high of $147 per barrel before the crisis, to a low in the $30 range, back up to about $110 as the supposed recovery was taking place, then dropping yet again in the $80 range in 2012, there is plenty of price movement with which to speculate on both the buy and sell side. But some ETF's such as *USO* and *OIL* have done less than a stellar job at tracking price movements on a comparable long term percentage basis. Take a look at a 5 year chart and compare it to the price movements of oil to see for yourself. However, over the short term, the percentage moves of the physical product compared to these ETF's is much better. Does this mean that you shouldn't have anything to do with an oil exchange traded fund? Not necessarily. It does mean however, that it may be best to use them for short term speculative purposes only. Before you buy or sell, make sure you do your technical analysis as outlined in the next chapter!

Natural Gas

Not all tangible asset classes would guarantee a profit, particularly if you don't buy right or your timing is off. There has been a tremendous amount of drilling for natural gas in the past few years, and it has been enhanced by the new hydraulic fracturing technology. Readers may want to think twice prior to sinking a bunch of money into new natural gas drilling unless they can find an immediate and guaranteed source for sale of the gas. The U.S. has new discoveries of upwards of a hundred year supply, which has driven wholesale prices to the basement, and many new discoveries are shut in until prices recover. Natural gas will be a great income generator for those who have it, but the question is when. If we expect to become energy dependant in the U.S., natural gas could well be a major part of the equation. If you are interested in natural gas investing, look for new and easy ways for end users to utilize it. When the oil price goes through the roof, natural gas will become a "go to" product. Start doing your homework early to profit in this sector later.

Having stated the above about drilling, it does not mean that you could not speculate in an attempt to catch an upward or downward price movement in the price of natural gas. By 2012, the price was at extreme lows. In the next chapter, we'll look at technical analysis that will help you to time an ETF purchase to catch such a move. For the same reasons stated above regarding oil, an EFT such as *UNG* could be used very cautiously for speculation, but should not be considered as a long term investment.

Rental real estate

We took a quick look at real estate earlier in the context of investment principles, but now let's examine what could be an excellent asset class for investment and cash flow in inflationary times.

Most people realize that the single family housing market has not been good; in fact, it has been disastrous. And you have undoubtedly observed retail stores going out of business right and left. There are vacancies at many strip plazas, and even many shopping malls are hollowed out. Factories have been shuttering due to kinder business environments outside of the U.S., and souring business conditions inside the U.S. Many residential rental properties have dropped in value in depressed areas. Does that mean you should you stay away from real estate investment like most of the public? NO! Remember, when no-one else wants something, that's the best time to buy.

The most important point to make with reference to real estate is that, regardless of the overall market, *each and every property stands on its own merits!* You are not buying the market, you are buying specific properties! Each property can be analyzed for its cash flow and profit potential, regardless of the scads of other similar properties across the city, county, state or country. The top suggestion regarding real estate is to *look for cash flow opportunities*. Many cities have been hit hard by dramatic price drops in single family housing, defaulted mortgages, and vacancies. Even after four years since the onset of the crisis, bank inventory of foreclosed homes or in threat of foreclosure is over 8 million properties. When banks do decide to sell a foreclosed property, many times it is at a fire sale price, further depressing the values of neighboring properties.

People who have been or about to be removed from their home have to live somewhere and most of them have turned to the rental market. What have rental rates done? They have escalated in a big way, making fat profits for those fortunate enough to own those properties! Both the market and the demographics in many areas are on your side, so try to exploit them to your benefit. Remember to *know your market before you buy*. Take the time and make the self-educational effort to wait for the right situation.

In the rental business, you have four sources of making money: cash flow via rents, mortgage amortization, tax benefits, and capital gains. You can easily get a return of 40 to 50 percent or more per year when you add these factors up after having bought right. Get help with the numbers if you have to. Remember, the game is to outpace inflation, not to tread water!

Bank loans have become scarce for most people since many banks still have a lot of toxic waste on their balance sheets. But many smaller banks have kept up their lending, albeit mostly to an upgraded quality of borrower than previously. So go to the smaller banks first for loan possibilities. And the Federal Housing Administration (FHA) is in the business of lending for multi-family projects with non-recourse loans! Non-recourse means that if you default they will simply take the property, and not chase your other assets for repayment. After all, this is the government we're talking about here! So if you can tolerate the bureaucracy, consider the FHA for your multi-unit financing. You can check the hud.gov website to learn all you need to know. Obviously *you'll need to identify your best sources for loans prior to spending too much time looking for something to buy.* For people with good credit, try to get pre-qualified for a certain loan amount, and then you'll know in which markets to look.

If the banks or the FHA aren't viable to you, *look for owner financing!* Remember, sellers are stuck too because of less bank lending, and many are just waiting to sell without actually listing their properties. Many sellers can't or don't want to put money into improving their property, making it that much less attractive! This is *perfect* for the buyer! Finding distressed sale situations accompanied by owner financing presents a major opportunity for buyers with the energy to make enhancements to the target property and to enhance the potential rents! Again, remember to *buy what is, not what could be.* Then, you can upgrade the property to its potential and profit accordingly.

With some rare exceptions, you should not look to become a flip (buy and sell quickly) artist. Rather, *look for properties to buy and hold.* Most areas of the U.S. will not be conducive to quickly turning properties over to new buyers at a substantial profit. Sure, there will be some areas that this could work, but for now, in most areas it won't. So you should be wary of using that strategy. Before the hyperinflation gets pronounced, it would be better to collect rents than to go after quick capital gains. This doesn't mean it can't be done, but your specific market will have to support such a strategy. This doesn't mean that you shouldn't cash in on a gain if you can get it. The point is that your focus for purposes of this suggestion should be on buying right, collecting increasing rents, and selling later when your market can support the effort.

For those with the time, money, and energy look to *conversions* for the potential of a huge profit. This means that you would change the usage from the property's prior use. Maybe it's a house that can become an office. Or maybe it's a retail store that can become a residence, or an industrial property that can become a party center. You get the idea; the possibilities are endless. Conversions can make you a lot of money in both capital gains and a superior cash flow. Clearly, making a conversion work requires extra homework in dealing with zoning, market studies, and prospecting for prospective users concurrent with your search for the right properties.

Finally, if you are well off enough to afford the travel, effort, and professional management, look to *buy real estate in foreign markets*. Again, go where the big wealth is going for investment, or go where you'd like to visit most often, and you may be able to do very well. All the same principles apply to foreign markets as they do in the U.S. But you'll also have to be up on local and national law in your area of interest, so that's where an agent would be very helpful. This is a bit different than the suggestion earlier with regard to becoming your own expert in your U.S. locale. Remember, most major economies of the world are inflating their own brand of currencies and this bodes very well for real estate prices in the high growth areas.

Buy diamonds and other precious gemstones

Many financial pundits and adept investors like diamonds as a superior store of wealth. So, for those of you who already have a good stash of gold and silver, diamonds or other gemstones would be a good way to diversify. But as in many sectors of investing, education and buying right is the key to success. One compelling factor for buying gemstones is that there is no paper market (like with gold or silver futures) which would make it easy for prices to be manipulated. Consequently, the right diamonds have escalated in value consistently for years, *handily outpacing inflation*. Any price corrections along the way have been mild and short lived. And rare gemstones are hard to mine, which makes them that much more compelling. Certified gemstones will help you to maintain your purchasing power in an inflationary environment. On the negative side, gemstones are not as widely accepted as a store of wealth as gold or silver, meaning that they could be less liquid in a time of personal financial distress. Although they represent a great store of value, their appeal for use in barter may be much more restricted than would be gold and silver. But for the wealthy, this should not be viewed as a deterrent, as the positives far outweigh the negatives.

Readers must know that this suggestion does not refer to diamond rings for you or for a significant other. There's too much air in the price due to the setting and overhead of your jeweler. So, look for loose diamonds and other stones (like rubies and sapphires for instance) that are certified. Certified means that they have been professionally inspected and pass for the real thing. You should only purchase diamonds or any other gemstone that are certified by either the Gemological Institute of America (*GIA*), or the American Gem Society (*AGS*), both of which have a long and strong track record. Additionally, their standards are consistent. Other certification services should be avoided, if for no other reason than the liquidity factor when you want to sell. Certification is critical in that it gives you comfort in knowing the authenticity of your purchases and a basis for price comparison. Not only that, the certification would also include the stone's exact measurements, weight, and information on its characteristics such as cut, clarity, and color. Readers should not confuse the certification with an appraisal. It is not an appraisal, but it would be the starting point for one.

If a jeweler or broker tries to sell you a stone without a certification by the two services listed above, don't buy it. Before considering your purchases, look for several gemstone brokers to find those who will give you the best pricing. As with other tangible asset investing, the key to gemstone investment is buying low. That means near wholesale, not retail. Use Google.com to find lists of reputable internet dealers that do business close to you. Some folks may even choose to go to New York to seek out the best prices. The internet can be your first resource for education and acquisition. Try to find an internet broker who is willing to help with your education as well as give you an opportunity to see the stones in person. Finally, check out your broker's refund and buyback policies. Furthermore, never buy a gemstone without seeing it with your own eyes and holding it in your hand. This means that television shopping offers should be avoided. Plus, you'll need to have a clear understanding of all the facets of the certification. This is due to the cost factor as mentioned above regarding dealer overhead. If you are a neophyte at gemstone purchases, you have to be that somebody. Somebody has to pay for it, and you shouldn't be that somebody. If you are a neophyte at gemstone purchases, you have some homework to do before you buy! But don't let this be a deterrent.

Just put in the necessary time and it could pay off handsomely over the longer term. Gemstones should not be considered for in and out trading. Buying and holding is preferred.

Start or buy a business

This suggestion definitely requires the mindset of an entrepreneur. If you don't think you can go it alone, get a partner. Partners should be those who could complement your particular skill set, or provide those skills that for whatever reason you couldn't possibly do on your own. Perhaps it could be a spouse or other family member. If you look to buy a struggling or existing business, make sure you have a strategy to make some changes for better profits. In all but exceptional cases, *don't buy just to keep up the status quo.* In the new economic paradigm, if you are in a business that isn't innovating, you will probably lose!

If you see a need that is not being met in your particular target market, consider making it happen. If you have to start your own enterprise to fill that need, that's fine. Fill the need!

Generally, *manufacturing is where the greatest wealth can be created.* Target your efforts here first before looking into the service sector. Either way, you'll want to somehow add value that the previous owner didn't offer. Once you've identified a possible target, *get your advisors involved.* The success or failure of any business is in the numbers. Good predictors can determine what the likelihood of success (or failure) would be just based on the numbers, *before they buy.* Sure, there are many risk factors that have to be understood and managed, but the first hurdle is the numbers. Too many times there are situations where advisors are called for help *after* the deed is already done. How could that be? Because the projections or assumptions used for making a rash decision were faulty in the first place, for whatever reason! The numbers simply didn't work. Don't let this happen to you. Double and triple check your numbers with your advisors and double check their related assumptions before you plunk down your cash. Does this sound obvious? Of course, but think about AIG, GM, Chrysler, Bear Sterns, Lehman Brothers, and Solyndra for example! The numbers and the underlying assumptions didn't work!

Because many baby boomer business owners are looking toward retirement, look for those who would like to slow down. Many would even like the comfort of the cash flow by providing you with the financing instead of your having to try to cajole banks into giving you a loan. Or, watch for government programs that provide loan money, as there will likely be plenty in the coming years.

If you don't have the money to buy a going concern, don't worry. If you have a valid idea, good numbers, and plenty of passion, you can make it work. Forget the naysayers. Many new businesses start on a shoestring or less. Many, many businesses such as Apple, Dell, and Hewlett Packard were started at home. Don't be intimidated, these are just examples. *You don't have to be an expert*, but you do need motivation, passion and a funding source. There could plenty of risks, but that's why the rewards are so high for those who succeed. If you are your own boss, your financial destiny is in no other hands than your own. In fact, being a business owner could actually represent less risk than working as an employee!

Finally, if you don't have the energy to own a business, but want to participate in a growth sector of the economy, *consider equipment or facilities leasing*. Many businesses with a new idea may not have the cash to re-tool their factory, or even have the space to do so. This is where an enterprising investor gets involved. With advisors as your backup, you can *become your own private equity concern* by looking for oursized profits without the attending hassles. You can place ads in trade journals or newspapers to search out parties who fit the profile, then bring in your advisors to double check the viability of the client's ideas, credit, collateral possibilities, and business plans. You might be surprised at the high returns available with a properly executed lease to a manufacturing concern.

Hands on is the key to huge profits

If it isn't obvious by now, the *best way to invest your money is direct investment*. Don't buy a packaged deal or a limited partnership plan from any broker or investment advisor or other huckster who takes the control and decision making out of your hands, with the possible exception of some Master Limited Partnerships (discussed later). When inflation really kicks into high gear, you'll see the market flooded with ideas to profit from commodities or real estate for hands—off investing. You know the pitch. They want you to cough up the cash, and send you a check along with all the other investors who you don't know and can't consult with various choices and decisions. There have been many, many types of indirect investment offerings over the years, but the chances of you making a superb profit on them are very poor, regardless of the hype in the prospectus or the other slick sales materials. With time and the help of pros in the business as partners, you can do the same thing and keep the profit in your pocket.

Don't think you can short-cut the road to extreme profit, because you can't. *Avoid all pre-packaged deals*, as they will most certainly provide you with a loss in purchasing power of your invested dollars.

Don't forget about taxes!

By the way, in no way should you buy tangible assets of any kind with the intent of avoiding income or capital gains taxes. Of course there can be many tax benefits such as depreciation and certain tax credits in those segments of the economy in which the government is trying to encourage growth. Just be aware that taxes have to be part of the profit (or loss) equation, and make your purchase and sales accordingly. If you want to buy and sell collectables check the tax rates and add the potential profits to your existing income on your tax return. Just make sure that the spread is there for you to make a profit well in excess of inflationary factors. By that I mean if you are already in a 28% bracket, add the possible gain of your collectable, and see how it affects your profit picture. If it isn't worth it to you, don't do it. But truly, *buying super low solves almost all problems in investing*. Even a novice can make good profits!

CHAPTER 15
PAPER INVESTMENTS

Extreme selectivity and specific strategies are the keys to success

Part II of 'Theft of the American Dream' has focused on tangible assets as a way to invest during a high inflationary environment. That's because it is the best way to defend your dollars from a dramatic loss of purchasing power. In a stagnant stock market, making a superior, inflation adjusted return is an iffy proposition at best. Throwing money at a mutual fund and hoping to outpace the true rate of inflation would prove to be disastrous almost every time.

Additionally, investing for a return to match the performance of the DOW or S&P will guarantee you a loss of purchasing power over the longer term. That's because in a bear market, even the best company names can and do drop in price. When liquidity dries up, the markets go down. Worldwide debt defaults and the lack of resulting liquidity are the reasons for central bank money printing. This money printing certainly finds its way into the stock markets, which makes some of the major indexes rise. Unfortunately, as soon as the QE efforts stop, the market could have a severe downtrend. For this reason, the utmost care and a different approach to stock investing should be used.

Retail investors have been fleeing the U.S. stock market for any number of reasons, particularly since the *flash crash of May*, 2010. That was when the DOW Index dropped by about a thousand points in a matter of minutes. Retail investors had pulled over $300 billion out of stock mutual funds in the first two years after that event. And the S&P 500 Index had gone nowhere for twelve years, and in fact presented a great risk to investors. When hyperinflation starts, many company stock prices will go up, but will still lag inflation by a wide margin. The stage is set for extreme disappointment in stock investing. But that doesn't mean you have to totally avoid stocks. However, it does mean that you have to be *very* selective and strategic. You *can* make money in a lousy and manipulated market, but it requires much more patience and fortitude. Here's an overview of some stock market statistics and strategies for investment success.

It's not your father's stock market

For 2011, computer program trading accounted for about 2/3 of the total volume on the New York Stock Exchange. This was about double the level experienced as recently as 2006. This leaves the typical retail investor at the back of the bus for timely information and good prices. What is of prime importance to the execution price is a type of program trading called *high frequency trading (HFT)*. HFT is used for quick profits based on the speed of executions on both the buy and sell side. The problem is that HFT is also used to place *dummy orders* to bump up the price bids, and then the orders are cancelled prior to the execution. This is called bid-stuffing. Meanwhile, the small time investor gets his order filled at a little higher price than otherwise would have been the case because the dummy orders jacked up the price. Not only that, the company putting in those phony bids to buy could actually be on the selling end to the retail public. We are talking about a matter of nanoseconds for all of this to happen before you get your trade executed. This is the likely reason that some investment banks made multi-millions of dollars on a daily basis for weeks and months on end after they got their TARP money.

How do you think some banks that were in such bad shape could pay the TARP money back so quickly? They were simply at a tremendous advantage with their high speed computers co-located at the New York Stock Exchange or at the COMEX in Chicago, and were able to use them to their price advantage on both sides of thousands or millions of trades a day. The money they made came directly out of the pockets of those not using the programs! This doesn't mean you should absolutely avoid stock buying and selling, just that you need to be a bit more knowledgeable when doing so.

You almost have to speculate to some degree to try to defend yourself and your savings from hyperinflation, and both stock fundamental and technical studies are in order. A recipe for disaster is eagerly complying with the suggestions of a broker with a big brokerage company without having done the attending homework. If you are buying a brokerage firm's recommendation, they could well be the one selling to you. This is not good, as they probably know something that you don't. By the way, this does not mean that your trusted broker knows what is actually going on in the higher echelons of his firm. He may not.

Another modern day risk of not getting the best prices for your stock picks is due to *dark pool* investments. Wikipedia.org defines dark pools this way:

"In finance dark pools of liquidity (also referred to as dark liquidity or simply dark pools) is trading volume or liquidity that is not openly available to the public. The bulk of these represent large trades by financial institutions that are offered away from public exchanges so that trades are anonymous. The fragmentation of financial trading venues and electronic trading has allowed dark pools to be created, and they are normally accessed through crossing networks or directly between market participants."

For retail investors, this means that you are at a big disadvantage due to the lack of transparency and genuine price discovery. One simply cannot tell who the buyers and sellers are much less the volume and prices involved. This also means that you could be up against a huge stock transaction which runs counter to your own buying or selling decisions. Simply, you could be on the wrong side of the trade and suffer an adverse price disparity in your transaction. If the volume involved is high enough, it could indicate a pending change in direction of the stock price. Dark pools are not deal killers for the little guys, but you'll definitely need some degree of technical analysis to confirm a buying or selling decision. Longer term price trends cannot be as easily swayed (manipulated, or managed if you like) as can short term trends. Think of it as the big boys getting better prices than you can get, and learn to deal with it.

Yet another risk to consider is *U.S. demographics*. Baby boomers are set to retire to the tune of over 4 million per year for the next 20 years or so. They could well be net sellers of stocks to help fund their retirement. This means less liquidity and potentially lower prices. Not only that, stock price movements are cyclical. Once the gravity of the U.S. and world financial conditions hit U.S. corporations, their profits could wilt along with their stock prices. Do not be fooled by the apparent progress made by Ben Bernanke's Quantitative Easing programs in bolstering stock prices. The fact is that trading volume and participation by the retail public has been waning since the crisis hit, and eventually that can only lead to lower prices. We know that the investing public pulled huge volumes of dollars out of mutual funds during 2010, 2011 and the first half of 2012, and that fact is significant. It takes money to float higher prices, as bid stuffing only goes so far.

Yet another risk is the *money availability and its movement* from central banks into the investing marketplace. This has made for exponentially higher volatility. With the complete unpredictability of the end result of OTC derivative creations and commodity futures side bets, there are mountains of funds that move electronically throughout the world in a matter of seconds. This can instantly and dramatically affect commodity prices, stock and bond prices, and interest rates. So the huge amount of savings in some of the resource-rich countries makes their investment moves more and more important to the individual investor. The amounts of money moving the markets are absolutely huge. Add to the mix the efforts by your government and others to manage both markets and consumer perceptions, and you have stock and bond markets that are fraught with peril. If you are caught on the wrong side of a stock or bond investment, you may find that by holding on to break even could take a generation or more to recoup your losses. Consequently, for most of your investment ideas in stocks, *"buy and hold" will not work anymore: you'll need more of a trading mentality.*

Retail investors must understand this basic fact: the stock market is devised to distribute stocks from the big players to the little players. You don't know what the big boys know, nor do you have the financial resources to guarantee yourself the best outcome like the big players can. You are simply a sucker if you think you can outplay the money mavens at their own game. The best you'd be able to hope for is to try to ride their coattails for a while and hop off before the price tops out. This is when they start to unload their positions to the retail public, and you can do it too!

Unfortunately, we could be in for years of sub-par stock index price performance in inflation adjusted terms, so you have to adjust your thinking. Using gold as a measuring stick, the market averages have actually declined about 80% in the past 10 years! In other words, if in 2001 you used gold as money to buy the 30 DOW stocks, after 10 years that purchase would now cost you 80% less in gold terms. This is a fact that the Washington and Wall Street crowd doesn't want you to know.

If you have become discouraged by the performance of your stock portfolio in recent years, that is understandable. Rather than to give up on stock investing, change you strategy to emulate a rifle shot rather than a shotgun. Selectivity is now the key. So, *invest in specifics, not "the market".* Self-reliance is all important. Too many investment advisors try to sell you stocks, bonds, other investments, and partnerships about which they, nor you, know anything about. That needs to change!

The facts about bull and bear markets

We've had a lousy market for big company stocks since 2000, as a quick look at the S&P 500 Index will attest. The U.S. stock indices have not nearly kept up with the true rate of inflation. Not only that, as soon as interest rates hit bottom the 30+ year bull market in bonds will be dead, and the rout will be on. Just realize that this is a normal part of the investment world. Asset classes inhale (go up), and they exhale (go down). The large money movements in a search for value see to that. But it is the investing public that makes the mistake of getting too enthusiastic by buying at the top, and capitulating into desperation stock sales at the bottom. It happens consistently. Your self-education and the *observance of both the investing actions of the pros as well as your uninformed friends will help you to avoid these traps.*

In a bear market, the price peaks keep getting successively lower and the price dips also keep getting lower. Smoothing out the main overall trend, one can observe that the prices are dropping. The notion that stocks will always go up in the long run is a bit too simplistic. Yes, for the past 100+ years the DOW has averaged over a 7 percent return, including dividends. This should offer investors absolutely no comfort. The 7 percent return doesn't account for long periods of lagging stock price performance. If you got in at the wrong time, it could have taken you *years* to recoup your losses if you had simply waited to break even!

Did you know that there were 3 different periods of 20 years each in the last one hundred years or so that there was virtually no growth in stocks? And now we're in another of those periods. Using the S&P 500 Average as our gauge, we can see that from June, 1901 to June, 1921 the average only gained .2% (*point 2* percent, not 2 percent) per year, for twenty years. This happened while the Great War and money printing by the Fed saw a big inflationary surge. Remember the phrase "what this country needs is a good 5 cent cigar"? That's because the price of a good cigar doubled in a couple of years during WWI. It was the first time the Fed ramped up money production. Then, from Sept, 1929 to Sept, 1949 the S&P only gained an average of .4% per year. That took U.S. through the Great Depression and World War II. Finally, from January, 1966 to January 1986, the S&P average recorded an annual growth of just 1.9% per year during a period of high price inflation and interest rates. Were stocks a good place to be during these times? No! Did people who bought in at the wrong time get this 1.9% return? No! People who just sat with a buy and hold mentality got nothing but a dramatic loss in purchasing power after inflation was factored in.

Your first and foremost objective in a bear market is that you *do not lose principal*, as is pretty obvious. If you have some losses, raise cash; take the loss. Now you'll be that much more prepared to invest in the next big thing that will certainly move up faster than the dog you were sitting on. And while you wait with cash on the sidelines, the asset or stock you are watching may well be getting cheaper. Guard your principal dearly, as this is the base you must have for building wealth. If some of your principal disappears, you will have that much more difficulty building your savings.

Let's say you have a 33% loss on an investment position. This means your positive return from then on has to be 50% just to break even. Or, what if you had a 50% loss? It is stressful to note that you'd have to realize a 100% return to get even at that point. So think this through. You made an investment, and did not have either the desire or discipline to sell once the investment went against you. You kept hoping that it would turn around so you could get out even. And it keeps going down. Now you are sitting there with that 50% loss. Get out! The reason is that if the investment went that far against you in the first place, how in the world do you think it would double any time soon, so you can get out even?

But that's not all. Even if you did have to wait because you were frozen by the prospect of losing money by selling, remember that the inflation time-bomb is still ticking. The point is that you could wait several years or more to break even, but really you haven't because your purchasing power has dropped due to monetary inflation. And finally, don't forget about the fact that because you were frozen into a loss by not selling at a predetermined price point, other investments that offer higher upside potential will leave you in the dust while you're waiting for your dog to come back to even. This is a bad plan!

Just for context, what about some statistics on bull markets? Amazingly, there were 3 periods in the past 100 years or so that actually provided over 100% of the total returns combined in the stock market during that entire timeframe. These periods were 1921-1929, 1948-1966, and 1982-1999. So we had raging bull markets of 8 years, 18 years, and 17 years providing fully 100% of total stock returns for the last century! What does this tell you about the 100 year stock investment experience? There was more sitting and waiting for the gains to happen, and praying for no more losses, than there were actual rising markets. You must sell your losers!

The bear lurks

Does this mean you shouldn't be investing in stocks until the crisis is over? No! It means that you have to be much smarter in doing so, that's all. The mantra for stock investing in a bear market is *education, education, education*. To outperform inflation, you'll need to learn to think and act differently than you have in the past. That means you've got to become more active in watching over your stocks investments and making some tough decisions. Most of all, you'll have to *control your emotions*. It is a big mistake to fall in love with a stock or mutual fund because it matches some ideology with which you agree. Certainly investment ideals are important, but that doesn't mean you'll make money on your pet idea.

Paper assets such as many stocks and bonds, and super leveraged assets like some real estate properties, are subject to deflationary forces as currencies fail and debt defaults occur. As asset prices drop, debt default becomes the norm. The destruction of debt is deflationary. And the *only* reason government bonds have not crashed after a 30 year bull market is that Mr. Bernanke has become the buyer of last resort, keeping prices up (and yields low) with artificial demand from his fresh new money.

Many hedge funds need to sell their best positions to pay off loans when they're called in. Many bankers have to do the same to meet collateral requirements. Countries now have the same problem. Think the PIIGS (Portugal, Ireland, Italy, Greece, and Spain), France, England, and the U.S. There is so much worldwide short term debt that has to be repaid or re-borrowed, that it's hard for everyone to come up with the needed new money all at once. Additionally, new collateral for refinancing purposes is scarce. Something has to give, so we must run printing presses 24/7 or assets must be sold to raise cash. Or both!

The U.S. stock market has a long way to go to real recovery (after factoring in inflation). Yes, many U.S. companies have a lot of cash on the sidelines just waiting to invest; and yes the health of many, many U.S. companies is really quite good. But that does not mean their stock prices will be outperforming inflation anytime soon. It takes big money to rush in to make stock prices accelerate to the upside, and that is the catch. Capital preservation is all-important in a bad market; *in a bear market, a winner is the one who doesn't lose money!* Good stocks get sold off with the bad ones, as there is little discrimination when the panic hits. Once the downside damage has been done to even the finest of companies, investor psychology is shattered. No-one even wants to think about stocks. That is when the pros jump in, and it is then that the retail investor is petrified and capitulates into irrational selling. This is the time to load up the truck with the best and cheapest companies.

Get an on-line trading account

In order to facilitate your education and investment abilities, you should *get an on-line trading account.* There are many quality companies that make it easy for you to get started. Whether it's for an individual or joint account, trust account, or IRA rollover, they can do it all. Real people are on the phone to facilitate the transfer of funds. It's truly easy, even for a novice. Once your account is ready to go, you can usually execute free trades for a little while or for a certain number of trades. And once you do have to pay for trades, the fees are virtually inconsequential, like under $10. These on-line providers don't just have a stock trading program. They also provide the research resources for you to delve into practically any company. Plus some of them are accompanied with nice technical charting capability. Everyone who has bank savings or investment money should do this, including retirees. These trading and research services aren't popular because they're hard to navigate! Providers make it easy for everybody. But where do you start? You start with the basics!

Innovation is where wealth is created

Look for *companies with profitable innovations.* In the stock market much of the innovation is taking place in technology, health care, and even energy and the companies that support these sectors. In a bear market there are plenty of companies that are innovating and bringing products to the market that are improving the lives of the consumer and business alike. Innovation does not necessarily have to be in electronics. It could be happening in practically anything. Keep your eyes open for those companies that seem to have a better idea, and a way to bring that idea to market *at a profit.* If the company isn't innovating, it is dying. Plodding along with little or no growth is not going to yield you the big capital gains. In fact, investing into non-innovative companies will destroy the purchasing power of your dollars.

It would be instructive for investors to study the facts behind the Facebook initial public offering. It is easy to see that the profit numbers (or lack thereof) did not support the offering price. Facebook is a great company with a quality idea and plenty of users. But it has to prove it can make sufficient profits to justify the lofty stock price! *Forget about investment in "concept" stocks.* These are the ones that seem to have a promising new idea to make investors fortunes, but to date have less revenues and profits than the hype surrounding them. Brokers can talk them up all day long, but when the money eventually stops going in to prop up the stock price, it'll drop like a rock if there are no sales or earnings to show for the prior stock performance. That was what the dot.com bubble was about; too many concepts with no earnings. Do you remember DoctorKoop.com? Many speculators have made big bucks riding the waves of concept stock movements. But it ultimately becomes a game not unlike musical chairs. Ultimately, no more suckers exist to buy into the concept, and then the stock will crash without warning. Also, beware of the fantastic stock "buy" ideas that may come your way via the internet, email or the fax machine. Many times the perpetrators of these stock hype efforts just *pump and dump*. And guess who gets stuck?

Step one - fundamental analysis

The key to success in stock investing is to perform both fundamental and technical analysis before you buy. *Fundamental analysis* can be defined simply as a study of those factors which lead you to believe that the investment in a certain stock could be a profitable one; like a solid industry, up and coming technology, good company earnings, dividends, growth, etc. These are important factors, but that doesn't mean the stock will go up, or continue to go up as it has in the past. If more people want to sell than to buy, no matter what their reasons, the stock will drop! Don't be the last investor standing with a high buy-in price! Remember, the big money got in when none of the retail public was interested. Now who do you think will buy those millions and millions of shares that the wise guys bought on the cheap? That would be the unwitting late comers!

*** An important guideline is to understand how, why and where a company makes money. This means that you should definitely *avoid most of the paper pushers*. These are the companies that make money in the financial industries. They act as gate keepers of sorts, and make money by shuffling paper between buyers and sellers. They don't manufacture anything. Their profits come from the pockets of others, and they try to leverage those profits by making their own investments. The problem for the investor is lack of transparency and understanding of business practices. This refers to most banks, insurance companies, finance companies, Wall Street investment companies and so on. It's not that they don't make money, because many of them do. The reason for avoiding these companies is that you do not have the wherewithal to really understand what they are doing to garner profits by trading in the derivative markets, making side bets, and trading off-balance sheet. As a matter of fact, many of them don't either. Think JP Morgan in the spring of 2012 with a purported hedging loss of $2 billion which morphed into something much worse. Even the CEO of the company could not immediately quantify his problem. A dire financial condition of any of these types of companies is hard to detect. Toxic assets and off balance sheet side bets consigns the investor to a dark closet, shutting out the knowledge of the actual investment prospects of these companies. Just because they report profits doesn't mean a thing. The accounting trickery going on in the financial industry is just too ingrained to be able to trust the financial statements. The simplest and safest thing to do is to avoid these companies.

*** Look for *leading edge manufacturers of products people want to buy, anywhere in the world.* The industry you invest in should have good prospects for growth. Think Apple, as an example. This doesn't mean you should hurry to your on-line account right now to buy Apple. But it offers an example of extreme stock price appreciation because of innovation and a tremendous cash flow. Also, have a genuine interest in the market in which you invest so complacency doesn't overcome your decisions. Understand the competition too. What you really want is transparency and simplicity. By searching out these types of attributes, you'll be able to determine *relative value.* This means that you can compare various companies in the same industry and attempt to pick the best one based on value. If it's not a good value, don't buy it!

*** If some sector of the market isn't growing, but your particular pick within that same sector is growing, you had better be wary. The game of shuffling dollars amongst competitors in the same stagnant market ultimately will not treat you well. Look for *industry growth,* and the gems within that industry. Remember, value investing in a lousy market is the way to go for both principle protection and profits.

*** By the time you hone in on an industry, and then to a company or two of interest within that industry, you are ready for step two. Think as though it were you running the company and ask yourself some *key questions* which could include: Is the company an industry leader? If the company is new with good prospects, do they have enough money to work a fast growth business plan? Has the company's earnings been growing faster than the true rate of inflation? Are there high barriers to entry into the product lines so that it would be hard for new guys to take some business away from them? Is the demand for the products stable, or is it more like a fad that could vanish quickly? Does the company have a good deal of cash reserves so it can protect themselves against adverse happenings? How much debt does the company have, how much does it cost to service that debt, and how does the debt service cost compare to the pre-tax profits? Does the company have relatively low fixed costs? What is the profit margin on each product they sell? Is the company relatively safe from a drop in sales due to cyclical downturns in the economy? Does it pay a dividend? Have company officers been buying stock? Are institutional investors buying the stock? The more positive answers you get in this regard, the better. What is nice is that you can find out all of the information on the internet.

*** If you identify a company you really like that has superior growth prospects and has suitable answers to the above type of questions, you could then even consider *investing in some of its suppliers*. This means that if a company has come up with a widget that people just have to have, you'll also want to consider investing in the parts manufacturers who supply that company. Getting in on the front end of the production cycle gives you the first heads up if things begin to go awry. If the supplier sales to the hot manufacturer are waning, this could spell trouble for the manufacturer, and you'd be in a good position to sell before adverse conditions accelerate.

In a lousy economy, the best performers are those which produce must-have products. These include companies that produce consumer staples, utility and energy companies, health-care companies, and so on. The growth of profits in these types of companies may not be outstanding, but you can be sure that stability would be there in a downturn. Does this guarantee that your return will exceed the true rate of inflation? Not necessarily!

*** Another attribute that you should seek out from a prospective investment are those companies which can demonstrate *strong pricing power*. That means that they can raise their pricing without adverse effects to sales. Of course at some point the consumers may rebel, but if your company has shown in the past that it's revenues can still grow in excess of its price increase, that's a big plus. This is important because that means that it could potentially raise prices in an ugly inflationary environment without serious damage to their sales prospects.

*** But that's not all. You must be aware that many companies can and regularly do game their earnings statements. This means they use accounting sleight of hand to manage their reported earnings so that they don't miss the projections that Wall Street analysts expect. Instead of concentrating on just the "bottom line", a couple of other measures are more telling than some version of "profit". Investors should *concentrate on the "top line" number as well as free cash flow.*

Of course profits are important. But equally important, if not more so, are sales. This means you need to check *gross revenues* which some analysts refer to as the top line. Look for accelerating growth in sales, as this is the real consumer or customer feedback we discussed earlier in the book. This is the money coming in the door from which all other expenses are paid. And just as important as the amount of revenues is the actual amount of units sold. If revenues are increasing simply due to price increases, this may or may not be good. Increasing units sold *and* increasing prices presents the ideal situation.

*** The real acid test for a solid stock investment is *excess cash flow.* This is the money that is actually left over once all expenses including taxes are paid. A public company should have a cash flow statement readily available for anyone to check. Investors should become acquainted with it before they make the plunge into a stock purchase.

*** A final note on company financial statements is that readers should always check the footnotes attached. This is the fine print that most people don't read, but can be extremely important. Footnotes on the financial statements reveal detail that could put an entirely different light on profits, liabilities and assets, so don't overlook them. Do you have to be an accountant to buy a stock? No, but if you don't know your way around the company financials, you should find someone who can explain the statements to you so you have your eyes wide open prior to purchase!

*** Another approach to seek out superior returns with your stock selection is to look at resource companies. Search out *companies that have a high level of natural resources* that may not be fully realized in the price of the stock. These could include mining companies, timber companies, coal, natural gas, or oil companies, etc. Investors should know that the prices of some of these companies tend to be somewhat volatile as they are subject to price swings in their underlying resources. But that's OK. Just act when the time is right and when the price charts scream "buy"! In a hyperinflationary environment, these companies could well make you a ton of money if you buy them right. But you have to do your homework, which includes a bit of technical analysis which we'll get into shortly.

*** In searching out hot areas for stock investing, try to seek out *pure plays.* This means that you are looking for the companies that will emphasize and profit the most from the new item of your interest. It would represent a major portion of that company's sales emphasis and growth. Is there more risk in this approach? Of course there is! But by taking educated risks, the rewards could be outstanding. Why not shoot for a 10 bagger instead of a measly 10% or 20% gain? Huge and quick gains happen all the time in stock investing, and they often come from pure plays.

For example, if a company like General Electric had a hot new item and dominated the market in that item, what would be the effect on its overall bottom line? It would not be that great because of all the other businesses in the mix that would have a muting effect on the overall picture. Conversely a company such as Apple which put out the I-Phone all over the U.S. and China without much competition had its profits absolutely soar. The company put major emphasis on that product, and it paid off handsomely for the company and for stockholders who saw the stock price move up by thousands of percent. But there are risks. If the pure play you have identified has competition in the wings, you had better be nimble with your purchase and sale of its stock. Only effective education about the company and its potential competitors will mitigate some risks of the pure play. But the time spent calculating your investment move can pay off handsomely.

*** Finally, don't forget to *look internationally* for a substantial portion of your portfolio of stocks. You have to go to countries where the growth is and where the currencies are strong, because that is where the wealth is being created. You'll find that these countries are tax and investment friendly, including several in Eastern Asia like Singapore, Thailand, Hong Kong, Vietnam, Malaysia, and others. China is a high growth possibility, but there are added political risks, so be aware.

If you have an on-line account as suggested, and if the stock you like isn't traded in the U.S., you can always get personal assistance by calling your on-line broker. Yes, the transaction fees will be probably be higher, but it'll pay off in a big way. Also there are plenty of EFT's for your consideration. These track the stock indices for markets in your subject country and are a decent way to participate in the overall growth of their stocks. Finally, those international corporate stocks that pay a superior dividend will offer added protection against purchasing power erosion as hyperinflation kicks in at home. Seek out the finest and the strongest!

*** For those who have the means, *moving some investment money offshore* should be considered. By doing so, you would have many more opportunities for investment and profit that would not be available in the U.S. and the rewards can be very high. However, the window of opportunity to move money offshore could come to an end soon. If you are so inclined, you would do well to act quickly, albeit rationally. In this case, you'll need not only tax advisors who can keep you in compliance with the rules and reporting requirements, but also an investment advisor who can point out ideas and investment opportunities. This does not preclude you from digging into ideas on your own however, which is always wise. But getting helpful direction from someone in your country of choice is also a wise move. Check references, and go to your countries of interest to meet the players before you do anything else. If you have no interest in traveling to a particular country, it would not be a great idea to park investment money there. Pick a place or places that suit your tastes and vacation plans for the future.

Having given the above suggestions about looking at the fundamental side of stock investing, this is only half the picture. Your education and homework also needs to consider technical analysis before you ever make your first purchase.

Technically speaking

When buying or selling *any* stock or ETF, you definitely should consider the *technical analysis* factors. Technical analysis is a study of the supply and demand (volume, momentum, etc.) factors on the price of the stock, leading you to more accurately determine the likely direction of the price based on prior experience. Of course, it is not a perfect science, but is nonetheless extremely helpful. At the very least it gives you a picture of where the stock price is in relation to its prior trading range.

*** Take the time to look at a *daily price chart* of each of your stock ideas or holdings. You will find three fine websites in the resource guide for easily calling up on your computer screen the chart of virtually any stock. Daily charts record the price action for each day and will typically go back 6 months to a year. You don't have to be a genius to see the direction the price of your stock is going. To help as a visual aid, you can even delineate a price channel for your stock. This is easily done by drawing a line on the chart connecting the two (or more) lowest price points on the chart. Extend that line out to the end of the graph. Then draw a line between the two (or more) highest peaks in price, and extend it to the end of the graph. Try to make the top line parallel to the bottom line, even if you have to fudge slightly on the upper line. Try not to fudge any on the bottom line, though. What you have done is to define the price channel in which that the stock is moving. It will be obvious. The channel will demonstrate one of three things: it can trend up, down, or it can look horizontal. And no matter what the channel direction, you'll be able to see price points for buying or selling your stock. Put another way, you have just determined the *trading range* of your stock. Do you really want to buy at one of those tops in the trading range? No! You want to buy at the *trough points*.

*** After you have examined a daily chart, look at a *weekly chart*. The weeklies will go back about 5 years, and will record one data point or trading range for every week of price action. Do the same exercise in drawing your lines at the top and bottom by intersecting the lowest price points and extending the line to the edge of the graph. Then do the same on the price peaks, extending through at least the top two points, and extend the line to the edge of the page. *Weekly charts are an excellent determinant of the longer term direction of your stock*, giving a more complete picture than the daily charts. What looks like a rising stock on a daily chart could well give you a totally different and opposite view on a weekly chart. You may actually be looking at a temporary up move on a daily chart that displays as a short term rally in the context of a larger down move on the weekly chart. Studying price movement in this fashion is the single very basic tenet of technical analysis, and you should definitely use it with each and every stock before you buy *or* sell. That way, it will be simple to see where you are in relation to the trend. If you are bullish and expect it to go up, you need to buy near the bottom of the trend channel. The converse applies to selling. If you plan to sell, a good time to do so is when the price is near the top of the channel you have drawn.

*** Most investors think stock trading is all about price. But equally important to trading success is *trading volume*. All charting services will enable you to look at total volume each day or week, as well as by the price paid for the time period covered in the chart. Use this information! You'll see where the most folks are getting on and off the boat. You can also follow the accumulation (big volume trades of institutional investors) versus distribution (small trades to retail investors). This is very important because you want to buy when the stock is being accumulated by the big boys, not when the big boys are selling to the little guys. And you can check the Chaikin Money Flow figures to see if money is actually flowing into or out of the stock on a net basis, regardless of price. It only takes a click of the mouse. If money is flowing in, that is bullish. If it is flowing out, that's bearish. Remember, a rising stock price on relatively low volume is not a good sign for future appreciation of your stock. The more shares that trade at a given price, the more likely it would be that the price will hold or go higher.

*** Another simple tool in technical analysis is the study of the *moving price averages* of your stock. Both the 50 day and 200 day moving averages, and their relation to one another, is very useful in looking at the shorter term. These are re-averaged each day to reflect that day's price change. On the 50 day moving average for instance, once today's closing price is added to the prior 49, the 50th day back gets dropped. It's the same for the 200. So what you'll get is a line that is either rising or falling to reflect the average price for the past 50 or 200 days. If the 50 line crosses *above* the 200 line, this indicates a break *up* in the stock price, and usually indicates friendly prices in the near future. If the 50 day line moves *below* the 200 day line, this could be ominous. Look for lower stock prices ahead.

One should note that using moving average studies works best in a stock price that is already *trending* to determine any potential change in direction. Trending means that the stock has either an up or down channel, but not horizontal. If the stock price has already been moving in a horizontal (sideways) channel, moving average studies don't work as well. It will be an exercise in frustration for you to attempt to trade stocks based on their moving averages that are moving in a sideways direction. Conversely, a trending stock that has experienced a moving average crossover as described above is a heads-up of a change in direction of the price action.

*** There are plenty more *technical indicators, oscillators and measurements* that you can look at that to add to your comfort level in trading stocks. Many websites can give you all the help you need with charting your stocks, as well as understanding what those charts are telling you. You can get a comprehensive tutorial on the how and what of technical analysis, using numerous indicators. Successful stock technicians pick their favorite tools out of the scores of indicators and measurements available to help them in determining their plan of action on any particular stock. With a little study in your spare time, you can do this too. But you can't know it all, so practice and experiment with your own go-to indicators, and use them consistently. That way you'll get more clues on what your stock is really doing, and what you might expect going forward. Finally, note that technical analysis is not for use with mutual funds, only with individual issues or ETF's.

And where can you get price charts? Check the resource guide for several suggestions. If you have an on-line account, most of the services have charting features. One free internet site that you could try is stockcharts.com. Another excellent service is found at decisionpoint.com. It has a lot more than just charts. It's an education in itself! Or maybe you can get printouts of charts from your broker, who will undoubtedly have access to any sort of chart you're looking for. But whatever you do, *don't ignore the price charts!* They are critical to your success in both bull and bear markets.

Have a plan, and stick to it

*** *Adopt a trading mentality.* By now you should understand that you won't be able to take the same investment approach as you did in the 1982-1999 bull market. You must adopt more of a trading mentality. That's why you need to become more educated and active with your investment decisions. It will have everything to do with making the purchasing power of your money grow.

During the Great Depression, the loss on the DOW average was a staggering 89% from the top to the bottom. Most people think the October 1929 crash was the problem. No, it wasn't. Up to the summer of 1930, the DOW had recouped a good portion of its losses from the famous crash. The real crash occurred after that. By the summer of 1932 stocks were down fully 89% from the top in 1929, not to recover the losses for years. Can you afford to wait for 10 or 20 years for your stocks to come back? If not, you'd benefit greatly by a change of thinking on your approach to your investments.

There's a big difference between having a trading mentality and playing the day trading game. Day trading is for fools or nerds only. This approach is not recommended. It involves getting in and out of a stock in a very short time frame, from the same day to a week or two. Forget that, as it's a prescription for frustration and losses.

Having the trading mentality involves taking some profits after a *cyclical* move. Basically, a cyclical move or trend is a price movement that would last for weeks to months, but not years. Many times, cyclical moves run counter to the main trend. It's pretty simple to spot the cyclical move on a daily chart, by looking at price channels on the stock charts, as we have just reviewed. Then there are *secular* trends, as opposed to the cyclical ones. The secular trend can typically only be seen on the weekly charts, covering 5 years or so. This can be defined as the *long term direction,* and if you are hoping to hang on to some or all of your stock for a huge profit, you'd better make sure you are betting on the right long term direction!

*** *Set buy and sell price objectives.* This requires discipline not disrupted by emotions. Many traders like to enter automatic computerized orders for buying and selling at certain prices. These are called *stop limits or limit orders*, and in theory this is a good idea. However, a mental stop limit objective along with strict discipline and with daily tracking of the price may be much better. Why? Because high frequency trading and bid stuffing can easily take you out of a position that actually doesn't meet your buy or sell criteria. You could find that the stock you just sold at its lowest point of the day goes back in its original direction after the computerized program swooped down to fill your limit order. Also, limit orders on the stock exchanges can do funny things at the end of a day, or when the buy and sell orders for a particular stock aren't balanced. You could unwittingly get whipsawed into or out of a position with pre-set, computerized limit orders. Remember, the sharks on Wall Street would know about your order, and can make the stock price get to your objective with no problem at all. Therefore, your buy and sell limits need to be in your head, not under the dutiful eyes of a vulture's computer!

Also, these same vultures have frequently been known to *front run customer orders*, since they are in position to know what the market is in that stock at any given time. This means that they trade for themselves just before completing customer trades. And because their computers are at the stock exchange, milliseconds can make the difference between your ability to get in at your desired price, or watching the price rise without you on board.

That's why mental stops are better than computer or even paper stop orders. But discipline and diligence are the keys to making this strategy work. Finally, when setting your limits, make sure that you consider the existing price channel of the stock before deciding on your buy or sell price objectives.

Once you have set your price objectives, sit. Then, if you have caught a nice move, take some profits. By taking 1/3 to 2/3 of your money off the table, you'll have funds available for later reinvestment in that same stock or a different one that later piques your interest. Don't jump out of the entire position if it is doing all you expected it to do. This assumes that you've been following the fundamental factors that led you to invest in the company in the first place. Once you have made your investment, keep track of both the technical and fundamental factors.

*** *Watch for breaks in the price channel both to the upside or downside.*

Upside breakouts indicate a possible risk in that a stock that goes too far too fast may be setting up for a sizable fall. If the upside breakout is accompanied by higher than normal volume, this is usually a good sign, in that more money is going into the stock. The bigger volume of buying at higher prices will tend to hold up the rising price. Conversely, if you have a channel break to the downside, this usually indicates a change in direction! If the downside break is accompanied by higher volume, this is not good unless you sold short!

Normally, you'll want to have the stock price stay above or below your limit price for at least a few days before your desired buy or sell transaction should occur. This way, you won't be in or out of a stock on a temporary variance from the prevailing price channel. Remember, you don't need to catch 100% of the move. If you miss out on a few points because you didn't buy at the very bottom, so what. The same goes for selling near the top. If you get only 80% of any move you'll be doing great, so adjust your thinking on this point, and you'll sleep a lot better.

The best situation is when a stock has been trading in a narrow horizontal channel for an extended period of time *after* having fallen from higher prices, and then the volume increases. An extended period of time means at least a couple of months. All the sellers have disappeared, and the volume has dried up. Many times a substantial volume increase on the tail end of such lethargy is a good sign that big money has moved in. And typically, the stock price increases due to this increased volume are minimal. This is a sign that the retail investors have capitulated, and the big money has stepped up its buying. When a stock demonstrates higher than normal volume after a big move in either direction, while at the same time moving horizontally, this almost always indicates a pending change in direction. This is when the big money gets in or gets out before the price ever budges! It is only a matter of time before the big price move will occur.

*** Finally, investors must be aware of what as referred to as *chart painting* by the pros and other gamesmen. Many of the Wall Street types and big money movers are very adept at the technical analysis techniques that are mentioned above, and many more. The most important thing to remember about using your indicators for buy and sell decisions is that make sure they are actually telling you what you think they are telling you. How would you know, being a rookie at technical analysis? Wait for verification and follow through!

Let's say you are following a stock and it has broken out of its trading channel, or crossed a moving average. As mentioned earlier, this *does not* necessarily mean that you should act instantly. It would be better for you to wait for a few days to a week or so to make sure the move is real. The reason is that it's easy to manipulate a stock over a short time frame with the computer program trading by hedge funds and big money types, to make it look like it is doing something it's not. In fact, it happens all the time. Say a stock breaks below its recent trading channel and you panic out of it immediately. You could very well find that within the next few days it reverses to the upside, and you got head faked out of your position. The pros do this quite often when they want to either sell on a breakout, or buy on a breakdown. They make the chart look like you should act so they can get their trade it at a super competitive price. Don't fall for it! This is why it's so important to know that getting 80% of a move is excellent. Leave the other 10% on the top and 10% on the bottom for others to fight over. So, if your position goes below or above your target by a little, don't succumb to fear or greed. Be coldly analytical, and wait to see what the stock does in the next few days. Most of the time you'll be glad you did!

More keys to successful trading

*** A big *mistake* people sometimes make *is buying on the good news* just announced on the internet or on the business shows that evening. The second worse thing is jumping in because you think something is good news, but in fact it isn't. Also generally to be avoided is buying on that good news at the opening bell in the morning. This will almost always cost you money in the form of a higher price paid than necessary. Once the news hits Wall Street, the individual investor would rarely get in just before a big jump in price. You aren't going to beat the high frequency traders and insiders, so don't even try. Instead, an axiom to be considered is to *buy on the rumor, and sell on the news.* That way you will have already made your purchase, homework, of course. This pre-supposes that you have done your and you can then sell to the masses when the news hits the street.

*** Another important guideline is to *buy on price weakness, and sell into strength.* This seems so obvious, but emotional investors get caught up in the excitement of a big up day in the market or on an idea, and then decide to buy *after* the big move. Forget it! If your favorite target for a portfolio acquisition has just jumped in price, sit tight. Don't worry because you'll have plenty of time to buy into certain price weakness. It might happen later that same day, or even in the next week or so. That's because the pros sell into the strength that the fish just bought! When the excitement drops off, so will the price.

Don't assume the stock price will run away from you to the upside and you just have to buy now. This is the wrong approach. It is the *greed* coming out in the human psyche, and most of the time it will *not work in your favor.* Wait until you are worried about your purchase or fear that you will be paying too much in the middle of a down trending price. Act like a pro by selling when you feel greedy, and buying when you are afraid. Under either circumstance, your education will bail you out. This is especially true when making precious metals investments, since they are regularly and continually gamed. Now can you see how important your technical and fundamental analysis is? The fundamentals lead you to the right stocks, and the technical analysis leads you to the right price, with better timing.

*** Investors should also learn to *play the downside* of stock movements. If the hedge funds, the Treasury Department's Exchange Stabilization Fund, commercial bankers, and the Wall Street types can do it, so can you. *Selling short* allows you to make money when a stock price is dropping! For an individual stock, this means that you borrow the stock from your broker, sell it in the open market, and put the money in your pocket. Then once the stock falls to your level of satisfaction, buy it back with some of the money you put in your pocket when you sold it in the first place. Return the stock to the broker, and keep the balance of the money in your pocket from the original sale. All brokers can accommodate this type of transaction in a seamless manner. You don't have to do anything other than place the phone call, or do it yourself online. The mechanism is the same as a stock buy, except you click on the sell box instead of the buy box. The rest will be taken care of for you. When you want to close out your short sale, click on the buy box.

Many people say that short selling seems to be unpatriotic or somehow wrong. But the fact is that short selling provides a guaranteed buyer of that same stock sometime in the future. If you are the short seller, then you will be that buyer of last resort after the stock tanks. Your first loyalty needs to be with your own finances. So learn how to play the short side of the market, just as you've played the long side for years! You probably realize that many times stocks drop much faster than they go up, so learn to use that to your advantage.

*** Also, *don't try to catch an anvil* thrown out of a second story window; wait till it hits ground first. We've covered this, but it bears repeating. If the fallen angel still shows signs of life, then cautiously pick it up. This means that you should not think a stock is a great buy just because it has dropped 50 or 60 or 80 percent or more. It's not a good buy until it has proven itself on the fundamental analysis, and subsequently hits bottom by leveling off on anemic volume. At that point it is likely sold out and ready to come back from the dead, albeit maybe not immediately. Just be very cautious about buying more when a stock goes against you. Check the price history with the trend lines on a chart as described above. Don't automatically think that you have to "average down". In a bear market this could be deadly.

*** Conventional wisdom has it that you would get more shares for the same dollar amount invested if the price action goes against you. This is called *dollar cost averaging*, and for a passive investor in a bull market, it would generally work. But in a bear market it is fraught with risk. The conclusion is that even if you have done your homework on the fundamental and the technical analysis, you may still want to take a hard second look before you buy more of a stock that's moving against you.

Conversely, if a stock price is rising more than you originally anticipated or has broken out of its price channel to the upside, consider buying more. But what if the price is higher you say? Well, don't you want it to go higher? Another mistake investors frequently make, assuming they are informed about their picks, is that they fear buying more because the price has risen well above their original buy price. In this context, fear is good. If previously they were trading within a specific price channel, and the stock has broken out and stays above that channel on good volume, serious consideration should be given to buying more.

*** *If hope plays a major part in your investment plan, change your plan.* This does not refer to being cautiously optimistic. Uninformed hope can do nothing but get you into more trouble than you may already be in. Of course, if you come up with some stock you like and you do the homework and make your move, sure, hope is OK. But if your plans have gone against you and you are now frozen by indecision and are hoping for the best, invariably the plan will continue to go the wrong way. This is why it is critical to set those mental stop limits on not only stocks, but any other investment you make, and stick to them.

*** Again, *take the emotion out of your investing experience. This is the* hardest piece of advice to follow and it means that you have to become your own expert. Fear and greed drive the markets, so beware of how you relate to experiencing them. Make knowledge and confidence your friends. Be tough, both on the upside and downside. Don't get greedy, but don't be a chicken either. Be knowledgeable, cold and calculating in the area that you have chosen for your investment.

*** Finally, *don't expect perfection*, particularly if you are new to the self-investment game. Not every one of your moves will pan out, and yes, you might just lose some money on some of them. Nobody said it was simple. But with time and practice it is eminently doable. So a good bit of advice is to cut your losses and most of all, *don't give up!* It's important that you analyze where things went awry in your plan, adjust, and move on. However, don't make major adjustments to your M.O. right away after having made a mistake or two; rather, just make small adjustments. Humans learn more from their mistakes than from their successes, so give it a chance. Remember, the ultimate goal is to outpace the ravages of the true rate of price inflation, and you'll be better off dealing with it yourself than to farm the work out to someone else.

Specific suggestions regarding paper investments

*** *Beware of Index Funds!* The proliferation of these funds has been astounding in the past 15 years, and it is mostly due to buyer interest. Investors who want to invest in the overall stock market have found that this method is the lazy man's road to riches. Or is it? When adjusting to the true rate of inflation, these funds have been marginal performers at best. For instance, it doesn't take a genius to see that the S&P 500 index has had no nominal growth since 2000. In the summer of 2000, the index was over 1400. In the summer of 2012, the index was less than 1400. It has had two major down trends of over 40% along with two ensuing up trends. Only those fortunate enough to have caught one of the two major price bottoms would have beaten inflation. But many investors using this type of index fund with a hands-off approach to long term stock investing have done nothing more than lose purchasing power of their investment dollars.

Index Funds are a proxy for investor sentiment, and the price movement is like a self-fulfilling prophecy. Just buy the index, and all the thinking is done for you; just ride the wave! But what advisors and investors don't seem to realize is that price performance is a direct result of the demand on the Index Fund. If investors with long term IRA or 401k money want to take the simple route, they just invest in the index. The fund manager must buy the stocks in the index, forcing the prices higher. The more that folks see a reasonable performance of the index fund, the more they are tempted to put more money in, forcing even more stock appreciation. This is all well and good until it isn't. Then the opposite occurs.

In a bear market, investors see continual stagnation or lower valuations in the prices of stocks, so they want out of their index fund. The fund manager has to sell the stocks in the index when you and others want to redeem your shares. So those stock prices comprising the index fund drop, encouraging more people to make the decision to sell. The fund manager is then forced into more selling, with lower prices ensuing. When does it stop? When people give up, that's when. In the stock business it is called *capitulation*, and it occurs when people want out at any price. Many become so disillusioned that they feel that they will never invest in stocks again. This is what the pros look for. The bottom is in, and the smart money takes over. This is when the investment bankers and Wall Street insiders step in to buy at bargain prices.

*** *Selling covered call options* is a viable idea in some cases. Many retirees and others hold stocks that, for whatever reason, they would never consider selling. These may have been passed down within the family, or a deceased person may have left company stock to the surviving spouse or family at death. But for whatever reason, people feel frozen with their stock position. Many times the stock will drop and not recover for years due to a plethora of reasons. And, maybe the dividend has been cut. So what should people do in a case like this to try to make up for the lost principle or income? Sell covered call options! What this means is that you agree to sell the stock at a higher price in the future, say 3 to 12 months or more from now. You pick the price at which you would sell, and when. Someone will pay you money for the right to buy your stock at that price prior to the contract date, and it is easily transacted with a broker, or even with an on-line account. The best part is that if the stock never gets as high as your proposed selling price prior to your specified timeframe, you get to keep the money the other party paid you. What is even better, you can then do it again! This way, you can have a guaranteed enhancement of income from your stock holding. You either keep the premium paid, or the stock goes up and gets called (thus the name call option) away from you; in either event, you made money! The only catch is that if the stock goes higher than your contract sales price, the buyer would get to keep the difference between the current higher price and the lower guaranteed transaction price to you.

*** *Whenever possible, invest in Exchange Traded Funds instead of Mutual Funds.* Very simply, you are not likely to make any serious return investing in most mutual funds in a stock and bond bear market. If only you could carve out the best sector or stock positions of a great mutual fund, things would be different. If only you could make money on the downside of practically any market or sector, that would make things more enticing. You can do this and more with Exchange Traded Funds (ETF's)! These investments try to match the performance, leverage the performance, or even take the short side for profit of practically any sector of the investment markets.

Because IRA or other retirement plan money cannot be used for short selling, the financial engineers on Wall Street came up with a solution. An Exchange Traded Fund can be used to play the downside in a qualified plan. ETF's are proxies for just about any investment objective. They look somewhat like a mutual fund, but trade on the exchanges just like a stock. And many ETF's are designed to play the downside on any number of investment classes. Do you want to short the Dow, or S&P? Can do! Do you want to short the Singapore stock index? Can do! Do you want to invest in the Singapore stock index? Can do! There are huge numbers of these ETF's just waiting for your attention, and they are able to hone in on very specific investment objectives, unlike most mutual funds.

What's even better is that all the charting services are able to generate the charts on ETF's just as they would with a stock, so you can watch any indicator you'd like to see. Investing in this manner isn't scary at all; it can actually be fun! There is one caveat though. *Many ETF's that track natural resource prices are simply used as manipulative devices by the big boys to guide prices of the physical resource.* The money elite can and do move the paper price down with the help of ETF's so they can go in the back door and buy the physical resource at the then discounted price. For this reason, some ETF's do not do an adequate job at tracking the price of the underlying resource. So when it comes to natural resource ETF's you may want to avoid them, or just buy the physical resource itself. Stick to industry sector specific or country specific ETF's and you'll be much better off.

Since you'd like to find the pure plays for your particular interest, ETF's will do the job, without other lesser attractive investments cluttering the picture. They're a great tool, particularly for investing in a sector as a whole. However, individual stock picking should not be ignored in favor of ETF's. Investors should consider both in an on-line investment account. Finally, investors should exercise caution when buying leveraged ETF's, as they are much more risky and volatile. Yes, there are derivatives and leverage, or both, in the multiple-percentage move ETF's. Unless you really understand the risk, make sure your ETF doesn't have any derivatives in it. Make sure it aims for a simple one to one match of the market sector of your interest.

*** *Forget about government bonds.* In this crisis environment, you don't want a government entity to owe you money. Government bonds have been going up in value for over 30 years. Remember when Paul Volcker was Fed Chairman and he took interest rates way up in the late 1970's? Thirty year Treasuries yielded in excess of 15%, and the prime rate was in excess of 20%. Money market funds yielded in the high teens. This meant that the principal value on government bonds was very low. Then yields started to fall, increasing the principal value. Fed Chair Alan Greenspan came along with his freshly repudiated gold standard; oh, that "barbarous relic". He dropped rates, over and over again. Sure, there were upticks, but the main direction was down, as we saw in Chart 3. Meanwhile, what were bonds doing? Obviously, they were on a tear. By the time Greenspan's successor Mr. Bernanke had lowered the Fed funds rates to 0% in 2009 shorter duration government bonds reached an all-time high. Then, with the Bernanke "Twist" plan of late 2011, even the long term bonds were making new highs. Like all time ever new highs. So do you think you should buy now? And where would the fuel be to send those bond prices higher? There are no more rate cuts to be had! When rates start to come out of the basement, there will be absolutely huge losses on invested bond principal.

Bonds are a guaranteed theft of your long term purchasing power. Yes, it looks like there are some attractive municipal bonds out there, and juicy yields on some select corporate bonds. But 'Theft of the American Dream' will not recommend that readers buy or even hold any bonds, period. T-bills are fine, however, as the risk of principal is almost nil along with the interest rate. You'll have to be your own judge and jury on putting your invested dollars to work there. Just realize that unsecured IOU's are not a place to be in a fiat currency crisis such as the one we are experiencing. What risks do you think are involved if some city or corporation out there wants to pay you 8% to borrow money? Financial analyst Meredith Whitney sees a huge number of coming defaults in the municipal bond market, which seems inevitable. Most local communities are short on cash, and their budgets are stressed. If you want to pick some up for a *short term* play, do your homework with your favorite broker, and be nimble. But overall, the bond market is not a favored sector going forward.

When you see the rates going up on government issues, it will be a warning signal that the U.S. budget deficit is about to explode, absent any severe austerity, as in the repudiation of promises. We know that Professor Bernanke assures the American public that he can keep long term yields low, which he has on more than one occasion. He says that he can do this by paying all time high prices for the T-Bonds in the open market with freshly printed money. That's just silly, and absurd. As soon as the Fed opens its pocketbook to buy bonds with freshly printed cash sellers come out of the woodwork to unload at high prices. When rates start to rise, it'll be like someone yelled "fire" in a packed theatre. Get me out of here! The world will be awash with U.S. currency, and hyperinflation will take off. Do not buy long term government bonds from any Western country.

*** This brings us to *bond mutual funds*. Forget it! The fact of the matter is that, once again, the bond funds have to comply with the objectives of their prospectuses, and they have to keep investor money invested, no matter what the market conditions. More importantly, bond funds don't mature like individual debt issues do. At least with the individual issues you know what to expect and when. You or your advisor can figure our what your yield to maturity actually is, depending on your purchase price on that bond. As to the high yields on corporate bond funds, they are high yield for a reason. You know, the higher the reward, the higher the risk. You may think top notch Fortune 500 company bonds are a good risk, but you really don't know what is hidden in those ivory towers. Legalized corporate accounting tricks and off balance sheet side bets should make potential bond buyers very skeptical.

*** *What about preferred stocks, or common stocks with high dividends?* Let's cite a couple of examples to understand the risk of counting on those supposedly solid dividend streams. The bailout of Citigroup consisted of the U.S. government getting preferred stock for its investment in the banking conglomerate. However those high preferred yields went by the wayside quickly once Citigroup proved it was still hemorrhaging cash. Bye, bye dividends, hello common shares with no dividend. Or how about GE, which had to slash its dividend by 2/3 after the advent of the crisis for the first time in 59 years? If you go fishing for high yield preferred or common shares with any company in the current economic environment, you need to be prepared for bad news. Preferred shares may just end up being a preferred way to lose a promised dividend. And when the dividend gets cut, the stock price will most definitely drop. The highest risk resides in the financial industry, where upwards of 40% of the big NYSE stocks trade paper for a living. If you want guaranteed dividends, look for companies that actually make a product or provide a needed service. Again, it is critical to remember that you are trying to achieve a total return in excess of the true rate of inflation. Trying to do so with both high dividends and stock appreciation is certainly possible in a traditionally inflationary environment. But when that inflation kicks in to overdrive, extreme caution is warranted. Tread lightly, do research, and get help here. Just realize that you'll need to do plenty of homework to be successful.

*** *Master limited partnerships* have also become a popular investment alternative. These are limited partnerships that trade like a stock on one of the exchanges. You can do the technical analysis on them, just as you would any other stock. They are run by the general partners, while the investing public, as limited partners, have no say in day to day decisions. The tax code mandates that these entities distribute 90 percent of their income, making their yields quite attractive. Many of them are involved in the transportation of natural resources. The good ones have provided stable incomes to the investors and appreciating stock prices as their revenues and distributions have increased. They do not have the risk of production or the risk of price volatility in the underlying resource. Although the stable nature of the demand for their services is desirable and attractive, they carry the same risks as any income producing stock in a rising interest rate or hyperinflationary environment. And they carry some of the risks of a nasty stock price downdraft in a cash starved bear market. Does this mean they should be avoided entirely? No! But it does mean that investors have to have a clear understanding of both the fundamentals of the business and the technical factors weighing on the stock price, as previously discussed.

*** For years, *real estate investment trusts* (REIT) have been favored by income seeking investors. These entities hold and rent out all kinds of properties. But in today's U.S. investment environment, REITs are not a sure thing. Making an after tax return well in excess of the true rate of inflation could be a tricky proposition. Like master limited partnerships, REITs are required by law to distribute 90% of their income. Investors should look under the surface before they jump in to get those apparently juicy dividends. Specifically, examine the funds from operations, and the actual cash that is left for distribution. Many of these investments actually return your principal as part of your dividend! Equally, if not more important, is the underlying net value of the properties held compared to the stock price. Since the debacle in real estate prices commenced, many properties in some popular REITs are underwater (having more debt than value). Unfortunately, this fact is not always reflected in the price of the stock. This means that you could easily have a REIT that looks like it is valuable in stock terms, but worth far less in property terms. Conversely, some newer REIT's have been started *after* the crash in property values and could present an outstanding opportunity! Investors should seek our the newer issues first for the best potential. Of course, the hands-on direct approach to real estate investing offers the best potential, and should be favored.

Also, foreign based REITs may also offer good opportunities for those seeking high returns. Look for the high growth areas internationally for high income and capital gain possibilities. This takes even more work on the part of the investor, but it could be worth the time. Finding solid REITs internationally with no leverage, high occupancy, and good pricing power is the way to go.

*** *Short term U.S. Treasury money market funds* are the preferred vehicle for a relatively safe place to park your cash. Forget about chasing yield to get an extra quarter of a percent interest. There is no free lunch here.

Clearly regular money market funds are now at risk, proven by the fact that the U.S. government decided to insure them up to $250,000 even though it would have to use the printing press to make good on the guarantee. But that guarantee is set to expire by the end of 2012. Guaranteed or not, if your fund has trouble satisfying its obligations (like honoring your check at $1 per share), you may well have an extended wait to become whole. So let's just make it a little bit easier. Get money market funds that are only invested in short term government treasuries. You are right; 'Theft of the American Dream' suggested that you not buy government bonds. But the money market funds that *only invest in short term treasuries (T-bills)* are safer than those that invest in corporate debt, repurchase agreements, and various forms of collateralized debt obligations (CDO's). Short term T-bills have no risk of principal. They are a cash substitute and the big money of the world uses them. Plus you can have check writing privileges in many of these funds, so you have instant availability of your funds. If the government defaults, we'll all have problems anyway, so don't worry about that. Just go on-line or ask a broker about this type of money market fund and go for it, as there are many to choose from. There may well come a time that you are glad you did.

*** *Be very wary of annuities and bank CD's.* Fixed rate annuities and CD's from banks give you a guaranteed rate of growth. But if the rate is less than the *true* rate of inflation, you are losing purchasing power even though your account balance continues to rise. This makes no sense to your long term prosperity. If you are risk averse, that is understandable, but it doesn't mean that you have to be a sacrificial lamb. What it does mean is that you'll have to educate yourself about alternatives, as suggested earlier.

What about annuities that offer high interest rate guarantees? There are actually plenty of them to be found, but there are also plenty of caveats. The high guaranteed interest rate has to come from somewhere, and that somewhere would be from the investor. It could be in the form of very high surrender charges for many years after your initial deposit, or it could even be tied to the necessity to annuitize (taking regular payments instead of a one-time, lump-sum redemption) at some point in the future. And there's the rub. The annuity payments are calculated on any number of factors including company expenses, their investments, and your own mortality factor as established by the company. When you annuitize, your sum of money held by the insurance company is multiplied by a factor calculated by the insurance company to determine your monthly, quarterly, or annual payout. This factor is where the insurance company is able to make up for that high rate of return that they offered you. By shopping your principal for the best annuity factor, you'll see for yourself. There is a HUGE disparity in annuity factors amongst insurance companies. Just know that you yourself will end up paying for that high interest rate guarantee! Think about it: how can a company offer you a relatively high guaranteed rate of interest when there are none to be found in the marketplace? You know the answer!

*** Should you buy *variable annuities*? No! These financial instruments allow you to invest in stock and bond funds, and defer the tax on any gains until your take the money out of the annuity. This sounds good; but again, investing in mutual funds in a bear market, whether tax deferred or not, will not work to your advantage for the same reasons stated above. Not only that, variable annuities usually have additional charges within to cover the cost of their guaranteed features such as a minimum return and a guaranteed death benefit. Additionally, the management fees of the investment funds within the annuity tend to put a damper on the rate of return to the annuitant. Finally, if you think the annuity would be a good idea to supplement your income stream if you decide to annuitize (take payments for a guaranteed period instead of your lump sum return of your money), think again. In a low interest rate environment, all you would do is to lock in that low rate for your entire payment period. Your best bet is to avoid variable annuities altogether and educate yourself on other ways to beat inflation by a wide margin.

*** There is one exception to the notion of avoiding bank CD's, and that is to *open a CD in a foreign currency*. We know that eventually all fiat currencies will end up in the trash bin, but before they do many will be stronger on a relative basis than the U.S. dollar. One U.S. bank that offers foreign currency CD's is Everbank (www.everbank.com), based in St. Louis, and it provides FDIC coverage like other U.S. banks. But this particular bank has many unique investment products, and offers CD's in about 20 different major currencies. This would allow you to realize the potential appreciation of that foreign currency against the U.S. dollar. How do you know which currencies would be most advantageous when you are ready to invest? Do your technical analysis as outlined earlier to find one in a solid uptrend! Begin by finding countries that have low debt and high income. They are out there! Not only that, but Everbank also has *commodity themed basket CD's* which would allow you to participate in currency appreciation in several asset rich countries concurrently. Click on the site map tab at the bottom of the home page to get information on the investment of your choice. Will any of the Everbank CD choices outperform in a super charged inflationary environment? This is doubtful. But until the situation gets to critical mass, a superior return is possible. This is not a paid advertisement!

Your retirement plan

*** It is a must is to *look at the portfolio choices in your retirement plan* at your place of employment. Many employers have set up a 401k for their employees, but don't attend to the investment choices as well as they should. Sure, you have some very high quality choices from any number of fund families, but that's not the point. The point is that virtually all of these choices invest for the upside. But too often they don't offer choices for the employee to invest on the downside. Remember, the majority of the 401k plans were set up during a bull market. But things are very different now. Witness the decimation in company sponsored retirement plans since the summer of 2008. Times have changed, and you need to change too.

*** Virtually all company sponsored 401k plans use strictly *mutual funds designed for bull markets* as their investment vehicles, making them very risky in a bear market.   These funds have prospectus stating their objectives. Check those objectives. Do they make sense for you? Be very cautious, as it will cost you money in a bear market if the bullish objectives of the fund are not met. Also, it may look like you have plenty of fund choices, but they're mostly variations on the same theme.   Plus, by the rules set out in the prospectus, the funds can only buy so much of any one stock (or bond). When the majority of the stocks are going nowhere, their own rules don't allow them the flexibility of piling on to their favorite stock picks. By definition, their performance will be relegated to average at best, and pathetic at worst through no real fault of their own. In a bear market, that's what happens.   Their job is to invest the money entrusted to them consistent with the fund objectives. They would find it most difficult to outperform the general market. Yes, we've had gurus in the market with outstanding results, like Peter Lynch, formerly of the Magellan Fund, or Warren Buffet of Berkshire Hathaway, but this occurred in a bull market. In a bear market, the majority of stock mutual funds will either drop or lose purchasing power, no matter their quality and wonderful fundamentals. So the paradigm has changed, and you need to change with it.

*** Put your money into a *fixed investment* within the plan until you are more than comfortable with your investment choices. Most sponsored plans offer a fixed principle, fixed interest type of investment as one of the choices. Don't get into a stock or a bond fund just because that's what everybody else is doing. First, do some serious homework on your investment choices. Then, pick the best of the best, and don't spread your money over more than the best two choices. If your account balance is too high to reduce your portfolio to two choices because you would be too uncomfortable in doing so, opt out of the plan! Diversification, particularly in an inflationary economic environment, will not prove to be a winning strategy. The stock market as a whole will be a buy at some point, but not until the public capitulation occurs, which likely won't happen until the DOW has far underperformed the rate of inflation. And, as you know, bonds are likely to lose money for years to come as rising interest rates erode the principle value. If you are not comfortable that any of the funds offered in your 401k are suitable for beating inflation, consider opting out of the plan even if there is some employer match. Then, you could roll the money into a self-directed IRA to give yourself a much better chance to make a superior return.

*** If your 401k provides a match *that is substantially higher than the percentage of Consumer Price Index* increase, then it's OK to continue to fund it with your own dollars to get that match. Continue to put enough money into the plan to just make it to the point where the company match would stop. *Do not put excess funding into a 401k that is not being matched.* Why? You can do better investing on your own by going with individual stocks instead of mutual funds. Go ahead; pay some capital gains taxes, but do your homework and you'll outperform your mutual funds every year. This will also allow you to become more competent in decisions regarding the retirement plan.

If your company does not offer some sort of match, you'll need to do some hard thinking on whether or not you want to continue to feed the bear market with your hard earned dollars. You'll have plenty of viable alternatives to invest outside of the 401k, and with some effort, your results will be far superior.

*** Other than investment choice risks, there are other *risks in all qualified plans*, and they are virtually *inevitable*. The first risk is increased taxes upon withdrawal. Remember, the U.S. is in dire financial condition, and its revenues are not coming anywhere near its current and planned future spending for entitlements. With the trillions of dollars sitting in these plans without having been taxed, politicians will devise ways to tap that huge pool of funds. Think higher taxes, for sure. And once the discussion starts in Congress, don't be surprised to see them pass something that is retroactive, so as to catch the people who had become concerned and exited before the bill is actually enacted. Retroactive measures have passed before, so don't be surprised to see it again.

*** Another risk is even more ominous, and it is also a good bet. That would be that the *U.S. government mandates that some or all of your investment inside the qualified plan be used to purchase U.S. government bonds*. That's right, those are the ones at 30 year high prices and 30 year low yields. Again, with the world-wide demand for our T-bonds dropping, the vast resources in qualified plans make for a prime and captured source of funds for borrowing by your politicians. You doubt that this wouldn't happen? Don't bet your financial future on it! Remember, Japan ruled the financial world in the 1980's before their crisis hit, and interest rates went to zero. That was in 1990. How did Japan sell more and more of its debt? It required its citizens to buy it in their retirement plans! In fact, by 2012, only about 8% of Japanese debt was held by foreigners! So the notion of mandated purchases is not far-fetched!

*** All investors should at least consider taking some or all of the money out of their qualified plans now, pay the tax, and look to reallocate that money in new-found investment interests for a far higher after tax and after inflation return. Prime candidates for this suggestion would be those who have already reached the age of 59 ½. In these cases, at least the 10% penalty for premature withdrawal would not be a consideration. This may seem radical and far from main-stream acceptable advice. But mainstream advice will change after the damage is already done, and you'll want to be ahead of the curve in your favorite tangible asset investments before the crowd pushes prices past the point of good value. In fact, you can sell yours to them! Of course everyone has their own unique set of circumstances to deal with. But if you are serious about maintaining and growing your purchasing power, a partial or complete withdrawal from your qualified retirement plan is a must for consideration.

CHAPTER 16
THE DEBT QUESTION

Is it good or bad?

The world is awash with all sorts of debt, and the U.S. is the leader of the pack. We have U.S. Government debt, along with massive unfunded liabilities such as Medicare and Social Security, state and municipal debt, mortgage debt, consumer debt, commercial debt, leveraged OTC derivatives, and the list goes on. But that's the big picture. What about you? Financial advisors and TV pundits think U.S. consumers should pay off their debts, and in many cases this is good advice. But in other cases it's not. Why not? It's a superior idea to *pay off debts with less valuable money* than was borrowed in the first place, just like the U.S. government does! A dollar repaid later will be worth less than the dollar that was borrowed earlier, so why not take advantage of the difference? That's exactly the plan of the U.S. government, and you can make it work for you too. If you incur new debt with a solid and workable plan for investment and subsequent repayment, that's a great idea. Conversely, unproductive debt (like credit for everyday purchases) appearing on your personal financial statement is not. Answers to some of the questions about good and bad debt, and what to do about them may require a serious mindset adjustment on your part. What follows is a brief recap on some of the basic issues and questions. There are not "one size fits all" solutions, so you'll have to decide what's right in your own situation.

In many cases, debt is good

We know that in general, you want to avoid holding bonds, particularly government bonds. Bonds are other people or entities owing you money, and the last thing you need is to be the holder of someone else's IOU with little or no security, and no solid income with which to pay you back. But, *in an inflationary monetary environment, you want to owe at least SOME money.* The caveat is the necessity that you have the means (income) to carry the debt, your own valid investment idea for which to use the money, and an actual plan to pay that money back. The word plan in this context is just that, including a "plan B" if the first plan doesn't work. Simply having an intention to repay debt really isn't good enough! Commit your plan to paper, and review it for holes with your business partner, spouse, accountant, or anyone else who would be affected. You'll likely want or need support for the idea by the important people in your life, so don't leave them out of the discussion.

Let's start by setting the record straight. Say you bought a $1000 government bond 10 years ago. Maybe the yield was, say 5 percent. So you have collected that $50 per year, but now the bond is maturing, and you expect to get your $1000 back, correct? Sure, but that $1000 won't buy nearly as much as it did 10 years ago. With a *true* inflation rate for the last ten years at around 6%, this makes that same $1000 worth less than $400 in today's dollars. The government only had to pay a fraction of its debt back, while you lost $600 in purchasing power; plus you had to pay tax on the interest! Why can't you do something like this with your own debt load? It's wise and advisable if you have solid income to cover the payments along with a good investment plan.

For *business owners and entrepreneurs*, judicious use of any available credit lines can be a great move. Many business owners wonder about the best places for them to invest their hard earned savings. The first place to look would your own businesses! If you can't invest in your own business idea with confidence, what else could you invest in with even more confidence? For business owners who aren't on the brink of disaster, it's advisable to invest in some new aspect, product, technology, or service in your business, and do it with borrowed money if you don't have the cash on hand. Look to the Small Business Administration and other newly devised government plans if your bank doesn't cooperate with your loan request. Let's look at a high profile example of an ancillary business idea in a lousy economy.

We all know about Starbucks and their thousands of stores selling cups of coffee for $5 and scones for $3. But we are now into some hard times. So granted, they did decide to close some stores, but only a small percentage of the total. The fact that McDonald's started to sell the same type of coffee products from its new McCafe's probably helped force Starbuck's hand. Instead of doing nothing, Starbuck's came out with a new product line featuring "instant" Starbucks coffee to go for about $1 per cup. This is a whole new market for them, and one that has been ignored for years. Instant coffee isn't that great, right? Well, Starbucks did extensive testing all over the country with its customers, and the feedback was impressive. So an idea was born as an extension to the existing product offerings. Businesses must always innovate, because if they don't someone else will beat them out of revenues in one fashion or another!

Can you think of a creative idea to fill an ancillary niche in your business? Entrepreneurs know that they are only limited by their imagination and work ethic, so the advice here is to go for it! Incur new debt to enhance your business and personal bottom line. If you don't, the tough times business environment will leave you in the dust.

Employers and entrepreneurs may have the mindset and risk tolerance for taking on more debt for a new idea, but what if you are an *employee*? You may not be used to risk. You're not used to borrowing money to invest. But your thinking may have to change. If you think nothing of borrowing to consume and accumulate more debt as a result, why not try to redirect that debt to something that has a better chance of paying itself back, and putting extra funds in your pocket at the same time?

This is not to say that borrowing money to re-invest for high returns is easy, but nor is it hard. The difficulty lies in the head of the individual. The difficulty is changing long entrenched habits and thought patterns. That's why there must be an emphasis on changing the way you think, along with added self-education. There is no question that your thinking has to change before your finances improve. For many this requires radical change, and the mental discipline for most people would be tough. But this is what it will take to thrive in the coming economic storm, so get used to the notion and act now. The environment for obtaining a loan after the crisis has been tough, but it will get much tougher as the financial system deteriorates. So search out investment ideas and sources for loans now. The rewards will surprise you!

Home mortgages and the market

We all have to be smart about our national insolvency and its consequences to our personal situations. Interest rates are so low, and the true inflation rate is so high and rising, that people *should not* automatically think they have to pay off their mortgage, without a very compelling reason. Again, this assumes a solid income stream. Even though it is time for saving and not consuming, most folks have to act much more intelligently than they have in the past when thinking about the issue of saving. Just as depositing part of every paycheck into the bank for a rainy day or for a collage fund is not going to do the job for you, nor will an accelerated plan to pay down the mortgage on your home. Both of these strategies ensure a guaranteed loss of purchasing power. Your disposable income *must be used to garner* a higher rate than that of the true rate of inflation. If you have *disposable income after the bills are paid*, you need to look for ways to have inflation work to your advantage, and to *use that advantage to grow your personal wealth*.

You should actually think about *obtaining a bigger mortgage* if you have the income and equity to qualify. After all, by 2012, U.S. mortgages had experienced the lowest interest rates on record! This is obviously not for everyone. However, there are many ways to earn a far greater after tax return than your mortgage rate. But these ways require some thought and a good action plan. Once you become successful at your wealth building plan, then you can revisit the debt payoff question with many more dollars than you would otherwise have had with which to make that payoff happen.

But what if you're *"upside-down"*? This refers to the homeowner who owes more on the mortgage than the current value of the home. Needless to say, this has morphed into a huge problem in the U.S. Mr. Obama proposed to fix the problem with a mortgage rescue plan that got enacted into law. That doesn't really matter, as it would never raise home prices. In fact, it probably won't even stabilize them, due to a continuing supply coming onto the market for the foreseeable future. However, the plan will eventually necessitate higher interest rates. It has to. With the shape banks are in, any concession they make to an existing borrower has to be made up elsewhere in their loan portfolio. If it isn't accomplished by government largess, it will eventually have to come from new borrowers. Fortunately, that eventuality is not likely to occur until Freddie Mac and Fannie Mae stops insuring over 95% of new mortgages!

Just after the appearance of the crisis at the end of 2008, about 8.3 million homeowners had negative equity and this had escalated to over 20% of all mortgage borrowers by 2012. The drop in equity values nationwide was estimated at an astonishing $2.4 trillion in 2008, with 5.4 million Americans in a delinquent or foreclosure status on their mortgages. By 2012, the total loss of equity came in at about $8 trillion! But the carnage was not equally dispersed. The higher growth areas have the biggest share of the problems, such as Nevada with 55% of homeowners under water at the peak. New York had the least damage, at only 4.7%

Many homeowners with excellent credit histories have decided to default on their mortgage payments because of the upside-down status of their home. This is called a *strategic default*. And many people have signed their deed back over to the bank as a "deed in lieu of foreclosure". They do this to try to keep in the good graces of the bank because the bank would not have all the cost and uncertainty of the foreclosure process. And yes, there was a great deal of uncertainty here simply because of the MERS (Mortgage Electronic Registration System) mess, whereby new versions of lost or destroyed documents had been signed by the thousands. Many courts disallowed the foreclosures due to the fact that the note and mortgage documents were split up when the loans were packaged by the sharks on Wall Street; when the banks tried to retroactively do new documents, it blew up in court! Only later was a deal struck between banks and State Attorneys General for trying to undo the problem.

Should you enact a strategic default? It depends on your timing and need for future loans for whatever reasons. Let's just say that there could be many reasons that a strategic default could actually be beneficial, and it depends on the individual circumstances. If you don't care about the hit to your credit score due to not having a future need to borrow from a bank, this may work for you.

If you are upside-down on your home mortgage, you need to strategize now. Homes don't pay for maintenance on their own, just as they don't pay the utilities, taxes, and insurance for you. Do you want to put in a new air conditioning unit on a negative equity home, or replace a leaky roof? Do you think the value of your home will bounce right back up so you have positive equity again pretty quickly? This is certainly possible in some very specific locales, but this will certainly *not happen* in most cases.

If you also have a lot of credit card debt along with an upside down mortgage, and a relatively low amount of savings or investments, you must seriously consider *bankruptcy.* Don't be afraid of bankruptcy; because even though it can be frightening in the short term, it would be your friend in the long run. The repair to your credit score won't be that arduous if you exercise good financial discipline going forward. Naturally, as you know from reading this book, the bankruptcy card is preferable and acceptable in a capitalist system as opposed to bailouts. This goes for the individual as well as businesses and government. Adjust your thinking, as it could work in your favor over the long term!

Of course you can go to your mortgage or credit card lender to see about getting relief, but this is not a permanent solution. If you do have some assets that can be sold to pay off some of the mortgage so that you can refinance at a lower amount, that could be a consideration. Or if you stand to inherit some money, maybe your benefactor could gift you some of that inheritance now. But this type of approach is like throwing good money after bad, particularly if home prices don't bounce right back up, which most won't. This would not be a favored approach, unless you were convinced that you wanted to stay in that home for the long term. Then it would be fine. Just remember, it took 10 years to get the housing prices into such a distended and overpriced condition and the comeback will not be a short or easy road. It will be long and tedious.

Reverse mortgages (RM's)

A great tool for the enterprising senior citizen is the reverse mortgage. Like any other suggestion in 'Theft of the American Dream', getting educated on the details is a basic requirement. Conventional wisdom would have it that you not borrow money for investing purposes. But in a supercharged inflationary environment, it is almost a must given the right circumstances, and the RM is a potentially awesome tool for doing just that. Or, if inflation eats into your purchasing power and you need to add to your monthly income, the RM could be a viable way to do so without having the onus of mortgage payments. Every senior who owns a home should look into this fabulous financing tool.

Reverse mortgages are strictly for homeowners over 62 years of age. The RM allows the homeowner to take equity out of the home either in a lump sum or in regular monthly *payments from the bank*, without the necessity to return any mortgage payments back to the bank as in the case with a conventional mortgage. *The proceeds withdrawn are not taxable.* The homeowner's only requirements are that the real estate taxes and routine maintenance be kept up, and that the owner of the home actually lives there.

Qualifying for a reverse mortgage is easy. There are no credit scores or income requirements to worry about, but your home does have to have equity. This doesn't mean that if you have a mortgage already that it can't be paid off with some or all of the proceeds of the reverse mortgage. It can. Like the conventional mortgage, there is a requirement for an appraisal as well as other closing costs. One additional requirement is that the homeowner must get counseling about the RM, but in many cases it can be done over the telephone.

If a senior takes all the qualifying equity out of the home, never makes a payment, and the balance owed after say, 20 or 30 years is far more than the value of the home, how does the RM loan ever get paid off? Since the home is required to be sold upon death or a move, the loan can be paid from the sale proceeds. If the sale of the home doesn't bring in enough to pay off the accrued principal and interest owed, the Federal Housing Administration (FHA) will make up the difference! This is not a free perk. Homeowners actually pay for it by adding about ½ of a percent to the loan interest. Conversely, if there is equity left over after the sale of the property, the property owner or the estate heirs would receive the balance.

Finally, seniors should know that Social Security and Medicare are not affected at all if you do an RM. However need-based government subsidies may be affected in certain situations.

Seniors who own homes should delve into the reverse mortgage idea. This doesn't mean that you have to borrow money right away. But if you owe nothing on your home right now, the RM could be set up like a home equity line of credit, and you could tap into that line of credit anytime you may need it in the future, without worrying about timing or qualification.

Credit cards and credit lines

It seems pretty obvious, but the only way to use credit cards is by *paying the total balance off each and every month*. Actually, with the benefits of airline miles, gas discounts, hotel points, etc. it makes sense to use credit cards. It even makes tracking your expenses easier. But if you are using credit cards, credit lines, or conventional home equity lines to fund *consumer spending* that you can't pay back at the end of the billing cycle, stop. If you can't pay off credit cards every month, you shouldn't be using up your sources of credit for things that don't even last as long as the time it takes to pay back the debt, like gas for the car or a meal at a fancy restaurant, for instance! If the debt is still there when the reason for the debt is gone, you have structural problems!

This is a bit like what your government does; but we know that paying regular bills with more debt doesn't work. Your government only has one favored method to pay its debts, and that is with more debt via the sale of bonds, depreciating the real value of its dollar obligations. But you can't do this, so a workable debt strategy is in order.

You want to pay off your debt with depreciated dollars too, but since you don't have the means to print your own money, you'll definitely need a better financial plan than your government has. We know that you can't consume with borrowed funds and not be the poorer for it in the future. There are millions of people who cannot pay off, much less pay down those credit card balances. For those folks, you must ask yourself right now, what is the long term plan? Most stuck in the trap of credit card debt would say they have no long term plan. If you don't have enough money saved to pay off your consumer related debts, and there is no plan of how it can be done, bankruptcy could be a viable alternative. If you are not really sure about avenues to help yourself to eliminate debt you can't afford to repay, perhaps a credit counseling service would be beneficial.

But if you default on credit card debts or file bankrupcy, what about your *credit score*? Who cares! You might just as well take the hit right now. Do you think your credit report will improve by your continuance of adding to the owed balances each month? Forget it! Look at all the money you'll save, which could now be invested in the future instead of the past. This strategy will only work if you swear off the use of plastic for regular daily consumer purchases. Better yet, just use a debit card, or even pre-paid credit cards; then the temptation wouldn't be there to revert to your old ways.

If you have *untapped credit lines*, or even an unused low interest credit card, or a home equity line at a reasonable rate of interest you are in good shape! With care, you can use these lines to earn a much greater return than the interest you'll pay. And with solid forethought and a good plan, the repayment will not be so hard, given that you'll be using depreciated dollars to pay off those debts. In a hyperinflationary environment, we all must become entrepreneurs. We are limited only by our imagination, guts, and wit. No one will take care of you through these trying times; that will be your job. That's why *effective debt management* is so critical. It can bury you, or it *can help you beat inflationary forces* and bring you back from the dead. Your job is to look for ways to *use debt to enhance your purchasing power.*

Private loans

Because the traditional banking system became widely dysfunctional to American savers after the fall of 2008, there has been plenty of income destruction in the form of anemic interest rates. Insurance companies have not proven to be a whole lot better with their annuity rates. Many retirees and other savers who count on interest from their savings as a necessary source of income have to tap principal every month to make up for this destruction of income. Meanwhile, regular expenses will continue to escalate like everyone else's. What can savers do? They can follow some of the recommendations in this book, plus they can *supplement their income by making private secured loans.*

For enterprising people, searching out *private sources of loan money* has become a necessary and viable strategy to fund entrepreneurial and other income and capital gain generating ideas. So both the private lender and the enterprising borrower might be able to craft a deal for the benefit of both! The deal could include both a decent rate of interest, security, and even some sort of profit sharing. Lenders should solicit help from their legal advisor on the best way to have the loan secured in the event of default or other non-performance issues, even if the deal is struck between family members.

Conclusion

Your next steps will be those which only you can take. Hopefully, 'Theft of the American Dream' has given you plenty of ammunition upon which to think and act. The problem with most people in our society is that they don't act until a problem is directly in their face. At that point their options are limited and time is not on their side. Don't let this happen to you. Start your financial survival plan now.

The good news is that the advice and approaches to your financial defense outlined within these pages do not have to come at an extra financial cost to you. You have what you have, and you can save what you can save. Just know that the winners in the coming upheaval will be those folks who have already changed their approach to their lifestyle and investing, and are conscientious enough to construct their own strategies. By putting those strategies to work into specific tangible asset classes, the rest should take care of itself. But it is a process. This means that it has to become part of your daily life and lifestyle, and that's the hard part. Dedicating the time to make your plan successful is absolutely critical. Have no doubt: if you apply yourself you can certainly do it in a way that no advisor could do for you.

A further note is in order. Don't let semantics get in your way when you are investigating your course of action. Some people define hyperinflation as 50% price increases per month. Some would think that even 15% per year is a hyperinflationary situation. It doesn't really matter what the number is. What matters is that your dollars are buying less and less each month and year, and our situation will not reverse itself anytime soon. It will get much worse. This is why financial education and lifestyle changes become so critical. If you fashion these factors to your advantage, you'll be much further ahead.

Finally, don't assume that you can't discover new and better ways to defeat inflationary forces that haven't appeared in 'Theft of the American Dream.' You probably can. Resourcefulness and motivation will be your best friend in the years ahead, so embrace it along with an entrepreneurial spirit. You'll be glad you did!

PART III

Resource Guide

WEBSITES

Your education continues right here. Much of the heavy lifting has been done for you in terms of screening various websites for accuracy and efficacy. This doesn't mean that you can't do more investigating on your own, but the sources listed here are almost a must for your financial education and survival. They'll give you plenty of what you'll need to know to defend your finances in the near and distant future.

King World News (http://kingworldnews.com)

The site features regular audio interviews moderated by Eric King with some of the smartest minds in the world on any number of financial subjects. The best part is that almost all of them are easy to understand, and that you can listen to them anytime. This is *the* prime site for your self-enlightenment. And, if you don't want to take the time to listen, you can quickly scan through the blogs by these same folks. They consist of key excerpts from the interviews. The interviews are invaluable because they cut through the mainstream media smokescreens and slanted hype of the bankers and politicians. Here is a list of just some of the participants and their areas of expertise, along with a mini biography for your consideration. Don't think that this is a comprehensive list, because it isn't. Virtually all of the people that Eric King interviews are top notch in their fields of expertise.

Jim Rickards – Mr. Rickards is an economist and lawyer with vast experience at the highest levels of the global capital markets. He has investment banks, private investment funds, and government directorates as clients. He has participated directly in many financial events of the past 30 years, and is regularly consulted on financial aspects of national security and department of defense initiatives. Rickards is also the author of the 2011 book 'Currency Wars'. This guy knows the meaning, motives, and moves of the bankers before they do it. Any chance you have to listen to his interviews or read his work, you should do so.

Chris Whalen – Mr. Whalen is the cofounder of Institutional Risk Analytics, a Los Angeles based provider of consulting services. He regularly works with regulators and financial professionals. He has also testified before Congress and the SEC on many subjects of their inquiry. He regularly contributes articles to publications such as The International Economy and American Banker. He is also a member of the Herbert Gold Society which is comprised of current and former employees of the Federal Reserve and Treasury Department. He is well connected, very smart, and a must listen interviewee.

Peter Schiff – Mr. Schiff is President and Chief Global Strategist of Euro Pacific Capital, and frequently appears on TV networks such as CNBC, CNN, Fox News, FBN and Bloomberg. He speaks in a clear and concise manner that allows regular people to understand his points. Since he is an Austrian economic school proponent, his insight is most valuable in this time of extreme worldwide financial stress. He is as smart as they come, and usually right on target with his predictions.

Gerald Celente – Mr. Celente is generally regarded as one of the world's top forecasters of social, political, and economic trends. He has been in too many media venues to mention. Celente speaks in a style that is really unique, irreverent, and entertaining, and is almost always spot on with his forecast of the macro picture and meaning of political and financial moves of the Washington and Wall Street elite. He is so entertaining yet insightful that once you hear him for the first time, you'll seek out more of his interviews on a regular basis.

James Turk – Mr. Turk is the founder and Chairman of Goldmoney. com. He has been in the international banking, finance, and investment business for 40 years and provides investment research to hedge funds and commodity trading advisors. He is also the publisher of 'The Freemarket Gold and Money Report', an investment newsletter. He has authored two books and many articles on money and banking. He is also the co-author of 'The Collapse of the Dollar'. When James Turk speaks, you should listen!

Zero Hedge (http://www.zerohedge.com)

This is a masterful site run by a former Wall Street insider. Writing under the pseudonym Tyler Durden, he brings to light the machinations of the international markets, banking and politics like no other site on the internet. It is a 24 hour commentary on the fly based on contemporaneous and instantaneous financial and political news reports. Please understand that this is not a farcical blog; it is very serious. You might even decide to drop your subscriptions to Barron's, the Financial Times, or the Wall Street

Journal once you become familiar with this website! If you want the news and want it now with critical insights and analysis, this is the site for you. The best part is that it cuts through all the "spin" and gets right to the pith. Guest writers contribute daily to the content as well.

Some of the issues are somewhat heavy, making them difficult to understand, but for many it will be a delight to comb through the headlines and check out which entries you'd like to delve into for the real story and its meaning. Under the headlines there is usually a teaser paragraph or two to give you a preview of what follows. The writing is clear and precise, with wit and apt criticism where necessary. Just click on the headline for more in-depth coverage and commentary on your item of interest.

The site also includes insightful charts on any number of issues that give readers a great picture of the written word. It is so comprehensive in subject matter that you could spend all day following it if you wanted to. It is updated on a constant basis. It is quite the education, and should be considered a "must" for the aficionado of the markets as well as for the novice. You can get as deep into a subject as you'd like to go. Do you want to become better educated on the economy and what the fiscal and monetary moves of the elite actually mean? Are you looking for macro ideas in your possible area of investment interest? Zero Hedge is a valuable tool in the pursuit of your financial defense. Use it often.

Mr. Gold's website (http://www.jsmineset.com)

Jim Sinclair is not internationally known as "Mr. Gold" for nothing. He is the man, and imparts daily financial and political wisdom on his website every day. He has a long history with various investments and gold, going back to the 1970's, and is truly considered to be the preeminent voice in the gold market today. As stated in his "about us" section of the site, "We are a service oriented teaching forum that uses the daily market as its text and blackboard, but every commentary carries a lesson. The spin really does stop here." Mr. Sinclair is also featured with regularity on the King World News website. Also featured on his site are contributors that add tons of value to the overall learning experience. Not only that, if you feel that you are not up to speed as much as you'd like to be with reference to gold, you can request his compendiums on CD which would be a great way for you to catch up. Finally, everyone should review "Jim's formula" published on the site. This is a 12 step process that has been self repeating, albeit getting much worse, to see how Mr. Sinclair sees the demise of the U.S.

economy happening. It was first published in 2006, and has been correct all along the way.

Decision Point (https://decisionpoint.com)

Decision Point should be your first stop to learn some basics of stock technical analysis. Carl Swenlin, developer of the site, is a master at his craft and he has shared the basics with the public through this forum. Remember, before you venture into any stock purchase, it is always best to look at pictures of price performance and understand what that picture is portraying. This assumes you have already done your homework on the fundamental analysis of companies you have interest in, as mentioned previously.

The Learning Center – This is a free service on the site. Click on the tab on the top of the home page to get started. The Learning Center is divided into four sections, all of which is recommended for your review, with emphasis on the first two which include an *Overview and Key Concepts* section and the *Basic Chart Patterns* section. Then, the Market Indicators and Miscellaneous Articles will be a good study to add to the basics. But the first two sections are critical to your stock trading success. Also, pay very close attention to the *Essential Analysis Steps* subsection. Then understand the construction of all of the Chart Patterns presented. Only then will the Market Indicators section be of added value. As to the Market Indicators section, don't expect to become an expert on all the indicators. This would be an exercise in frustration for almost anyone. Rather, you should concentrate your efforts on just a few of them and use the same ones on a regular basis for each buy and sell decision. This allows you to become relatively attuned to the nuances of the ones that you are used to, and your chances of using them successfully will increase.

Basic indicators such as Moving Averages, the Price Momentum Oscillator, BB's (Bollinger Bands), RSI (Relative Strength Index), MACD (Moving Average Convergence/Divergence), and Volume by Price are all very useful. Although the BB, RSI and MACD are not covered by Mr. Swenlin in his tutorial, you can practice their use in almost all of the charting services. Also, it is many times instructive to look at Chaikin Money Flow and Accumulation/Distribution overlays. These cut through the price action to tell you if money is actually going into your stock or coming out, and if it's the big boys or the small fries doing the buying and selling. Make sure you're buying when the big boys do!

Top Advisors Corner – This is a great resource. You can tap into some of the best minds in the stock business on a regular basis, all for free. Among frequent contributors are Dr. Joe Duarte, Tom McClellan, Gene Inger, Steve Todd, Carl Swenlin, Alan Newman, John Kosar, and Harry Boxer. These guys have stood the test of time as to their efficacy. Also valuable is the *ETF Tracker* which was devised by Swenlin. This allows you to follow the performance of scores of ETF's and see which are doing the best at the time. In fact, a visit to this page alone could save you a tremendous amount of time if you are searching for the next hot market sector for investment. And if your targeted company for investment is not in a sector that is doing too well, it may save you some grief and money too! The ETF Tracker is another screening tool for success.

Chart Spotlight – This section highlights one chart every week or two, with a narrative on what it is telling Mr. Swenlin. Typically it is a big picture view of a certain market segment, be it in stocks, bonds, the dollar, gold, or whatever. It is definitely worth a few minutes of your time.

Member Section – Has a lot of charts, both current and historical, with the capability for the user to develop his/her own charts on thousands of stocks. The cost for this added section is $20 per month. Recognizing that some readers may not want to pay for a subscription to develop their own charts to follow their stock selections, a couple of alternative, less comprehensive free sites are listed below. But please do not miss the benefit of the services that Decision Point provides for free.

Bigcharts.marketwatch.com

This is a great site for free charting. In the center top of the home page, you'll see 3 buttons for "basic chart", "advanced chart" and "interactive chart". For strictly technical analysis, you should use the "advanced" chart. This allows you the same type of capabilities as the other service mentioned above. However, the "interactive" chart section is not to be ignored either. When you put in your stock symbol for this section, you can actually use the cursor to scroll horizontally across the chart and it will give you the prices as you go, and relevant news stories related to that particular stock. If you see a big move in the stock and you want to look at any related news, you can click on "news stories" and see what is amiss. Not only that, on the top left side of the page, you can click on numerous displays and technical indicators you'd like to see and they come up instantly in the chart. And no matter what timeframe or indicators you have up on the screen, you can scroll horizontally through the chart and it will give you price levels of each and every indicator interactively. It's really a neat feature. Don't be intimidated by the above narrative here, as this site is very easy and user friendly! Give it a try!

Stockcharts.com

This is another good site for free charting. Go to the upper right hand side of the home page under the "start a chart" section. For most people, the "sharp-chart" should be sufficient, although there are options for point and figure charts as well, which is a bit more sophisticated for the budding experts and enthusiasts. Once you get your basic chart up on the screen, you can scroll down to the "chart attributes", "overlays", and "indicators", sections to refine your chart for timeframes and to plug in the indicators you want to follow. Practice and become your own expert!

Shadow Government Statistics (http://www.shadowstats.com)

There is no doubt that 'Theft of the American Dream' has created a lot of noise about government and it's fudged (to be kind) economic statistics. After examining this site and its free offerings for non-subscribers, you'll see for yourself. For those of you who can afford the $175 per year for a subscription to the full range of services, it is highly recommended. But developer John Williams offers quite an education for free. On the home page, you can access primers on government economic reports, his special 'Hyperinflation Update', and much more. Mr. Williams keeps track of data the old fashioned way before the statistics starred to become massaged after 1980, and more particularly after 1990. Just look at the numbers in pictorial form to see for yourself. These are an eye opener. Under "alternative data" on the right side of the home page, he charts the GDP, CPI, Unemployment and Money Supply. For year-end 2011, this is where you'll discover the true inflation number of 7% instead of the reported 3% or so; this is where you'll find the true unemployment number at a staggering 23%; and this is where you'll see that the real GDP growth has been falling since 1984, and indeed has been in negative territory for the last ten years (meaning actual contraction instead of falling growth)! When you access any chart, just click on it for a larger version so you can see the details. If this site alone doesn't convince you that you need to protect your invested assets from the ravages of inflation, nothing will, with the possible exception of the next site suggestion.

Daniel Amerman (http://www.danielamerman.com)

This is a tremendous site for convincing you how inflation really works for the government, and by definition, against you. Even though we may see some selected consumer prices drop before hyperinflation actually kicks in, you'll need some serious preparation for the inevitable, and this site will get you into the right mindset. Additionally, Mr. Amerman presents general economic issues of the day in easy to read presentations. These free offerings by the super sharp site developer are a staggering and sobering look at reality. You simply must read the free sections, and sign up for his email posts. He does not give specific investment recommendations, but rather presents *"a conceptual exploration of financial and general economic principles"*, and he does it in a manner that any neophyte can grasp. For starters, you can sign up for his free 'Turning Inflation into Wealth' series of lessons, accessible on the home page. There is so much good information on this site that it will take you some time to go through it all. But going through it is a must for your financial survival. Just click on each of the gold boxes on the front page to get to the related subject matter. Again, this is a superior resource that should not be ignored.

St. Louis Fed Website (http://research.stlouisfed.org/fred2/)

Cleary this resource has been used for many charts and data in 'Theft of the American Dream'. You can do the same, and update the data as your curiosity dictates. Follow this website for your information so you don't have to rely on political or media blather. You can even customize the information as to the time-frames you want to see, just as was done on numerous charts included earlier. It is really simple to do; all you have to do is click on "edit graph" and you can put in your own parameters on thousands of data series.' The categories include money, banking, finance, tracking GDP, the CPI and many others. And there's financial tracking for almost every sector of the economy. Business owners may want to check their particular industry to follow the trends. Just click on the blue highlighted areas on the front page and you'll be on your way. For the more avid researchers, you can read their publications and working papers. Just click on the tabs near the top of the home page. It's all free.

Lew Rockwell (http://lewrockwell.com)

This is a great website for education in many areas including politics, investing, health, freedom, Austrian economics, and other miscellaneous subjects. There are usually about 10 new essays posted each day with a sentence or two regarding their subject matter on the home page. You can quickly scan the list for anything that may interest you. It is a good site to visit for light reading and a great education to boot! Although it is likely considered a conservative site with anti-government intrusion themes as a frequent subject matter, it is a great place to pick up the thoughts of modern day experts in their many diverse fields.

Gold Anti-trust Action Committee (http://www.gata.com)

This is the site for gold bugs! According to GATA:"The Gold Anti-Trust Action Committee was organized in the fall of 1998 to expose, oppose, and litigate against collusion to control the price and supply of gold and related financial instruments. The committee arose from essays by Bill Murphy, a financial commentator on the internet (LeMetropoleCafe.com), and by Chris Powell, a newspaper editor in Connecticut." Their biggest claim to fame is the complete documentation of gold price suppression tactics used by Western governments, including the U.S., and they have all the proof you'd ever want to see or hear. They also feature daily analysis and insight on any number of financially related issues. This is a great resource for the investor interested in wealth preservation and understanding of precious metals price movements.

Kitco (http://www.kitco.com)

This is a great website for metals market enthusiasts. You can get all the latest worldwide gold news, commentaries by many experts on various subjects, press releases, metals quotes, stock quotes, currency quotes, technical charts and much more. And you can buy and sell your metals at their on-line store. It's a one stop shop for all things gold and silver!

Gold-Eagle (http://gold-eagle.com)

This is a great site, if for no other reason than reading their contributed editorials. There is so much good content in the editorials that you must simply spend some time on them on a regular basis. And the editorials are not just metals related as the site name might lead you to believe. They are a superb collection of easy to read economics lessons, market analysis, and yes, even politics. They are updated on a daily basis, and many expert authors post their essays there, including many listed just below. The ones listed below are among the best of the best. Whether you find them at Gold-Eagle, Kitco, King World News, or any other site that offers contributed commentaries, take the time to follow a few of them and you'll be glad you did.

OTHER EXPERTS

Without going into detail on the biographies and expertise of the following gentlemen, here are more superior resources for your edification in all things financial. Most publish regular articles that you can read for free, although they also offer extended services for a fee. If you see the name, read and heed their advice.

Jeff Clark (www.caseyresearch.com)
Dr. Antal E. Fekete (www.professorfekete.com)
Chris Martenson (www.chrismartenson.com)
Jeff Neilson (www.bullionbullscanada.com)
Gary North (www.garynorth.com)
Michael Pento (www.pentoport.com)
Richard Russell (www.dowtheoryletters.com)
Steve Saville (www.speculative-investor.com)
Daryl Robert Schoon (www.survivethecrisis.com)
Graham Summers (www.gainspainscapital.com)
Stewart Thomson (www.gracelandupdates.com)
Dr. Jim Willie (www.goldenjackass.com)

Essays and Articles

Listed below are links you can use to further your pursuit of financial education. You may notice that some of the articles are dated. But those same articles are timeless as to their value, and therefore are included here. Also, it may be that some of the addresses will no longer get you to the article you seek. That's just the nature of the internet. If that is the case, just do a Google search for author and subject matter.

Austrian Economics

The Bailout Reader; this link includes a tremendous list of other links to numerous subjects touching on the financial crisis, and how they may be viewed from an Austrian economics standpoint:
http://mises.org/daily/3128

Murray Rothbard on Ludwig Von Mises; the basics of his brilliance:
http://lewrockwell.com/rothbard/rothbard272.html

The Austrian view of "forced money" verses "natural money":
http://www.usagold.com/whithergold.html

Antal E. Feteke – Read this brief review of the history of money and the gold standard, capital formation, hoarding, the gold bond, and derivatives. A must read for "the basics":
http://mises.org/daily/3340

Read 'A Free Market Monetary System' by Frederich A. Hayek. How would it look, and how it could happen. The problem is not the idea, but rather getting there:
http://mises.org/daily/3204

Gary North on the deficit reduction debates and Austrian economics:
http://lewrockwell.com/north/north1055.html

Do you think like an Austrian economist? Take a 25 question test for quite an education:

   http://mises.org/quiz.aspx

Depression of 1920

History verses theory on the treatment of economic depressions. Watch this instructive and revealing video by Tom Woods for an explanation of the 1920 crisis and how it was handled by government:

   http://www.youtube.com/watch?v=czcUmnsprQI&eurl=http%3A%2F%2Frightwingnews.com%2F2Fmt331%2F2009%2F05%2Fwhy_youve_never_heard_of_the_g.php&feature=player_embedded

Exchange Stabilization Fund

Zero Hedge provides the links to a 5 part video presentation on the ins and out of the ESF. This is a great primer on the ESF and a "must view" to understanding why many markets are not free:

   http://www.zerohedge.com/news/presenting-exchange-stabilization-fund-5-parts-real-plunge-protection-team

The Federal Reserve System

The New York Fed- How it operates to control the entire system. Its bylaws:

   http://www.newyorkfed.org/aboutthefed/ny_bylaws.html

The author of 'Money: Sound and Unsound' explains its true nature:

   http://lewrockwell.com/wile/wile25.1.html

San Francisco Fed Research Paper- the Fed is powerless to foster additional employment:

   http://www.zerohedge.com/news/san-francisco-fed-admits-bernanke-powerless-fix-unemployment

Ron Paul on the need to audit the Federal Reserve:

   http://lewrockwell.com/paul/paul769.html

Former Fed VP on how the Fed bails out European Banks with currency swaps: A Zero Hedge posting:

   http://www.zerohedge.com/news/former-fed-vp-accuses-bernanke-bailing-out-europe-currency-swaps

How the Fed commits fraud by selling put options on Treasuries to keep rates low, by Eric Decarbonel:
http://www.youtube.com/watch?v=ZnZnkaq8Nf8&feature=playe
r_embedded#at=31

How the Fed bails out foreign banks:
http://theeconomiccollapseblog.com/archives/unelected-
unaccountable-unrepentant-the-federal-reserve-is-using-your-money-
to-bail-out-european-commercial-banks-once-again

How the Fed was creating new money to buy more than 60% of U.S. debt issues by 2012:
http://www.moneynews.com/Headline/fed-debt-
Treasury/2012/03/28/id/434106?s=al&promo_code=E8AA-1

The Financial and Banking Crises

An insightful article on Zero Hedge on how the world's second and third largest economies plan to bypass the dollar in trade:
http://www.zerohedge.com/news/worlds-second-and-third-largest-
economies-bypass-dollar-engage-direct-currency-trade

Gordon T. Long on the systemic collateral contagion in the banking industry, bank runs, shadow banking, etc, with charts and a link to his work 'Thesis 2012: Financial Repression':
http://www.scribd.com/doc/7661019/Article-Collateral-Contagion

A Zero Hedge posting by Charles Hugh Smith: Three unspoken truths about the U.S. financial system:
http://www.zerohedge.com/news/guest-post-our-fragile-hothouse-
economy

Former Fed Chair Paul Volcker tees off on our financial system and its various "issues" (June 2010):
http://blogs.wsj.com/economics/2010/09/23/volcker-spares-no-one-in-
broad-critique/

2005 Bernanke video- If ever there were proof that the good Professor Bernanke did not have a clue as to the coming housing and mortgage crisis, this is it:

http://austrianfilter.blogspot.com/2009/04/zero-credibility.html

Gordon T. Long explains how accounting tricks mask the true condition of our banks and financial system, with numerous links included:

http://home.comcast.net/~lcmgroupe/2010/Article-Extend_Pretend-Accounting_Driven.htm

Gordon T. Long explains the box in which Bernanke has placed himself with regard to "tools" to help rescue of the U.S. economy:

http://www.gold-eagle.com/editorials_08/long042111.html

Jim Sinclair Blog; Get a view from 2011 of the extent of overstatement of bank balance sheet assets, showing that the crisis continues, over 2 years after the problem was supposedly fixed:

http://www.jsmineset.com/2011/05/20/jims-mailbox-703/

The Market Oracle; the underlying problems with banks have not been addressed, regardless of media and punditry stories. Understanding how corruption and economic misconceptions rule:

http://www.marketoracle.co.uk/Article15412.html

Weiss Banking White Paper; learn of the dangerous unintended consequences of bailouts of the banking system. Check out this comprehensive review by Martin Weiss:

http://www.moneyandmarkets.com/files/documents/banking-white-paper.pdf

'The Most Important Chart of the Century' by Nathan A. Martin; learn how debt saturation has now come into clear focus, and what it means to our economic system going forward:

http://economicedge.blogspot.com/2010/03/most-important-chart-of-century.html

Understand the rise and fall of the U.S. mortgage and credit market; a comprehensive analysis of the meltdown by the Milkin Institute:

http://www.milkeninstitute.org/pdf/Riseandfallexcerpt.pdf

Treasury Secretary Geithner's plan to "fix" the banks: why it could not work due to 5 basic misconceptions, by economist James Galbraith:
http://finance.yahoo.com/tech-ticker/article/216311/Part-I-Geithner%27s-Plan-%22Extremely-Dangerous%22-Economist-Galbraith-says?tickers=^gspc,dji,c,bac,jpm,WFC?sec=topStories&pos+2&asset=TBD&ccode=TBD

Bernanke and Paulsen quotes: during the height of the crisis, both leaders were either hiding the facts or simply ignorant of the extent and depth of the crisis. Read some choice quotes here:
http://austrianfilter.blogspot.com/2009/04/zero-credibility.html

How Bank of America attempts to dump derivatives losses on the U.S. taxpayers; a Zero Hedge offering:
http://www.zerohedge.com/contributed/federal-reserve-and-bank-america-initiate-coup-dump-hundreds-billions-dollars-losses-ame

Bond king Bill Gross of PIMCO explains in a Zero Hedge posting why you can't solve a debt crisis with more debt:
http://zerohedge.com/news/bill-gross-latest-monthly-thoughts-pennies-heaven-or-can-you-solve-debt-more-debt

How U.S. taxpayers are on the hook for potentially trillions of dollars in losses bank derivatives:
http://seekingalpha.com/article/503761-details-of-the-291-trillion-in-derivatives-to-which-american-taxpayers-are-exposed

How the Fed used swaps to bail out foreign banks. A Mises Institute posting:
http://mises.org/daily/6002/The-Feds-Swap-Bailout-of-the-Eurozone

Gold and Silver Investing Privacy expert Mark Nestmann on legally moving metals out of the U.S.:
http://lewrockwell.com/nestmann/nestmann31.1.html

Politics of historical silver manipulation; read some history surrounding the LBJ initiative to remove silver coinage from circulation:
http://www.silver-investor.com/charlessavoie/cs_march06_lbjgwbsilver.htm

Jeff Clark on the role and value of gold in past, and the value of ownership today:

http://caseyresearch.com/editorial.php?page=articles/greatest-bubble-history-our-doorstep&ppref=CRX422ED1011A

A short history of gold use as money:

http://www.kitco.com/ind/Mills/20120615.html

A fabulous presentation with charts on gold as compared to currencies, the loss of purchasing power, and irreversible trends causing gold price escalation:

http://www.bmgbullion.com/lib.pl?rm=show_document&record_id=996

Antal Fekete on the Chinese economy and their lust for gold:

http://www.gold-eagle.com/gold_digest_08/fekete101911.html

Jeff Clark of Casey Research on how political risk should not be ignored when investing in gold:

http://lewrockwell.com/clark-j/clark-j36.1.html

On leverage, risk and gold, by Paul Nathan; the lessons of a gold standard:

http://www.kitco.com/ind/Nathan/dec192011A.html

Gold and Silver Price Suppression

Gold Anti-Trust Action Committee; listen to a relevant radio interview regarding gold price suppression:

http://www.kingworldnews.com/kingworldnews/Broadcast_Gold+/Entries/2009/10/2_GATA.html

The Fed has undisclosed gold swap agreements. Check out the mounting evidence of price manipulation by reading this post and following the provided links:

http://www.gata.org/node/7819

Citations and links to more articles and proof of gold price suppression:
http://www.fgmr.com/new-dynamic-in-the-gold-market.html

The Rosetta Stone for gold price suppression, with all documented links in this work by Chris Powell:
http://www.gata.org/node/10554

JP Morgan, takeover of Bear Sterns silver short position and the CFTC:
http://www.scribd.com/doc/6730783/Silver-Gorillas-CFTC-Etc-1#

Jeff Nielsen on silver shorting; a Gold-Eagle posting:
http://www.gold-eagle.com/editorials_08/nielson11411.html

A Zero Hedge posting by Tyler Durden: The Fed on Gold Manipulation:
http://www.zerohedge.com/article/smoking-gun-fed-controlling-gold

Goldman Sachs

Learn how Goldman Sachs and other firms can easily take money out of your pocket pennies at a time while garnering hundreds of millions in profits weekly:
http://zerohedge.blogspot.com/search?q=goldman+sachs+domination+of+program+trading

Check out Elliot Spizer's view of the AIG payment to Goldman Sachs at 100% on the dollar, even though other creditors would receive far less:
http://themessthatgreenspanmade.blogspot.com/2009/11/elliot-spizer-on-tim-geithner.html

Goldman Sachs is under the microscope regarding European money dealings:
http://jessescrossroadscafe.blogspot.com/2010/02/simon-johnson-goldman-faces-special.html

Read how Goldman Sachs alumni dominate the European money scene:
http://www.independent.co.uk/news/business/analysis-and-features/what-price-the-new-democracy-goldman-sachs-conquers-europe-6264091.html

Why did Hank Paulsen secretly meet with Goldman Sachs board in Moscow while he was Treasury Secretary? Read this:

http://blogs.reuters.com/felix-salmon/2011/11/29/hank-paulsens-inside-jobs/

Hank Paulsen gives hedge fund managers (prior Goldman Sachs alumni) a heads-up on the pending failure and nationalization of Freddie and Fannie so they could profit by shorting the stocks:

http://www.bloomberg.com/news/2011-11-29/how-henry-paulsen-gave-hedge-funds-advance-word-of-2008-fannie-mae-rescue.html

MF Global sold assets to Goldman only 4 days before it collapsed; an essay by Reuters:

http://www.yahoo.com/mf-global-sold-assets-goldman-collapse-sources-002332058.html

The Great Depression

Inflation vs. deflation debate of the 1930's; Daniel Amerman demonstrates how the government can create inflation during even the worst of times, and clarifies 3 common fallacies:

http://www.gold-eagle.com/editorials_08/amerman021209.html

Chart of pompous prognosticators; what they said and when they said it from 1927 to 1933. This demonstrates the lack of understanding and foresight during the boom and bust cycle:

http://www.ritholtz.com/blog/2006/11/1927-1933-chart-of-pompous-prognosticators/

Revisionist history and the Great Depression, by Andy Sutton:

http://www.gold-eagle.com/editorials_08/sutton102111.html

Alan Greenspan

Read this classic essay on Mr. Greenspan's true feeling on the role of gold as a monetary instrument, as it was published in 1967 in Ayn Rand's work 'Capitalism, the Unknown Ideal':

http://www.usagold.com/gildedopinion/greenspan.html

How Alan Greenspan wanted to keep the discussion about the housing bubble under wraps, by Ryan Grim:

http://www.lewrockwell.com/spl2/greenspan-kept-secrets.html

Greenspan says the Fed's QE program did not help the economy, and that it will destroy the dollar:

http://www.thedailycrux.com/Article/37759/Inflation

Historical data

Links to all sorts of historic inflation, price and money statistics:

http://libguides.asu.edu/content.php?pid=5241&sid=32617

This is the most important chart of the century. How the debt to GDP ratio shows us the uselessness of incurring more debt to stimulate the economy:

http://economicedge.blogspot.com/2010/03/most-important-chart-of-century.html

Debt saturation is here and now. Taking on more debt has become harmful, not helpful:

http://www.gold-eagle.com/editorials_08/long042711.html

Hyperinflation

Check out this short essay on the Argentina debacle of the 1998-2001:

http://www.gold-eagle.com/editorials_08/ulivi021809.html

Understand the parallels between Weimar Germany and the actions of Bernanke. Check out this comprehensive look at 1920's Germany and the U.S. today:

http://economicedge.blogspot.com/2010/03/most-important-chart-of-century.html

Read Steve Saville on the two prerequisites for hyperinflation:

http://www.gold-eagle.com/editorials_08/saville112211.html

James Turk in video conversation on hyperinflation, with Adam Fergusson, author of 'When Money Dies':

http://www.goldmoney.com/video/fergusson-turk-interview.html?gmrefcode=gata

Peter Warburton on the debasement of world currency and what it really means:

http://www.gata.org/node/8303

Money and Investing

How Quantitative Easing gooses the stock market higher:
http://lewrockwell.com/barnett/barnett39.1.html

Doug Casey on how to get money, and how to keep it:
http://lewrockwell.com/casey/casey93.1.html

Daniel Amerman on how you can actually lose purchasing power when the DOW rises dramatically:
http://www.gold-eagle.com/editorials_12/amerman011212.html

A must read; Dr. Jim Willie on fraudulent investor traps:
http://lewrockwell.com/spl3/fraudulent-investor-traps.html

Another Jim Willie posting with a comprehensive look at corruption in the U.S. financial system:
http://www.silverbearcafe.com/private/07.12/corruption.html

An insightful interview with an insider to high frequency trading:
http://www.zerohedge.com/news/interview-high-frequency-trader

An historical look at the evolution of paper money under the Federal Reserve regime in the U.S.:
http://www.Friesian.com/notes.htm

What is the best sector by far of any in the U.S. stock Market? It's the gold and silver miners. A guest post on Zero Hedge dated 12/7/2011:
http://www.zerohedge.com/contributed/gold-and-silver-mining-stocks-offer-best-value-any-sector-far-and-wide-marg

Chris Marrenson on how to position yourself for the future (2 parts); a Zero Hedge post:
http://www.zerohedge.com/news/guest-post-how-position-yourself-future-step-1-financial-security

Doug Casey on how to prepare for when money dies:
http://www.gold-eagle.com/editorials_08casey092711.html

New World Order and the demise of the reserve currency

The Rockefellers, Council on Foreign Relations, and the Trilateral Commission, by Andrew Gavin Marshall:
http://lewrockwell.com/orig10/marshall14.1/html

The future of the USA-2012-2016: an insolvent and ungovernable U.S. Scroll half way down the page for this grim assessment by GEAB:
http://www.leap2020.eu/Global-systemic-crisis-usA-2012-1016-An-insolvent-and-ungovernable-country_a8481.html

Historical quotations from politicians to philosophers enlighten the reader on the significance of the devolution of U.S. governance:
http://www.scribd.com/doc/16449032/HistoricalQuotationsRegardingtheNewWorldOrder

Brandon Smith on recognizing the signs of cultural change:
http://www.zerohedge.com/news/guest-post-breaking-points-recognizing-signs-painful-cultural-shift

Daniel Amerman on the collapse of the Euro and its short and long term consequences in the U.S., in 2 parts with a link to part two:
http://www.gold-eagle.com/editorials_08/amerman100711.html

Ten survival tools to have ready for survival preparedness:
http://readynutrition.com/resources/shtf-survival-10-survival-tools-that-should-be-in-your-survival-pack_10102011/

The death of the dollar: a provocative interview of Eric Janszen by Chris Martenson:
http://chrismartenson.com/page/transcript-eric-janszen-we-are-witnessing-death-dollar

A Zero Hedge posting by Brandon Smith on the new Asian Union and the fall of the dollar, with relevant links provided:

http://www.zerohedge.com/news/guest-post-new-asian-union-means-fall-dollar-0

Outgoing President of the World Bank calls for a new central bank of BRICs nations:

http://www.telegraph.co.uk/finance/newsbysector/banksandfinance/918037 3/Robert-Zoellick-calls-for-Brics-bank.html

The barter items and trade skills you'll need after a dollar collapse:

http://www.shtfplan.com/emergency-preparedness/top-post-collapse-barter-items-and-trade-skills_06102011

Essay by Lew Rockwell on the threat of fascism and how the U.S. stacks up on eight points of reference:

http://lewrockwell.com/rockwell/facist-threat192.html

The real numbers

Check out the real cost of living increases tracked by the American Institute for Economic Research. Type "everyday price index" in the search box to see the complete list of consumer goods and services:

http://www.aier.org

A New York Post writer looks at the unemployment numbers:

http://www.nypost.com/p/news/business/how_nation_true_jobless_rate_is_N4E6MjtfhnMcCi537pucaJ

Check the numbers and facts showing how the middle class is being squeezed out of existence:

http://lewrockwell.com/rep2/U.S.-middle-class-rapidly-shrinking.html

Top 100 statistics about the collapse of the economy that Americans should know:

http://lewrockwell.com/rep2/100-stats-collapsing-economy.html

Be very careful of big up moves in bear markets! Review the evidence:

http://tycoonreport.tycoonresearch.com/past_issues/710357249

Read of the collapse in shadow banking system assets (Money Market Funds, etc), and how it is treated by the Fed. Pictorials included:

http://www.zerohedge.com/news/scramble-U.S.-safety-europe-imploded-offset-357-billion-plunge-q3-shadow-banking

Very distressing facts about the U.S. debt picture:
http://lewrockwell.com/rep2/34-shocking-facts-about-U.S.-debt.html

Mike Shedlock on the farcical way that GDP is distorted by hedonics and imputations:
http://globaleconomicanalysis.blogspot.com/2005/05/grossly-distorted-proceedures.html

The Regulators

The irrepressible Matt Taibbi of Rolling Stone Magazine on the covered up investigations at the SEC:
http://www.rollingstone.com/politics/news/is-the-sec-covering-up-wall-street-crimes-20110817

Learn why William Black, PHD (who cleaned up the S&L mess of the 1980's) believes the banking system is "rotten to the core":
http://www.financialsense.com/contributors/william-black/2011/11/25/banking-system-rotten-to-the-core

Listen to this 4 minute interview of William Black, one of the regulators who prosecuted hundreds of fraud cases in the S&L crisis, and how he compares that situation to the complete lack of prosecution of the fraudsters in the current crisis:
http://wwwyoutube.com/watch?v=4XJe7O-3QBc&feature=channel_video_title

Peter Brant on MF Global and how the government failed to protect investors:
http://peterlbrandt.com/mf-global-proof-that-the-u-s-government-is-not-able-or-willing-to-protect-investors/

Gary Gensler (Goldman alum) at the Commodity Futures Trading Commission (CTFC); an expose posted on Zero Hedge:

http://www.zerohedge.com/contributed/gary-gensler-u-boat-sent-cftc

The real reason that MF Global investors will not get their money back is that the money was hypothecated away:

http://newsandinsight.thomsonreuters.com/Securiites/Insight/2011/12_-_December/MF_Global_and_the_great_Wall_St_re-hypothecation_scandal/

The SEC accuses Freddie and Fannie of causing the financial crisis:

http://online.wsj.com/article/SB100014240529702047911045771081
8367763S076.html?mod=WSJ_Opinion_LEADTop

Forbes Magazine article on how the regulators block the truth about MF Global:

http://www.forbes.com/sites/francinemckenna/2012/01/09/the-neverending-mf-global-story-regulators-block-the-truth-from-coming-out/

Eric Sprott; The Financial System is a Farce. A Dodd-Frank reform indictment:

http://zerohedge.com/news/eric-sprott-financial-system-farce

Elizabeth Warren; learn how accounting changes mask the true financial condition of the banking system from someone who ran the Congressional Oversight Panel:

http://www.businessinsider.com/henry-blodget-elizabeth-warren-we-have-a-real-problem-coming-2009-8

A foreign bank insider discusses the failure of the Volcker Rule:

http://www.zerohedge.com/contributed/volcker-failure

The Stimulus Spending Spree

Why the Obama stimulus plan was doomed to failure:

http://www.gold-eagle.com/gold_digest_08/fekete033009.html

Read how stimulus jobs went to illegal immigrants:
http://www.humanevents.com/article.php?fc_c=137&334x289823&x1
47028636&id=31063

Go inside the Solyndra/Obama scandal:
http://www.zerohedge.com/contributed/solyndra-obama-connection

Bigger Government is not stimulus. Watch this 7.5 minute video from the Cato Institute on government "stimulus":
http://www.youtube.com/watch?v=VoxDyC7y7PM

Troubled Asset Relief Program

Treasury Dept had no metrics to measure TARP goals:
http://www.marketwatch.com/story/panel-treasury-has-no-metric-for-its-tarp-goals-2010-01-14

The TARP money was not used for commercial loans to customers; article posted on Market Oracle:
http://www.marketoracle.co.uk/Article15412.html

How the Fed solves the short term debt and high inflation dilemma, by Daniel Amerman. This is a must read:
http://danielamerman.com/articles/Flawed.htm

U.S. Treasuries

Wall Street selling imaginary Treasuries! Learn how "failure to deliver" is the same as selling something you don't own or can't produce; call it counterfeiting:
http://www.marketskeptics.com/2009/04/wall-street-selling-imaginary.html

Jeff Neilson on fraud in the U.S. Treasuries market:
http://www.gold-eagle.com/editorials_12/nielson010312.html

Bud Conrad on how foreigners are losing confidence in the U.S. treasury market (scroll down to middle of page for start of article):
http://www.caseyresearch.com/cdd/are-foreign-banks-losing-confidence-U.S.-treasuries

A Zero Hedge posting showing how foreigners are dumping Treasuries, with charts included:

http://www.zerohedge.com/news/foreigners-dump-record-amount-treasuries-past-month

Historical U.S. Interest expense on the national debt:

http://treasurydirect.gov/govt/reports/ir/ir_expense.htm